Liberating Oedipus?

Liberating Oedipus?

Psychoanalysis as Critical Theory

Filip Kovacevic

LEXINGTON BOOKS

A division of
ROWMAN & LITTLEFIELD PUBLISHERS, INC.
Lanham • Boulder • New York • Toronto • Plymouth, UK

LEXINGTON BOOKS

A division of Rowman & Littlefield Publishers, Inc.
A wholly owned subsidiary of The Rowman & Littlefield Publishing Group, Inc.
4501 Forbes Boulevard, Suite 200
Lanham, MD 20706

Estover Road
Plymouth PL6 7PY
United Kingdom

Copyright © 2007 by Lexington Books

All rights reserved. No part of this publication may be reproduced, stored in a retrieval system, or transmitted in any form or by any means, electronic, mechanical, photocopying, recording, or otherwise, without the prior permission of the publisher.

British Library Cataloguing in Publication Information Available

Library of Congress Cataloging-in-Publication Data

Kovacevic, Filip, 1975–
  Liberating Oedipus? : psychoanalysis as critical theory / Filip Kovacevic.
    p. cm.
  Includes bibliographical references and index.
  ISBN-13: 978-0-7391-1148-2 (cloth : alk. paper)
  ISBN-10: 0-7391-1148-5 (cloth : alk. paper)
  1. Oedipus complex. 2. Psychoanalysis. 3. Critical theory. 4. Freud, Sigmund, 1856–1939. 5. Lacan, Jacques, 1901–1981. I. Title.
  BF175.5.O33K68 2007
  150.19'5—dc22   2006023954

Printed in the United States of America

∞™ The paper used in this publication meets the minimum requirements of American National Standard for Information Sciences—Permanence of Paper for Printed Library Materials, ANSI/NISO Z39.48-1992.

Contents

Acknowledgments		vii
Introduction		ix
1	Freud's Theses	1
2	The Liberation Thesis	59
3	Lacan's Theses	107
4	Post-Lacanian Theses	157
5	Contemporary Lacanian Theses: The Liberation Thesis Revisited	193
Conclusion		225
Bibliography		231
Index		239
About the Author		245

Acknowledgments

I would like to thank Professors Patrick Peritore, Ellie Ragland, and Joseph Bien who inspired me by their examples. I will remember their seminars as the anchoring points of my work as a theorist.

More generally, I would like to thank my parents, Ljupka and Srdja Kovacevic, whose love has been a beacon of hope in the years of separation from my native land when this book was written. They raised me in an environment where the best and most beautiful things human beings are capable of were properly valued. I would also like to thank my colleagues, friends, and girlfriends with whom I have discussed this work in its various stages.

I dedicate this work to those who innovate and take risks so that the children of tomorrow will live a better life in a better world.

Introduction

> Therapy of neuroses is only one of the uses of psychoanalysis; perhaps the future will show that it is not the most important.[1]

When taking stock of the existing literature on psychoanalytic social and political criticism, I concluded that Paul Robinson's classic book on the Freudian Left, originally published in the 1960s, is in need of an expansion and an update.[2] In fact, I think that what is needed is a book that covers recent developments in this field and connects them to the kind of Freudian radicalism Robinson discussed. For instance, one should go beyond the usual suspects of Freudian radicalism, such as Reich and Marcuse, and take a theoretical step backward and then a step or several steps forward. First, what is necessary is to go back to Freud's writings and show the promises and limits of his own conceptualizations for the advance of radical thought. Secondly, in order to take account of the post-1960s developments, the most prominent psychoanalyst after Freud, Jacques Lacan, should also be included on the list of Freudian radicals. Since there are theorists who find the emancipatory potential of Lacan's theories problematic, this thesis cannot simply be asserted, but must also be demonstrated based on textual evidence. Lastly, it is necessary to examine the utility of Lacanian formulations in contemporary debates in critical political and social theory.

These are precisely the things that I hope to have accomplished in the present work. In fact, my analysis shows that a critical perspective grounded in a Lacanian interpretation of Marx and Freud is the best model for theoretical and practical engagement in changing existing social and political realities.

I have entitled this work "Liberating Oedipus," because I think that these two words, the two signifiers—Oedipus and liberation—condense quite well the multiplicity of issues that I have set out to explore. I take Oedipus to be the metaphor of any individual (male or female) who lives within the confines of a world whose particular conditions (consistencies and inconsistencies) he or she does not wonder about. Just like Oedipus, this individual is cursed insofar as his or her fate is predetermined. Without wonder, which inspires questioning, he or she is always at the mercy of circumstances (social and/or psychological, as the case may be). This Oedipus, who is no more than a puppet of the obscure forces whose existence he or she is unable to understand and confront, is the true subject of this work. Under what conditions, if at all, he or she can gain a measure of assertiveness over his or her fate is the key question I am asking. This is what I mean by "liberation"; it is the ability to choose and shape the contours of one's fate. In other words, "liberating Oedipus" stands for making a metonymy out of a metaphor, a displacement out of condensation, the emergence of desire out of the rock of congealed *jouissance*.[3]

Is this possible? The short answer to this question is "yes, but it is far from simple"; the long answer is this work itself. I begin with Freud and with an issue that more or less provides the background for my reflections throughout: the inquiry about the genesis of values, the dominant values of a given community (in this case, of the contemporary Western sociopolitical configuration). I think that understanding how something comes to be provides at the same time understanding how that which is, can become something else; I stress the importance of understanding the primary conditions or constitutive elements, since, as I see it, this also implies understanding the modalities for changing them.

Concerning the origin of values, Freud emphasizes the Oedipal relation: the imposition of paternal values on each subsequent generation. At times, in his works, Oedipus appears as the transcendental condition of civilization. However, the apparent inflexibility of this statement needs to be modified by the fact that the masculine and the feminine trace out two different Oedipal paths, which is precisely what provides for the possibility of the subversion of Oedipal norms (as is testified by the work of Lacan). In fact, taking into consideration the structural conditions of sexuation (that is, of sexualized subjectivity) is, as I show, a necessity in any contemporary model for critical social and political theory.

In my chapter on Freud (chapter 1), I present a chronological examination of Freud's works, from his letters to his friend Wilhelm Fliess to his works on the psychoanalysis of culture, a span of more than forty years. I do so to elaborate the emergence of the key concepts of psychoanalysis, and also to position Freud on the issue that motivates my work: the possibility of a political and cultural improvement in the existing state of human affairs. I find that, with respect to this issue, one can draw a distinction between the early Freud and the late Freud, the dividing line being, in my opinion, the experience of the World War I.

The early Freud emphasizes, what I call, the primacy of a positive relation to the Other, which establishes a framework for the relations with other individuals throughout one's lifetime. The frustration of this initially good relation leads to the emergence of aggressivity; hence negativity toward others is a derived phenomenon, a psychological defense mechanism. The bad is the absence of the good; it does not have an ontological status in its own right. What this means for social and political theory is that there is nothing eternal about the prevailing climate of political instability, insecurity, and violence, considering that these negative phenomena are the products of a specific set of social and economic circumstances (scarcity, alienation, atomization, and so on). In other words, human nature reveals itself as bad because of its disappointment at the lack of the good. The early Freud, therefore, does not rule out the possibility of beneficial changes in the conditions of social life, and it is not surprising that his insights are incorporated by the theorists openly committed to such changes, whom I refer to as the theorists of the Liberation Thesis.

However, the early Freud is not the only Freud that one needs to account for. After World War I (influenced, it seems to me, by the horrific extent of suffering and destruction), Freud began approaching the issue of the I-Other relation from a different perspective. Whereas in his early works, the drive for union and togetherness (Eros) is primary and the opposing drive (Thanatos) derives from it, now the two are postulated to exist side by side, each grounded ontologically in the autonomous aspect of the psyche: Eros in the sex-drives and Thanatos in the death drive. This dichotomy marks all subsequent Freud's works on the nature of social and political phenomena; he no longer offers hope that aggressivity and violence can be eradicated from human affairs. From this period in Freud's work stems his explicit polemic with Marxists (and the Liberation Thesis *avant la lettre*), in which he argues that no change in economic and political conditions of life, no matter how radical, can eliminate envy, jealousy, and competitiveness, considering that these psychological states are instinctual, not rational.[4]

Still, Freud does remain open to the modifications of the death drive by Eros, by the life force that combines existing entities into a greater unity. In this respect, Freud stresses the importance of the leadership dynamic, especially concerning the leader-follower relation. Freud shows that a benevolent leader (i.e., the psychoanalyst) can advance quite far in shaping the values and attitudes of those whose trust he or she had gained. The internalization of the good authority figures and their subsequent integration into the individual's super-ego are the only paths that Freud envisions for the genesis of progressive social and political changes. Even though these claims can hardly qualify Freud as a revolutionary, it must be kept in mind that his underlying thesis that human drives are malleable and prone to a wide variety of vicissitudes opens itself for the possibility of a radical interpretation.

Precisely this kind of interpretation is applied to Freud's insights by the thinkers whose overall thesis I call the Liberation Thesis. Wilhelm Reich, Herbert Marcuse, and Norman O. Brown, all in their slightly different ways (which I discuss in chapter 2), work to unfold the radical potential of psychoanalysis. The key question that they try to respond to is whether a civilization without discontents is possible and if it is, what kinds of measures need to be put in place to make a transition from the existing state of power domination and exploitation to such a civilization. All three of them endeavor to effect a synthesis of the Freudian and Marxian corpuses, showing, in essence, that neurotic repression is a product of a specific economic and cultural configuration (i.e., capitalism), and not at all a transhistorical phenomenon.

Committed to a naturalist framework, Reich makes a case for the existence of natural or self-regulatory needs that are consequently badly warped by existing social and political mechanisms. Influencing the later works of Marcuse and Brown, he underlines the liberating power of sexual expression and fulfillment as a way of access to suppressed needs. He sees the liberation of the body as a necessary first step toward the liberation of the mind. This is why, in his therapeutic case histories, Reich stresses the development of an ability to enjoy the movements and capacities of the human body, including genital sexuality. Reich claims that a fulfilled human being will know how to recognize and avoid the traps of mystifying and myth-making ideologies that in an irrational way have separated and continue to separate human beings from each other (religion, nationalism, fascism, and so on). However, Reich is aware that the fight against "the little fascist" in oneself is an arduous one, and that the prospects for success are not all that bright.[5] In this respect, he chronicles the failures of revolutionary emancipation in the Soviet Union, and enunciates the inevitability of its collapse fifty years before the event.

Marcuse follows Reich in stressing the transformative potential of erotic drives. He coins the concept of libidinal rationality which postulates the reconciliation of the rational and the sensual (the sensuous) faculties in a way that will preserves the truth of the senses.[6] However, this reconciliation is, according to Marcuse, prevented by the forces and demands of the capitalist status quo, the status quo that extols the virtues of hard (read: alienated) work and repression for the sake of an ever-proliferating commercialized pleasure. The powers of Eros reveal the untruth and unfreedom of capitalism by stressing the value of pleasures that money or status cannot buy. They provide for a possibility of the development of an aesthetic consciousness, which refuses to participate in any and all activities not conducive to individual well being.

Brown extends the call for the necessity of intellectual autonomy and sensual self-discovery by attempting to connect psychoanalysis with a set of Nietzschean insights. This is particularly difficult to do considering that Freud and Nietzsche defined certain basic building blocks of their theories, such as, for instance, the concept of desire, in a way that minimizes compatibility.[7] However, Brown's endeavor succeeds in so far as his use of Nietzsche is selective and centers on the metaphors that have to do with the liberation of human erotic potential. Brown stresses Nietzsche's commitment to the constitution of a Dionysian ego, which, when translated into the language of psychoanalysis, turns out to be nothing else than the abolition of repression and the impetus for the creation of a new type of personality structure. In contrast to Nietzsche, however, Brown insists that the ultimate outcome is a more egalitarian social organization, and not the loneliness and isolation of the *Übermenschen*.

In final analysis, one can perhaps define the main orientation of the Liberation Thesis of Reich, Marcuse, and Brown as affirming the claim that psychoanalytic insights, incarnated in psychoanalytic theory and practice, point a way toward the transcendence of social and political status quo. The affirmation of this claim is important, because it allows me to set up a framework for approaching correctly the sociopolitical importance of the psychoanalytic thought of Jacques Lacan (chapter 3). In contrast to several key works of recent scholarship, I argue that the relation of Lacan's work to the critical orientation of the Liberation Thesis is positive. Lacan is no less of a radical thinker than Reich or Marcuse. I demonstrate the validity of this claim through a three-pronged examination of Lacan's *écrits* and seminars, which, in a certain sense, fits the preoccupations of the early, middle, and late periods in Lacan's teaching. I begin by focusing on the ethics of psychoanalysis, then move on to the discourse theory, and finish with the discussion of the logic of sexuation.

In essential agreement with the theorists of the Liberation Thesis, Lacan considers erotic desire as the key coordinate of the ethical field. This is so, because, according to Lacan, desire represents most authentically the essential determinations of one's subjectivity. In other words, in my desire I am as I am, and in fact also as I should be, that is to say, the conscious appropriation of my desire marks my highest ethical act. This is why Lacan translates Freud's famous statement on the task of psychoanalysis—*Wo Es war, soll Ich werden*—as "There where It was, it is my duty that I should come into being."[8] In other words, the subject enters the dimension of truth when it reveals itself as desiring. This leads to the establishment of a standard of truth independent from the standards, norms, and values of the existing social and political order, and hence opens an ethical dimension for refusal and revolt. In this respect, Lacan refers to the figure of Antigone as the prototypical heroine of radicalism. Antigone subverted the imperatives of her immediate political environment in order to honor a commitment that could be best described as the commitment of desire.

Lacan designates the discourse of the desiring subject as the discourse of the hysteric. The discourse of the hysteric is one of four discourse structures (in addition to the discourse of the master, the university, and the analyst) that, in Lacan's view, all human communication that establishes "a social link" can be reduced to.[9] Lacan sees the task of psychoanalysis as enabling the emergence of the discourse of the hysteric in the public and private realms. In fact, as I show, the discourse of the analyst is a necessary structural link or permutation between the discourse of the university (the discourse of linear/positivistic knowledge as the basis of social division of power, the most dominant discourse today) and the discourse of the hysteric. In other words, psychoanalytic theory and practice has an indispensable role to play in modifying the prevailing discourse structure so that it becomes more open to the truths of individual subjectivity linked to the unrealized social potential. The subversive nature of psychoanalysis shines through this facilitation of the return of the repressed.

The discourse of the hysteric is also rooted in Lacan's conceptualization of sexual difference, which he refers to as the logic of sexuation. Lacan's distinction between the masculine and the feminine is not established on the basis of biology or of sociological/cultural roles, but is instead founded on the basis of the knowledge of the structural incompleteness of the social Other (the particular sociopolitical configuration). In other words, the masculine and the feminine are distinguished in terms of whether their horizon of being is confined to that which a given social Other deems possible or impossible and necessary or contingent. The masculine is on the side of the possible/necessary dyad, on the side of that which conforms to the norms and values of the status quo. In contrast, the feminine is on the side of the impossible/contingent dyad, and therefore structurally grounds the possibilities for radical social and political change. Here is found the void or the hole in the Other through which what is truly new enters into history. It is therefore not surprising that the hysteric, as the agent of dissatisfaction and revolt, is to be located on the feminine side of sexuation, the side that approaches the particular social Other as insufficient and lacking, as the not-all (*pas-tout*). In the best Marxian dialectical tradition, the hysteric is the one who rejects or refuses that which is for the sake of that which could be.

This is why I speculate that the one who speaks the discourse of the hysteric is to be considered a genuine revolutionary agent, the primary mover behind all that is different from what the forces of socialization and habit made to seem an eternal human nature. The hysteric demands that his or her desire be represented by the social Other and, in this way, motivates the creation of new signifying chains that lead to the reconfiguration of the Other itself. The hysteric's activity makes present or tangible the worlds forever imprisoned by the one-dimensional dictates of the status quo. These worlds are ridiculed as impossible by those who hold the reigns of power and by their academic ideologues, which can be seen, for instance, in the charges of "utopianism" concerning the social constellation described by Marx and Engels in a passage of *German Ideology*.[10] But the new world, as imagined by Marx and Engels, is in fact the example of a world whose realization could be brought about by the relentless and faithful insistence of hysterics. The exchangeability of social functions as the principal axis of orientation in such a world is something to which the hysteric is always already committed, even within the world as it is today. This is so because the only way to preserve one's desire and at the same time oneself as a desiring subject (as the hysteric) is to recognize the necessity of the existence of the variety of objects which can act as the aims of desire. Here once again we see the radical nature of psychoanalytic insights in that they locate the truths of humanity in the concept of multiplicity rather than monotony, emphasize discontinuity rather than continuity, and elaborate the construction of the new beyond any particular blueprints, all this in a clear opposition to the tranquilizing (gradualist) quality of the prevailing popular and university discourse.

Yet, as I show in chapter 4, the claim regarding the radicalism of psychoanalysis is far from being accepted as valid in all contemporary theoretical quarters. In this chapter, I confront two readings in particular, two strains of thought that converge on the idea that psychoanalytic theory and practice are ineffective or even obsolete in terms of their relation to the movements of sociopolitical change. The first reading is by Gilles Deleuze and Felix Guattari, whom I take to be the representatives of what has come to be known as Nietzschean post-structuralism. I approach their critique of Lacanian psychoanalysis within the general framework of an inquiry as to which theoretical perspective is more appropriate to, or consistent with, radical praxis. I argue that Deleuze and Guattari's interpretation of desire (which, on my reading, is a direct derivation of Nietzsche's will to power) is less capable of providing a foundation for an ethic of revolutionary subjectivity than the classical psychoanalytic notion of desire as lack. This is so because desire as will stresses the self-sufficiency of the subject and his or her essential indifference toward "the outside," while desire as lack is always already deeply implicated in the relation with the Other, with that which beyond the subject holds the possibility of his or her satisfaction. In my opinion, only the latter perspective can inform a theory of individual and social change because, rather than giving its stamp of approval to the proliferating repetition of the same, it is slanted in the direction of the Other and, in this way, genuinely oriented toward creating difference as value.

Once this conservative core in the work of Deleuze and Guattari is revealed, it becomes easier to understand why their theory of emancipation and the models they offer to support it do not exhaust the critical potential of psychoanalysis. For instance, it is not clear how the praxis of schizoanalysis, which they put forth as a more radical and radicalizing substitute for psychoanalysis, can advance beyond the solipsistic universe of psychotic articulations.[11] If the task is to free desire entangled in the mechanisms of the status quo (which psychoanalysis, as I have shown, is far from disputing), what necessity is there to ground one's theory in the discourse of the schizophrenic? In my view, the hysteric remains committed to the liberation of desire in an exemplary fashion, and there is therefore no need to find one's inspiration in the cases that cross into the shadowy territory of mental illness. The problem is that desire as will is found in its purest manifestation only in psychosis, and the theoretical commitment to this interpretation of desire makes Deleuze and Guattari articulate the model that, I think, is of questionable utility for sociopolitical change.

The second reading critical of psychoanalysis that I confront in chapter 4 comes from another important contemporary perspective. Here I deal with a critique from the perspective of a feminist, Luce Irigaray, who sees psychoanalysis as yet another instance of the male dominated philosophical discourse whose more or less explicit aim is to deny or minimize the importance of a specifically woman's point of view. I defend psychoanalytic endeavor against Irigaray's attacks, demonstrating a set of problems with her critique. My general claim is that psychoanalysis contains within itself a feminist dimension, considering its commitment to the emancipation and demand recognition of all human beings, regardless of their substantive characteristics (sex, class, ethnicity, and so on).

I dispute the necessity of what I see as a biological or essentialist aspect of Irigaray's work and suggest that a more promising direction for critical theory is that of structuralism, which I find exemplified in the work of Lacan and of Lacanian thinkers whose work I discuss in chapter 5. This is so, because, considering that discourse structures depend on the chains of signifiers, they are more conducive to change than biological determinations. At the same time, in my view, structures represent the ways in which we approach or read biology, and therefore exert a direct influence on that which we call human biological nature. Hence it seems to me that critical social and political theory should help bring out this structural dimension in human affairs rather than take the path of that which appears to be derivative.

In this respect, I disagree with Irigaray's effort to ground certain psychoanalytic concepts in bodily or organic realities, such as, for instance, the concept of the phallus.[12] Here I stress that the phallus is far from being the derivation of an organ and that therefore the role that it plays in psychoanalytic theory does not privilege the masculine over the feminine. In fact, I enunciate conditions under which precisely the presence of the phallus marks the positions of the masculine and the feminine in a way that demonstrates the emancipatory potential of the latter. In the structural relations of sexuation, as defined by Lacan, the feminine represents (to an extent) the beyond of all symbolic orders, and is hence revealed as a source of the possibilities for their reconfiguration.

I give a final articulation of my claim that psychoanalytic theory and practice ought to be the key components in any project for the radical leftist re-thinking of the existing sociopolitical order in chapter 5. Here I discuss the contemporary uses or applications of psychoanalytic theory and show how they illuminate the important aspects of social and political life in the spirit of what I have called the Liberation Thesis.

I begin with the work of Slavoj Žižek and the issue of ideology. I show that, in contrast to a traditional definition of ideology as a distorting, illusionary emanation that covers over the more complete or true nature of things, there is no other reality "behind" ideology; it embodies a structure in which all lack has been filled and is consistent and complete in itself.[13] This means that it can be designated by a specific psychoanalytic concept, the concept of fantasy. As elaborated by Lacan, fantasy is a structural relation ($\$\lozenge a$) where the subject ($\$$) persists in his or her belief that he or she found an object (a) that will forever fulfill his or her desire. What this means for social and political theory is that it is ideological to believe that any set of arrangements, norms, and values can provide for a sociopolitical system that could stop the permutations of history, including the possibility of leftist revolutions. However, precisely such a belief dominates contemporary social and political life in regard to the postulated blessings of transnational capitalism and its political double, liberal democracy.

As in a typical psychoanalytic session, the only way to dissolve or transcend this belief (which, in a technical sense, is a fantasy) is to traverse or work through it. This enables the uncovering of the structural elements underlying the belief and reveals their contingent nature (especially the contingent nature of the object). In terms of sociopolitical application, this means that what needs to be done is to examine the conditions, which have led to the formation of a capitalist liberal democratic social structure. Žižek calls this process "historicizing historicism," because it involves the search for a principle that, by its presence or absence, structures a given empirical content, that is, a particular sociopolitical configuration, which, for historicists, is the only horizon of truth.[14]

I argue that psychoanalytic theory is specially suited for the effort of transcending such a particularistic perspective, because one of its fundamental assumptions is that no sociopolitical configuration, no social Other, is complete in itself. In other words, there is always an element that remains repressed or excluded in order for a given reality to take shape. The element that is excluded is always the one that could expose the fundamental incompleteness of the Other. In terms of our liberal universe, this element is embodied in those whose demands and desires are not represent by dominant signifiers, those who are beyond the laws of any political sphere (undocumented immigrants, for example). It is a hope of those who, for one reason or another, think that liberalism is the ultimate word in the history of humanity that it can accommodate even the inclusion of such an element. However, as psychoanalysis shows, the genuine inclusion of the repressed content can never be accomplished by a simple process of integration, since this content, if it is to be freely articulated, necessitates an entirely different framework, an entirely different structure. Hence capitalist liberalism as a framework must undergo a fundamental change in order for those who currently suffer under its institutions to be given their due.

Drawing on the work of Lacanian scholars Ellie Ragland and Alain Badiou, I attempt to chart more precisely the course of this transformation. In this respect, what I find is that a structural transformation of this kind would necessitate a shift in the dominant social logic from what, in Lacan's theory of sexuation, is called the masculine pole to the feminine pole. The masculine pole is marked by the belief in the permanence of hierarchical symbolic structures, the belief in the truth of the given as such, and hence is always blind to the emergence of the genuinely different. Within this pole, which I argue is akin structurally to the ideology of liberal multiculturalism, everybody must play by the same rules or risk condemnation. In contrast, the feminine contains an element that represents the incompleteness of the Other, the limitless source of possibilities. It is here that the true relation of universality resides, universality which is not implicitly tied to any particular content, but which is oriented toward the inclusion of all human potentialities across the board.

I see the commitment to the representation of this kind of universality in social life as the most important task of critical political and social theory today. In psychoanalytic terms, this commitment requires working towards the re-articulation of the relationship between the symbolic (what is) and the real (what is not, because its being is repressed by what is). The critical theorist therefore should assume the position designated by Badiou (and Marcuse) as that of "the no . . . but."[15] In other words, a given structure is rejected so that another structure, a structure that can incorporate more of the hitherto excluded and repressed, can be engendered. Nothing happens or can happen until the Other, which with its ideological (fantasmatic) apparatus conceals its void, is confronted in this way. As confirmed by psychoanalytic theory and practice, it is this act in the present that determines both its own past and its own future.

I argue that here once again we encounter as the principal model the figure of the hysteric, somebody who does, in fact, refuse to play the game of the Other, and demands of the Other to produce something different, something new, something that may provide for the hysteric's satisfaction.

In other words, the hysteric's desire is not fulfilled by the *jouissance* provided by the Other. This is why I contend that the discourse of the hysteric represents the only way to break apart or dissolve that which I have designated as the rock of *jouissance*, that is, the enjoyment congealed in the existing sociopolitical structures, in the existing ways of acting and being (political/economic system, nationality, and so on). That it is our duty to enjoy this *jouissance* is precisely what the hysteric refuses to accept. In my opinion, this is also the only attitude underwritten by a *bona fide* radicalism. If the hysteric is thus the prototypical subject in revolt, then psychoanalysis must be an indispensable component of critical theory of society, since its primary commitment is, as I noted previously, "to hystericize" individuals. The liberated Oedipus, to whom I dedicate this work, is none else but the individual (*any* individual) who speaks the discourse of the hysteric.

NOTES

1. Sigmund Freud, *The Question of Lay Analysis*, trans. Nancy Procter-Gregg (New York: Norton, 1950), 121.
2. Paul A. Robinson, *The Freudian Left: Wilhelm Reich, Geza Roheim, Herbert Marcuse* (New York: Harper & Row, 1969). The proof that this particular theoretical configuration has hardly lost contemporary relevance is Robinson's book being re-issued by Cornell University Press in 1990.
3. *Jouissance* is one of the principal concepts coined by Lacan. It is typically translated as enjoyment; in the sense that I am using it here, it represents the particularity of the established ways of living, thinking, being, and so on. See chapter 3.
4. Sigmund Freud, *Civilization and Its Discontents*, trans. James Strachey (New York: Norton, 1961), 70–71.
5. Wilhelm Reich, *The Mass Psychology of Fascism*, ed. Mary Higgins and Chester M. Raphael (New York: Farrar, Straus, and Giroux, 1970), xvi.
6. Herbert Marcuse, *Eros and Civilization: A Philosophical Inquiry into Freud* (Boston: Beacon Press, 1955), 227.
7. I discuss this point in great detail in chapter 4 where I enunciate the critique of a Nietzschean orientation in the works of Gilles Deleuze and Felix Guattari.
8. Jacques Lacan "The Freudian Thing, or The Meaning of the Return to Freud in Psychoanalysis," *Ecrits: A Selection*, trans. Alan Sheridan (New York: Norton, 1977), 128–29.
9. Jacques Lacan, *Le Seminaire, Livre XVII, L'Envers de la Psychanalyse*, ed. Jacques-Alain Miller (Paris: Seuil, 1991). See also Jacques Lacan, *The Seminar of Jacques Lacan, Book XX: Encore*, ed. Jacques-Alain Miller, trans. Bruce Fink (New York: Norton, 1998), 14–25.
10. "Nobody has one exclusive sphere of activity but each can become accomplished in any branches he wishes. . . . [It becomes] possible for me to do one thing today, and another tomorrow, to hunt in the morning, fish in the afternoon, rear

cattle in the evening, criticize after dinner, just as I have a mind, without ever becoming hunter, fisherman, shepherd, or critic." Karl Marx and Friedrich Engels, "German Ideology," in *The Marx-Engels Reader*, ed. Robert C. Tucker (New York: Norton, 1978), 160.

11. Gilles Deleuze and Felix Guattari, *Anti-Oedipus: Capitalism and Schizophrenia*, trans. Robert Hurley, Mark Seem, and Helen R. Lane (Minneapolis: University of Minnesota Press, 1983), 322–82.

12. Luce Irigaray, *Speculum of the Other Woman*, trans. Gillian C. Gill (Ithaca, NY: Cornell University Press, 1985), 46–90.

13. Slavoj Žižek, *The Sublime Object of Ideology* (London: Verso, 1989), 11–55.

14. Slavoj Žižek, "Class Struggle or Postmodernism? Yes, Please!" in *Contigency, Hegemony, Universality: Contemporary Dialogues on the Left*, ed. Judith Butler, Ernesto Laclau, and Slavoj Žižek (London: Verso, 2000), 106–10.

15. Alain Badiou, *Saint Paul: La Fondation de L'Universalism* (Paris: PUF, 1997), 59–68. Marcuse, Herbert, *One-Dimensional Man: Studies in the Ideology of Advanced Industrial Society* (Boston: Beacon Press, 1964), 203–57.

1
Freud's Theses

> One need not be an anarchist to see that laws and ordinances have no sacred or unimpugnable origin.[1]

Freud himself did not subscribe to emancipatory leftist ideas. However, I argue in this chapter that his work provides a set of hints, which, in my opinion, can ground a theory and a practice critical of the liberal capitalist status quo (the Liberation Thesis). For instance, I argue that the early Freud (that is, the pre-1920 Freud) is more open to the ideas of transformative political and social change than the late Freud, the Freud who has come down to us in the works such as *Beyond the Pleasure Principle* and *Civilization and Its Discontents*. Yet, even in these two works, I find that Freud voices a commitment to the potential of erotic drives to counteract and prevail over all the aggressive and hateful individual and social activities.

My inquiry in this chapter begins with Freud's answer to the question—"how do children acquire values?" What is at stake here is not simply the content of values, but also the form or manner in which they are passed on. For Freud, the acquisition of values is the process of psychological combat, in which one side has all the resources at its disposal to make the other submit. But the submission marks those who submitted for life. The name Freud gives to this unequal struggle is the Oedipus complex. My claim is that the flexibility of the Oedipus complex provides both the promise and the limit of Freud's contributions to the Liberation Thesis. In other words, if the Oedipal hierarchy is necessary for normal psychological functioning, then the prospects of the Liberation Thesis are slim, indeed. If, on the other hand, Oedipus can be modified through Eros,[1] then we can hope for a more egalitarian and less violent civilization.

RIVALRY AND JEALOUSY

On May 31, 1897, Freud wrote to his friend and confidant Wilhelm Fliess[2] the following words: "[A] presentiment tells me, as though I already knew—but I know nothing at all—that I shall soon uncover the source of morality."[3] About four and a half months later, on October 15, 1897, Freud sent to Fliess the rough draft of a structure, which he would later refer to as the Oedipus complex.

What led Freud to Oedipus was the existence of a childhood phenomenon he noted in his patients: the love of the mother and the jealousy of the father.[4] Even his own childhood was marked by it.[5] But, in addition to this personal recognition, Freud found the justification for his formulation in the common reaction of the theater audiences to the performance of Sophocles' *Oedipus Rex*. According to Freud, this common reaction was provoked by the murder of the father and the incest with the mother and consisted of horror mixed with revulsion. These affects, says Freud, are not accidental, but come into being because each member of the audience was "once a budding Oedipus" and now, in the course of the tragedy, is faced with the repressed Oedipal wishes being played out in the light of day. Expressed horror shows the extent of repression and underwrites the truth of the existence of the postulated twin emotions directed toward the parents.[6]

Another manifestation of the truth of Oedipal feelings, in Freud's view, is found in Shakespeare's *Hamlet*. Freud argues that Hamlet hesitates to take revenge on the murderer of his father, because (at some point in his past, presumably in his childhood) he himself entertained similar murderous attitude. In fact, what is at the root of his hesitation and self-doubt—his moral impulse—is nothing but a creature of (in the sense of being created by) the unconscious sense of guilt for this attitude.[7] In other words, the actual murder of the father brings the memory of the repressed wish to the surface, cutting through the layers of repression, and, as a result, Hamlet is literally paralyzed by the irruption of guilt. His conscious mind (his ego, to use Freud's later, more precise terminology) is overwhelmed by the underside it had repressed—though without conscious awareness—and Hamlet never quite regains the upper hand. The proof that he is ultimately drowned by his guilt, according to Freud, is that he ends in the same way his father did: his being poisoned is the work of his father's murderer, that is, Hamlet punishes himself by getting himself killed.

THE OEDIPAL CLAIM

In the letter to Fliess cited above, we see Freud claiming for the first time that the structure that grounds morality has an Oedipal nature. But did he, at this point, offer enough evidence to support his point of view? Did he give us a convincing rationale? This is indeed the question that needs to be examined before proceeding to link up Oedipus with other sociopolitical insights of psychoanalysis.

Oedipal morality, according to Freud, is derived from the existence of childhood love for the mother and jealousy of the father. But shouldn't the child's love toward parents, as his or her primary caretakers, be unopposed? What could bring about the affect of jealousy? To support his case, Freud offered the following: his personal history, the theater audience reaction to the performance of *Oedipus Rex*, and the attitude of a fictional hero, Hamlet. In my opinion, the examination of the latter two provides us with an insight into the theory of mental functioning that Freud held at the time.[8]

The conscious manifestation of a strong negative emotion was, in Freud's view, a revelation of the strength of the repression of its opposite. For instance, the audience's explicit horror at parricide and incest is a sign of their having repressed their desire for them. After all, if parricide and incest were not psychologically significant, one would expect the audience to be indifferent to their being presented on the stage. What Freud did not say was which one of these deeds inspired more horror: parricide or incest. Which one would the individual conscience (moral impulse) find more difficult to deal with? In other words, which one is primary and which one is derivative in its relation to the psychic life of the individual?

It seems to me, however, that Freud did hint that, in a certain way, the murderous jealousy toward the father was derived from the existence of the love for the mother. This then means that the latter is to be considered more significant than the former. One could therefore say that a prohibition against incest is more fundamental (more primordial) than a prohibition against parricide. Or, in general terms, the ground of morality is a prohibition against incest and all other prohibitions are derived or flow from it.

And yet, the example of Hamlet that Freud brought up was not about incest, but about parricide. Even so, I think that Freud's position here is not contradictory. This is so, because Freud viewed the father as the agent of incest prohibition, as the enforcer of the taboo, which must not be transgressed. The argument therefore remains consistent: the enforcer is less primordial than the crime he forbids, since it is the existence of the possibility of such a crime that leads to the necessity of the enforcer.

On another level, this also means that the repression of sexual (love) feelings has a more important role to play in the formation of a moral individual than the repression of aggressive urges. In fact, that is what Freud states in a letter to Fliess that followed shortly after the letter on Oedipus and Hamlet. In this letter (November 14, 1897), Freud identifies morality with the presence of sexual repression.[9] Here one sees him connect the psychological fact of repression to the physiological phenomenon of the shrinkage of the number and scope of the body's erogenous zones from the period of childhood to that of adulthood.

In childhood, according to Freud, the sources of sexual excitation are less "localized" and "perhaps [extend to] the whole surface of the body." Eventually certain zones are abandoned (at this point, Freud leaves out the question of the dynamic of this process; his vague reference is to "development"), but the memory traces of their having been the sources of pleasure remain in the unconscious. When these memory traces are brought into consciousness by being triggered or re-activated by some external event, the conscious mind is beset by the "thou shalt not" types of commands. And, at the same time, at the level of physiology, what is felt is displeasure and disgust. As Freud vividly puts it, "the memory actually stinks just as in the present the object stinks."[10] In other words, the nose of the conscious mind wants to escape the malodorous intrusion and therefore mobilizes its powers to repress the memory even more forcefully. As a result, the feelings of shame and sexual revulsion are formed and gain strength. Indeed, Freud concludes that even a great variety of what he calls the intellectual processes of development come to be "at the expense of extinct sexuality."[11]

But this is only a part of the story, though, in my opinion, Freud seems not to have recognized it at this point. Surprisingly, Freud did not connect his discussion of morality in this letter with his earlier elaboration on *Oedipus Rex* and *Hamlet*. This is strange, considering that it is very plausible to consider the performance of *Oedipus Rex* as the external event that can trigger the bringing to consciousness of an unconscious memory trace (the incest prohibition). There is something more as well. In his interpretation of *Hamlet*, Freud considers guilt as formative of moral impulse or conscience. Hamlet's guilt, however, is not primarily an outcome of repressed sexuality, but instead comes about as a result of repressed aggressive, murderous desire. Even though the neurotic personality such as Hamlet may be prone to amplifying this sense of guilt, it cannot be denied that repressing aggression constitutes a component even in the formation of morality in non-neurotic individuals. This is especially so, if the love of the mother and the jealousy of the father are considered to be universal. Therefore, it remains a puzzle why Freud did not incorporate this insight into his discussion of morality in the November 1897 letter.

Freud also did not take any note of the possibility that sex difference might make a difference in terms of the Oedipal attitude. The audience he talked about is considered as a collectivity; presumably individuals of both sexes experience the same reaction. On the other hand, Hamlet is a male hero and his attitude towards his father seems to be a reflection of the fact that in his early childhood he had considered his father as a same sex rival for the love of the wife/mother. This (in addition to the mention of Freud's own early experiences) could be taken to imply that what is talked about here is the formation of morality in a male child. And yet Freud postulates the existence of Oedipal emotions as a universal childhood event. Therefore it seems safe to conclude that Freud's Oedipal theory of morality was, at this point in the late 1890s, still in need of a great deal of thinking through.

INTERPRETATION OF DREAMS

If the transitions from one century to another are marked by the advancement in the understanding of human spirit (and I am by no means arguing that such is the case), it is perhaps fitting that Freud published his first major work *The Interpretation of Dreams* in the last months of 1899. The key premises of this book that dreams are "a royal road" to the unconscious, and that as such they provide access to a kind of logic, which though not of the same cloth as consciousness, influences the conscious mind are, it seems to me, an epochal discovery worthy of underscoring the century change. Thus perhaps one can say that if the nineteenth century opened so many areas of daily life to the inquiries of consciousness, the twentieth century would expand the horizons of understanding into a region so far unconquered—the life of the night, the realm of that which remains different and apart from the conscious.

What this meant, in Freud's case, is that the essential phenomena of the night—dreams—contained a meaning that could be deciphered by those who cracked the code, by those who uncovered the grammar of their secret language. As I have shown in the case of his letters to Fliess, Freud had already grown convinced of the existence of repressed wishes circulating in the unconscious. In *The Interpretation of Dreams*, he took another step along the same path: he argued that dreams are manifestations of those repressed wishes in which the wishes themselves appear as fulfilled.[12] He claimed that the degree of distortion in a dream depends on the extent of the repression of the particular wish that motivated the dream's formation. In addition, distortion—in the guises of condensation and displacement—could be influenced by the events and consciously recognized emotions of the preceding day.

Freud noted that there existed several categories of "typical" dreams, which meant that the repressed wishes that stimulated such dreams had a universal character. In light of his statement that the feelings of love and jealousy toward parents were the universal features of childhood which later underwent varying degrees of repression, it is to be expected that these feelings found their manifestation in typical dreams. It is therefore not surprising that the most prominent subsection in the section on typical dreams is entitled "Dreams of the Death of Beloved Persons."

DEATH AND THE DREAM

In this section, Freud endeavors to show that dreaming of the death of a beloved family member (while at the same time feeling pain and anxiety) reflects quite accurately the meaning of the repressed wish. In other words, at the certain point of time, the dreamer had actually desired such a thing to come to pass. This does not mean, as Freud is quick to add, that the dreamer consciously entertains such wishes at present, but it does mean that what had once been desired broke through the layers of repression and is now seeking conscious recognition by the dreamer. In Freud's poetic words, repressed wishes are "like the shades in the Odyssey which awaken to a certain degree of life as soon as they have drunk blood."[13] And this blood is usually found in the memory-residues of the events of the previous day.

Freud is aware that his claim that the dreamers actually desire the death of the beloved persons will encounter a great opposition in his readers. So he sets out to substantiate his claim by references to empirical observations of early childhood behavior, and also to his own psychoanalytic work with neurotics.

Freud first tackles the issue of dreams of the death of siblings (sisters and brothers). He attributes the cause of these dreams to the feelings of rivalry inspired by the sibling's presence. In Freud's view, child behavior is marked by consistent egoism, that is to say, by a strong commitment to one's own pleasure and well-being.[14] Hence siblings are considered rivals for parental affection and material comforts. Freud notes a case of a child who, upon being told that the stork had brought her a sibling, reacted by saying: "The stork had better take it back again."[15] Or another child who, at every mention of his new born sister, exclaimed: "Too (l)ittle, too (l)ittle," thus implying that his new sister is not worth much attention and nurture compared to himself. Several months later, his sister having grown at a rapid pace, the same child commented to Freud: "But she hasn't any teeth!"[16] It is the evidence of this sort that makes Freud conclude that adult dreams of the death of siblings stem from the re-activation of such childhood wishes.

Freud, however, makes an important qualification regarding the child's understanding of death. He argues that children have no perception of suffering and pain that the path to death entails. In other words, they have no understanding of "the horrors of decay, the shivering in the cold grave, the terror of infinite Nothing" that plague many adults when they position their mind's eye in such a way as to consider the end of their earthly journey.[17] For a child, "being dead" is equivalent to "being gone" and being gone means that the departed person is unable to obstruct the child's own enjoyment, freedom, and comforts. A child wants the unwanted rival to disappear and therefore chooses to wish him or her out of sight.

Yet Freud does not explain why precisely the metaphor of death is invoked and not the metaphor of a (simple) absence, for instance. One can perhaps attribute such a dramatic aspect of the child's wish to its egoism (or narcissism). For the little tyrant, it seems that "every inconvenience constitutes the crime of *lese majesté*" with only one possible punishment—death.[18]

The notion of child as tyrannical implies that it is only through the repression of its primary impulses that he or she could become a member of a functional community. Hence Freud refers to the necessity of education or training in morality.[19] But this also means that on the theoretical level Freud posits an inevitable conflict between nature and society, between what is primary in the individual and what is necessary for a society to be established. The morality as a social creation is imposed (stamped) upon the desires of the individual. It is therefore to be expected that the deepest layers of the psyche will consider it as something external, as a yoke that it is imperative to overthrow given any possible escape from punishment. This means that, according to Freud, at the unconscious level human beings are beings with an insatiable desire for self-satisfaction, a desire whose strength persists regardless of a social price for its fulfillment. In Freud's view, it is precisely this unconscious propensity that the dreams of the death of beloved persons show or demonstrate clearly.

Such a narcissistic orientation of the unconscious becomes even more perceptible when Freud investigates the child's attitude toward those who are considered to be its primary educators: its parents. Here he continues his discussion of Oedipus and Hamlet he first unfolded in his letters to Fliess.

OEDIPUS AND HAMLET REVISITED

Freud begins his discussion of the dreams of parental death with a puzzle. How is it—he asks—that a child who has just been defined as the perfect egoist, as a being that wants to get its way at all times, would desire the death of persons who actually provide it with the possibility of fulfilling all its egoistic wishes? In order to deal with an obvious contradiction, Freud thinks that his original claim (the actual unconscious desire for parental death) requires a modification and, for the first time, he introduces the sex difference into his theorizing of this issue. He now states that what generally takes place is not the desire for the death of both parents, but only for the death of the parent of the same sex. This is so, according to Freud, because the child considers the same sex parent as a rival in love.[20] In other words, boys will desire the disappearance of the father, while girls will harbor similar feelings towards their mother.

Freud argues that the everyday interaction of parents and their children bears witness to the existence of such partiality in love and hate. He states that in many families it is the father who holds sway over the issue of the son's autonomy and independence, while the mother plays the same role regarding the daughter of the family. The nature of such power relations engenders the state of disharmony, especially as children and adolescents push for more freedom than parents are willing to give them.[21]

Freud also refers to something he calls "a natural tendency" on the part of the parents to meet the child's emotional attitudes halfway. This tendency finds its expression in the widely observed phenomenon that fathers are more favorably inclined toward their daughters, while mothers frequently take the side of their sons. This is perhaps not unrelated to the issue of independence and control that Freud brought up first, but, in any case, it confirms and strengthens the child's own attitudes. Freud, however, skirts around the issue of priority in that he does not say whether parental attitudes determine those of children, or it is vice versa. It seems, however, that his hints go in the direction of postulating the sex differential in the child's affection to be an expression of the child's own "nature," rather than as something that comes into being by environmental influences.

This is confirmed by the examples Freud notes to substantiate his case. He refers both to the observations of children and of neurotics. One four-year-old girl, for instance, exclaimed at the social event Freud attended: "Now mummy can go away; then daddy must marry me, and I will be his wife."[22] Another case Freud cites concerns a neurotic young girl who suffered attacks of convulsions and vomiting. After the work of analysis was able to put a stop to their occurrence, Freud speculated that these attacks were stimulated by the presence of the unconscious rivalry with her mother. Interestingly—but in line with the theory of the unconscious present, as I have shown, even in Freud's early letters to Fliess—the last incarnation of her neurosis was in the expression of the intense and excessive concern for the mother's well-being. This psychological phenomenon, which Freud calls "reaction-formation," pointed to the efforts that the girl's conscious mind was making to deny and repress the unconscious impulses clamoring for recognition. Yet the path to recovery opened up only when the girl confronted all these evil "shades that have drunk blood," and saw them for what they are—the expressions of repressed childhood wishes for her mother's disappearance.[23]

Not only do repressed childhood wishes haunt the subsequent life history of the individual, but also—continues Freud, adding another brick to the edifice of his argument—their content and structure reveal a high degree of correspondence (affinity) with the artistic and creative products of the early stages of civilization (its mythology). In Freud's view—and this will remain true for many of his later writings on society and culture—the prehistory of the individual contains a set of remarkable structural similarities with the prehistory of human society.[24] This is so because in both cases (the personal and the social) the processes of (imposed) external repression have not been firmly established. In other words, that which will later be exiled into the depths of the psyche can still, under certain conditions, appear on the surface.

According to Freud, this kind of development marks the essential difference between Oedipus and Hamlet. Oedipus actually lives through that which every male child desires—the sole possession of the mother and the murder of the one who could prevent or interfere with it, the father. Hamlet also harbors the same wish. Moreover, Freud claims that this wish is universal and transcends history or, in his own words, "the oracle laid upon us *before our birth* the very curse which rested upon [Oedipus]."[25]

Yet, according to Freud, what separates antiquity and modernity, what distinguishes Oedipus from Hamlet, is not a mere passage of time, but also "the progress of repression in the emotional life of humanity."[26] In other words, as modernity takes hold, unconscious wishes (desires) that infringe upon the socially imposed norms and ways of behavior find it more and more difficult to gain expression and representation in daily life. In the adult life of the modern individual (Hamlet, you, me), such desires (while not losing their intensity) are forced into the depths of the psyche, breaking loose on occasion and emerging in the shape of a neurotic symptom.

We infer the existence of unconscious desires based on the structure of the symptom. In the case of Hamlet, for instance, his hesitation and vacillation about taking revenge for his father's murder point to the existence of an unconscious complicity with the murderer. The murderer had fulfilled the foremost of Hamlet's childhood wishes, and no wonder Hamlet is unwilling to strike him down. In Freud's interpretation, "the loathing which should have driven him to revenge is thus replaced by self-reproach, by conscientious scruples, which tell him that he himself is no better than the murderer whom he is required to punish."[27] As a result, the feelings of guilt brought about by self-reproach prove too much to take, and Hamlet—one could almost say willingly—submits himself to being murdered in order to atone for the murderous impulses he himself entertained.

I think that Freud takes Hamlet's case to exemplify the tragedy of the modern moral individual. The court of neurosis condemns him or her to severe punishment in earthly life, since he or she is always being out of sync, unable to act or else over-reacting. Only the work of psychoanalysis can present enough evidence for the modern individual's acquittal, as Freud never tires from reminding his readers, and which is of signal importance for the emancipatory potential of psychoanalytic theory and practice. But Freud cautions that even such an acquittal requires a probationary period to which no limit could be assigned or known *a priori*. This is so because, in Freud's view, the drives of infantile sexuality—making up the repressed of the unconscious—never find a permanently comfortable home among the edifices of modern civilization.

INFANTILE SEXUALITY

As I see it, the issue that provides the foundation for Freud's understanding of the relations between mental processes and moral attitudes is the issue of infant and child sexuality. This issue, as Freud points out in his *Three Contributions to the Theory of Sex* (1903), had for a variety of reasons been neglected in the study of infant and child development.[28] One of these reasons, in Freud's view, has to do with an extremely curious fact that most of that which occurs in early childhood is not remembered in the later adult life of the individual. This childhood amnesia is rather puzzling, considering that during the period that is subsequently forgotten the child was far from being a passive observer of events. It intervened actively in all kinds of activities, and its quickness and acuity of the mind are later fondly recalled by those adults who witnessed it. So what happened? Freud makes us ask.[29]

Freud argues that these impressions are not wiped out at all, but are instead prevented from coming to the recognition of consciousness. The combined forces of organic development (growth) and education (i.e., social norms and conventions) establish or constitute what Freud refers to as "dams" in order to keep the infantile drives under control in the darkness of the psychic underworld. This is so because the nature and content of infantile impressions and attitudes is such that the conscious mind (as the agency largely shaped by social standards and educational norms) wants nothing to do with them. In other words, the conscious mind (as it comes into being) confronts and strives to defeat the polymorphous and perverse character of infantile drives.[30]

But—at the same time—the conscious mind is also forced to feed off its "enemy" in order to generate enough energy for its own activity. This means that the psychological phenomena of reaction-formation and sublimation which, according to Freud, underlie the formation of all moral and aesthetic values and judgments are also based on the functioning of sexual drives. Freud hints that he considers sublimation especially relevant for the flourishing of arts and other cultural attainments, but he leaves the account of its psychological genesis undeveloped.[31]

The notion of the child's uninhibited pursuit of gratification for its own sake, discussed in *The Interpretation of Dreams*, finds a more specific elaboration in Freud's essay "Infantile Sexuality." Here Freud chronicles the origin and development of various erogenous zones. He notes their original dependent (anaclitic or "lean-on") connection with the self-preservative bodily functions. The erotic gratification of the oral zone, for instance, is first linked to the taking of food, but after a short while it takes an independent path as is manifested in the wide-spread childhood practice of thumbsucking.[32] The rhythmical movement that leads to the feeling of pleasure remains the same, though the food is now absent (the satisfaction becomes virtual). Freud explains this development as expressing the infant's attempt to take control over the sources of his pleasure. Since the infant after all cannot depend on being fed each time it desires to eat, it re-directs its drives toward its own body (the body that is always there), and engages in gratification that it can give itself without the actual presence of others.[33] Analogous developments take place in the formation of the anal and genital erogenous zones.[34]

THE PRIMACY OF A RELATION TO THE OTHER

However, it is important to note that Freud assigns the initial impetus that sets the infant on the path of the pursuit of self-gratification to the involvement of others (cf. dependence on—and absence of—his caretakers). In my opinion, this means that one could postulate the existence of the object-relation (the relation to the other) prior to the envelopment in autoerotic practices. As a result, then, the infant's relentless narcissism can be seen not as a primary phenomenon, an *a priori* phenomenon of childhood, but as a derivation that points to the priority of the communal presence. In other words, narcissism could be theorized as a defensive mechanism due to the failure of community to come to the infant's aid.

In fact, the priority of object-relations seems to be the gist of Freud's statement that "object-finding [in adult life] is really a re-finding."[35] It is a re-finding of that primary bond with the object that first inspired desire—the maternal breast—and also of the feeling of contentment and satiety that this object (through its magical presence) could bring about. In other words, in the search for the object, the infant perceives a glimpse of a total union (oneness) that awakens and determines the path of its desire. From this, it seems to me safe to conclude that the first movement of desire is towards the other, and that even though desire soon afterwards becomes entangled in one's own body (the other having remained distant), it is essentially searching for the repetition of the other in and to oneself.

If therefore, in this way, the social (the communal; the other-relation) gives birth to the individual, then the social cannot be represented (or conceptualized) as solely a sum of all the individuals (as in classical liberal theory). It seems to me that hence the implications of this line of thought ally Freud with a strand of communitarian thinking, such as one finds in Rousseau's *Social Contract* and, as I will show in chapter 2, in the writings of the theorists of the Liberation Thesis. Rousseau, for instance, argues that the general will (the universal; the social) establishes the condition(s) for the possibility of the existence of the individual, who, if stripped of the veil of his or her particularity, will discover (or, we could say, re-discover) the social essence within. If forcing somebody to be free, in Rousseau's sense, means instilling the clear awareness of the tie that frames the social, then forcing somebody to be free, in Freud's sense, means instilling the clear awareness of that which is really looked for in what is found; in other words, what is looked for in the object of desire is the relation to the other.

But, for Freud, this also means the recognition (and acceptance) of the fact that what is found is always at one remove from that which is looked for. In his presentation, one can almost sense certain Platonic overtones in that the primary object-relation "participates" in all the object-relations of adult life, but it is not fully materialized in them. It seems to me that if this were not the case, we would know nothing but the darkness of the cave (or, perhaps, the fatally blinding light of the Sun).[36]

Or, in other words, the individual always has to choose twice. The object choices of childhood and the drives oriented towards them undergo a wave of repression during the latency period that precedes puberty. In Freud's view, the relation to these objects does not disappear, but—in a situation that does not lead to neurosis—emerges in the attitudes of honoring and esteeming and, in this way, represents "the tender stream of the sexual life."[37] The events of puberty establish another "stream" which comes to contain the drives and objects of adult sexuality. The functioning of the conscious mind as well as the existing social norms keep the two streams wide apart. It is only in neurosis that the partial convergence (that is, the influx of the primary into the secondary stream) takes place. What neurosis shows, as Freud keeps pointing out, is the persistence of the libidinal attachments to the childhood objects of desire.

THE THEORY OF THE LIBIDO

Freud defines the libido as the energy or force that stems from sexual sources and that transmits sexual excitement throughout the body.[38] However, this should not be taken to mean that all psychic energy is exclusively libidinal or sexual. For example, Freud refers to component or partial drives that only in later development come to be submerged under the sway of sexuality.[39]

One such component-drive, Freud argues, is the drive for mastery, which finds its empirical expression in cruelty often observed in the behavior of infants and young children. In fact, it seems to me that Freud's presentation of early childhood narcissism explains this type of behavior rather well.

However, his claim that sympathy or empathy toward others should be taken as a reaction-formation of such infantile (primordial) cruelty appears not to be consistent with his assertion of the existence of the primary bond with the object of desire (with the other) examined in the previous section. On the contrary, what emerges is the fact that the drive for mastery and its manifestations are not all that primordial, but come into being only after the primary bond with the other is broken. Therefore, I think that one does not rupture the Freudian framework if one argues, as I do, that cruelty can be understood as a reaction-formation of initial love that has been frustrated and not vice versa. This is also the position of those thinkers who subscribe to the Liberation Thesis. Clearly what is at stake here is not only the issue of the psychic transformations of drives, but also and more importantly the issue of priority. Or, in other words, the question here is whether there is an original other-regarding quality to the being of the human being.

However, if this is admitted to be the case, then it becomes difficult to consider the drive for mastery free from the libidinal tendencies and sexuality. In fact, I think that Freud's discussion of sadism and masochism shows to what extent control and domination on one side and submission and subservience on the other come to be invested with libidinal energy.[40] The conclusion, which seems inescapable, is that even these at times violent practices represent nothing else but two paths that the drives open up in the search for gratification in the ever-elusive object of desire. In other words, even masochism and sadism are the modes in which a relation to the other is established, and they remain no more and no less than the carriers of libidinal messages from oneself to the other and back.

One could therefore say that the relation between cruelty and the libido is not as clearly cut as claimed by those who sought to make of Freud a cynic, a conservative judge of humanity.[41] In other words, the child's component drives seem to be motivated by the libido (by an erotic relation to the other) even before the conscious efforts of parents and educators. In fact, I think that Freud's own statement seems pertinent here. Freud states that "the different paths along which the libido moves, behave one to another from the beginning like communicating pipes, and one must therefore take into account the phenomenon of collateral streaming."[42] In other words, just because animosity seems to prevail over cooperation in contemporary society does not mean that this animosity does not flow out of libidinal bonds among people, and could not therefore be modified by the redirection of the libido.[43] It is here that psychoanalysis can play a role supportive of transformative political and social changes, since it is the only theoretical and practical enterprise that knows how to deal with the cadences of libidinal flows.

THE OBJECT-LIBIDO V. THE EGO-LIBIDO

It seems to me that Freud was aware of the social significance of psychoanalysis and that is why he made a fundamental distinction in the types of libido based on the location of its investments or occupations (occupations in the military sense; also referred to as *cathexis*). In this respect, he postulated the existence of the object-libido and the ego-libido.

The object-libido, according to Freud, is the type of libido that structures the individual's relations to the world beyond his or her inner life. Its workings could be conceptualized as the fixations on a variety of objects of desire, and one of the main tasks of psychoanalysis is to guide the object-libido from the choices that may impede the psychological well being of the individual to those that will enhance it.[44] The ego-libido, in contrast, is the libido which is narcissistically invested in the psychological processes of one's conscious mind (one's ego). Its excessive accumulation at the expense of the object-libido leads to serious psychological disturbances, including psychoses. This is so because excessive libidinal investment pushes the ego to cut off all the ties with the external world, as if by an impenetrable theater curtain, and, as a result, spin in the orbit of the world of its own making. In other words, the ego becomes its own stage without any relation to that which also exists for others. Therefore a selfish individual who consistently disregards the concerns of others can be seen as manifesting a psychological attitude formally similar to the elements of psychosis, and therefore I would argue requires a certain degree of psychoanalytic care. In this sense, selfishness is revealed to be a psychological pathology.

However, even though one can glimpse the liberatory potential of Freud's theory of the libido, one should still keep in mind that it is modeled along the lines of mechanistic physics and classical economics. These two influences pervaded the scientific enterprise at the turn of the last century. In his later works (see below), Freud transcends the linear conceptualizations of Newtonian physics. However, as I will show in subsequent chapters, it will be left to those following and extending the Freudian path to modify the libido-economics based on Adam Smith with a bit of Marxism.

THE SEX DIFFERENCE

Another Freud's thesis significant for psychoanalysis as social and political theory, which is for the first time systematically presented in *Three Contributions*, is his conceptualization of sexual difference. It is should be noted at the start that this aspect of Freud's thought has been judged most deficient by many contemporary commentators, especially those allied with feminist thought.[45] The essence of feminist argument is that Freud's theorizing shows a distinct male bias because the model of male sexual development is taken as the standard and the female development is then derived from that of the male. It seems to me that one could defend Freud by pointing out that he himself admitted the extensive focus on male sexuality, but justified it on the account of social and cultural conventions of his day that prevented women from speaking freely and openly on the issue of sex.[46] In other words, one had to use for theoretical elaboration the empirical material that was at hand; there was not any other.

In this respect, I find it important that Freud distinguishes the psychoanalytic meaning of the notions of the masculine and the feminine both from the biological and the sociological meaning that they carry. He therefore makes it clear that his conceptualization does not concern the presence or the absence of specific organs,[47] nor does it directly derive from the behavior of actual men and women. Instead, in Freud's view, the masculine signifies activity, and the feminine means passivity.[48] While this formulation may be perceived as having an air of misogyny, it is far from being a value judgment (i.e., Freud does not say that it is preferable to be active). The formulation is but a shorthand and, in addition, Freud is quick to point out that in psychoanalysis there are no pure types; the psyche of every individual contains a mixture of active and passive attitudes, that is, a mixture of masculinity and femininity. These attitudes are then manifested in the object-choices of one's libidinal tendencies.

It should also surprise no one that Freud states that the libido is always masculine; this means no more than that the propulsion of libidinal energy is always active. Even so the libido, though itself active, might become invested with a passive aim. This situation is, for instance, amply demonstrated by the examples of psychological and physical masochism. Or, in a more dramatic formulation, every masochist is a sadist who derives pleasure from aggressive transgressions towards oneself.

However, sexual differentiation is made manifest when the existing social norms and the prevailing standards of adult sexual behavior are taken into consideration. These, according to Freud, require a more active disposition on the part of the man than on that of the woman. Considering that the childhood of both sexes is marked by active (masculine) pursuit of the chosen sexual objects, Freud sees it necessary to postulate the occurrence of "a wave of repression" at the time when the girl reaches puberty. Freud connects the genesis of this repressive tendency to social factors underlying the education that girls receive during the latency period. This makes it likely that for a girl sexual relations may carry a more intense sense of shame and (perhaps) loathing than is the case with a boy.[49] The implication here is that if these social factors were somehow changed, the attitudes toward the sexual act in both sexes could reach some sort of a positive equilibrium. In other words, Freud seems to be saying that change in social values can easily make an impact on the expression of masculine and feminine sexuality.

In addition to this, however, Freud links the repression occurring in the girls' puberty to a factor that apparently has an organic basis. He thinks that in order to feel pleasure during the heterosexual intercourse, each girl must make a transition from the clitoral to vaginal sexuality.[50] In other words, while the clitoris is the sole genital erogenous zone in childhood, in adult sexuality this zone needs to be extended to include also the vagina. This extension necessitates the disengagement of the part of the libido from the clitoris (accomplished in the guise of repression) which is then, in the years of sexual activity, re-invested into the vaginal area.

In Freud's view, the reason that the boys do not undergo this type of libidinal repression during puberty and therefore generally preserve their active, grasping (aggressive) disposition is that there is no necessity for them to abandon the infantile genital erogenous zone—the penis. In fact, for Freud, the clitoris is akin to the penis in terms of its importance in childhood sexuality: the only difference is in size. The size, however, seems to matter greatly, as I will show below in my discussion of the Little Hans case history. The penis becomes a symbol of value for the little boy and the Oedipal relation with the threat of castration that it carries, Freud argues, remains a very important marker in his psychological development. The little girl, on the other hand, adjusts to the fact that she does not have the penis by desiring it, and this is what sets her on the path of finding varying substitutes for it.[51] Freud refers to this attitude on the part of the little girl as "penis-envy," and this term has certainly generated an immense amount of controversy over the years. However, the little girl's recognition that she does not have the penis also means that she has nothing to lose in confrontation with paternal authority. In essence, she finds herself in the position of being able to subvert the law of the Father without being weighed down by guilt or by unconscious fear of punishment. In other words, her psychological development is free from most Oedipal anxieties and the burdens that they entail. A strategy that one can mark as revolutionary therefore seems to grow out of the logic of the feminine.[52]

However, it seems to me necessary to keep in mind that Freud's account of female sexuality depends on his claim that the clitoris remains the sole genital erogenous zone in the young girl's childhood. Freud bases on this claim the conceptualization of the girl-boy relations as well as the emergence of sex-specific repression in the girl's pubescent period (responsible in part for engendering a passive disposition). If, on the other hand, the little girl experiences libidinal excitement also in the vagina, as Karen Horney argued soon after the publication of Freud's thesis, then his argument loses its founding stone.[53]

It is beyond the scope of my concerns in this chapter to adjudicate the dispute between Freud and Horney, but I brought it up in order to underscore the fact that, for psychoanalysis, sexual difference makes a difference in terms of the positioning of the two sexes toward the potentialities of the political and social status quo.[54]

CASE HISTORIES

Aware of the widespread skepticism that psychoanalytic theories generated when first published, Freud thought that his theorizing (as, for instance, in *Three Contributions*) needed to be supplemented by the publication of extensive case histories that would demonstrate the validity and practical application of psychoanalytic concepts. His elaborate five case histories—written in the style reminiscent of detective novels—were intended for this job.

The first published case history, entitled "Dora," was to illustrate the psychoanalytic understanding of hysteria; the "Little Hans" was to show the essential elements of phobia; the "Rat Man" was to shed light on obsessional neurosis; the "Wolf Man" dealt with infantile neurosis,[55] while the "Doctor Schreber" made bold strides upon the land of psychosis. While all these case histories contain the material of interest for the study of the genesis of moral values (having of necessity to dip into the childhood of the respective patients), I find two of them particularly pertinent. These two are the Little Hans and the Wolf Man.

THE LITTLE HANS

Freud refers to the four and a half year old Hans as "the little Oedipus,"[56] and in this way, from the very beginning, links this case history to his earlier theoretical ruminations on the role of the Oedipal attitude in the socialization of children. It seems to me that the choice of Hans (and not, for instance, his younger sister Hanna) also shows Freud's adherence to the claim that girls are, in a sense, released from having to carry Oedipal burdens directly. After all, the focus in the Little Hans is on the (emerging) attitudes toward parents on the part of a young boy. But does this also mean that the fear and hatred of the father and the love for the mother (typical of young boys) are more essential to the development of moral values than the reverse attitude prevalent in young girls? Freud does seem to think so, even though he does not state it directly. This implication, however, adds wind to the sails of feminist critics that Freud sneaks in the male development as the norm. The way Freud pieces together the components of Hans's phobia shows that it would not have come into existence, if he had been a little girl.

But this also means that, in that case, Hans's childhood would have been all the less traumatic.

This is so because the little Hans's fundamental fear, which manifested itself through a variety of symptoms, was that something might happen to his "widdler," a nickname he used to refer to his penis. He considered his widdler an object of significant value because it had given him intense autoerotic satisfaction. He was so preoccupied with it in frequent masturbation that at one point his mother uttered what (to Hans) sounded like a castration threat.[57] This threat came to play a significant role in the constitution of Hans's phobia because it drove the point home that the behavior and attitudes not sanctioned by adults might bring about serious restrictions on his enjoyment. In other words, the explicit parental message was that Hans had to moderate (and deflect) his libidinal investments if he was take his place in the world of adults without being reproached or punished.

Freud contends, however, that Hans's phobia was not set into motion by the mother's castration threat but by something a bit different. The precipitating event was the birth of Hans's sister Hanna and the rather exclusive preoccupation of his mother with Hanna's well-being. By seeing the great deal of his mother's affection now directed towards his sister, Hans was reminded of the period in his early years when he himself had been the sole center of such maternal love.[58] Freud argues that it is this that led to a great release of libidinal energy, which however at this point could not reach its intended aim. This was so because Hans encountered a rival to his libidinal desire to spend more and more time near his mother (for instance by sleeping next to her). This rival was nobody else but his dear father.

The problem for Hans was that his father was also his great friend. They would spend hours talking and walking together, and Hans derived a great pleasure in playing all kinds of games with his father. Therefore, Freud claims, the aggressive feelings that arose in Hans as the result of the frustration of the original libidinal aim could not be openly expressed. He had to repress them with all his conscious energy, though they were forcefully surging forward.[59] For—Hans thought—if the father found out not only would he stop being affectionate towards him, but he would also most likely retaliate by punishing him, even perhaps by taking away his widdler from him. Hans had an inkling that there were living beings without widdlers, and therefore his fears that he might lose this source of enjoyment seemed to him to be justified. As a result, Hans found himself in a psychological quagmire and no wonder that something had to give way: the smooth functioning of libidinal flows was blocked (analogously, a computer that is given several contradictory commands at the same time will shut down). The way of getting out of the deadlock, the compromise-solution, was the emergence of a neurosis in the shape of phobia whose most prominent manifestation came to be the fear of horses.[60]

The object of a phobia could be almost anything, and the reason that in Hans's phobia horses played the principal role is based on several environmental influences. These include witnessing the death of a horse, living across from the Customs House where there was plenty of horse traffic every day, playing games of horses with other children of his age at a summer retreat and so on. The formation of a neurotic phobia (and not some other neurotic disorder) was determined by the fact that since Hans's libido could not attain its aim (of exclusive maternal love), it had to be bound in some other way. This binding was accomplished by the imposition of a set of internal prohibitions that outwardly manifested itself as a phobia.[61] In fact, the horse—in Hans's fantasies—was his father; his fear of horses, translated from the language of neurosis, meant the fear of paternal retaliation and punishment.[62]

It was only by making peace with the fact that the father's affection for the mother has the right of precedence and by re-deploying his libidinal investments elsewhere (the study of music, for instance) that Hans was able to overcome his phobia and face horses without fear. In this he was no doubt helped by his father's warm attitude towards him. Important also is his father's friendship (analysis) with Freud, so that Freud was able to intervene from time to time from behind the scene. In fact, after a session with Freud, the little Hans exclaimed: "Does the Professor talk to God, as he can tell all that beforehand?"[63] Hans clearly felt that Freud could understand and help him deal with unresolved tensions boiling up in his soul. But the battle that was waged was ultimately one that he fought with himself. He had to recognize the necessity of curbing his libidinal impulses, pleasurable though they were, for the sake of learning how to deal with the limits imposed on him and other children for the sake of preserving existing social values.

And this essentially is the dilemma of moral development. At what price must one square one's libidinal tendencies with the exigencies and requirements of civilization? The transmission of the accomplishments and values of civilization demands a certain level of libidinal repression on the part of each individual, on the part of each new being that faces this gigantic enterprise of many generations. On a psychological level, in Freud's view, the imposition of values without understanding their meaning represents the essence of repression, and therefore the kernel of a possible pathology. It is hence the task of psychoanalysis to bring about a genuine enlightenment, a revelation of why it is necessary to channel libidinal investment in one way and not in another. But this, according to Freud, does not mean that what the individual is given in terms of rationale will ever lead to his or her complete acquiescence. The individual will in a way continue to suffer (provoking a sense of malaise), but he or she will know why this is so. One can therefore say that Freud believed that it is the conscious knowledge of who we are and how we came to be the way we are that could set us free (to the maximum extent possible under circumstances). There is a bit of us that will always remain unknown to ourselves, but this bit or this part of our psyche does not have to be the one that fully determines our behavior. Or, in a more enigmatic re-statement, the outline is sometimes as useful as the completed work. And, in fact, isn't it precisely the existence of something that is outside, something that is left out and left over that leads us to search on with a renewed energy and enthusiasm? Is it impossible (even from our imperfect knowledge) to envision the utter desolation and futility that a complete fulfillment would bring in its wake?[64]

The outright rebellion against civilization also remains in the cards, however. In his essay "'Civilized' Sexual Morality and Modern Nervous Illness" written in 1908, (in what is admittedly a very fragmentary reference) Freud refers to a possibility that a few individuals may boldly refuse to shoulder the burdens of civilization, those stones that always roll downhill as soon as the more or less weary brothers and sisters of Sisyphus roll them up to the summit.[65] These individuals who make refusal the focus of their being Freud designates as "heroes," as those who establish new civilizations and new worlds of being and thinking. But, according to Freud, the capacity of these individuals to do so is determined by their having "a high social position and/or exceptional abilities." Otherwise, they may also turn out to be great criminals or outlaws.[66] In a sense, however, the heroes or the masterbuilders of the new, are always considered outlaws by the standards of that which they work to replace. Therefore, the aura of criminality surrounding their name can hardly be avoided. But, in my opinion, the criteria on which their work can be judged—and Freud does not do so in this essay—is whether their newly established values and institutions present an improvement in the overall social and political conditions when compared with those values and institutions that have been dissolved.

Of course, it is much easier to see the work of heroes in a positive light if one subscribes to a Hegelian/Marxian philosophy of history and conceptualizes the movement of history as the progressive extension of freedom (embodied in a set of institutions and laws governing a given community). However, Freud gives no indication that he understands history in this way. Instead, as I have shown, he sees history as the process of internalization of a set of moral prohibitions. In other words, what Sophocle's Oedipus could do in deed, Shakespeare's Hamlet can only accomplish in thought, in the neurotic confusion of his psyche. It seems difficult to determine whether that makes Hamlet more or less free. It certainly paralyzes his activities and therefore makes him less suitable to be a builder of any sort.

THE WOLF MAN

Perhaps the neurotic *par excellence* in the world of Freud's case histories is the Wolf Man. This is not to say that the neurosis of Dora or of the Rat Man was less painful or with less severe consequences for their adult life. However, if the essence of neurosis is constructed out of one's childhood experience, the most pristine form of neurosis—the neurosis *par excellence*—is the one caused solely by the content of that experience.[67] This precisely is the case with the Wolf Man. The most crucial issue of his childhood—the Oedipal issue—failed to find a successful resolution. In other words, I think that I could go so far as to say that the Wolf Man is the little Hans whose treatment has failed. His case history could be read as the description of the fate of those who do not renounce and sublimate their Oedipal libidinal tendencies, but at the same time fail to attain a heroic stature.

This unfortunate man whose adult life was literally held captive by the strands of an unresolved childhood dynamic was nicknamed the Wolf Man by Freud because of his particular phobia of the wolves. As can be seen right away, in this, his psychological development mirrored that of the little Hans who also had an equally strong animal phobia. And, as Freud noted in the Little Hans case history, the objects of these animal phobias (no matter what animals are chosen) at the level of the unconscious mental processes represent the figure of the father. They act as the father-surrogates or father-substitutes.[68] This is so because at the time that the phobias usually emerge in a child's life (around the age of four), the child is undergoing an intense questioning of its attachment to various family members based on its own internal psychological needs and libidinal tendencies. Before this age, there is, in Freud's view, an unquestioned love for the father in the life of a typical male child, which is manifested in the expressions of identification with the father (or another male family member that acts as a father substitute). For instance, in the case of the Wolf Man, this could be seen in his exclamation that when he grew up he would like to be "a gentleman like his father."[69]

Soon, however, there clamors for conscious expression a contrary attitude toward the father (representing the hostile trend) connected to the re-activation of the love for the primal love-object (the mother), and influenced by the vicissitudes (stages) of infantile sexuality and environmental factors (the birth of a new sibling for the little Hans, for instance). This hostile aggressive trend is the consequence of what is perceived as the rivalry with the father. It may be displaced onto a phobia to alleviate the attacks from two fronts: the fear of the father's wrath and, at same time, the love trend that, though subordinated to hostile tendencies, continues to be present. Freud argues that the successful resolution of these psychic conflicts is ultimately brought about by the recognition of the conflicting tendencies, and by conscious renunciation of those that obstruct the ongoing development of oneself into a psychologically mature individual. For instance, one aspect of this kind of maturity, in Freud's view, is the adult object-choice that is relatively free from the repressed libidinal investments in the family dynamic or "the family romance" (as it has been called by various commentators).

However, what happened in the case of the Wolf Man, is that his particular awakening to what a love for the father entails was a particularly brutal or violent one. His psychological reaction to it was a vigorous repression of this recognition, which of course greatly complicated the matters. Essentially, based on a slow and lengthy analysis of a dream from the Wolf Man's childhood, Freud showed that the content of latent dream thoughts, and the particularly strong attack of anxiety (and the phobia) that followed, pointed to a likelihood that the Wolf Man, at an early age, witnessed the act of sexual intercourse between his parents (the Primal Scene).[70] This was a particular type of intercourse—the intercourse from behind—that, as Freud speculated, allowed the child a possibility to see his mother's genitals, and also to remember the whole act as one abounding in violence and outright sadism. At the time the act was witnessed—at the age of one and a half (according to Freud)—it could have meant nothing to the child, but the memory of it did not disappear and was instead deposited in the recesses of his unconscious.

It was only at the age of four that this memory found its way into latent dream thoughts, and hence came to consciousness in the shape of a dream (the dream of wolves that Freud analyzed). By acting through what Freud calls the deferred effect, this memory led to the emergence of anxiety and the constitution of the phobia.[71] The reason for this was that at the time of the dream, the Wolf Man was in the midst of what could be referred to as the genital stage of sexual organization, with its intense libidinal investment in the genital organ. He therefore cherished his penis as an object of particular value. However, the memory of the Primal Scene brought him to a realization that the love for the father on his part might well mean having to identify with the position of his mother vis-à-vis the father. Considering that he saw his mother's genitals as lacking the penis, he interpreted the intercourse he witnessed as an act of castration. His anxiety therefore derived from his fear for the loss of the valued genital organ.[72]

On a more general level, the question for the Wolf Man (or any other male child) was whether to choose autonomy (the rebellion against the father and the preservation of the organ) or submission (love for the father, but also castration). Freud contends that—in the life of modern man—this question is never fully resolved by the definitive victory of the autonomous path, even though in psychic constitutions that successfully deal with neurosis, such a path tends to predominate. In these cases, the action against the father is taken, while ultimately a portion of paternal norms is also internalized. In other words, the identification with the father is accomplished without the surrender of one's potential for active object-relations and libidinal investments.

In the case of the Wolf Man, however, the submissive or passive tendency was especially powerful and battled mercilessly against the opposing narcissistic (active) tendency. As psychoanalysis shows, when two such equally strong opposing currents encounter each other, the result is the creation of the symptom. Indeed, the Wolf Man's symptoms ranged from the wolf phobia to the compulsive acts connected to religious belief, the spending of his father's money, and intestinal problems.[73] Ultimately, they were all connected to the particularly intense ambivalence regarding the paternal relation. The Wolf Man's love for his father did not abate even though he was faced with the reality of the price that had to be paid for it. At the same time, however, the narcissistic interest in his autoerotic satisfaction also held ground. The Wolf Man hence became a prisoner of rapid attitudinal shifts from one to the other unconscious libidinal tendency, and it took several years of daily psychoanalytic therapy with Freud to bring him to the conscious recognition of the positions taken up by his libido. In the end, one could think of his case as demonstrating the consequences of the failure to resolve (or consciously settle) the Oedipal relation while still in childhood years.

In his conclusion to the Wolf Man's case history, Freud refers to a puzzle that will preoccupy him in his only study in psychoanalytic anthropology, *Totem and Taboo*, written at the same time or shortly before the case history. This is the issue of whether something like the Oedipus complex (essentially, the predominantly hostile father-son relation) represents a transcendental category, a "phylogenetically inherited schema" that determines individual experience.[74] In other words, if the male child had the most lenient father in the world (e.g., the passive father who would never interfere with the child's desires), would this prevent the eruption of the hostility against the father, would this somehow mute the existence of the Oedipus complex?

Freud's answer is in the negative. He argues that the same schema will be played out in the life of every male child, even if the environmental influences diverge from case to case (as they of course do). In Freud's view, if reality does not favor the establishment of Oedipal relations, childhood fantasy (connected with the fear of the loss of something valuable) will provide the necessary material. Freud therefore sees the Oedipal schema as genuinely transcendental in a Kantian sense; it represents the condition of the possibility for the experience of being a man. It is in *Totem and Taboo* that Freud raises this issue to another level of analysis and approaches it from the standpoint of the origin and development of culture.

TOTEM AND TABOO

One could say that *Totem and Taboo* represents Freud's first sustained attempt to apply the insights of psychoanalysis on a level that goes beyond the clinic and the psychopathology of the individual. As I have shown above, his earlier works contain numerous references to social and cultural phenomena, but the basic focus of these works is elsewhere. It is found, for instance, in the elucidation of the structure of dreams or the components of neurosis, and not in the discussion of the origin and development of social laws and institutions. But, in *Totem and Taboo*, the latter—cultural mores, norms, customs—become the object of study. They become a fair game for the psychoanalytic "working-through." In fact, just as the goal in the individual analysis is to make the repressed, unconscious wishes conscious, so in the study of cultural phenomena the goal is to expose that which behind the screens (so to speak) determines the phenomena's coming into existence.

But approaching the study of culture in this way reveals quite clearly the fundamental assumption that grounds Freud's project. I think that this assumption could be formulated as follows: cultural phenomena are determined by psychological needs of those who have constructed them.[75] In other words, in their essence, cultural phenomena represent individual attitudes projected onto the external world. They represent strategies and procedures sanctioned by the community to deal with and help resolve psychic conflicts that plague the individual. Freud turns to anthropological studies of the indigenous societies to show that this in fact is the case.

The notion that anthropological evidence is useful in a psychoanalytic study is one of the key claims of Freud's book. In a sense, what he strives to accomplish is to establish the lines of similarity among three (in his view) only apparently different psychological attitudes: that of the indigenous person (the member of a tribal society), that of the child, and that of the neurotic.[76] The link between the latter two—the child and the neurotic—is the one Freud takes for granted, having demonstrated its existence in his earlier works (as I have shown above). Briefly stated, what connects the two is the fact that neurosis is to a great extent caused by unresolved conflicts among the libidinal investments of early childhood. What remains for Freud to do in *Totem and Taboo* is to furnish the evidence for the similarity between the attitudes of the indigenous person and the other two. It is clear that if he is successful in doing so, he will have shown the relevance of the psychoanalytic method for the study of the origin and development of social norms and customs. In other words, he will have firmly and justifiably staked out land beyond the clinic for psychoanalytic excavation, which is something that the critics of psychoanalysis have always disputed. With this goal in mind, Freud turns to investigating the social customs of the tribes from all over the world.[77]

However, at the same time, Freud endeavors to deal with the fact that his project may be attacked on two fronts: for reductionism, and for pathologizing and/or infantilizing the life of the indigenous tribes. To the first charge, Freud replies that what he wants to show is the similarity in psychic structures and mechanisms based on a careful examination of evidence, and this, of course, does not entail the reduction of one phenomenon to another. However, once this similarity is established, one is, according to Freud, justified in postulating that perhaps similar motivations underline both.[78] This is exactly how Freud proceeds in linking up the taboo rituals of the tribes and the symptoms of obsessional neurosis.

To the other charge, Freud retorts that he is cognizant of the fact that the tribal societies are "just as old as" the European ones and that therefore there is no way to know to what degree they have preserved the customs of the dawn of civilization.[79] In fact, the odds are that their customs and norms have undergone many processes of elaboration, distortion, and omission so that at this point it is unclear how their most pristine social organization looked like. Even so, the way these societies are organized preserves a certain degree of affinity with how one is led to conceptualize the earliest social forms. Here Freud refers to the three-fold division of the worldviews popularized at the turn of the century by hermeneutic philosophers, such as Wilhelm Dilthey.[80] This division into the animistic, the religious, and the scientific worldview has the worldviews ranked in a stage-like order (one following the other). Tribal societies are postulated to belong to the animistic stage—based on their use of magic inspired by the beliefs in the omnipotence of thought and the ultimately animate nature of the physical world—which was later followed by the religious and the scientific stages.[81] And, according to Freud, the belief system of animism is remarkably similar to that of children and neurotics.

THE QUESTION OF TABOO

Freud frames his foray into anthropology by sustained attention to the most prominent and universal social institution of the tribal world—the taboo. The question he asks is why precisely this is so. Why is the taboo the principal structuring mechanism of tribal societies? Freud's starting point is the claim that the taboo must serve very important psychological needs of the members of a given community. Yet the taboo is a special sort of an institution, because, in its essence, it is a set of prohibitions or reservations directed toward specific aspects of social life. Therefore the taboo's function must be fairly specific as well—to impose restraint or limitation on the way that the members of the community live and carry on their daily interactions. In fact, Freud's premise here is fairly simple. He states that the reason something is prohibited explicitly (that is, by the establishment of a taboo) is a sign of its having been desired.[82] The stronger the desire to transgress, the stronger the prohibition. Hence, according to Freud, a particularly severe penalty for the violation of a given taboo demonstrates the fact that there has existed—or still exists at some level of psychological functioning—an imperatively strong desire to violate it. The penalty of death, for instance, shows how high the stakes need to be in order that the tabooed object remains intact, or out of reach of those who want it.

One of the most frequent taboos found in tribal societies has to do with incest. The taboo on incest prohibits the expression of sexual feelings for those who are, psychoanalytically speaking, one's primary objects of love. In Freud's view, the universal existence of this taboo reveals the universal existence and particular strength of incestuous feelings. By being compelled to impose a block on the expression of such feelings, the individual is pushed out of the "family romance" (the mommy-daddy-me triangle) and into the social life of a greater community. In fact, Freud postulates the existence of the incest taboo as the necessary condition for the formation of social units that extend beyond the confines of the family.[83] More technically stated, the incest taboo enables the formation of exogamic practices, which extend one's social unit and hence enable more sophisticated division of labor, development of technology and so on.[84] In terms of a general claim, it seems reasonable to conclude that the restriction on the immediate gratification of genital sexuality provides the grounding for the emergence of cultural creations. The incest taboo becomes the prototype of all other taboos in which the social triumphs over the narcissistic gratification of sexual intercourse.

Freud locates the apparent dichotomy between the social and the sexual as the causative factor in the genesis of neuroses. Indeed, what causes neuroses is precisely the fact that one's sexual drives conflict with the socially sanctioned ways of gratification. The neurotic symptom hence represents sexual gratification by other means. It seems to me that, in a certain way, it also represents an attempt to forge a culture that would suit one's demands for pleasure; it is the neurotic's attempt to be the heroic master builder. What can be glimpsed in this is that the neurotic is unconsciously motivated to push for changes in the status quo, and that, though his or her efforts may be appear ridiculously absurd in light of the Reality Principle, they represent nonetheless the passionate commitment to the emergence of new forms in social and political life.[85]

Freud contends that the proper way to approach symptomatic behavior is to become aware of that which one desires (the object choices), and then to transform these libidinal tendencies consciously in accordance with the greater good of the community and culture of which one is a part. In other words, one's psychological efforts should be made in order to contribute to the good of all (cultural capital) and to fit one's contributions into the edifice of civilization.

In Freud's view, the necessity to conform to a given culture, which differs from making a contribution to it, recommended above as the goal, weighs more heavily on the modern individual than on the member of an indigenous tribe.[86] This is so because the external agent of prohibition in the shape of a taboo has become internalized in the modern individual; it has been supplemented, if not replaced, by an internal agency. In other words, the successor of a taboo appears to be a moral conscience. This may explain the loss of prominence that explicit taboos underwent in modernity.[87]

In my opinion, this is a daring speculation and the evidence for its validity cannot be conclusive. Even so, the functional similarity between the taboo and moral conscience is striking. In both cases, the emphasis is on the restriction of desire by a psychological source endowed with extraordinary strength, but whose origin is unknown.[88] For instance, the members of the indigenous tribe may not know the reason why something is tabooed, but they still feel the strong impulse of guilt—even to the point of inflicting self-punishment—if they violate the taboo. In the similar way, the obsessional neurotics are compelled by their conscience to perform various rituals, and then to justify their performance by convincing themselves that something bad will happen either to them or the persons they love if the rituals are not performed. The reason behind these rituals remains obscure to the neurotic, but the sense of guilt that is felt is real.[89]

Freud thinks that it is the existence of guilt that provides a proof for the presence of the desire to violate a taboo. Libidinal investment in the object of the taboo is particularly strong and when it encounters an obstacle (either social or internal), it transforms itself into anxiety that requires expiatory or atoning practices in order to go away. The psychological dynamic here has the form of a paradox: one desires and feels guilty at the same time.

On a more general theoretical level, this means that the psyche itself is capable of containing opposing attitudes toward the same object. Freud—following a suggestion of Bleuler—calls this state of affairs *ambivalence*. In other words, the emergence into consciousness of the negative feeling towards something depends on its positive counterpart's (the feeling that affirms desire) being repressed into the unconscious.[90] But the triumph of conscience—in its essentially negative, prohibitory dimension—is never complete, because the desire that opposes it also clamors for conscious expression. If, in a certain case, this desire succeeds in breaking through the controls imposed by conscience and finds gratification, the scope of its dialectical relation with its opposite comes into full view. In other words, its gratification is followed by the strong reassertion of the tendency, which acted to prohibit gratification. In law enforcement, for instance, this situation is described by the saying that "the criminal always returns to the place of his or her crime."[91]

THE GENESIS OF SOCIETY

Freud claims that precisely this kind of desire-guilt dynamic led to the emergence of society. In trying to conceptualize the birth of the social, Freud follows in the footsteps of the social contract theorists, such as Hobbes, Locke, and Rousseau (among the most famous), who first made this issue an object of study in the field of political and social philosophy. Freud's narrative grafts the psychoanalytic finding of the ambivalence of emotions onto the 'Darwinian' hypothesis of the primal horde and Fraser's descriptions of totemistic practices of indigenous societies.[92] The primal horde hypothesis states that the primary group in which human beings lived was one in which one man—the primal father—controlled the women and denied sexual satisfaction to his sons. Freud is not explicit as to why the primal horde does not represent a genuine society, but I think that it is safe to assume that it does not, because the existence of the horde depends on the brute force of one person with only violence binding the members together.

It seems to me that this claim of primal violence is (still) within the orbit of social contract theorists. However, Freud departs from social contract theory with his further claim that the birth of the social came, not through a contract to contain existing violence, but instead through a violent act itself, the act of murder of the primal father. In other words, the sons conspired, killed, and ate their father (hence the postulated similarity with totemistic rituals where the animal, otherwise tabooed, is consumed collectively). The sons (or brothers) physically incorporated the father, having desired his strength and power while under his control. And yet when they overthrew paternal authority, no orgiastic free-for-all (anarchical fulfillment of desire) took place. They imposed a set of renunciations on themselves, almost similar in scope to those imposed on them by the father. In other words, they consciously chose to renounce that which in the past was forbidden to them by other means.

I think that it is very important to emphasize that the brothers' act is not to be interpreted on purely utilitarian grounds. It is true that genital satisfaction, in Freud's view, is ultimately private (or asocial), and that therefore the continual orgies might have infused an element of chaos into the newly emerged brother-clan. Thus it may appear on the surface that such a satisfaction is best renounced, or confined to specific and controlled rituals, for the sake of social utility. However, while plausible, this is not the main reason why the brothers were compelled to renounce orgiastic sexual enjoyment, according to Freud. Freud contends that upon committing their deed, the brothers suddenly became plagued with the feeling of intense guilt. This was so because after their hostile tendency toward the father was gratified and therefore temporarily put out of play, the opposing tendency—the one that decreed love for the father according to the law of ambivalence—asserted itself. In other words, hate consumed itself in the deed, and what was left over was love.

However, since the deed had already been committed and the father killed, love for the father had to erect another object for itself, an object in which it could find gratification once again. This object took the shape of totemistic prohibitions and rituals that the brothers imposed on themselves, which (collectively imposed) mirrored those imposed by the father. Thus it can be said that the father in his death continued to rule over the living.[93] Or, stated differently, the father's death was not definitive—he continued to exist by other means. The actual reality was replaced by psychic reality; the external entity was internalized and became a proto-conscience that (from then on) surveyed the psyche's work and pronounced its judgment on it as it saw fit.

As I see it, therefore, two components of Freud's narrative of the origin of society distinguish it from those put forth by social contract theorists. First is the traumatic nature of the actual beginning. It is the murder that makes the contract possible; the accomplices in crime become the pioneers of the new order. Perhaps such a violent rupture was necessary in order to constitute the organization of human life along different lines. Entrance into another dimension often requires the radical overturning of the existing one. At the same time Freud also observes that the memories of trauma and imagined or actual transgressions into the forbidden form the essence of neurotic and psychotic disorders. Does this mean that society (civilization) itself is in some sense a neurotic phenomenon, the entrance into which is paid in the currency of mental health? If Hamlet is the prototypical modern individual (as Freud seems to indicate), then this may be the case. But are there any alternatives to this state of affairs? Freud leaves these issues unresolved in *Totem and Taboo*, but returns to them in greater detail in his late 1920s works on culture and society, *The Future of An Illusion* and *Civilization and Its Discontents*, which as, I will show, are marked, on the whole, by a spirit of pessimism regarding the possibility of a non-repressive civilization. This is precisely the key point of disagreement between Freud and those who will bring a leftist orientation to his work, as I emphasize in chapter 2 when I discuss the Liberation Thesis.

The second significant component of Freud's narrative is his claim that there is a psychological cost to rebellion against authority.[94] This cost is experienced as a sense of guilt, and a compulsion to atone for whatever is done. The case in point are the acts of the members of the brother clan who, upon the murder of the father, decided to re-institute paternal prohibitions. Yet, what I think should be kept in mind is that this claim presupposes a particular view of mental functioning. In other words, it depends on the conceptualization of the psyche as governed by the law of ambivalence.

Whatever is hated is also loved. In fact, in Freud's view, conscious hatred is possible only through the repression of love into the unconscious and vice versa. Both hostile and affectionate tendencies co-exist in the unconscious, but only one can be brought to consciousness at any given time. The conscious gratification of one tendency weakens the strength of its libidinal investment, which results in the re-assertion of its opposite. The cycling therefore continues, and there is never more than a temporary equilibrium. Perhaps this is one of the main reasons why social revolutions have failed to construct the world of fulfillment that their slogans promised. After all, the question that the law of ambivalence makes us ask is—the fulfillment of what?

Even so, I think it would be a mistake to interpret this insight as a condemnation of rebellion against authority. It seems to me that the value of the insight is that it underscores the psychological complexity of a rebellious act, which must be taken into consideration in any model of social and political change.

For Freud, the nature of social authority has a specific root within the primal family. In other words, authority is generated out of the father-son dynamic (the Oedipus Complex).[95] The son's relation towards the father's strength and power determines both his striving for emancipation (becoming-the-father) *and* his falling back into the orbit of paternal world (guilt and atonement). In fact, on my reading, Freud's understanding of this relation seems to contain an element that remains unaffected by the usual dialectic of psychic life. Freud designates this element as the longing for the father.[96] This father who is longed for is the all-protective father who represents Divine Providence, and is therefore distinct from one's own father who is subject to the ambivalence of one's feelings. In other words, as Lacan remarks, there are always two fathers. It is therefore clear that radical social transformation, considered in chapter 2, would require the overthrow of both paternal figures: the question is whether such a thing is doable or, in other words, humanly possible.[97]

FREUD AND THE DEATH DRIVE

It has been said that how we live, to a great extent, shapes how and what we think. It so happens in the life of a theorist that external circumstances act as a kind of a wake-up call for certain obscurities in his or her theoretical endeavors. The new material makes one aware of the puzzles that necessitate new answers or at least the modification of the old ones. I think that this is what happened in the case of Freud's understanding of aggressive drives. In his original theory of the mind, he did not assign them an autonomous existence or, in other words, a place in the psyche in their own right. It is true that in his *Three Contributions*, Freud recognized the presence in the ego of the impulse for mastery (a sadistic tendency) that worked against the drive for union and combination so typical of the erotic (love) tendencies. It is also true that his subscribing to the law of the ambivalence of emotions made it easy to see that love is always counter-balanced by hate at the level of the unconscious. Even so, for Freud at this time, the drive for mastery was no more than a component drive frequently swayed by or merged into the pursuit of an erotic aim. And the hate-side of the ambivalence of emotions could result simply from the exhaustion of erotic drives rather than from a source separate from them. In other words, aggressive drives could still be conceptualized as the children of Eros. Even in *Totem and Taboo*, while the brothers are seen as actually committing a violent act, its repercussions and consequences show that love soon re-asserts itself with a vengeance (perhaps in a more powerful light than ever before). As I have argued, this is precisely the Freudian heritage that the theorists of the Liberation Thesis refer to in their works.

However, soon after the publication of *Totem and Taboo* in 1913, Freud modified his understanding of the derivative nature of aggressive drives. In my opinion, the experience of World War I influenced him to do so. In fact, on my reading, Freud's World War I essay "Thoughts for the Times on War and Death" represents a transitional point between his pre-1914 formulations on the sources of aggression and the formulations in the works that followed the war. It is worth mentioning that it is in his first major post–World War I work, *Beyond the Pleasure Principle*, that Freud postulates the existence of the death drive in its own right, unmixed with any traces of the desire for life.

WAR AND DEATH

Freud's frames his essay on war and death from the perspective of a non-combatant shocked that the attainments of civilization have been so quickly trampled underfoot by the war machines of European powers.[98] He is dismayed that the intellectual resistance to the war effort so easily gave way to the uncritical support for it. Such a fact, in his view, reveals the work of civilization as shallow and superficial, and points to the presence of instinctual forces in the psyche that favor violent and aggressive resolutions. Indeed, Freud proposes to re-visit his view of the development of moral conscience in order to attempt to give an explanation of why this is the case. Here for the first time Freud explicitly examines the genesis of the modern ethical subjectivity.[99]

Freud begins by saying that the origin of conscience is to be found in the fear of communal reaction.[100] Under the pressure of this fear, the hostile tendencies are repressed into the unconscious or modified to an extent that fits with the exigencies of social life. The hostile—or, more specifically speaking, narcissistic—tendencies therefore do not disappear; it is only that their manifestation in daily life is restricted. Here, however, Freud goes on to make a distinction between the internal and external factors that make their influence felt in modifying the individual's drives. As is to be expected, the internal factors make a more lasting impression on the goodness of instinctual aims. According to Freud, what happens in this case is that narcissistic tendencies become socialized by being mixed with the erotic drives.[101] For the sake of the love of other people, the individual, out of his or her own will, re-models the paths to pleasure and satisfaction. The compulsion to change is actively desired, and therefore the modifications made are usually difficult to overturn.

However, the situation is otherwise with the factors that remain solely external and are never taken into the psyche as its own. Here Freud refers to the utilitarian reward and punishment dynamic. If the individual complies with the regulation of society only due to the fear of punishment, then the danger exists that as soon as he or she realizes that the punishment is not forthcoming, the prohibited deed will be committed. In fact, Freud designates such an individual as a hypocrite, considering that he or she is "living, psychologically speaking, beyond his or her means."[102] In other words, in the times of crises or war, it will not be difficult for such an individual to throw off civilization's precepts and indulge his or her narcissistic instinctual disposition to the fullest.

In addition, aggressive drives seem to be present even in those who are not swayed by the vicissitudes of national or international conflict. Even pacifists have a quota of aggression that pushes for expression. At this point, Freud leaves out of the picture the consideration of how aggressive drives are handled within different character structures. But one can already see the glimpses of his second topographical model of the mind (the id—the ego—the super-ego) whose formulation, I think, was necessitated precisely by the problem of aggressive warfare.

Freud re-states a law of the ambivalence of emotions (so forcefully argued for in *Totem and Taboo*), but this time he puts much more emphasis on death wishes and aggression directed against those whom one loves. In fact, he theorizes that the first ethical propositions and commandments were brought into being "beside the corpse of the beloved" as a reaction against the realization that even in one's grief for this death, there was a sense of another tendency being gratified.[103] In other words, the flip side of the coin of ambivalence—the hatred of otherness as a threat to one's narcissism—found its way to consciousness. Combating it and re-sending it into the unconscious requires putting up external—discourse or symbolic—barriers. Hence, Freud argues, various rules of social life emerged, all in order to keep aggressive sadistic impulses in the depth of the psychic underworld.

Most dramatically, it appears to Freud, held captive to the depressive war atmosphere, that this struggle is uneven and bound to lead only to partial successes for the side of virtue. In other words, since the forces of virtue are heterogeneous (made up both of the internal erotic impulses and external social precepts), it is possible that more compact and homogeneous internal aggressive drives will be able to drive the wedge between the two, and then triumph in the ensuing confusion. The diversity of social groups makes it probable that aggressive narcissism will always find the possibility for open and unrestricted discharge. And while civilization is generally a block to aggression, it may in certain cases—such as in warfare—become subordinate to it, making the mix deadly. To the mental life, governed as it is by the pleasure principle, what matters is the quantity of libidinal gratification, and its objects and ways of coming about are secondary. Thus it appears that, in the proverbial blindness of the unconscious, the pleasures of death are equal to the pleasures of life. In fact, Freud seems to hint that the former may have an upper hand, considering the strength of narcissism, which alienates the ego from any genuine object-choice. At the level of the unconscious, says Freud, "we are . . . simply a gang of murderers."[104] Death is our most intimate business.

Yet, in this 1915 essay on war and death, Freud does not go so far as to postulate the existence of the death drive. The elaborate theoretical justifications for the death drive appear in his first major post–World War I work *Beyond the Pleasure Principle*. In essence, the phrase "the death drive" is a dramatic designation for that which Freud comes to see as the tendency of most drives.[105] This tendency is marked by their striving to return to a prior state of being, a state in which they can come to rest.[106] What motivates drives—in their "blind" surge forward—is the presence of an external tension, which they want to lessen and overcome. But the only way to transcend this tension completely is to still the drives—and this is death. According to Freud, the drives are, however, constrained to follow the path to death particular to the living organisms in which they subsist—they are blocked from plunging into death in the manner that is the shortest and always available—self destruction.[107] This is so because the very fact of life positions itself as a resistance to death, as a barrier to the actualization of the ultimate tensionless state. In Freud's view, an entire set of drives comes to embody this process of the resistance of the living against the general urge to discharge and disappear. These are the sex or erotic drives.

THE ROLE OF EROS

According to Freud, the function of sex drives is to perpetuate life. However, they are also constrained to carry out their assigned function within the framework of what is essentially a conservative nature.[108] What this means is that they have a tendency to strive to return to a prior state. However, this return in the realm of sex drives does not mean an allegiance to death. Instead, it means that the life whose carriers they are is forced to pay the price of repetition. I would even say that repetition is the currency in which the immortality of Eros is expressed. Each new organism (each new life) has to start from the very beginning, and to repeat (however briefly) the logical (not biological) stages that were prior to the development of the kind of organism it is. Its path is therefore permeated by a certain concession to the death drive, and is ultimately limited and cut off by it. However, in the time period between its birth and its demise, during the time that in one way or another Eros guides its functions, the organism will be enabled to give life its due by generating sex-cells or gametes (Freud calls them the germ-cells).[109] The germ-cells are the investment that life makes in the possibility of its own continuation. Perhaps, in a fashion analogous to the formation of the symptom in neurosis, the germ-cells are a compromise solution between the forces of life and the forces of death. Death of course calls the final tune for every organism, but on the other hand the life process itself is not ended by it.

Even the development of increasingly more complex organisms (more complex combinations of living matter) can be explained from the standpoint of this perspective. Freud claims that the changes in external environment threatened the tasks of Eros, the tasks which revolve around the protection of the path of life. The response of Eros was to make the organism more suitable for survival by making its life functions more complex and, as a result, more flexible in adapting to environmental changes. The combination into a greater unity—or, in other words, making the one out of the many, the homogeneous out of the heterogeneous—is therefore recognized by Freud as the principal characteristic of erotic processes.[110] The death drive, on the other hand, strives to dissolve bonds established in this way, and to separate components that originally went into making the phenomena of life possible. In it the primal heterogeneity of the world (the muteness and immobility of disparate pieces of matter) manifests its return.

One can rightly call the preceding reflections "meta-psychological."[111] However, Freud is careful to stress their derivation from—their grounding in—the actual practice of psychoanalysis. He refers to several phenomena observable in analysis that pointed him toward the conceptualization of the death drive. The most dramatic of these phenomena Freud calls the repetition compulsion. In fact, the repetition compulsion shows that there are mental processes that go beyond the pleasure principle.[112] Repetition concerns the actual re-enactment of events in one's life that could not be characterized as pleasant (either at the time when they originally took place or at the time when they are repeated). Freud brings up the case of traumatic neuroses (such as the war neuroses) in which the traumatic situation returns again and again in various guises destroying the psychic stability of the sufferer.[113] Freud sees this repetition of the trauma as an effort on the part of the psyche to assert its mastery over the situation in which it had been so unmercifully—and in most cases unexpectedly—hurt. In other words, the psyche attempts to change its position from being a passive material on which the trauma is inscribed to being an active agent who works through the trauma in order to come to terms with the injury. Freud compares the traumatic situation to a burst of unbound (psychic) energy that broke through the established psychic mechanisms.[114] The task of repetition is then to bind this alien energy into something that the psyche could actually handle in its normal functioning.[115] It is precisely in this function of binding the energy that has been introjected (or forced through) from the outside, which in turn diminishes the tension present in the psyche, that the repetition compulsion does the work of the death drive.

Paradoxically what this means is that the death drive has more affinity with the pleasure principle than does the life drive or Eros. The pleasure principle, according to Freud, is always oriented toward keeping the amount of tension in the psyche at the minimum.[116] In fact, what causes pleasure is precisely the release or discharge of tension. In addition, to follow this line of thought further, even though, as stated before, the repetition compulsion may be beyond the pleasure principle (in the sense of being different from it), its goals are not incompatible with those of the pleasure principle. One could even argue that something akin to the principle of repetition established the conditions necessary for constituting the psyche, which can function along the line of the pleasure principle.[117] This makes sense because, in Freud's view, the earlier psychic processes (the primary processes) are completely made up of unbound (free) energy. Their binding would therefore be accomplished by the repetition compulsion, which would then lead to the formation of the secondary processes. The secondary processes—the conscious re-working of the unconscious impulses—are, according to Freud, precisely the mental processes in which the sway of the pleasure principle is indisputable. But here the key question arises for Freud—what is the task of Eros if both the pleasure principle and the repetition compulsion seem to favor its adversary?

At times it seems that Freud hints at the possibility that even Eros is motivated by the drive for the eventual self-dissolution. He does state at one point that "the goal of all life is death."[118] Yet once this statement is considered in terms of the context in which it appears, I think that it becomes clear that Freud simply means that all life ends in death (the absolute tensionless state). He has already emphasized that striving to release tension accumulated in the course of the life processes is akin to the work of the death drive. But the work of Eros is something different.

As already pointed out, Eros, according to Freud, combines the living substance into a greater unity. This means that Eros actually increases the possibility for the existence of tensions in the organism. It builds up something that the death drive is intent on destroying. In a certain way, Eros shows that the whole is more than its parts in that "more and more complicated detours" have to be made for the death drive to reach what it desires.[119]

In other words, I think that Freud links Eros to whatever combines the particular into the universal. Its existence is, in Freud's view, just as tangible in the evolutionary development of life forms as it is in the development of human societies. In fact, for Freud, what holds any given society together is not only the strength of interest for vital self-preservation, but also the presence of erotic (libidinal) ties between its members. In other words, Eros reaches beyond *Ananke* (necessity). It is precisely to this insight that Freud gives careful consideration in his subsequent writings on group psychology and psychoanalysis of cultural phenomena. What becomes a necessity for his work after *Beyond the Pleasure Principle* is to find a way to connect the conclusions about the dual nature of the drives to human behavior in social contexts. This, as I will show, leads Freud to develop a new model of the mind in which the social component, embodying the forces of parental and other extra-individual influences, receives a prominent position.

GROUP PSYCHOLOGY

In the early 1920s, Freud replaced the model of the mind (the unconscious-the preconscious-the conscious) first postulated in the 1890s by the new tripartite formulation (id-ego-super-ego). The greatest change occurred in that both the preconscious and conscious components of the old model were integrated under the concept of the ego. The super-ego (or, in earliest formulations, the ego-ideal) was conceptualized as being formed as a portion, a split-off part of the ego itself under the pressure of the immediate environment in which the infant finds itself. The unconscious remained represented by a separate agency—the id.[120]

I think that a possible interpretation of Freud's rationale to reformulate the psychoanalytic model of the mind is found in the fact that in this period he increasingly came to concern himself with social issues, or, in other words, with the interaction of the individual and society. Thus he wanted to find a way to show the psychological impact of society on the life of the individual. One of the ways of doing so was to postulate the existence of a mental agency that represented the interests of society at the level of the psyche. In addition, the existence of such an agency proved all the more necessary for explaining social progress and overall development of civilization considering that Freud had already postulated the inevitable presence of individual aggressive and destructive drives. In other words, this agency, which Freud referred to it as the ego-ideal or the super-ego, could be seen as a tool of society for inhibiting or repressing all anti-social individual strivings and desires.

In Freud's view, studying the super-ego's interconnections with other two mental agencies (the ego and the id) would provide a way for psychoanalysis to enter into a more sustained study of collective or group interactions in society. No more would the family be the limit of psychoanalytic investigations; the study of the wider social field could now also come under its purview. Interestingly enough, psychoanalysis would eventually find this wider social field also stamped by the family dynamic of early childhood.[121]

Freud defines group psychology as the study of individual behavior in institutional settings that possess an identity separate from that of the individual.[122] He finds that the identity of the group interacts in psychologically complex ways with the identity of the individual. For instance, Freud notes that the individual's membership in any group (e.g., national, religious, professional, revolutionary and so on) affects and modifies orientations or attitudes the individual considers his or her own. I think that this should not be interpreted to mean that Freud thinks that the individual was the self-enclosed monad at some point of his or her life (even in the earliest infancy). Instead, what Freud contends is that the group membership reshapes whatever the individual was before joining—or being compelled to join—a given group. The key question for group psychology is therefore how and to what extent the behavior of the individual is altered under the influence of the group.

A particularly dramatic example Freud offers to illuminate the effect of the group on the individual concerns the members of a revolutionary terrorist group.[123] According to Freud, these individuals may be drawn by their membership in such a group to commit certain acts against other individuals that they are likely to condemn when approached apart from the group. In other words, their membership in the revolutionary group makes it more probable that their aggressive tendencies towards others will find actual fulfillment in reality. In Freud's view, this is so because the group membership gives the individual a sense of reckless power, a sense of fearlessness that facilitates the rapid discharge of unconscious hostile impulses that had been repressed for the sake of tranquil communal life and social progress.[124] The individual feels protected by the numerical strength and ideological power of the group and is therefore unafraid to act out his or her unconscious wishes without the fear of punishment. Supported by the love of the group, the individual finds it uncomplicated to strike out brutally at his or her fantasized enemies.

Freud argues that what happens at the level of the psyche in such a situation is that the ego-ideal or the super-ego—which usually acts as the depository of one's sense of responsibility and other ethical/moral values—is dissolved by the invasion of the pleasure-seeking impulses from the unconscious. The similar psychological mini-revolution (the return of the repressed, as it is often called) also takes place during the social events aimed at the collective expenditure of the libido, such as the carnivals, festivals, costume balls and so on.[125] In other words, since the external check on libidinal satisfaction is suspended, the internal one that derived a part of its strength from it, is also put out of action, and as a result a certain number of detours imposed on drives on their path to satisfaction disappears. From the standpoint of the id, the restrictive parental (that is, paternal) authority that underwrote the establishment of the super-ego is dethroned and the doors of intense enjoyment are widely open for it.

Yet, as I have already stated, Freud maintains that there is a price to pay for a libidinal overthrow of the internal and external sources of authority, however transitory and provisional the triumph of Eros has been. Once the so-called magic spell of a revolution or a carnival is broken with the onset of tranquility (and the libidinal energy exhausts itself by gratifying both its aggressive and sexual manifestations), the trumpets of guilt begin to echo in the ears of the former revolutionaries or revelers. This of course can mean only one thing: the structures of the super-ego—which, in Freud's view, can only be suspended, but not altogether abolished once they are put in place—have re-asserted themselves. This is why, from a psychoanalytic viewpoint, the phenomena of revolutions "eating their own children," in terms suicide or psychological instability of those brought to political power in their wake, are not particularly surprising. The sense of guilt, which marks the return of the repressor (the super-ego), is their principal motivating factor.[126] As I show in subsequent chapters, the theorists of the Liberation Thesis have devised a variety of approaches to counteract and overcome the vengeance of the super-ego.

As Freud points out, however, no study of group psychology is complete without trying to uncover the underlying factors in the formation of social groups that are more enduring than those formed in the midst of a revolution or a ritual celebration of Eros. This is so especially because in many cases the more enduring groups represent a psychological platform from which (or in opposition to which) the less enduring ones are established.[127] Among these enduring groups, Freud singles out the Church and the army as the groups that embody the features typical of all.[128] According to Freud, the key question with which one should approach the study of these two groups is "what holds them together," or, in other words, "what makes them endure and thrive." Freud contends that the glue that binds their structures is not their institutionalized power to ostracize and otherwise punish the members for non-compliance, or, alternatively, reward them for compliance. Freud therefore explicitly refutes the argument of those who think that the group formation can be explained solely by the reference to the rational self-interest of the members.[129] The factor that Freud considers a necessary condition for the endurance and smooth functioning of groups is the existence of libidinal ties on two levels. In other words, for a group to persist over time the strong libidinal ties or bonds must be established both between the group members and their leader, and between the members themselves.[130]

THE LIBIDO AND THE LEADER

As already pointed out several times,[131] Freud defines the libido as a life enabling energy that acts as a force behind the emotions of love.[132] While the libido's essential orientation is toward sexual gratification, Freud contends that the libido can and does get deflected from its original orientation or aim. For instance, in an insight that I will show is much elaborated in his *Civilization and Its Discontents*, Freud asserts that this quality of the libido is what made possible the development of civilization. In other words, civilization owes its attainments to the fact that it was able to accumulate and channel the libidinal energy for the performance of asexual and non-sexual tasks. Freud calls this process of the deflection of the libido "aim-inhibition," and considers aim-inhibited libidinal impulses as the glue that holds any group together. In fact, Freud argues that it is precisely aim-inhibited libidinal drives that underwrite the establishment of enduring group bonds. This is so, because the actual attainment of libidinal aims (that is, libidinal gratification) results in a considerable decrease of built-up and accumulated energy. The glue that holds the group together—the continually reinforced ties of libidinal energy—would therefore be subject to frequent corrosion or dissolution, if libidinal gratification became more than a temporary or fleeting state of affairs.[133]

Freud contends that one can uncover the fundamental structure of enduring social groups. Namely, all such groups represent a collection of individuals who "have substituted one and the same object for their ego-ideal [or super-ego] and have *consequently* identified with one another in their ego."[134] What I think should be noted right away is that Freud's model highlights the priority of vertical identification. It is on the basis of such identification with the ego-ideal, represented by the group's leader, that horizontal identification between the group members can successfully take root and unfold. Therefore, implicitly, the structure of group psychology is that of the Primal Horde from *Totem and Taboo*. Brothers identify with each other and enter a social pact on the basis of their ambivalent emotions towards the slain father. In each of them, the father lives on as an ego-ideal, and their social bond acquires its strength from such a primary identification. In other words, they relate not simply because they are brothers, but because they are the sons of the same father. Or, to put it in yet another way, they share "a similar love [and hate] of the same object."[135] The bond that structures their clan, therefore, survives the proliferation of disagreements and envy inevitably engendered by daily mundane tasks, because it is grounded in something that remains outside of it, in the transcendent object now internalized as the voice of conscience, the ego-ideal.

Freud shows how in contemporary social groups the position of such an object is filled by the group leader. In fact, he explicitly refers to the leader as "a father surrogate."[136] In the way reminiscent of the Primal Father, the leader dazzles the group members with his power and imposes on them various types of libidinal aim-inhibitions.[137] These inhibitions make possible the performance of social and political tasks, but they come at a price of repression and possibly result in aggressive perversion. Yet the compensatory mechanism is also in place, according to Freud. The group members are not simply forced or coerced to follow the commands of the other, of an alien being that towers above them and displays its unrivalled power. In fact, if such were the case, the group life would become untenable; soon enough such a situation would lead to an outright rebellion and the murder of the one who commands.

On the contrary, what happens is that the group members identify with the leader by incorporating the qualities they value in him or her into their own psychic structures. In Freud's words, the group members' egos "assume the characteristics of the object."[138] In this way, the imagined qualities of the leader—who seems omnipotent—become internalized substitutes for what the group members desire, but have no hope of ever reaching. Such internalization (though, in essence, castrating) enables group members to obtain vicarious satisfaction and compensates them for frequent failures and setbacks in daily life. It becomes possible for them to enjoy indirectly all that they have desired to be or have, because the leader now stands for their own ego-ideal. A part of them remains a beacon of success no matter how badly fate has treated them otherwise.

In certain cases, however, the object (the internalized figure of the leader) never ceases to make strenuous demands upon the ego. One can conceptualize these demands as the price that the object exacts for its presence (cohabitation) within the psyche. The object strives to dominate the ego and soon enough exhausts it by demanding constant obedience. Freud designates this phenomenon by the term "fascination."[139] He compares what happens in these cases to the hypnotic situation, where all reality-testing is suspended temporarily at the command of the object of fascination (the hypnotist). In other words, in the groups constituted on the basis of fascination, the group members become the hypnotized followers of their leader. This state of affairs is especially frequent in tightly organized movements led by charismatic leaders. The fascist movements of the late 1920s come to mind as well as the variety of cultist groups in the late twentieth century.

According to Freud, in cases such as these, the ego-ideal of group members, which was in place before the fateful encounter with the leader, is completely annihilated. The leader, the newly internalized object, has taken up its place. It is precisely this situation that makes it psychologically impossible for group members to voice (or even think of) the criticism of the leader's actions. In other words, their critical faculties have been occupied by the image of the leader.[140] To describe this state of affairs, Freud coins a particularly dramatic formulation—"the object has consumed the ego," he says.[141] As a result, the leader can do no wrong. He or she hovers omnipotently in the realm of supreme goodness and is followed with a secure and peaceable sense of mind, happily even onto the path of individual and collective destruction.[142]

Freud contends that, on the basis of their identification with the leader (vertical identification), the group members also identify with each other (horizontal identification). Horizontal identification is therefore not primary, but represents a derivation. This makes it less intense and less durable. In other words, if one takes Freud's formulation a step further, it seems that the groups without a leader not only have less chance of enduring over time, but also provide less psychological goods—in terms of security and vicarious enjoyment—than those with a leader (especially if this leader is genuinely noble and heroic).[143] In fact, Freud refers to "the psychological poverty" of leaderless groups. In light of the unlimited praise that the groups of Tocquevillean civil society receive in contemporary social and political theory, it may be surprising that Freud singles out precisely the groups of this type as the most blameworthy culprits for the psychological narrowing of horizons. In such groups, in Freud's view, horizontal identification represents the only glue holding the group together, and the individuals with leadership qualities do not attain positions necessary to assure the group's coherence and persistence over time. In these cases, the ego-ideal is equated with the ego, and therefore no obstacles are imposed on the ego's relentless and selfish search for immediate gratification. Freud darkly remarks that "the present [1920s] cultural state of America would give us a good opportunity for studying the damage to civilization which [from this] is to be feared."[144] In essence, Freud maintains that no products of culture that transcend the limited horizons of momentary self-interest could be created by American-style groups. I think that this explicit concern for the fate and future development of cultural and civilizational goods that could be seen as the main motivating factor behind Freud's two key treatises on cultural matters: *The Future of an Illusion* (1927) and *Civilization and Its Discontents* (1929). In these two works, Freud takes a theoretical position that diverges from his earlier works as well as from the claims of the Liberation Thesis.

CULTURE ON THE COUCH

Freud begins *The Future of an Illusion* with the premise that culture is that which distinguishes human beings from animals.[145] In this work, he is less concerned with the origin of culture or the transition from nature to culture since he has devoted his earlier work *Totem and Taboo* to this problematic. Instead, Freud proposes to examine culture as a fact already in existence. That is, his intention is to explore the psychological underside of the cultural phenomena of modern society in which we live. However, in order to do this, he first needs to elucidate the main structuring mechanisms of culture, or, in other words, its functions.

Freud sees the functions of culture as essentially twofold. First, culture involves a collective regulation of the individuals' relation to nature, and secondly, it involves a collective regulation of individuals' relations with one another.[146] It is clear that any sort of regulation requires stabilization and coordination of libidinal (erotic) energy. This energy, as Freud points out repeatedly, is in limited supply and therefore directing it to one set of goals means withdrawing it from another set. This issue would remain unproblematic if those libidinal goals that individuals are "by nature" drawn to—for instance, the pursuit of pleasure and the avoidance of pain, according to the utilitarian calculus of the ego—are the same as those that underlie the functions of culture. However, according to Freud, this is not the case. He dramatically pronounces his judgment: "every individual is virtually an enemy of culture."[147] And yet without culture the individual's growth and development would hardly be imaginable. It is this and only this that, in its paradoxical simplicity, constitutes the tragic dimension of culture.

The individual is the enemy of culture because those tendencies of his or her personality that are charged by the libido are governed by laws fundamentally different from those that govern the institutions of culture. The discharges of the libido follow the pleasure principle, while cultural forms embody the functioning of another principle, under whose grip pleasure has no choice but to yield. This principle is the reality principle. In Freud's view, the interaction between the pleasure principle and the reality principle is best seen in the process of the ego formation.

Freud contends that for up to several months after its birth, the infant has no means at its disposal to distinguish itself from the external world. In this period, there is neither inside nor outside; rather, all there is (all that there could possibly be) is inside.[148] The infant feels the world as the extension of its body. The world is the body, whereas in maturity the body comes to be at the mercy of the world. Yet soon enough the infant's perception changes due to increased development of the ability to locate the sources of stimuli. The infant becomes aware that it can exercise more control over some sources of stimuli than over others. It begins to glimpse the existence of something other than itself on which, however, it depends for the satisfaction of its needs—at this stage primarily limited to the quelling of hunger and thirst.

As pointed out earlier, Freud refers to this first other as the primary object. The primary object (i.e., the mother's breast) brings blissful contentment when present. But that precisely is the issue: at times the primary object is absent and its absence forces upon the infant the experience of frustration. This experience first confronts the infant with a situation in which it is clear that it is not alone in the world, that there is a difference, a line, between it and the world. No matter how urgent the need for satisfaction, sometimes satisfaction simply is not there. Hence the primary object could be seen as the first representative of the reality principle. It blocks immediate fulfillment of the libido and opens up the possibility of libidinal re-direction to purposes that delay gratification.

In Freud's view, the ego does try hard to minimize the impact of the reality principle and remains oriented towards the pursuit of that which will bring it pleasure.[149] However, through the repeated experiences of frustration and privation in early childhood, it learns that playing the game of reality (in other words, of culture) is the safest way for a certain amount of assured fulfillment. The fulfillment that culture offers is a far cry from the bliss of early infancy, and it is frequently inadequate even to satisfy the most essential psychological needs (warmth, love, etc.). Yet the ego's making peace with it is the only way to avoid slipping into psychopathologies. There is no escape, says Freud, from the conclusion that culture will make individuals permanently discontented and that no matter what they do, no matter how they chart their life's course, a certain level of discontent (of malaise) will remain.

THE MALAISE IN CIVILIZATION

Culture inevitably involves instinctual repression, says Freud, and this is so, even in its products most obviously related to the pleasure principle, such as religions or arts. He suggests that therefore a measure of coercion seems to be a necessary condition of all cultural endeavors.[150] In other words, individuals would not follow the precepts of culture (perhaps most strikingly articulated in the cultural demand for manual and mental labor), if their non-compliance did not entail painful consequences. They would be worse off, if they did not conform: and that is why they do conform. Force and repression (in certain cases, attenuated through the process of sublimation) can therefore be seen as the *sine qua non* of culture.

Freud is aware that critics might attempt to historicize this argument and he takes a stand against such attempts.[151] He asserts that the reasons for the fact that individuals cannot feel one with the demands of culture are not to be found in the particular configurations of any given culture. Instead, one finds them in the individuals themselves, that is, in the conflicts that rage in the world of the psyche. Therefore, even a culture established along the lines much different from modern liberal capitalist democracies would also entail a certain degree of coercion, repression, and consequently libidinal frustration. However, Freud does not distinguish between the necessary and surplus repression, and therefore opens himself for the possibility of a reading proposed by the Liberation Thesis.

Freud does dispute the general Marxian argument that the abolition of private property in the means of production would usher in the era of harmonious inter-linking between nature and society and between the individual and the community.[152] He notes that it is not only inequality in property distribution and economic power that leads to the presence of a large quota of aggressiveness and radical dissatisfaction in contemporary society. Aggressiveness is innate. It is an expression of the ineradicable death drive (Thanatos), and economic conflicts—class struggles—are only one way in which it is manifested. Were capitalist property relations to be abolished in future proletarian society, individuals—though liberated from the shackles of alienated labor—would seize upon other communal relations as means through which they could act out their aggression. Freud, for instance, points out that sexual competition (based on physical appearance and intellectual skill) might be one of the relations that transcend purely economic determination.[153]

Freud does admit, however—and it is one of the key findings of psychoanalysis—that the drives are extremely malleable or, in other words, that they are capable of undergoing endless vicissitudes. This means that through a concerted and sustained effort of the cultural and political elites (that is, of individuals who occupy the high pole of vertical group identification), the drives of the vast majority could perhaps be directed (channeled) from destructive to erotic modes of fulfillment.[154] However, Freud expresses doubt that something along these lines would actually take place, considering the corruption of those in power in whose interest it is to preserve the status quo.[155] Yet even if the elites desired to modify the status quo, the question is whether this would involve a slow cultural metamorphosis rather than any sort of rapid revolutionary change. Freud seems to contend that revolutionary process would be too sudden and too fleeting to effect a genuine change in the drives and their vicissitudes.[156]

However, though Freud does not endorse the necessity of a radical social and political revolution, I do not think that this means that he is content with all cultural matters being the way they are. In his view, there are things and relations within culture that individuals can well do without, if they are to live a more aware and psychologically truthful existence. The dissolution of such relations would not only be a step toward a more wholesome psychological health, but would also free a great deal of libidinal energy for many practical social and political tasks. In this respect, religion seems to be the cultural relation that bears the brunt of Freud's critique.

THE PROBLEMATIC NATURE OF RELIGION

Religion, for Freud, is an example of a cultural practice grounded in illusion. The psychological mechanism of illusion comes into being when reality is mixed with one's wishes. In other words, a reality perceived as true and genuine is distorted by what one wants or desires. Wish fulfillment takes place of truth.[157] Gaps in logic and inconsistent thinking are covered over in order to make such an illusion feasible or at least superficially consistent. One is not supposed to question but rather to submit and believe. It is this rejection of reason as the ultimate arbiter of truth that troubles Freud the most concerning religious relations.[158]

This is so because he sees his life work—psychoanalysis—precisely as an endeavor whose primary task involves dispelling untruths or half-truths about the nature of the self and its relation to other beings and the world. According to Freud, the only procedure conducive to such an endeavor is the rational (scientific) one, because it is the only one that leads to generating repeatable (universal) insights that transcend the idiosyncrasy of any particular observer. It is true, Freud contends, that scientific procedure is rather removed from the demands of the pleasure principle,[159] but this makes it all the more capable of grasping that which follows the laws quite different from those of the psyche—the reality principle of the natural and social worlds.

Religion acts as a protective psychological device (or defense) from the realization that nature is not there for individuals, that life is full of hardships and pain and that moments of happiness are few and far between. Freud's conclusion on the nature of life is therefore not far from that of Hobbes.[160] Hobbes, it is to be recalled, described life as essentially "brutish, nasty, and short." However, while Hobbes limited this description of life to the state of nature and hoped that the establishment of civil society would make a difference, Freud seems to extend it to the state of civil society as well. Otherwise, why would a practice such as religion, illusionary as it is, have been able to exercise such a hold on human imagination and social life over countless historical epochs? The reason must be that the need for compensation of suffering has been overwhelming.[161] The guiding and all-knowing hand of Providence was hallucinated in order for individuals to be able to give meaning to physical and psychological stresses that seemed to have no end.

In this respect, it is interesting to compare Freud's critique of religion to that of Marx. Both thinkers, as children of Enlightenment—the process, in Kant's words, of "man's emergence from his self-incurred immaturity"—unmasked the process of religion as essentially a smoke and mirrors trickery. For instance, Marx's catchphrase from "The Contribution to the Critique of Hegel's *Philosophy of Right*: Introduction" that religion is "the opium of the people" has become famous even among those who have never read Marx. But I think that we should not be misled by appearances: the agreement of Marx and Freud is only partial. While both Marx and Freud agree on a diagnosis, their understanding of the overall outcome of the realization that religion is an illusion is very different.

For Marx, this realization leads to jubilation and opening up of the horizons of infinite possibility. "The abolition of religion as the *illusory* happiness of men is—he says—a demand for their *real* happiness."[162] Once the illusionary sun of religion is extinguished, the individual will be able to actualize his or her real potentials to the fullest extent. Together with other equally enlightened individuals, he or she will work towards building a new (qualitatively different) social and political world in which the individual will "revolve around himself as his own true sun."[163] In a Marxian world, at the end of (class) history, man will become akin to God, with his inauguration/deification taking place—what else than—under the sounds of the finale of Beethoven's Ninth Symphony.

For Freud, however, the disclosure of religion as illusion does not lead to the poetic effusions of Romantic humanism. In contrast, he sees it as no cause for celebration, but instead for humbleness and resignation. With religious dogmas out of the way, the individual is forced to come to terms with his or her essential insignificance and smallness in light of the forces of the universe.[164] The wings of narcissism become permanently clipped and the quest for meaning has to be grounded in the here and now with all their uncertainty and unpredictability. Alienation from other individuals—once cleverly concealed under the guise of religion or political ideologies—is revealed in its full immensity. Freud does not share Marx's belief that it is possible to transcend such alienation in any genuine way apart from the comfort of illusionary thoughts. The overall tenor of his late works seems to approach the stern *Homo homini lupus*. And even science ultimately fails to carve the path for the individual's elevation to the status of his or her own sun: the individual becomes "a kind of prosthetic God"[165] inaugurated by the sounds of Bartok and Shoshtakovich.

Freud is not content solely with examining the function of religion, but also concerns himself with the possible sources and motivations for religious belief. He traces the genesis of religious attitude to the experiences of early childhood. The infant feels powerless in the face of daily experiences and therefore relies on parental figures to help him or her out. In other words, their presence assures the infant that everything will be as it should be, that his needs and wants will be taken care of, and that therefore there is no reason for fear and anxiety.[166] Freud argues that maternal protection—mother is the first protector—is soon eclipsed by that of the father figure. In Freud's view, this transition, from exclusive reliance on maternal authority to extensive reliance on the father, stems from the infant's perception of the father's strength and his more aloof and hence more feared status in early interactions with the infant.[167] The father is, in many ways, a stranger and therefore his ways and aims become a prototype that the infant will unconsciously relate to the inscrutable ways of God. For Freud, religion becomes patterned on the relations of childhood dependence, because life itself provides the adult human being with challenges and sufferings similar to those that faced him or her in childhood. Powerlessness, uncertainty, anxiety are all found in adult life, and it seems that the only path for the ego in defending itself and finding consolation is in the regression to the time when a great deal of support and help was assured. The religious adult realizes that in a certain way "he [or she] will remain a child forever" and that therefore the support and guidance from the Divine Father is indispensable.[168] In Freud's view, the longing for the certainty of such protection underlies all religious devotion and provides a reason for the persistence of religion in all forms of human societies.

Religion (or the religious relation) therefore has a hierarchical structure that resembles the structure enunciated by Freud in his analysis of the leader-follower relations. In its essence, it is an Oedipal relation in which the son submits to the father and if he does not, he is forced to pay a steep price. His hubris demands self-sacrifice. However, if the same argument is extended to the level of society, it may be interpreted to mean that the overthrow of religious traditionalism might lead to the eruption of anarchy. This of course is a favorite argument of religious conservatives and disillusioned rationalists. "If there is no God, everything is permitted"—concludes Dostoevsky's hero Ivan Karamazov. If there is no transcendent being to ground ethics, then appetite and fancy rule the day and fairly soon the only standard that emerges is that might makes right.

Freud is aware that his argument might be appropriated by the conservatives to justify the continued dominance of religion in social and political life. Therefore he takes a great deal of care to distinguish himself from them and yet preserve both the theoretical claim for the Oedipal structure of social relations and his belief that religion needs to be discarded.[169] For Freud, ethical values are possible without the blessing of the divine hand, and yet they are far from being innate or natural. Cultural mechanisms are necessary to instill them and the only question is as to the nature and direction of these mechanisms. Freud thinks that while the paternal position remains the axis around which the establishment of ethical values revolves, the way it is utilized needs to be reversed. In other words, instead of externalizing the father (in the image of God), the individuals need to internalize him (in the structure of the super-ego). This internal balance of power (internal psychic cosmology) makes the external one superfluous. The necessity of living in an illusion (religion) disappears because the task of monitoring, channeling, and restraining the drives is increasingly accomplished by an agency which is itself a part of the individual's psychic life (the super-ego).

THE BIRTH OF THE SUPER-EGO

The super-ego, according to Freud, comes into being as the result of the interaction of the infant's ego with its environment. One could perhaps conceive of the super-ego as a component part of that which Freud calls "education to reality," and which he suggests should replace the teachings of religious dogmas.[170] The super-ego plays the role of the strict guardian over both the ego and the libidinal processes of the id. The tensions between the ego's hedonistic orientations and the super-ego's close monitoring engender the feelings of guilt.[171] In Freud's view, guilt seems to be the fundamental by-product of civilization. It acts as an externally conditioned internal check to the sway of desire and aggression; even though it tries to tame and subdue both Eros and Thanatos, it shares more affinity with the latter. Like Thanatos, guilt stops desire in its tracks; it freezes expansive push of desire and re-routes aggressive impulses towards oneself, towards one's own being. The accumulated guilt finds its expression in submission, and will to self-punishment. As Freud points out, what sometimes appears as a particularly malignant hand of fate is no more than the individual's own psychic conflict played out with recourse to the events of the external world.[172] The world itself becomes a part of the macabre game the super-ego plays with the ego. The pleasure principle comes to be subverted from the inside, but with the help of external means.[173]

According to Freud, the constitution of the super-ego involves the alienation (or splitting-off) of the portion of the ego.[174] It is one of the first cracks in the shell of primary narcissism, because it represents the price that the ego is forced to pay for the sake of its survival in the world in which it is powerless to fulfill its basic needs. The ego depends on others (on parental figures) to help it survive, and the formation of the super-ego is a way of establishing a permanent coordinating link between these indispensable guardians and the ego. In other words, the ego experiences anxiety and fear at the prospect of this assistance being withdrawn and therefore forces itself to conform to the expectations parental figures have of its behavior and attitudes. This means that, for instance, the quota of aggressive energy striving for expression is blocked from its potentially destructive pursuit of an external outlet (in other beings or things), and is re-directed towards the ego's own being. This makes the ego a *bona fide* party to the pact entered into with those who help its survival. One can say that the super-ego acts as the guarantor and enforcer of this pact.

Freud contends that the process of the formation of the super-ego is affected through the mechanism of identification with parental figures. This implies that the force motivating the whole process is not simply a utilitarian calculus of costs and benefits, but also involves the presence of a love relation.[175] Identification is always based on an unconscious attraction and desire to be like the one who is being imitated. The establishment of the super-ego therefore represents a willingness to become like the one who can and does provide for one's own survival; it is a sign of determination to engage creatively with the world and overcome undue dependence on others.

On the other hand, Freud argues that the lack of a strong super-ego opens up possibilities for individual violation of cultural conventions. The super-ego, as the guarantor of respect for norms and values, is not installed in its seat of honor, and so ego's pursuits, fueled by libidinal energy, find no obstacles.[176] The world becomes a free space for the actualization of the ego's fantasies. These fantasies may possess a destructive, narcissistic core and as such affect the existing culture in a manner that negates its attainments. Freud makes it clear that even though he is aware of the inevitability of discontents within a culture, he cannot give his stamp of approval to any radical re-fashioning of its structures. Radical revolution would likely lead to a regression to the level of culture already surpassed both in terms of intellectual and ethical values. Nothing but pain and misery would be gained by revolution; none of its attainments could rival those that slow technological social evolution would bring about. Therefore resignation rather than revolt is the strategy that Freud in his late works counsels the individual to adopt in response to structural social and political ills. It is perhaps this conclusion that can be interpreted as sealing Freud's fate to orbit the galaxy of conservative thinkers. And yet, as will be shown in subsequent chapters, the theorists of the Liberation Thesis were able to read Freud against himself in this respect and, in my opinion, were correct in uncovering the radical liberatory kernel of psychoanalytic teachings.

CONCLUSION

In the end, it could be said that Freud's social and political theory, expressed in his late works, postulates the inevitability of conflict both in the external and psychic life of human beings. In fact, Freud rejects the existence of any firm dividing line between the inner and the outer and considers the social and psychic conflicts as mutually reinforcing. However, due to the presence of innate opposing drives, the conflictual nature of the psychic life seems to be primary and it essentially spills over into the social and political realm. The possibility of harmonious social relations therefore becomes illusive, and alienation and reification the facts of daily life in all human communities.

Freud also stresses the inevitability of the Oedipus complex in the formation of ethical values. The psychological submission of the child to (paternal) norms and hierarchies already in existence represents an unavoidable condition for its ability to live, love, and work in a way that precludes physical and psychic suffering. The price of the refusal to acquiesce is neurosis. Neurotic individuals are therefore especially sensitive to the weight of the status quo inscribed onto their minds and bodies, but Freud, in opposition to the theorists of the Liberation Thesis, thinks that their protests are ineffective in generating radical social improvements.[177] This is so, because he contends that their truth is the truth of individual subjectivity and as such likely to be captured by the specter of solipsistic narcissism. There is little likelihood of genuine (altruistic) collective strategies in Freudian universe. As Freud points out in *Civilization and Its Discontents*, "every man must find out for himself in what particular fashion he can be saved."[178] And yet, Freud also never tires stressing the creative and indestructible communal power of Eros that may, however briefly, overcome the abyss separating the self from the other, and the unconscious from the conscious. It is precisely this insight that will be amplified by the theorists of the Liberation Thesis.

NOTES

1. Sigmund Freud, *The Question of Lay Analysis*, trans. Nancy Procter-Gregg (New York: Norton, 1950), 101.

2. The correspondence between Freud and Fliess lasted for more than seventeen years, from 1887 to 1904. Some of the most fundamental findings of psychoanalysis saw the light of day in the context of this correspondence.

3. *The Complete Letters of Sigmund Freud to Wilhelm Fliess*, trans. and ed. Jeffrey Moussaieff Masson (Cambridge, Mass.: Harvard University Press, 1985), 249.

4. Moussaieff Masson, *The Complete Letters*, 272.

5. For the in-depth investigation of the significance of this admission, see Peter L. Rudnytsky, *Freud and Oedipus* (New York: Columbia University Press, 1987), 54–93.

6. Moussaieff Masson, *The Complete Letters*, 272. Note Freud's line of reasoning here; the seemingly paradoxical nature of psychoanalytic insights has baffled many over the years. Yet it is precisely that which appears paradoxical or nonsensical to the

ego, schooled as it is by the prevailing Reality Principle, which reveals the subversive thrust of psychoanalysis. This insight will be stressed over and over again by the theorists of the Liberation Thesis, see chapter 2.

7. Moussaieff Masson, *The Complete Letters*, 273.

8. For the examination of Freud's personal history, I refer the interested reader to the three-volume biography by Ernest Jones, *The Life and Work of Sigmund Freud* (New York: Basic Books, 1953-1957).

9. Moussaieff Masson, *The Complete Letters*, 279.

10. Moussaieff Masson, *The Complete Letters*, 280.

11. Moussaieff Masson, *The Complete Letters*, 280.

12. Sigmund Freud, *The Interpretation of Dreams* in *The Basic Writings of Sigmund Freud*, trans. A. A. Brill (New York: Random House, 1938), 208-16.

13. Freud, *Interpretation of Dreams*, 298.

14. Freud will later designate this attitude as narcissistic.

15. Freud, *Interpretation of Dreams*, 299.

16. Freud, *Interpretation of Dreams*, 300.

17. Freud, *Interpretation of Dreams*, 301-2.

18. Freud, *Interpretation of Dreams*, 302, fn. 2.

19. Freud, *Interpretation of Dreams*, 298, 308.

20. Freud, *Interpretation of Dreams*, 303.

21. Freud, *Interpretation of Dreams*, 304.

22. Freud, *Interpretation of Dreams*, 305.

23. Freud, *Interpretation of Dreams*, 305-6.

24. This, however, is not to be construed as the argument that the biological development of the individual somehow recapitulates the development of humanity in general, which scientific findings have discredited. The affinity in question is structural (analogical) rather than physical or biological.

25. Freud, *Interpretation of Dreams*, 308, italics mine. The phrase "before our birth" conveys the sense of structural predetermination. See chapter 3 on how Lacan re-articulates this sense in his concept of the symbolic register.

26. Freud, *Interpretation of Dreams*, 309.

27. Freud, *Interpretation of Dreams*, 310.

28. For a survey of contemporary theories of sex and sexuality, see Mildred W. Weil, *Sex and Sexuality: From Repression to Expression* (Lanham, Md.: University Press of America, 1990), and Paul R. Abramson and Steven D. Pinkerton, *With Pleasure: Thoughts on the Nature of Human Sexuality* (New York: Oxford University Press, 1995).

29. Sigmund Freud, "Infantile Sexuality," *Three Contributions to the Theory of Sex* in *The Basic Writings of Sigmund Freud*, trans. A. A. Brill (New York: Random House, 1938), 581.

30. Freud, "Infantile Sexuality," 592.

31. Freud, "Infantile Sexuality," 584 fn. 2. See also Jeffrey B. Abramson, *Liberation and Its Limits: The Moral and Political Thought of Freud* (New York: The Free Press, 1984), 83-98.

32. Freud, "Infantile Sexuality," 585. See chapter 3 for Lacan's remedy of this weakness in Freud's overall argument.

33. Freud, "Infantile Sexuality," 586.

34. Freud, "Infantile Sexuality," 589–90.
35. Freud, "The Transformation of Puberty" in *Three Contributions to the Theory of Sex*, 614.
36. In the 1897 Draft N, Freud says: "The incest is antisocial—civilization consists in this progressive renunciation," *The Complete Letters*, 252. This dynamic of the relation between the I and the other as the object of desire will be revisited in chapter 3 with the introduction of Lacanian concepts such as the object small *a*.
37. Freud, "Infantile Sexuality," 599.
38. Freud, "The Transformations of Puberty," 611.
39. Freud, "Infantile Sexuality," 593–94.
40. Freud, "The Sexual Aberrations," in *Three Contributions to the Theory of Sex*, 569–70.
41. See Philip Rieff, *Freud: The Mind of a Moralist* (Chicago: University of Chicago Press, 1959).
42. Freud, "The Sexual Aberrations," 564, fn. 2.
43. Or, as the popular slogan goes, "make love not war."
44. Freud, "The Transformations of Puberty," 611.
45. On a feminist encounter with Freud, see chapter 4 where the work of Luce Irigaray is presented and discussed.
46. Freud, "The Sexual Aberrations," 565.
47. This in fact is the point that almost all critics of Freud's thesis on sexual difference seem to disregard.
48. Freud, "The Transformations of Puberty," 612–13, fn. 3. For a list of problems with linking activity and masculinity, see Imre Hermann, "The Use of the Term 'Active' in the Definition of Masculinity: A Critical Study," *International Journal of Psychoanalysis* 16 (April 1935): 219–22.
49. Unless perhaps these feelings are sublimated in some artistic form.
50. Freud, "The Transformations of Puberty," 613–14.
51. Freud, "Infantile Sexuality," 595.
52. This is a very important point, which I will enunciate more substantially in relation to Lacan's concept of sexuation in chapter 3. As I see it, the psychoanalytic understanding of the feminine represents one of the nodal points which link psychoanalysis with radical social and political theory.
53. See Karen Horney, "The Denial of the Vagina," *International Journal of Psychoanalysis* 14 (January 1933): 57–70.
54. Perhaps one can take the contemporary political phenomenon of "the gender gap" as an empirical manifestation of this psychological trend.
55. Hence its intricate connection with "the Little Hans" case history, on which I will insist below.
56. Sigmund Freud, "Analysis of a Phobia in a Five-Year Old Boy," *Collected Papers Vol. III*, trans. Alix and James Strachey (London: Hogarth Press, 1953), 239, 253.
57. Freud, *Analysis of a Phobia*, 151.
58. Freud, *Analysis of a Phobia*, 273.
59. Freud, *Analysis of a Phobia*, 253–54.
60. Freud, *Analysis of a Phobia*, 165–68, 192–93, 264–65.
61. Freud, *Analysis of a Phobia*, 258–59.
62. Freud, *Analysis of a Phobia*, 187–88.

63. Freud, *Analysis of a Phobia*, 185.

64. Freud's later works on this subject, such as *The Future of an Illusion* and *Civilization and Its Discontents*, become, for the reasons that I will discuss, more pessimistic regarding the possibility of a less dichotomous relation between the individual and the social. This will become an issue of disagreement between Freud and the thinkers whose works will be presented in chapter 2.

65. "We must imagine Sysyphus happy," says Albert Camus. A voice of resignation and (subtle) defeatism, no doubt! I would rather ask Sysyphus *himself* how he is feeling and then start from that. Sysyphus, after all, may turn out to be a masochist.

66. Sigmund Freud, "'Civilized' Sexual Morality and Modern Nervous Illness," *The Standard Edition of the Complete Psychological Works Vol. IX*, trans. and ed. James Strachey (London: Hogarth Press, 1953–1974), 187.

67. The neuroses of Dora and the Rat Man were precipitated by the events taking place in their adult life.

68. Sigmund Freud, "From the History of an Infantile Neurosis," in *Three Case Histories*, ed. Phillip Rieff (New York: Collier Books, 1963), 306.

69. Freud, "Infantile Neurosis," 210. It is one of the postulates of psychoanalysis that every time there is an expression of comparison in a spoken discourse, there is also an identification at the level of the unconscious (at this level, the speaker actually is the person he or she compares himself or herself with).

70. Freud, "Infantile Neurosis," 213–34, esp. 228–31, fn. 13. Freud argues that even if the Primal Scene never took place in actuality, but was pieced together by the child through other environmental influences, the Wolf Man's neurosis would still have taken the same course. See 243–48.

71. Freud, "Infantile Neurosis," 303.

72. Freud, "Infantile Neurosis," 275–76.

73. Freud, "Infantile Neurosis," 249–72.

74. Freud, "Infantile Neurosis," 314.

75. Sigmund Freud, *Totem and Taboo* in *The Basic Writings of Sigmund Freud*, trans. A. A. Brill (New York: Random House, 1938), 890.

76. Freud, *Totem and Taboo*, 827, 904–5.

77. Freud relies on anthropological material from the studies of the renowned anthropologists of his day, such as Fraser, Lang, Reinach, Westermarck, and Wundt.

78. Freud, *Totem and Taboo*, 827.

79. Freud, *Totem and Taboo*, 886, fn. 2.

80. This speculative division has first appeared in the works of French thinkers Saint-Simon and Compte.

81. Note that the simple linearity of this model is highly problematic, and is in fact subverted by Freud in his effort to establish the similarities between neurotics and the members of the indigenous tribes.

82. Freud, *Totem and Taboo*, 831.

83. With this claim, Freud anticipates the findings of structuralist anthropology (cf. Levi-Strauss).

84. Freud, *Totem and Taboo*, 812–14.

85. See Lacan's discourse theory in chapter 3.

86. Compare this with Freud's previous discussion of Oedipus and Hamlet.

87. Freud, *Totem and Taboo*, 860.
88. Freud, *Totem and Taboo*, 859.
89. Freud, *Totem and Taboo*, 860-61.
90. Freud, *Totem and Taboo*, 854. Freud makes the same point for the first time in the Dora case history. He says: "There is no such thing at all as an unconscious 'No.'" *Dora: An Analysis of a Case of Hysteria*, ed. Phillip Rieff (New York: Collier Books, 1963), 75.
91. Perhaps Raskolnikov from Dostoevsky's *Crime and Punishment* can be taken as the prototype of a person who finds himself subject to this kind of psychological dynamic.
92. Freud, *Totem and Taboo*, 914-19. The primal horde hypothesis is not genuinely Darwinian, because Darwin's theory rejects the concept of group selection. In fact, as Jean Laplanche argues, Freud's conception is neither Darwinian nor Lamarckian, since it treats of the transmission of memory traces in a way different from both. Jean Laplanche, *New Foundations for Psychoanalysis*, trans. David Macey (London: Basil Blackwell, 1989), 33-34.
93. Freud, *Totem and Taboo*, 917.
94. Freud, *Totem and Taboo*, 926.
95. Freud, *Totem and Taboo*, 927.
96. Freud, *Totem and Taboo*, 920.
97. In *The Future of an Illusion*, Freud himself considers the consequences of taking a stand against the existence of the Divine Father (see below).
98. Sigmund Freud, "Thoughts for the Times on War and Death," *Civilization, War and Death*, ed. John Rickman (London: Hogarth Press, 1953), 2-4, 13-14.
99. Freud will examine this issue in greater detail in *Group Psychology and the Analysis of the Ego* and in chapter 7 of *Civilization and Its Discontents* (see below).
100. Freud, "Thoughts on War and Death," 5-7.
101. Freud, "Thoughts on War and Death," 8.
102. Freud, "Thoughts on War and Death," 11.
103. Freud, "Thoughts on War and Death," 20.
104. Freud, "Thoughts on War and Death," 23.
105. See below on the distinction between the ego-drives and the sex drives.
106. Sigmund Freud, *Beyond the Pleasure Principle*, trans. James Strachey (New York: Bantam Books, 1959), 67.
107. Freud, *Beyond Pleasure*, 72.
108. Freud, *Beyond Pleasure*, 74.
109. Freud, *Beyond Pleasure*, 79-81.
110. Freud, *Beyond Pleasure*, 78. This characteristic of Eros is particularly emphasized by the Liberation Thesis. See chapter 2.
111. See the discussion in Paul Ricoeur, *Freud and Philosophy: An Essay on Interpretation*, trans. Denis Savage (New Haven: Yale University Press, 1970), 281-302.
112. Freud, *Beyond Pleasure*, 38.
113. Freud, *Beyond Pleasure*, 28-31. Other instances Freud brings up to make the same point are the transference neuroses in which certain traumatic events from childhood are re-enacted during analysis with the analyst as the representative of the parental figures, and also the play of a sole child in the absence of his or her loved

ones. The latter involves the widely cited *"fort-da"* game played by Freud's great nephew (Freud, *Beyond Pleasure*, 32-37).

114. What has to be kept in mind is that those who suffer from traumatic neuroses generally have gone through the traumatic experience without any permanent physical or bodily injury. This is why Freud is justified in treating trauma as essentially a psychic injury rather than a condition caused by certain somatic disturbances. In fact, Freud claims that a bodily injury as a place into which a strong narcissistic libidinal investment could be made (binding the unbound energy brought along by the actual event) works against the onset of a traumatic neurosis. Freud, *Beyond Pleasure*, 29.

115. Freud, *Beyond Pleasure*, 64-65, 107-9.

116. Freud, *Beyond Pleasure*, 21-23.

117. Freud, *Beyond Pleasure*, 107.

118. Freud, *Beyond Pleasure*, 70.

119. Freud, *Beyond Pleasure*, 71.

120. The literal English translation of German *das Es* is "the it." The *it*, I think, is a more adequate term for the unconscious, because it faithfully denotes its radical otherness within the psyche.

121. This claim becomes in later years a favorite target for those who for various reasons critiqued psychoanalytic enterprise. For a response to this critique, see chapter 4.

122. Sigmund Freud, *Group Psychology and the Analysis of the Ego*, trans. James Strachey (London: The International Psychoanalytic Press, 1922), 3. See also Robert Bocock, *Freud and Modern Society: An Outline and Analysis of Freud's Sociology* (New York: Holmes & Meier Publishers, 1976), 56-64.

123. Freud, *Group Psychology*, 9-10.

124. Freud, *Group Psychology*, 28. See Mikkel Borch-Jacobsen, *The Freudian Subject*, trans. Catherine Porter (Stanford: Stanford University Press, 1988), 128-46.

125. Freud, *Group Psychology*, 105. A literary example that comes to mind here is Thomas Mann's description of the celebration of the Walpurgis Night at the International Sanatorium Berghof. See Thomas Mann, *The Magic Mountain*, trans. H. T. Lowe-Porter (New York: Alfred A. Knopf, 1961), 322-43.

126. See, for instance, the treatment of this and related issues in Edward Glover, *War, Sadism, and Pacifism* (London: Allen & Unwin, 1948), Franco Fornari, *Psychoanalysis of War*, trans. A. Pfeifer (Bloomington: University of Indiana Press, 1975), and Vamik Volkan, *The Need to Have Enemies and Allies: From Clinical Practice to International Relations* (Northvale, N.J.: Aronson, 1986).

127. This point is made clear by Mitscherlich. See Alexander Mitscherlich, "Group Psychology and the Analysis of the Ego—One Generation Later" *Psychoanalytic Quarterly* 48 (1978): 1-23. See also Borch-Jacobsen, *The Freudian Subject*, 153-73.

128. I think that it is important to keep in mind that the Church and the army are in essence bureaucratic structures, and that therefore, even though Freud does not mention other types of bureaucracy, the insights he derives from the study of the Church and the army are applicable to them as well. Hence his list could be extended to include the police, the diplomatic corps, political parties, trade unions, university administrations, and so on.

129. Rationality in this sense is taken to mean an instrumental (means-end) attitude.

130. Freud, *Group Psychology*, 82.

131. See the section on the theory of the libido.

132. Freud, *Group Psychology*, 37.

133. Freud, *Group Psychology*, 78. As I pointed out, the Liberation Thesis is critical of this conclusion. See subsequent chapters, especially chapters 2 and 3.

134. Freud, *Group Psychology*, 80, italics mine.

135. Freud, *Group Psychology*, 87.

136. Freud, *Group Psychology*, 43.

137. Freud, *Group Psychology*, 99.

138. Freud, *Group Psychology*, 64.

139. Freud, *Group Psychology*, 76. Borch-Jacobsen, *The Freudian Subject*, 146–52.

140. As Freud is fond of repeating, the libidinal "occupation" (*Besetzung*), in its forcefulness and unwillingness to compromise, greatly resembles the military one.

141. Freud, *Group Psychology*, 75.

142. Freud, *Group Psychology*, 102. For the application of this insight to a particular historical situation, see Peter Loewenberg, "Psychoanalytic Origins of the Nazi Youth Cohort," *American Historical Review* 76 (1971): 1457–502.

143. This qualification as to the goodness of the leader seems crucial to preserve the coherence of Freud's claim and to avoid its plunge into a contradiction. In other words, if the leader has evil intentions, is it not much better *not* to identify with him?

144. Sigmund Freud, *Civilization and Its Discontents*, trans. James Strachey. (New York: Norton, 1961), 74.

145. To avoid terminological confusion, it is proper to state at the outset that Freud uses the terms "culture" and "civilization" interchangeably. In fact, he contends that he "disdains to separate culture and civilization." Sigmund Freud, *The Future of an Illusion*, trans. W.D. Robson-Scott (New York: Doubleday, 1953), 3.

146. Freud, *Future of an Illusion*, 3–4. See also Freud, *Civilization*, 42–43.

147. Freud, *Future of an Illusion*, 4.

148. Freud, *Civilization*, 13–14. Freud argues that the so-called "oceanic feeling" that is often connected to religious or mystical ecstasies has to do with the bringing into consciousness of this primary period of ego development. Freud, *Civilization*, 20.

149. Freud, *Civilization*, 35.

150. Freud, *Future of an Illusion*, 5, 7–8.

151. One can say that here Freud anticipates and responds negatively to the attempts to mix his teaching with Marxian postulates, seen in the works of the theorists of the Liberation Thesis, which will be examined in chapter 2. The explicitness of this disagreement is what I claim distinguishes the early Freud from the late Freud.

152. Freud, *Civilization*, 70–71.

153. Freud, *Civilization*, 71.

154. As will be shown in subsequent chapters, this claim is the claim that the theorists of the Liberation Thesis will greatly elaborate.

155. Freud, *Future of an Illusion*, 7, 18–19. Note Freud's left-leaning discussion of how the liberal capitalist elites manipulate cultural ideals (i.e., national achieve-

ments) in order to rally mass support for their attempts to extend elite control over more and more regions of the globe and subdue the "less developed" countries.

156. Perhaps Trotsky's idea of the necessity of "permanent revolution" was not too far off the mark in terms of human psychology. Only such a sustained process of building up and destroying, Trotsky argued, could effect lasting attitudinal changes. However, in all social revolutions so far, a period of upheaval was rapidly replaced by a period of stabilization.

157. Freud, *Future of an Illusion*, 52-54.

158. Freud, *Future of an Illusion*, 56.

159. In fact, in a short 1910 article on psychology of love, Freud says that "science is the most complete renunciation of the pleasure principle of which our mental activity is capable." Sigmund Freud, "A Special Type of Choice of Object Made by Men," *Standard Edition XI*, trans. James Strachey, 165.

160. On the similarities and differences between Freud and Hobbes, see a detailed examination in Jean Roy, *Hobbes and Freud*, trans. Thomas G. Osler (Toronto: Canadian Philosophical Monographs, 1984).

161. Freud, *Future of an Illusion*, 24, 28.

162. Karl Marx, "Contribution to the Critique of Hegel's *Philosophy of Right*: Introduction" in *The Marx-Engels Reader*, ed. Robert Tucker (New York: Norton, 1978), 54.

163. Marx, "Contribution to the Critique," 54.

164. Freud, *Future of an Illusion*, 57.

165. Freud, *Civilization*, 44.

166. Freud, *Future of an Illusion*, 26-27, 31.

167. Freud, *Future of an Illusion*, 39.

168. Freud, *Future of an Illusion*, 39-40.

169. Freud, *Future of an Illusion*, 60-62.

170. Freud, *Future of an Illusion*, 88-89.

171. Freud, *Civilization*, 89. See also Ricoeur, *Freud and Philosophy*, 211-29.

172. Freud, *Civilization*, 88; Freud, *Beyond Pleasure*, 44-45.

173. As will be shown in chapter 3, Lacan coins the adjective "extimate" (external + intimate) to describe the psychological dynamic of this sort.

174. Freud, *Civilization*, 84.

175. Freud, *Civilization*, 85.

176. Of course the question needs to be asked whether these norms and values are worth protecting. This is one of the principal issues confronted by the theorists of the Liberation Thesis. See subsequent chapters.

177. In affirming the social and political utility of neurotic opposition, see for instance my discussion of the Great Refusal and the discourse of the hysteric in subsequent chapters.

178. Freud, *Civilization*, 34.

2
The Liberation Thesis

> The man who would not prefer to build a world by his own strength, to create the world and not simply remain in his own skin—such a man is accursed by the spirit, and with the curse goes an interdict, but in the reverse sense: he is cast out from the sanctuary of the spirit, deprived of the delight of intercourse with it and condemned to sing lullabies about his own private happiness, and to dream of himself at night.[1]

> Both for the production on a mass scale of this communist consciousness, and for the success of the cause itself, the alteration of men on a mass scale is necessary, an alteration which can only take place in a practical movement, a revolution; this revolution is necessary, therefore, not only because the ruling class cannot be overthrown in any other way, but also *because the class overthrowing it can only in a revolution succeed in ridding itself of all the muck of ages and become fitted to found society anew*.[2]

The issue of the potential ability of individuals within a social group to transcend "the muck of ages" represents the focus of this chapter. For Marx, such an event is a necessary condition for the establishment of a qualitatively different society. Since the way he describes this event indicates a radical psychological change, a transformation in attitudes and beliefs, the question that I plan to investigate here is whether the possibility of this transformation can be grounded in psychoanalytic concepts. Is there anything in Freud's work that would provide a justification for Marx's claim? Can it be considered legitimate in light of psychoanalytic discoveries? To what extent and under what conditions does psychoanalysis affirm and support the possibility of radical social and political re-structuring that leads to more egalitarian institutions, not encumbered by alienation and class division of labor? Or, on a more dramatic note, does psychoanalysis envision the possibility of its own obsolescence, the establishment of a society where it ceases to be necessary?

In the previous chapter, I have focused extensively on the issues surrounding the Oedipus complex, the complex that, in Freud's view, underlies the formation of ethical value systems. As I have shown, Freud thought that unconscious repression and conscious renunciation of sexual and aggressive drives, effected as the outcome of the Oedipus complex, play an important role in the construction of any cultural or moral system. For him, the conflict model of the psyche (the super-ego; the ego; and the id) and the dichotomy between Eros and Thanatos were universal and transcendent; one could discern them just as easily in the pre-modern as in modern societies. As a result, according to Freud, the possibility of a culture or society in which individuals would not be subject to a pattern of hierarchical (Oedipal) authority relations, though not to be discarded out of hand, was still very slim.

Hence while Freud does not entirely preclude radical social and political change, he is much less optimistic about its possibility compared to Marx. In fact, I think that Freud is inclined to agree that the muck of ages is most likely to remain with humanity, and perhaps, in certain cases, get even more burdensome, as Freud seems to hint in his comparison of the characters of Oedipus Rex and Hamlet. Can we conclude from this that there would not be any rescue in sight apart from an occasional analytic session? Or that the only options open to individual conscience would be either to wallow in guilt, drown its cares in intoxication, or exhaust itself in the perpetual pursuit of pleasures, none of which can please for very long? In other words, the key question is the following: should psychoanalysis be rejected by those interested in social change and the creation of better political worlds? Has Freud condemned himself to the company of pessimistic conservatives such as Oswald Spengler and Leo Strauss?

I claim that the answer to this question is negative, and that there exists a group of thinkers who showed how Freudian insights could be harnessed for the causes of social betterment and fairer human existence. I designate the claims of this group of thinkers, which, in my account, includes a practicing analyst Wilhelm Reich, a philosopher Herbert Marcuse, and a classics professor Norman O. Brown, under the heading of the Liberation Thesis. As I define it, the Liberation Thesis is the thesis that psychoanalytic concepts offer a supportive basis for leftist revolutionary projects. In order to draw its contours, I have chosen to focus on Reich's early researches on sexuality and their subsequent Marx-inspired application to the realm of social and political phenomena, Marcuse's bringing together Marxian critique of alienation with Freud's stress on the deleterious consequences of libidinal repression, and Brown's eclectic blending of psychoanalytic and

Nietzschean insights. Even though there are differences in Reich's, Marcuse's, and Brown's positions vis-à-vis certain psychoanalytic formulations (which I will point out in the course of the chapter), they all share the fundamental belief that psychoanalysis is, to an extent underestimated by Freud, open to leftist appropriations. However, these appropriations, as I intend to show, cannot come about without the modification of certain Freudian positions.

INTRODUCING WILHELM REICH

Wilhelm Reich was a young medical student in post–World War I Vienna. He became interested in Freudian discoveries by way of sexology. It seemed at the time that only psychoanalysis was open to a frank study of sexual matters, which were considered a taboo in the essentially conservative Viennese medical establishment. Reich decided to set up a sexology study group and contacted Freud about the possibility of providing the group with psychoanalytic literature on the subject. Their first meeting took place shortly afterwards. As Reich relates in his autobiographical book *The Function of the Orgasm*, he was truly impressed by Freud. Though already quite famous, Freud "did not put any airs, [but] . . . spoke like a completely ordinary person."[3] He was curious to learn about the projects of Reich's newly founded group and gladly supplied him with the special editions of several of his best known works. Freud also agreed with Reich that the study of sexuality was impeded by the prejudices of the dominant scientific community. This encouraged Reich to double his research regarding the exploration of links between physiological, psychological, and social aspects of sexuality. As I will show, the conclusions arising out of this research motivated Reich to declare himself a Marxist in the late 1920s. In fact, Reich was the first to bring Freud and Marx together in a work of radical political orientation, therefore establishing the theoretical foundation for what I call the Liberation Thesis.

THE IMPORTANCE OF GENITAL SEXUALITY

As discussed at length in chapter 1, one of the most important Freud's discoveries is that children are not as asexual as the late nineteenth century medical science depicted them. On the contrary, childhood is pervaded by sexual concerns. The first steps of intellectual development, for instance, are brought about by trying to find answers to certain sexual enigmas (from the question of sexual difference [male/female] to the question of sexual origin [where do the babies come from?]).

Freud divides up this questioning, motivated by a desire for knowledge, into two phases, each with its psychological and physiological manifestations. He calls these phases the pre-genital and the genital, in reference to the body areas or zones that provided the chief source of excitement.[4] The pre-genital sexuality revolves around the oral and anal drives, which are, after a period of maturation, encompassed—in a relation that, in Freud's view, always remains incomplete—by the genital drive. However, in contrast to Freud, Reich disputes that the incomplete subordination of other drives to that of the genital is a biological necessity. In fact, Reich's insistence on the complete substitution of the pre-genital drives by the genital provides him with an opening for a critical intervention in Freud's conceptualization of neurosis. In my opinion, Reich's intervention makes a theory of neurosis more concretely related to the problems encountered by individuals in a capitalist system marked by egoistic competition.

Reich's principal claim is that the core of every neurosis has to do with the actual disturbance in adult genital sexuality.[5] Here Reich knowingly elides the distinction that Freud draws between actual neuroses and psychoneuroses, such as hysteria or obsessional neurosis. For Freud, only actual neuroses are brought about by sexual inadequacies in adult life; in contrast, psychoneuroses are grounded in the unresolved tensions of early childhood. What puzzled Reich, however, was the question of energy that motivates the formation of symptoms in both psychoneuroses and actual neuroses. What are the sources of this energy?[6] The libidinal energy that can find no satisfactory outlet is the source of the latter, but what if the same type of energy represents the source of psychoneurotic symptoms as well?

In other words, Reich asks whether perhaps one's feeling of impasse in relation to childhood events derives from the difficulties one is presently experiencing in one's daily life. What if, rather than being shaped and framed by childhood traumas, adult psychological problems shape those traumas retroactively? What if the recollections of childhood (inevitably fragmentary, with gaps filled in by fantasy) represent a psychological defense against failing the demands of adult life? What if the present shaped the past more so than the past shaping the present, as was common to assume in psychoanalytic practice?

If the present shaped the past retroactively and the problems of the present were fixable, then it is reasonable to argue that a solution to an individual psychological crisis and to a variety of social problems is within reach. What should not be overlooked, however, is that Reich goes one step further and zeroes in on what he thinks is the primary cause of the problems of the present: the unfulfilling satisfaction of genital sexuality. Several case histories of Reich's patients from *The Function of the Orgasm* show this to be the case.[7] But, at the same time, what becomes clear upon reading these case histories is that the type of genital satisfaction

Reich talks about has little in common with what ordinarily passes for genital sexual intercourse. As Reich points out, "people [tend to] confuse 'fucking' with the loving embrace."[8] In other words, it is not just more genital sex that can cure individual and, by extension, social ills; what is offered as a solution instead is a different and better genital sex—the loving embrace.

According to Reich, the most important element of the loving embrace is orgastic potency, defined as "the capacity to discharge completely the dammed-up sexual excitations through involuntary, pleasurable convulsions of the body."[9] In other words, two processes occur simultaneously: there is the loosening of conscious control over the sexual dynamics combined with relaxing body postures. In addition, the discharge of bound-up energy is complete so as to preclude the possibility of subsequent symptom formations.[10]

The question that arises at this point is what precise techniques or practices can bring these processes into being. If we follow Reich, orgasmic potency and its beneficial effects are quite uncommon, or else there would not be as many neuroses. The reason for the infrequency of orgasmic potency, Reich argues, is found in the fact that humanistic disciplines and social sciences (including the psychoanalysis of Freud's followers)[11] look for the solution of psychological tensions in the ego, in the calculative aspects of individual rationality. However, Reich stresses that the key to orgasmic potency is in the body, in the potentially inexhaustible supply of its libidinal energy.

This is so, because, according to Reich, repression is not solely a psychological process, but it also involves a somatic or physiological dimension. This dimension is evidenced by bodily rigidity or muscular spasms and by conscious and unconscious bodily gestures and movements that prevent spontaneous and smooth expression. Hence in his therapeutic techniques, Reich devises ways that deal not only with the content of the repressed, but also with the manner or the form of repression.[12] In this respect, Reich contends that loosening the manner of repression, which generally manifests itself in bodily movements and attitudes (such as holding one's breath, tensing one's abdomen, or closing one's eyes) is more likely to lead to positive results than the sole emphasis on cognitive remembering and free association. For Reich, it is not only the mind that remembers and speaks about trauma, but the body does also. In his words, every muscular rigidity (or armoring, as he sometimes refers to it) "contains the history and meaning of its origin."[13] This history, expressed in the progressive deadening of the body, could be traced back to moments when a spontaneous bodily reaction was interrupted due to fear or external prohibition. Reich cites a comment that one of his patients made about her perpetually "stiff" cheeks. "My cheeks are heavy with tears"—she said.[14] Her tears were invisible; it was her rigid cheeks that told the story of emotional reactions that had to be held back and repressed.

The task of Reichian psychoanalytic therapy, renamed vegetotherapy, since it seeks to harness the energies of life, is to loosen bodily rigidities and to vivify, so to speak, the petrified and dead body parts. In this way, the undistorted expression of that which these rigidities and bodily distortions express is made possible. In an interesting take on the age-old philosophical debate on the nature of the mind-body connection, Reich shows how the loosening of a muscular spasm (let's say in the head and neck muscles) may lead to the emergence of a cognitive memory associated with the formation of this spasm. In other words, the patient may suddenly recall a traumatic childhood or adult experience (anger at an older sibling, for instance).[15] In contrast, according to Reich, a merely "intellectual interpretation" would be unable to reveal the full extent of such a feeling, because it would lack the means to tackle and loosen the symptomatic bodily spasms. Words, in Reich's view, are not as therapeutically effective as actions (in contrast to Freud's claims).[16] The patient, Reich contends, needs to be shown the manner in which he or she is acting in order to change it; thus, one of the main techniques of vegetotherapy is the imitation by the analyst of the bodily movements and gestures of the patient.[17] In other words, the interventions of the analyst transcend the sphere of speech to which Freud confined them.

Overall, Reich argues that a successful vegetotherapy does not represent a creation *ex nihilo*, but instead enables a constitution of the "natural" or unrepressed way of functioning of the human organism (which may never have existed, except as an ideal).[18] I find that this argument has significant implications for Reich's conceptualization of the nature of social relations. In other words, he seems to say that individuals possess a capacity to express their erotic feelings spontaneously and fully through attaining orgastic potency, and therefore can establish genuinely meaningful relations with others. The reason that at this historical period social interactions are not based on collective eroticism and individual sexuality is far from orgastic potency is, according to Reich, not due to the limitation to love and eroticism found in human nature. Instead, Reich correlates the disharmony and unfairness of communal relations with the impact of social and political arrangements. These arrangements impose all kinds of detours and renunciations on the path that otherwise would be taken spontaneously. Therefore, in Reich's view, they are to be indicted for fostering the misery of the human condition. In this respect, his view conflicts with the view of human nature expressed by Freud in his post-1920 meta-psychological texts but, as I have shown in chapter 1, not with the views of the early Freud. As will become clear in the following section, Reich is particularly critical of Freud's notion of an innate destructive impulse, or the death drive.

THE DEATH DRIVE AND REICHIAN SOCIAL THEORY

Freud introduces the concept of the death drive in 1920 with the publication of his *Beyond the Pleasure Principle*. In this work and others that followed, he revises his earlier claims about the derived or socially conditioned character of aggression and now maintains that it is grounded in human nature. Freud notes that the death drive as such represents a key aspect in the constitution of personality. In contrast, Reich opposes this claim both on therapeutic and philosophical grounds.

From the point of view of therapy, Reich claims that the postulation of an entity like the death drive can be easily used by mediocre analysts to excuse the inadequacy of their knowledge and the superficiality of their techniques.[19] In other words, an analyst can always claim that the patient is not getting better because his or her death drive (the drive to be sick, to destroy oneself) has gained the upper hand. And since the death drive is an irreducible fact of nature, nothing can be done to stop or reverse mental anguish or decline. In addition, the concept of the death drive could also act as an intellectual barrier (a block of non-thought), stifling the development of new innovative techniques with a more consistent and reliable therapeutic success. Reich therefore concludes that Freud's concept of the death drive should be taken as "a hypothesis," a speculation that may be rendered obsolete by the progress of psychoanalytic knowledge.[20]

Philosophically, in line with his commitment to the Liberation Thesis, I think that Reich was hesitant about affirming the concept of the death drive, because it severely narrows the range of possibilities for social and political change. If people are by nature bad and aggressive, how can any social and political arrangement undo those tendencies? In fact, this would make a non-exploitative political order impossible, considering that people would have to be forced to give up their "nature," who they really are. Not even something as extreme and horrifying as revolutionary terror could "force men to be free." Yet his analytic experience convinced Reich that such claims are false. As a successful psychoanalyst, he clearly witnessed transformations of individual character. For instance, a chronically depressed individual would recover the ability to feel the joy of life once again, or somebody who for years could not form a fulfilling relationship would find happiness in love. Case histories such as these motivated Reich to question the necessity of renunciation and discontent that, in Freud's eyes, seemed an inevitable accompaniment of culture and society. In fact, Reich came to consider Freud's claims, not as the true expression of his opinion, but as a resigned attempt to make psychoanalysis palatable to the political powers that be. These powers, according to Reich, had a stake in perpetuating the existence of a political and social system in which the manipulative emphasis on the supposed presence of eternal conflicts prevents the demands of those who are repressed and exploited from being taken into consideration.[21]

Reich of course did not deny the existence of a great deal of destructiveness and violence in political relations; what he rejected was the conceptualization of these attitudes as components of human biological or psychological givens. His analytic practice led him, just as it did the early Freud, to consider all expressions of what was termed the death drive (destructiveness, violence, meanness, bad faith) as secondary or derived psychological phenomena. In other words, they appeared as the outcome of the lack of gratifying fulfillment. In Reich's words, "the desire to destroy is merely the reaction to disappointment in or loss of love."[22]

Therefore, according to Reich, the social phenomena such as reckless violence and sadism are not ingrained in human nature, but are instead consequences of the way of life structured around alienation, exploitation, competition, and anxiety (i.e., capitalism). Not only does this way of life offer few possibilities for genuine gratification, but—and this is far more serious—it has made individuals unable to contemplate what this genuine gratification would look like.[23] Reich is aware that this may cause his demand for orgastic potency to be misunderstood and vulgarized (as, in fact, it has been).[24] However, he persists in unfolding his case for a type of society where the genital character would replace the neurotic character as the predominant character structure.

According to Reich, one of the main features of the genital character structure is that its behavioral and psychological attitudes and expressions are not based on prohibitions (as is the case with neurotics), but instead on the recognition of spontaneous or "natural" needs.[25] In the genital character, these needs, which Reich defines in terms of complete libidinal energy discharge, guide individual behavior. In other words, the psychologically painful contradiction between "I want" and "Thou shalt not" disappears together with all other forms of social and cultural alienation. The principle of conventional bourgeois morality is replaced by the principle of self-regulation.[26] Harmony and happiness, and not competition and conformity, become social norms of the highest standing. Work that is mechanical and repetitive is rejected out of hand, while creativity and creation become the features of the work process embraced by all.[27]

This may sound utopian, but Reich bases his belief in its possible realization on a great deal of success that he attained in individual therapy. Encouraged by this success, he applied the insights gathered from his analytic practice on two social fronts: anthropological and political. In terms of anthropology, his key works are *The Invasion of Compulsory Sex Morality* and *The Sexual Revolution*, both originally published in the 1930s. His explorations of the political dimension are most explicit in *The Mass Psychology of Fascism* (1936). As a way of entry into the examination of the significance of these three works for the Liberation Thesis and psychoanalysis as political and social theory, I will use Reich's critique of Freud's twin works on culture *Future of an Illusion* and *Civilization and Its Discontents*.

CULTURE V. NATURE: FROM HERE TO ETERNITY?

In his late 1920s texts on the psychoanalytic interpretation of culture, Freud maintains an antithesis between culture (social relations, political systems, intellectual productions) and nature (individual desires, drives, and wants). In essence, he states that in order to have culture, nature either needs to be repressed outright, or modified through a variety of mechanisms of cultural control (religion, ideology, education). Sublimation—transmuting raw libidinal energy into cultural or artistic production—is a viable alternative only for a few; it is, according to Freud, beyond the reach of the masses. In his opinion, masses in every society remain at the level of greater or lesser infantilism, and are tutored by their corrupt elites. Moreover, Freud does not find in either group a genuinely democratic and emancipatory potential.

Reich agrees with Freud insofar as this state of affairs is the empirically observable reality of the day, but he disputes the idea that there is anything eternal or natural about it. Reich claims that the infantilism of the masses and the corruption of the elites are the results of a specific configuration of social and educational policies designed to perpetuate capitalist relations of production. It is true, Reich admits, that people frequently appear "corrupt, slavish, faithless, full of empty slogans, or simply dried up . . . [but] they had become this way through the conditions of life. . . . [These] characterological contradictions reflect the contradictions of society."[28] In other words, individual character structure is made to conform to the general social pattern: an exploitative and unjust society will bring up exploitative and unjust individuals.

However—and this is one of the key points of the Liberation Thesis—there is in each individual a potential for creative change even after years of educational conditioning. Freud recognizes this potential when he speaks about a powerful, unyielding individual demand for being happy: he perceives the goal of human life as the attainment of the state of contentment and well being. Reich affirms the existence of this unceasing demand for happiness and endeavors to unshackle it from detrimental social and political influences. In other words, he believes that this demand for happiness will, once liberated from repressive techniques of the status quo, lead to the emergence of a set of self-regulatory needs, needs that can be fulfilled in harmony with oneself and others.[29] In other words, while Freud's ultimate advice (found for instance in his *Civilization and Its Discontents*) is to modify one's desires to fit into an existing social framework even at the price of discontent or malaise, Reich calls for the opposite. He contends that no discontent is genuinely necessary, that it is liberal capitalist system that needs to be modified and rationalized so that it can correspond to what fulfilled or liberated individuals want to make of it.[30]

The notion of fulfillment, in Reich's understanding, includes, as one of its main components, sexual (genital) fulfillment. In other words, Reich treats with suspicion Freud's claim that extensive libidinal expenditures may decrease desire for work and therefore endanger the continuation of social life. In contrast, Reich maintains that in his analytic work he witnessed the positive correlation between sexual fulfillment and cultural productivity.[31] Hence, his conclusion, which I see as one of the fundamental articulations of the Liberation Thesis, is that sexual freedom is repressed, not because its unimpeded expression would lead to the end of culture, but because it would lead to the end of a specific culture, a culture in which the sexual needs of the majority are dictated by the political machinations and ideological demands of the ruling, corrupt minority. Sexual repression, according to Reich, serves the interests of those in power; it is essentially geared toward the creation of conformist attitudes toward established political authorities. Reich compares its consequences to "a psychic castration" that leads to the generation of psychosomatic pathologies on a mass scale. In fact, these pathologies become so widespread that they turn into "a somatic (bodily) innervations (inscriptions)," and enter the status quo definition of the natural and the normal.[32]

In essence, therefore, for Reich, in contrast to Freud, it is conceivable that there could be or have been cultures without sexual repression. In order to offer a body of evidence for this contention, which would complement his analytic findings, Reich turns his attention to the anthropological and ethnographic findings of his day. I think that his researches in this area represent an equivalent to Freud's own foray into anthropology—*Totem and Taboo*—which Reich critiques, especially regarding the hypothesis of the Primal Horde and the murder of the Primal Father.

THE ORIGINS OF REPRESSIVE SEXUAL MORALITY

In the late 1920s, a book appeared that seemed to mirror Reich's insights about the possibility of non-repressive societies. It was a work by a Polish-English anthropologist Bronislaw Malinowski entitled *The Sexual Life of Savages in North-Western Melanesia* (1929). Malinowski spent years in Melanesia, particularly in and around the Trobriand Islands, and wrote voluminously about all aspects of indigenous life. The facet of life that he was most interested in, and not the least because it had a clear reference to theoretical debates going on in Europe at the time, involved indigenous sexual practices.

What Malinowki finds and describes is, in a word, something that to his eyes resembles "a happy, free, Arcadian existence, devoted to amusement and the pursuit of pleasure."[33]

According to Malinowski, the inhabitants of the Trobriand Islands knew of no sexual restrictions apart from the incest taboo. In other words, no other prohibitions were made regarding childhood, adolescent, and adult sexuality. Social life on the Islands was structured around sexual and ritual practices in which all tribal members would partake in freely chosen and unobstructed sexual intercourse. For instance, during a festival called the *kayasa*, in Malinowski's words, "sexual acts would be carried in public on the central place; married people would participate in the orgy, man or wife behaving without restraint, even though within the hail of each other."[34] Not only was adult sexuality openly embraced in this way, but, in this and other situations, even the young adolescents could play all kinds of sexual games without the public and private condemnation that routinely faced and still faces their European or American counterparts.

Both Malinowski and Reich claim that this free and public expression of sexuality has shaped the psychological make-up of the Trobrianders in a decisive way. In other words, it has eliminated all sexual and other psychosomatic pathologies from the Island tribes.[35] These were truly the people who gathered the fruits of that which, in *The Function of the Orgasm*, Reich calls self-regulating sexuality or orgasmic potency. The denial and repression of the open display of genital sexuality, endemic in Western countries, was replaced here by "a simple, direct approach." Hence there was no external necessity that would motivate the emergence of psychologically unhealthy phenomena. Unrequited love, anger, jealousy and other trigger-points of pathological behavior did not have a rationale to come into existence; tribe members were genuinely content with themselves and their bedfellows.[36]

Reich admits that in a certain way some contemporary Western cultural practices retain a hint of this kind of sexual freedom. He points to a profusion of masked balls, carnivals, peasant dances, youth excursions and travels so frequent in Europe of his day.[37] However, as I see it, this hint remains no more than an illusion of freedom, since these events are bound to be crassly commercialized and are usually geared toward increasing rather than decreasing sexual tension.[38] Moreover, the increase of sexual tension without an outlet which can provide more than illusory, or to bring up an appropriate Marxian term, reified gratification can only intensify already existing pathological traits.

Granted that this line of argument is true, the question arises as to how we got from there, from the time of unrepressed sexual life, to here, to the repressive sexual attitudes of modern societies. In order to answer this question, Reich starts out from the Marxian (Marx-Engels) hypothesis about the formation of social values. Within this general framework, he develops his own theory of value formation, which he then contrasts with Freud's Oedipal hypothesis.

Marx and Engels claimed that the dominant values of a society are the reflection of the relations of production. In other words (put in very simple terms), what people do determines what they think and feel; the values of a hunter-gatherer society will differ from those of an advanced industrial society. Thus, even in one of their earliest joint collaborations—*The German Ideology*—Marx and Engels contend that "what [the individuals] are coincides with their production, both with *what* they produce and with *how* they produce. The nature of individuals thus depends on the material conditions determining their production."[39] Almost two decades later, in a preface to his *Contribution to the Critique of Political Economy* (1859), Marx states the same argument in even more explicit terms: "The mode of production of material life conditions the social, political and intellectual life process in general. It is not the consciousness of men that determines their being, but, on the contrary, their social being that determines consciousness."[40] In other words, a given set of economic relations will generate a set of social and political values appropriate to its perpetuation.

What makes this conceptualization so important and attractive for those who, like Reich and other Liberation Thesis theorists, demand anti-capitalist changes is due to what the other side of the coin implies. This important implication concerns no less than the dynamism of historical process; in other words, the implication is that as soon as the relations of production change, other sets of social and political relations among individuals will change as well. If the change in the relations of production is geared toward greater freedom and individual well being (i.e., the change from capitalism to socialism), this positive turn of events will be mirrored in other communal relations, making them more conducive to a fulfilled life.

This process, Reich contends, parting company to some extent with the more optimistic Marx and Engels, can take on a negative direction as well. In other words, the amount of freedom present in social and political relations can actually decrease in relation to the emergence of more exploitative economic practices. This claim can explain why the life of the Trobrianders is less repressive than contemporary European or American life. Reich argues that certain economic practices prevalent in Western world have extinguished freedom and creativity that once upon a time were present there as well.

Reich locates a specific economic practice that he thinks is responsible for giving an initial impetus to the increase of repression regarding sexual and other matters. Drawing on Malinowski and the earlier ethnographic studies of Morgan and Bachofen, Reich concludes that the practice of the marriage gift, provided to the husband by the wife's family, led to the conceptualization of marriage as a set of property relations. Conceptualized in this way, the institution of marriage is likely to have given rise to the tightening of moral norms regarding sexual expression outside the marriage bond.[41] In other words, marriage came to be related to the accumulation of material possessions. Whatever was seen as threatening to marriage began to be associated with economic loss and impoverishment, and was therefore resisted and restricted by those who stood to lose the most—the husbands. According to Reich, new norms of behavior developed including an emphasis on premarital chastity, hurtful puberty rituals, and various sorts of punishments for adultery, the deadliest of them reserved for "unfaithful" wives.[42]

More generally speaking, economic and political power shifted from the maternal clan to the paternal one, from the family of the wife to the family of the husband. Reich follows Morgan, Marx, and Engels in claiming that this meant a world-historical transition from a matriarchal to a patriarchal form of social organization. However, even if the subsequent twentieth century anthropological research turned out no evidence for the historical existence of matriarchies, I think that the orientation of Reich's argument remains valid. In other words, we can discount the claim about matriarchy and still argue that what took place was the shift of economic power from one social group to another in whose interests was to insist on restrictive social norms in order to maintain and perpetuate its rule.

THE GENESIS OF THE INCEST TABOO: THE TWO CLANS HYPOTHESIS

The question that I think should come into play here is the following: how can Reich's interpretation explain the origin of one of the key institutions of indigenous societies—the incest taboo? Isn't it the case that the incest taboo came into being before the emergence of the practices of wealth accumulation? After all, as I noted above, it is also found among the Trobrianders whose free and public sexual practices are praised by Reich as one of the highest peaks of human liberation. Can one devise a hypothesis of the incest taboo that is line with Marxian claims discussed so far? As I will show in this section, Reich's answer is affirmative.

What Freud has to say about this issue is clear: he derives the incest taboo from the mythical murder of the primal Father and subsequent expiatory actions of the sons. Reich, on the other hand, finds this hypothesis problematic for several reasons.[43] First, Reich contends that a social group organized along the lines of the Freudian Primal Horde would have great difficulty maintaining itself for any extended period of time. This is so because the Father kept the sons, that is, at least a half of the productive members of the Horde in the extreme state of subjection. In addition, even when he was overthrown and killed, no sexual gratification and the loosening of the conditions of privation took place. According to Reich, this state of affairs leads to several unresolved dilemmas. Whom did the sons mate with if not with those whom they found near (the Father's wives)? How could the group perpetuate itself and, moreover, generate a culture and a set of ritualistic norms if its members could not reproduce? To simply assume that there was another tribe nearby would be an all too easy post-hoc addition.

Secondly, Freud finds the motive for the sons' rebellion and subsequent remorse in the psychological phenomenon of the ambivalence of feeling. Yet Reich is not convinced that we are justified in assuming that the primitive man possessed the same psychological make-up as the present day individual. Were the intermixed feelings of love and hatred as prevalent in the primeval past as they are today? Reich argues that, on the contrary, the ambivalence of feeling is a recent phenomenon brought about by worsening social and economic conditions. He draws on Malinowski to show that, for instance, jealousy, envy, and spite were very rare amongst the Trobrianders. Moreover, another question that remains unanswered by Freud is how the sons' guilty feelings can represent the origin of morality, when guilt itself can come about only as a response to an already existing moral ideal. The sons' guilt seems to presuppose a "morality" before one is actually formulated.

In the final analysis, Reich finds Freud's hypothesis contradictory and offers his own instead. This hypothesis, he says, is likely to be more historically accurate, since all hypothesized events could in all likelihood have taken place. This is a requirement that Reich needs to satisfy in order to fit his hypothesis in a general Marxian framework, which necessitates the historical grounding of its assumptions.

Reich's hypothesis starts out with the existence of two tribes, which lead a self-contained and autarkic life and practice incest.[44] Due to an external event, such as a natural catastrophe, for instance, one tribe is forced to infringe upon the lands of another. This leads to a violent conflict over supremacy in which one tribe emerges victorious. The victorious tribe then imposes on the defeated a set of slave like practices, including the prohibition of sexual relations among its members. Reich believes that this prohibition can be interpreted as an expression of the victors' desire for more sexual access, or perhaps is due to the fact that the female population of the victorious tribe was decimated in the conflict. In any case, this imposition means that, from now on, sexual relations can be entered into only with strangers, that is, with the members of another tribe. In other words, incestuous relations are forbidden and the practice of exogamy, which is one of the principal features of all subsequent human societies, according to contemporary anthropology, comes into being.

As I see it, Reich's hypothesis is of particular significance for the Liberation Thesis, because it can buttress the claim that a non-repressive and non-exploitative society is historically possible. What Reich shows, on my reading, is that those who imposed the incest taboo are different from the actual Father or fathers of the tribe: they are strangers who have no familial links with those who are forced to obey their authority.[45] Translated into more precise psychoanalytic terms, this means that the Oedipus complex is not necessarily equivalent to the formulation of the incest taboo. In other words, the Oedipus complex and its demand for a rigid submission to the established, paternal authorities can be conceptualized as a later cultural development, linked with the unequal accumulation of wealth on the part of the tribal chiefs. The incest taboo can anchor social life even without the Oedipal relation. For instance, the presence of the incest taboo did not impede the freedom of the Trobrianders, which would inevitably have been restricted had they established the social relations of Oedipal nature. In the final analysis, this means that the transcendence of Oedipal hierarchies may not necessarily lead to anarchic social chaos that Freud imagined in his most pessimistic moments, since it would not mean the rejection of all social values, but only of those that are injurious to freedom, fairness, and individual well being. Stated in another way, Oedipal family structure neither is nor has to be an eternal accompaniment of human civilization.

THE END(S) OF OEDIPAL FAMILY

Reich elaborates his critique of the traditional Oedipal family structure in a book entitled *The Sexual Revolution* and published in the 1930s. In this book, Reich claims that political and social conservatism, together with other variants of conformity to the status quo in all social classes and especially in middle-classes, can be linked to the functioning of the traditional family.[46] According to Reich, the traditional family (the father-mother-child model) is a mini-relay station of dominant political ideology, and hence shapes the character structure of children in line with the more or less codified dictates of the powers that be. The family transmits to the children the socially sanctioned set of values, which are typically the values of patriarchal nature. This means that the children learn to respect and fear paternal authority, and, in this sense, are being taught how to fit into a framework that facilitates their adult submission and morbid or irrational attachment to all types of social or political authorities (i.e., from the boss to the general).

Families in which the father is the only parent who is employed, as was generally the case among the Western middle classes in the first half of the twentieth century, are especially likely to impose a set of strict, authoritarian norms on the children. In Reich's words: "Owing to the contradiction between his position in the production process (servant) and his familial function (master), [the father] is logically and typically a drill-sergeant type."[47] In other words, the father is forced to be slavishly obedient to his workplace superiors, but, then, in order to compensate for the non-recognition in the public sphere, he rules with a hard hand at home. And in cases in which both parents are employed (the typical family today), it is likely that this diabolical dynamic affects them both. As a result, economic uncertainty and parental frustration, in addition perhaps to marital difficulties, combine to increase the amount of repression imposed on young children.

Repression comes in the shape of a variety of prohibitions enforced by the threat of or by actual punishment. According to Reich, the most affected—and with the most serious implications—is the children's sexual life. Genital explorations, such as "playing doctor," and masturbation, even though they are natural expressions of children's curiosity about themselves and others, are prohibited and punished. Since there is no outlet for their sexual feelings, children learn to repress them and therefore lay a foundation for a future pathological character structure.[48]

Reich argues that even the very structure of the traditional family—the triangle—(with two figures towering above the child) works toward intensifying repression and is very conducive to the establishment of adult fascination with persons of authority. The triangular Oedipal bond, which even with the most ideal parents quite easily turns into a hopelessly unequal power relation, may represent a serious psychological challenge to adult democratic thinking and expression. In other words, the triangular model, when it becomes an explicit model of political life, is a manifestation of dictatorial rule. The familial Oedipal relation therefore establishes an unconscious authoritarian propensity that translates into political attitudes of the same nature.[49]

This propensity, Reich contends, cannot be dissolved without first dissolving childhood paternal fixations. Otherwise, the Leader will always remain a loved and feared father-substitute described by Freud in his *Group Psychology and Analysis of the Ego*. In other words, he or she will continue being seen as a mysterious person, beyond good and evil, that the helpless child-man/woman identifies with in order to share vicariously in the perceived mystery and power.

Reich devotes to the study of authoritarian identification what many scholars regard as his most radical book *The Mass Psychology of Fascism*. In the same book, he is also most explicit about possible solutions and remedies. For Reich, as the key theorist of the Liberation Thesis, believes that the hierarchical Oedipal relation of value formation is historical, and therefore replaceable by a relation both egalitarian and emancipated. In the words reminiscent of the early Marx, Reich describes this relation as one in which "nature and culture, individual and society, sexuality and sociality, would not longer contradict each other."[50]

THE STRUGGLE AGAINST FASCISM WITHIN AND WITHOUT

Reich calls his approach to the study of social and political patterns and processes "sex-economy," which he defines as a study of "the way in which society regulates, promotes, or hinders gratification of sexual needs."[51] Reich thinks that all social phenomena (religions, political ideologies, cultural ideals) have a sex-economic basis, that is to say, they contain an underlying conception of how sexual needs of individuals should be organized. This conception is in more or less conflict with the self-regulatory way of sexual expression, which, according to Reich, represents the only hope humanity has of breaking out of the endless historical cycles of wars, violence, and cruelty. However, the layer of the psyche governed by self-regulatory or natural sexual and other needs, according to Reich, lies deeply buried under two other layers that have come into existence due to the cultural or social changes over thousands of years.

The psychic layer[52] that lies closest to "the surface" manifests itself in the daily life of the modern individual, at the level of ordinary social discourse, punctuated with petty demands and superficial tolerance and civility. This layer also contains a set of defense mechanisms, disguised as conventional ethical norms, designed to contain that which finds its location immediately underneath it—that which Reich calls "the Freudian unconscious."[53] The Freudian unconscious is a source of attitudes hostile to the work of society in a manner both destructive and self-destructive; it motivates the emotions of envy, hatred, violence, and brutality—*Homo homini lupus*. It is unsuccessfully contained by the first psychic layer (especially in times of economic and political uncertainty), while it distorts the expression of the third and most concealed layer of the psyche—the layer of self-regulatory or natural needs and expressions governed by genuine solidarity, peace, and love.

Reich attributes the repression of the third layer to social and political forces—the ruling minorities—in whose economic and political interest it is to restrict the fulfillment and well being of the majority in order to increase their own enjoyment, both in terms of quality and quantity.[54] The second layer, the Freudian unconscious, formed as the repression of the third, while the first layer represents the most recent psychological acquisition. It came about as a psychological compromise with the powers that be, enabling a degree of social stability, at the price of being unable to address the roots of psychological discontents in any meaningful way. On my reading, the only position that Reich sees as consistent with the Liberation Thesis is not that which works for the strengthening of the first layer (conventional ethical norms, tolerance, and so on), which would characterize those who consider themselves liberal democrats. Instead, the liberatory position means confronting the hostile, sadistic layer in a daring struggle and neutralizing it by allowing the imprisoned human potentials to find expression.[55] Unless this is done, I would say, there is no telling whether a great portion of humanity may not once again fall prey to authoritarian ideologies such as fascism and ethnic and religious fundamentalism.

Reich claims that ideologies based on hatred of difference appeal to the gratification of tendencies and drives populating the second layer of the psyche. They tap into the envious, intolerant attitudes of the average person, whom Reich calls "the little man."[56] The little man has a fascist character structure. He is in awe of authority, for instance, the authority of the military and other hierarchical organizations, and craves to be "saved" by this authority from internal demands that are oppressing him. He is therefore a willing prey of mysticism and messianism, both in religions and in political propaganda. He yearns for the resolution of tensions, yet is not willing to make a responsible effort to attain it. He is generally passive and waits to be told what to do and how to do it. This makes the little man "incapable of freedom," because genuine freedom presupposes the responsibility and willingness to be accountable for one's choices.[57]

From the standpoint of the Liberation Thesis, it would be a mistake to think that the little man inhabits only those countries that actually developed fascist political regimes. Reich's characterization is more widely applicable than that. In fact, Reich claims that wherever the majority of people show a great deal of reverence for the religious message, the little man is alive and well. Like Freud, Reich sees religion as perpetuating into adulthood an essentially infantile relation of helplessness and dependence.[58] For Reich, dependence on God is a derivation of childhood dependence on parents and as such prevents the development and realization of maturity. This dependence entails the denial of responsibility for the consequences of one's actions, which, when translated into the realm of political action, can lead to horrifying outcomes. In this respect, consider the common defense of Nazi officers after World War II—"I just followed orders from my superiors," or "That is what I was told to do." As in the case of the Nazis, the denial of responsibility frequently leads to the non-recognition, and even the infliction, of real suffering on fellow human beings.

Reich contends that the longing for God is a distorted psychological expression of the longing for release, generally for the release of sexual tension.[59] Religions, with their rituals and practices, seek to divert libidinal energy from sexuality. This is in line with the basic psychoanalytic claim that all human activities depend on libidinal investments; however, compensation received by religious individuals in return for repression of sexuality is psychologically unfulfilling. Misery and discontent are perpetuated to such an extent that fanaticism, outright sadism and intolerance come into being.

Even though religious excitation is a poor substitute for genuine sexual release, so many individuals still follow the religious message. How can this be explained? Reich thinks that the main reason lies with "that fascist in oneself"[60] who is more willing to wallow in conformity and dependence, because it is safe and others do it, than "to take arms against the sea of troubles / and by opposing, end them," as Shakespeare put it in *Hamlet*. Or, as Camus states in his novel *The Fall*, for the vast majority of humanity "the fall begins at dawn," when they wake up and have to get up to go out into the alienated world that tortures them in more ways than one.

Even being non-political or not interested in politics is, for Reich and the Liberation Thesis in general, not an innocent social phenomenon. Reich claims that what on surface appears as passivity, as a mere non-participation in political matters, is actually the sign of an active defense against social responsibility, with deeper roots in sexual anxieties.[61] Those who are not political are not thereby protected from falling into the trap of enchanting political propaganda. In fact, because they lack the experience of social responsibility, the experience of what it means to work together with others toward a common goal, these individuals are easily taken in by the siren-like voices of political demagogues. In Reich's words, "if, now, such a self-encapsulated person meets a propagandist who works with faith and mysticism, meets, in other words, a fascist who works with sexual, libidinous methods, he [/she] turns complete attention to him [/her]."[62] This is why those who are non-political represent a great potential reservoir of authoritarian reaction that may break the established liberal democratic regimes, which, exploitative and corrupt in themselves, can do nothing to alleviate it.

However, even this outcome does not exhaust all the possible varieties of fascism. According to Reich, even those who in public, political life take the banner of liberation, such as Western Communist or Socialist parties, may not be up to the task of addressing fascism adequately. In his view, a typical Party politician sees "only 'the working class,' which he wants 'to infuse with class consciousness.'"[63] In other words, the approach of such a politician is as external, abstract, and abusive as found in any other ideology or religion of salvation.

Reich contrasts this approach with the approach he himself has taken as a scientist committed to the advancement of genuine freedom in the world. Explaining his position, Reich says "I saw man as a creature who had come under the domination of the worst possible social conditions, conditions he himself had created and bore within himself as a part of his character and from which he sought to free himself in vain."[64] As I see it, the second part of this statement is crucial. Reich says explicitly that the oppression of human beings is their own creation that has become internalized, while all attempts to lift it and attain liberation, in order not to be condemned to futility, must break with the status quo through radical articulations in theory and practice.

Reich finds these radical articulations in the works of Marx, Engels, and Lenin, especially in terms of their emphasis on the disappearance of the political apparatus, the disappearance of the state. In other words, Marx and Engels, as well as Lenin in his work *State and Revolution*, contend that the state as such has become so tainted by the abuse of power and manipulation on behalf of the capitalist class that in the new type of political democracy that they propose, it would simply have to "wither away."[65] What Marx, Engels, and Lenin suggest is that the responsibility for running public affairs fall into the purview of the daily life of citizens. In this way, democracy would cease to be a merely formal framework in which citizens' participation ends with an act of voting or where politics is seen as a professional enterprise maintained by scores of "experts," but would come to mean active participation of all in social tasks at hand. This end-goal represents a rationale behind the necessity of "the dictatorship of the proletariat" as conceptualized by (later) Marx, Engels, and Lenin. The proletarian seizure of political power is to be a transitory period supposed to establish social and ideological preconditions for the eventual disappearance of all political mechanisms, which are not oriented toward the fulfillment of vitally necessary practical tasks. It spells the end of political rhetoric for rhetoric's sake, and opens up new horizons for the solution and resolution of all social problems, from poverty to war.

Writing in the early 1940s, Reich is aware that the Soviet Union, presented by Stalin as the actually existing dictatorship of the proletariat, grotesquely failed to accomplish the goals charted by Lenin in *State and Revolution*. The soviets, initially hailed as the true-to-life successors of the cells of the Paris Commune, in fact never came close to fulfilling their purpose, which was to extend political and social participation as widely as possible.[66] The soviets' power was absorbed by the Communist Party functionaries who exhibited the same tendencies to manipulation, corruption, and abuse that their ideological enemies, the tsarist bureaucrats, had been known for. Far from withering, the Soviet state apparatus was enlarged and strengthened. The Soviet Union became not an oasis of peace and freedom in a cruel bourgeois world, but a brutal dictatorship that punished even the freedom of thought. The question, then, that needs to be asked in reference to the Liberation Thesis, and that Reich indeed takes time to consider is what this kind of outcome means for the praxis of liberation.

Reich claims that what the sad failure of the Soviet Union shows is that economic reorganization coupled with intense ideological propaganda is not enough to effect needed changes in human psychology. In other words, the character structure of most of those who went through the Revolution remained essentially unchanged. Therefore no new, more emancipatory political and social outcomes could be expected. For Reich, in contrast to some strands of Marxist theory, class identity does not make much difference in terms of the character structure. In his words, "it is not as if we had revolutionary angels on one side and reactionary devils on the other, avaricious capitalists as opposed to generous workers."[67] And this precisely is the human predicament; for the lack of the progress of freedom, the blame is to be divided up among all the groups, it is not a sole burden or possession of the particular ones.[68]

Reich therefore sees the cause of the collapse of the liberatory project in the Soviet Union in what he diagnoses as the principal feature of the authoritarian character structure: the avoidance of social responsibility, the state of dependence of the majority on the few charismatic manipulators whose private interests dominate the public agenda. Reich finds blatant evidence for the failure to transcend the authoritarian character structure in the repressive organization of Soviet labor force. In other words, in opposition to Marxian insights, basic work in Soviet factories and elsewhere was performed under the conditions of compulsion.[69] No genuine link existed between the worker and his or her product, which meant that the essential characteristics of alienation were firmly in place.

In addition, the Soviet Union did not overcome traditionalist prejudices concerning sexual morality. The access to contraception and housing for young adults remained a great problem, while childhood and adolescent sexuality were denied appropriate outlets. Hence, as one of Reich's principal claims goes, without a gratified sexual life, it is impossible to develop "an urge to activity" that is creatively productive and socially affirmative.[70] An inescapable conclusion emerges that given these shortcomings, the hopes and dreams of the 1917 Russian Revolution had to remain unfulfilled.

Yet Reich does not mean by this that the entire project of liberation is to be abandoned, crumpled up, and thrown away into the dumpster of history. As other thinkers of the Liberation Thesis, he emphasizes that all illusions that liberation is at hand, or that it is the province of a particular group or class, need to be abandoned, while the reality of hard facts needs to be faced. As things stand now, the majority is not capable of freedom; most individuals are not capable of taking into their hands the responsibility for rational self-administration. The solution that the Liberation Thesis underwrites is that social and political energy should be used to enable this capacity to develop. Reich, for instance, argues that this capacity is here already, present or immanent in each individual, but that there are obstacles that have to be removed before it can flourish.

These obstacles are found not only in class and political disparities, but also in an overall mechanistic tendency of contemporary Western civilization.[71] The mechanistic organization of work, leisure and conceptions of life establish a restrictive framework for the practice of social and political life. The machine makes the living being subservient to itself, until the living being in its most intimate expressions and activities comes to mirror the machine. In this way, life is distorted or denied, while the most precious thing, the self-regulatory nature of spontaneous growth, is lost.

Spontaneity is a mode of existence that Reich most resolutely wants to make emerge. However, he knows that spontaneity cannot be imposed from above, by political leadership, for instance. In contrast to Rousseau, Reich does not think that people can be forced to be free. Their freedom must come into being organically, by itself for itself. What those committed to the advancement of freedom need to do is to create the conditions in which such freedom can take place. Reich calls the totality of such conditions—work-democracy.

Reich does not conceptualize work-democracy as a political system; in fact, it appears that there would be no politics in it. He states that the notion of work-democracy is neither leftist nor rightist, but transcends all ideological divisions.[72] For Reich, ideologies only add fuel to the fire of human irrationality. If this irrationality is to be rooted out, work-democracy must be faithful to the articulation of a process that takes place behind all ideological sweet-talk. This process refers to a set of natural or self-regulatory needs that could support an emancipated social life. According to Reich, these needs are centered around love, as expressed in non-repressive social interaction, functional and pleasurable work, and the pursuit of knowledge about oneself and others.[73] As the motto that Reich has chosen for all his books declares: "Love, work, and knowledge are the well-springs of our life. They should also govern it."

INTRODUCING HERBERT MARCUSE

Wilhelm Reich and Herbert Marcuse were members of the same generation; Reich was born in 1897 and Marcuse in 1898. Both witnessed first hand the horrors of the World War I, yet neither was drawn to a type of pessimism depicted, for instance, in T. S. Eliot's poem "The Hollow Men." Instead, both committed themselves to working for political changes so that the tragedies of war would never be repeated again. Though their professional activities differed—Reich was an analyst and Marcuse a philosopher—the content of their thinking regarding the utility of psychoanalysis as critical theory, shows a great deal of similarities, as I intend to show. These similarities justify the inclusion of both thinkers under the banner of what I have called the Liberation Thesis.

In the early 1930s, after having studied with some of the best-known German philosophers, such as Edmund Husserl and Martin Heidegger, Marcuse joined the Institute for Social Research in Frankfurt. Under the leadership of Max Horkheimer, the Institute supported theoretical and applied research oriented in the traditions of humanistic Marxism and the critique of political economy. The focus was on the so-called social and cultural categories (i.e., ideology, science, art, family and so on), and the task was to show to what extent these categories of social life shared in the perpetuation of the capitalist status quo or, conversely, represented tendencies and possibilities that transcended it. The Institute soon came to be known as the Frankfurt School and the specific theoretical perspective associated with its work was termed a critical theory of society.[74]

Marcuse's work spans all major areas of philosophy and social and political theory; in this section, however, I am interested in presenting only an aspect of his work that shows an affinity with, or is explicitly concerned with, the conceptual framework of psychoanalysis. This is why I have chosen to start this examination by looking at a less known essay from the late 1930s and, then, move on to the discussion of Marcuse's major contribution to psychoanalytic social criticism, his book *Eros and Civilization*. I will follow this discussion by an examination of a set of published lectures, which Marcuse delivered in the late 1960s and early 1970s and which, in my opinion, add new insights to his research into the emancipatory potentials of psychoanalysis.

HEDONISM AND MARXISM

In 1938, Marcuse published an essay on the philosophies of hedonism in the journal of the Institute for Social Research.[75] His principal claim regarding the Cyrenaic and Epicurean hedonistic philosophies is that to a certain extent—Marcuse's phrase is "in an abstract, undeveloped form"—they anticipated the revolutionary insights of Marxian critical theory.[76] In other words, they showed more theoretical similarities with Marxism than any other ancient or modern philosophies, including here the philosophies that Marcuse designates as bourgeois idealism (primarily Kant and his early twentieth century followers Ernst Cassirer and Hermann Cohen).

According to Marcuse, what distinguishes hedonism from other philosophies is its emphasis on the actual needs and desires of the individual. Hedonism considers individual gratification as the highest good. The Cyrenaics, for instance, claimed that bodily, especially sexual, pleasures should be seen as ends in themselves, an insight that Reich would have agreed with. How different this claim is from the "official" Platonism and Aristotelianism of antiquity that relegated bodily pleasures to the lowest and most base realm of the psyche! A quick look at Plato's dialogues *Phaedo*, *Republic*, and/or *Philebus*, and Aristotle's *Nichomachean Ethics* will convince even a philosophical dilettante of the truth of this statement.

Marcuse links up the claims of the Cyrenaics with Marxian demands, demands that call for the transcendence of a society in which individual gratification becomes the plaything of the profit motive, in which pleasure and pleasuring are doled out as reified commodities. In Marcuse's words, in a capitalist society, sexual pleasure is "rationalized and appears as a mere means to an end lying outside itself, in the service of a smooth subordination of the individual to the established form of the labor process."[77] The individual, together with the substance of his or her wants and desires, is sacrificed to the forces beyond his or her control. The irrationality of these (economic) forces generates the ephemeral nature of enjoyment and leads to general malaise or discontents in civilization diagnosed by Freud.

Even capitalists, the main material beneficiaries of the system, stand to lose in this kind of social arrangement. According to Marcuse, it is likely that they experience "a social guilt feeling," manifested in not being able to enjoy their easy at-hand enjoyments and leisure activities, since these come to seem as "a burden or duty."[78] In other words, their duty to enjoy takes vitality and creativity out of the freedom from the blatant abuses of capitalist labor process that they do in fact have. Their sense of unfulfillment is of course not as great as in those who sell their labor as their only commodity, but it is present and may even take on a pathological bent (masochism, *schadenfreude*, waste, ennui, gratuitous violence, and so on).

Marcuse is aware, however, that having or not having an access to means of gratification is only a part of the issue. Another important aspect is the content of that which is gratified, of wants and desires that the individual (whether bourgeois or proletarian) possesses. The Cyrenaics, as he points out, did not distinguish between pleasures, and this landed them in the realm of ethical relativism whereby each pleasure is as good as any other. In contrast, Marcuse and other Liberation Thesis theorists believe that, in light of the necessity for social and political change, it is justifiable to establish a hierarchy of values. This is why Marcuse parts ways with the Cyrenaics and appeals to a later version of hedonistic philosophy (the Epicureans) and also to later dialogues of Plato, where the concepts of true and false pleasure are introduced for the first time.[79] The capacity for making a judgment on the nature of different pleasure is, according to these philosophies, found in reason or the rational faculty.

While Marcuse agrees that reason needs to play a key part in discerning the quality of pleasures, he does not accept the way in which either Plato or Epicurus employ the concept of reason in defining what a true pleasure is. He finds in both philosophers a justification for what is essentially an escape from the uncertainty of social and political realities. Neither the Socrates of the later dialogues nor Epicurus and his followers are willing to bear social and other responsibility for communal concerns. This, according to Marcuse, is the repressed underside of their claims that happiness, together with truth, finds its true abode in "the inner man."

Marcuse claims that a good example of escapism is the life style of the Epicurean sage. The sage uses his reason not in order to critique the existing state of social relations (which, for Marcuse, is the primary function of reason), but instead makes it busy with "the calculations of risk and the psychic technique of extracting the best from everything."[80] In a fashion typical of what will in the bourgeois epoch come to be known as "possessive individualism," the Epicurean sage abandons the search for a rational understanding and critique of the social and political order and spends his days devising cunning strategies for minimizing pain.

On the contrary, Marcuse stresses that the key task of reason is to enable individual and collective emancipation from the conditions of suffering. Faced with the irrationalities of exploitation and injustice, reason needs to represent a spur for political action and social change. In this way, existing wants and needs can be transformed, since, under the light of critical reason, "the faults and blemishes of the objects of enjoyment" inevitably appear.[81]

Though reason has an important role to play in social transformation, at the same time Marcuse emphasizes that this does not mean that sensual and sexual enjoyment are to be downplayed. Like other thinkers of the Liberation Thesis, Marcuse contends that the demand for this kind of enjoyment may in fact provide a spark that will mobilize a universal political revolt, since libidinal investments ground the functioning of the rational faculty. This may be especially true in regards to generating opposition to the capitalist labor process in which enjoyment is undermined by an intense focus on productivity and antagonistic competition. Work as enjoyment rather than profit is a rare oddity in capitalism.[82]

Neither Freud nor psychoanalysis are specifically mentioned in Marcuse's essay on hedonism, but I think that in his emphasis on the wants and desires of individuals Marcuse endorses key psychoanalytic concerns. To some extent, Marcuse departs from Freud in that he accentuates the possibility of the eventual overcoming of tensions between individual demands and social frameworks, and also among individuals themselves. This shows his theoretical affinity with Reich. For Marcuse, civilization without discontent is possible, but it is a possibility repressed by existing civilization. Therefore, in order for a different civilization to come to be, existing civilization must be transcended or, in Hegelian terms, *aufgehoben*. The *Aufhebung*, according to Marcuse, can be motivated by demands that resemble the demands of ancient hedonistic philosophies, in other words, demands inspired by Eros, the same ones, it should be remembered, that enable a recovery from individual psychological pathologies.

EROS IN CIVILIZATION?

Freud defines Eros as a drive "to preserve living substance and to join it into ever larger units."[83] Marcuse approvingly quotes this definition and bases on it his claim about the significance of social and political practices and activities motivated by Eros.[84] Eros affirms the values of life and stands for communal coming together. According to Marcuse, this makes Eros besieged on two fronts. On one hand, its strivings are checked by its eternal enemy, the death drive (Thanatos), and on the other, it is impeded by the bourgeois (capitalist) form of Western civilization.

As pointed out by Freud, the goal of Thanatos is the dissolution and destruction of whatever is bound by libidinal energy. This feature, Marcuse claims, makes Thanatos into an ideal supporter of capitalist civilization with its emphasis on mechanization, conquest of internal and external nature, and alienated labor. Hence capitalism acts as a support of social and political phenomena that appear as manifestations of Eros' enemy. Aggressive behavior in daily life, sadistic crimes, and wars stem, according to Marcuse, from the imprisonment or repression of Eros within the social and political status quo.[85]

Marcuse contends that repression of Eros is not a psychological necessity. He criticizes the post-1920 works of Freud for giving the concept of the Reality Principle, with its emphasis on the necessity of renunciation and resignation, a historically transcendent status. In Marcuse's view, there is no one eternal Reality Principle to which the ego must submit in order to sustain the life of the individual, but the case is rather that the Reality Principle is historically conditioned. The flip side of this is that if the Reality Principle is shaped by historical processes, then it is possible to transform the existing Reality Principle by making it less repressive and more open to the gratification of erotic demands and wants.

Marcuse calls the Reality Principle historically compatible with capitalism "the Performance Principle," since what counts in a capitalist system is the quantity of tasks performed rather than their intrinsic worth or quality.[86] This feature of capitalism is manifested in the processes of alienated and underpaid labor, which are meaningless from the standpoint that goes beyond the perpetuation of mere existence. Marcuse argues that existing Western civilization possesses enough material resources to put a stop to all repetitive and unfulfilling work practices. Like Reich, Marcuse does not believe that work as such is incompatible with Eros; what is incompatible with Eros is alienated work, work that breaks the link between the producer and that which is produced, work that distorts and diminishes, instead of fully expressing the personality of the worker.[87] Marcuse posits as the ultimate goal the kind of work that is an end in itself rather than a merely functional means for the satisfaction of wants that an unfree society extols above all others (for example, a consumerist life-style).

According to Marcuse, the development of social practices that support creative and freely chosen work may lead to the formation of an aesthetic, loving attitude toward the world and all human and non-human beings that inhabit it. This is so, because in the routinized labor processes of capitalist civilization, the human body is "desexualized," and its libidinal or sexual energy is invested into performing well and getting *the job* done. In this way, individual libidinal investments are made to serve the needs of the overarching economic apparatus.[88] Marcuse contends that if the time taken up by alienated labor diminishes, a certain amount of libidinal energy will become available for re-investment into other areas, areas that can conceivably combine work and pleasure. For instance, the individual might choose to direct the liberated libido toward his or her own body, making it "a thing to be enjoyed," or toward social activities with other libidinally free individuals.[89] The freedom to make and unmake libidinal investments is supported by both Marcuse and Reich and, as such, represents one of the most important components of the Liberation Thesis.

Marcuse also agrees with Reich that libidinal energy, which is, in this manner, "returned" to the individual, should be dispensed with knowledgeably. Individuals must by all means avoid falling prey to what he labels as "organized leisure activities."[90] Such activities are guided by the profit motive and therefore just as constraining to individual freedom of libidinal choice as capitalist labor processes themselves. If the investments of libidinal energy are the tools of raising individual freedom to a higher, more meaningful dimension, then whatever is chosen as gratifying must not come at anyone else's expense.[91]

In order to defend the beneficence of free libidinal investments, Marcuse coins the concept of libidinal rationality. This concept implies that a genuinely free libidinal gratification is not chaotic, brutal, or wild. It essentially follows the erotic trend of "joining living substance into greater wholes" (Freud). Libidinal reason may even avoid immediate gratification so that by constructing its own obstacles, it increases the yield of enjoyment bound up with overcoming them.[92] In other words, libido itself, in Marcuse's view, contains tendencies that Western civilization (and Western philosophy) understood as the sole province of reason.

In fact, as I see it, by emphasizing the existence of libidinal rationality, Marcuse attempts to eliminate tensions between the rational and the sensuous faculty in a way that will preserve the truth of the senses. He admits that, in the realm of idealist philosophy, Kant and Schiller have attempted such a task. Therefore, it is not surprising that, in developing his own argument, Marcuse extensively quotes from Kant's *Third Critique* and Schiller's *Letters on the Aesthetic Education of Man*.[93] However, for Marcuse as well as for all other theorists of the Liberation Thesis, the reconciliation of reason and the senses in the sphere of the mind or, in practical terms, only for capitalist elites who can afford the enjoyment of refined artistic products, is sorely inadequate. What Marcuse demands is that this reconciliation becomes the basis of the daily life for all individuals.

NARCISSUS AND ORPHEUS

Marcuse is aware that this demand for the meaningful co-existence of the mind and the body requires a radical "transvaluation of all values," which means that contemporary social and cultural frameworks, built on the split between the two, must be founded on "qualitatively different principles."[94] In order to help this process along, Marcuse suggests that the old archetypal "culture-heroes" be replaced.[95] For instance, he considers Prometheus and Hermes the archetypal heroes of capitalist civilization, since their mythic undertakings glorify the dutiful performance of tasks imposed by society. Prometheus and Hermes also stand for an active renunciation of sensual enjoyment for the sake of an ever distant, but increasingly mechanized and rationalized, future. Marcuse argues that a qualitatively different civilization needs to frame its cultural heritage by reference to a set of mythological heroes with very different range of accomplishments. Specifically, he means here Narcissus and Orpheus.[96]

According to Marcuse, the elevation of Narcissus to the status of a culture-hero reveals a positive dimension of narcissism, a dimension that seems to have been little emphasized by conventional psychoanalysis. The positive dimension of narcissism is repressed in a capitalist system, because it goes against the prevailing standard of economic and political competition. On the other hand, it can only find its expression in practices that motivate the feeling of an unbroken bond with the whole universe, when all beings, both animate and inanimate, are approached as resonating with a part of one's own self, as an indispensable complement to one's own being.[97]

Freud comes close to identifying positive narcissism when he speaks of "the oceanic feeling" in the first chapter of *Civilization and Its Discontents*.[98] However, he considers it a fragmentary recollection of the early stages of the ego development, and does not think that it can become one of the principal features of adult life. Yet, as I see it, the question remains whether this kind of a narcissistic attitude may be able to restrain and transform the destructive tendencies of the death drive. Does it not represent a necessary ally in the effort to minimize the impact of Thanatos?

In my opinion, Marcuse's theoretical quest is directed to a great extent toward the question of what can modify the death drive, whose existence he does not deny.[99] This, I think, is one of the reasons he chooses Orpheus as the other culture-hero that a qualitatively different civilization would need to adopt. Recalling the myth of Orpheus, one finds that its most memorable feature is the ability of Orphic songs to pacify the wild beasts and extinguish suffering and pain. According to Marcuse, the quality of his songs enables Orpheus to liberate both the human and the natural world from external determination, that is to say, from the antinomy between freedom and necessity—"the things of nature become free to be what they are."[100] In other words, brutality and destruction now terrorizing daily life are diminished: nature itself becomes "humanized" at the same time as the individuals (for the first time) attain genuine humanity.[101] In Marcuse's view, a new civilization, which would in this way cherish the intimate links of everything with everything else, actualizes the Beaudelairean fantasy of the imaginary land of love in which *"tout n'est qu'ordre et beauté / luxe, calme et volupté."*[102]

THE SUPER-EGO, SURPLUS REPRESSION, AND REPRESSIVE DESUBLIMATION

However, Marcuse does not downplay psychoanalytic insight that the great enemy of the *calme* and *volupté* resides—and in great style—within each individual psyche. This enemy is no other than the psychic agency of the super-ego. Marcuse agrees with Freud that the super-ego's alliance with the ego as against the id is the most powerful motivator of aggression, intolerance, and cruelty in contemporary civilization. At the same time, the liberation of the libidinal impulses, in the case that they manage to express themselves, is also distorted by the presence of the punishing super-ego. In other words, individuals do not enjoy activities that, objectively speaking, they should find highly gratifying.

Marcuse conceptualizes this process of not enjoying one's enjoyment as an outcome of what he calls social "surplus repression." Surplus repression is the amount of repression, which is not necessary for the development of human personality (i.e., learning of basic norms of behavior), but which is put in place in order to perpetuate the essential characteristics of a contemporary capitalist civilization.[103] Surplus repression increases as the glimpses of a possible liberation become more frequent, since the ultimate goal of liberation is to expose the fallacy of believing that the existing character structure is eternal and universal, a transcendent fact of nature that existed unchanged over the centuries. Repression in excess to that which is necessary makes civilization accumulate more and more discontents until they are discharged in interstate warfare and intrastate hostility, racism, sexism, and xenophobia. Surplus repression checks Eros on all fronts, turning the human condition into "a vale of tears."

The question that arises at this point concern the ability to know what amount of repression and renunciation is necessary. Marcuse explicitly rejects a possible criticism that in developing his criteria, he is articulating partisan or ideological goal. On the contrary, he contends that an objective basis for the necessity of overcoming repression is discerned as soon as the first layers of contemporary political manipulation by capitalist elites are dismantled. The objective basis is found in "the material and intellectual resources [of the attained stage of civilization], and they are quantifiable and calculable to a high degree."[104] For instance, in contemporary capitalist civilization, the basic needs of *all* individuals could be satisfied by the re-orientation of social resources and by eliminating the practices of alienated labor. Marcuse contends that the rationale of scarcity or of putting the blame for failure on the disadvantaged themselves, which are used to justify the persistence of capitalist status quo, are no more than cynical myths.[105]

Marcuse's message, as well as the message of all the theorists of the Liberation Thesis, radiates, what I would call, an optimism of possibility. This, however, does not mean that Marcuse believes that a more equitable social and political world is around the corner. He is aware that there are many factors that may delay the actualization of these possibilities, the most salient of which he calls "repressive desublimation."[106]

Repressive desublimation designates a type of libidinal gratification, which is content to remain within the confines of the status quo, and maintains that the existing world is the best of all possible worlds. In other words, even though it may appear radical, in actuality, it does not threaten established political and social reality. Perhaps an appropriate example is that of anti-globalization protesters who after leaving the protest get their dinner at a fast-food restaurant chain.

While discussing repressive desublimation, Marcuse confronts the dilemma that I already mentioned in connection with Reich, namely how does one speak of liberation to those who consider themselves to be free?[107] In this respect, Marcuse argues that those who consider themselves free in a capitalist civilization have fallen victim to an illusion. In other words, their experience and judgment have been manipulated by existing political elites to such an extent that they acquiesce in their own repression. Marcuse locates the culprit for this state of affairs in "the overpowering machine of education and entertainment [which produces] . . . a state of anesthesia from which all detrimental ideas tend to be excluded."[108] Individuals are simply prevented from seeing that which opposes the perpetuation of the system. It is true that contemporary capitalist civilization seldom uses brute force to enforce its point of view, unless it is dealing with outside enemies—"the rogue states," as they are called. Yet this is so, according to Marcuse, because its technological sophistication allows it to fine-tune repressive measures by mixing them with activities that in a different context would greatly advance the cause of liberation.

The case in point here is the issue of sexual freedom. It is fairly easy to see that Western civilization has grown less restrictive about sexual practices and life-styles; in this respect, one could for instance compare the waning decades of the twentieth century with the Victorian Era. Yet, as Marcuse points out, the hold of capitalism is not any looser today than a hundred years ago. The reason for this is that the manifestations of sexual freedom have become thoroughly commercialized; the pursuit of Eros has been distorted into conformist gratification dependent on the interplay of market mechanisms and new technologies.[109] Even the language of tenderness and emotion reflects the dominant role of markets in contemporary society. In Marcuse's words, "in their erotic relations, [individuals] 'keep their appointment'—with charm, with romance, with their favorite commercials."[110] As a result, the space for a genuine discourse on social and political liberation, for free thinking and free love, has become smaller and smaller and, in some areas of social life (i.e. the news/entertainment industry), almost non-existent.[111]

THE FAMILY AND ITS DISCONTENTS

Marcuse argues that the shrinking of intellectual freedom and autonomy in contemporary capitalist civilization is related to the transformation of the social function of the family.[112] In the past, the family represented the chief agency of socialization, and Oedipal dynamics between the child and the parents provided the basis for the development of the child's individuality. Responding to parental idiosyncrasies, it was to be expected that the child would develop personality traits that would mark him or her as an individual uniquely different from others. In this way, the space for being different, or for being a social non-conformist, remained a real possibility for the child.

However, Marcuse claims that the processes of capitalism, starting with the practices of the 1930s "organized" or monopolistic capitalism, have undermined the function of family as an autonomous agent of socialization. The forces of capitalism have co-opted or made obsolete the role of the parents in shaping the character structure of children. The super-ego has come to be a creature of the agents outside of the family, such as the radio, television, and other types of mass media, and this has led to the co-ordination or similarity of its features in the psyches of individuals across social groups.[113] In other words, the same standard—the standard consistent with dominant social and political ideology—has become the source of values, the ground of good and evil for all.

I think that this outcome poses a difficult question to all critical theory, to all theory that finds the social status quo problematic and lacking. When dominant ideology represents the grounding of the individual super-ego or the basis of the individual value judgments, how can the individual see anything wrong with it?[114] As I see it, this is why Marcuse and other thinkers of the Liberation Thesis find an ally in the id, in the erotic drives of the psyche. The id is the only source or generator of libidinal energy, and therefore it is conceivable that it could "refuse" to channel this energy for the support of the existing super-ego. The super-ego would then in essence wither away and there would be a possibility of replacing it with an agency containing a different set of values and standards, an agency governed by the rationality of Eros—libidinal rationality. This, for instance, could be accomplished in a society whose culture-heroes are Narcissus and Orpheus.

I see this as the happy ending for the current unhappy state of affairs. However, another type of ending is also possible; in fact, some of its tendencies have already become the facts of contemporary social life. For example, in all advanced industrialized countries, the processes of standardization and the enforcement of conformity have gained an upper hand when compared with emancipatory social and political activities. Marcuse refers to "frozen gestures" and shallow daily conversations among individuals; he speaks of meaningless questions accompanied by equally meaningless replies. In one of the most dramatic formulations of his entire *oeuvre*, he asserts that "the antenna on every house, the transistor on every beach . . . are as many cries of desperation—not to be left alone, by himself, not to be separated from the Big Ones, not to be condemned to the emptiness, or the hatred, or the dreams of oneself."[115] I interpret this to mean that the mass media have become the parents whom the individual seeks to please, whose love he or she desires to gain and without whom life is seen as a failure, a misfortune, a disappearance into nothingness.

The flip side of this, for Marcuse, is that the praiseworthy individual qualities such as creativity and independence of thought have come close to extinction. However, I do not think that they have been completely eradicated as is evidenced by the support that Marcuse's work garnered from various social and political groups over the years. It seems that the spirit of critique that Marcuse and the Liberation Thesis strove to keep alive has still not taken flight into the underworld of lost dreams and fragments of possibilities.

THE GREAT REFUSAL AND THE PROMISE OF AUTOMATION

To those who desire to take a stand against the odds, against the system that continues to provide the blessings for the few on the basis of the alienation of the many, Marcuse counsels the Great Refusal. The Great Refusal means saying "no" to the rules of the capitalist game, no matter how difficult that is.[116] To refuse is to engage in a political practice that "reaches the roots of containment and contentment in the infrastructure of man."[117] In other words, only through the act of refusing to settle for what is given can one open up a space for something new to emerge, considering that existing social situation denies more than it fulfills. Both the will and its objects have to be transformed, says Marcuse, and this cannot be accomplished without activist critique of the present state of affairs.[118]

In fact, those who are materially and tangibly on the outside of the capitalist system already, those who have been rejected as unfit and undesirable before they could choose their path, represent a symbol, or provide an example, for others to join the effort for political and social change. As Marcuse elaborates in the last pages of *One-Dimensional Man*, the opposition of outsiders and of the persecuted "hits the system from without and is therefore not deflected by the system; it is an elementary force which violates the rules of the game and, in doing so, reveals it as a rigged game."[119] Existing ideological manipulations are revealed because the system is unable to integrate such opposition and cannot continue with business as usual. For the same reason, political measures that the system uses to deal with the opposition are brutal. Marcuse contends that brute violence and mercilessness of the system's reaction may act as catalysts for other individuals, for those who have hitherto been contained and contented, to reconsider their own social and political position. This would enable the possibilities and ways of doing things that are repressed and made impossible by the status quo to spring forth.

I interpret this as a subjective or a voluntarist side of the possibility for a generalized social revolt. Marcuse contends, however, that there is another side to the same possibility, a structural or objective side, related to technological development and innovation, especially the progress of automation, that is, techniques and machinery that do not require human labor.

I find this claim very interesting, in light of the generally a-technological aspect of the Liberation Thesis, and find it best to begin its examination with Marcuse's dialectical formulation in *Eros and Civilization*. In the last sentence of a chapter on the dialectic of civilization, Marcuse states: "The elimination of human potentialities from the world of (alienated) labor creates the preconditions for the elimination of labor from the world of human potentialities."[120] For Marcuse, "the elimination of human potentialities from the world of labor" stands for the acceleration of the processes of automation or automatization. In other words, in the daily routines of the production of goods and services, machines (and computers, we can add from our early twenty-first century standpoint) replace human labor. The implications of these developments for a capitalist system seem to be paradoxical. In short, according to Marcuse (as postulated earlier by Marx), capitalism depends on the extraction of surplus value from human labor. However, only human labor, due to its intrinsic qualities, that is, its relation to human "essence" or vital energy, can produce surplus value, that is, profit, for those who exploit and harness it in capitalist work relations. Hence, if human labor disappears from the sphere of production in the wake of automation, the entire edifice of capitalism may easily enter a time of crisis and collapse, since it will be precluded from making profits.

In his later lecture on utopias, Marcuse comes back to the same point. He maintains that "the technification of domination means that if we rationally think through technological processes to their end, we find that they are incompatible with existing capitalist institutions."[121] In other words, capitalism in the full unfolding of its essence contains the seeds of its own consumation or ending. As is clear, this formulation represents a very good example of Hegelian logic in which each given reality contains a negation within itself.

The question, however, arises as to what the use of critical psychoanalytic theory and practice is, or what purpose is served by the Liberation Thesis, if capitalism as a set of economic and social relations is bound to self-destruct. Do we just need to sit around and wait for the inevitable? Or are we not perhaps asked to trust the World-Spirit to usher in an era of greater freedom? And if that is the case, where does that leave the erotic dimension and the playful practices of Narcissus and Orpheus? In this respect, Marcuse seems to want to have it both ways. If the subjective or voluntarist liberation of Eros does not lead to desired social and political changes, then the objective or structural factors are called in to make the progress of the cause (appear) more realistic. On this particular reading, Marcuse turns out to be a cynic (to say the least).

However, I think that these two sets of claims can be compatible, or that, for instance, it is preferable that one precedes the other. Just contemplating the term "the technification of domination" for a moment makes it easy to see that social strategies and practices that seek to unshackle libidinal impulses should be favored over waiting for the absolute technological conquest of nature. In other words, Narcissus would hardly be able to be Narcissus, if there is no pond of clear water in which he could observe his image. In fact, as I see it, the main theoretical significance of Narcissus is precisely that he merged the fascination with his own beauty with the framework of natural environment in which it took place. It was only in this way that he could affect the desired and longed for oneness with nature—nature within with nature without—or, to state it a bit differently, show that there is no dichotomy between the two.

At times, however, Marcuse implies that the subjective liberation of Eros has against it forces that may be impossible to overcome and that, by default, structural changes show more emancipatory promise. This is perhaps so, because the (traumatic) past history may be a closed book to whatever the future eventually turns out to be. The argument here seems to be that the trauma itself can never undone; that which it crushed cannot come to life again. This may be the reason why Marcuse ends *Eros and Civilization* by saying that "even the ultimate advent of freedom cannot redeem those who died in pain. It is the remembrance of them, and the accumulated guilt of mankind against its victims, that darken the prospect of a civilization without repression."[122]

Yet is this really Marcuse's final statement? I would argue that it is not, since he has shown that collective guilt can not only be alleviated, but also re-configured through the engagement with the (re)generative power of art.[123] In fact, Marcuse emphasizes that art as a libidinal (erotic) vehicle of remembrance can conquer even time itself.[124] And once "time loses its meaning," it must surely be possible to atone for the sufferings of the past. The cycle of repression would finally be broken, and a new era of creative, collective Eros come into being.

INTRODUCING NORMAN O. BROWN

Before settling on a set of general conclusions on the role of the psychoanalytic Liberation Thesis in critical theory, I would like to discuss a portion of the work of an American scholar, Norman O. Brown, since, in my opinion, he offers an aspect of the emancipatory psychoanalytic perspective not explored so far. For several decades, until his retirement in the 1980s, Brown has been a distinguished professor of classics at several U.S. universities. His work has ranged from the studies of Greek mythology to the metaphysical reflections on the nature of time. However, the portion of his academic work relevant to my concerns here is limited to two contributions: *Life Against Death* (1959) and *Love's Body* (1966). In fact, considering the peculiar stylistic techniques he had employed in composing the latter work, making it a pastiche of quotes and aphorisms, it is likely that I will be able to sketch out most of his argument based on *Life Against Death* alone. Nevertheless, I think that *Love's Body* also deserves the attention of a theoretical gaze, because, in certain places, it strengthens the argument advanced in the earlier work.[125]

Brown's argument is significant, because it has to do with the establishment of the link of philosophical affinity between Freud and Nietzsche, and this in a special way. What Brown does is to tie together psychoanalysis as critical theory and the philosophy of transformation and overcoming in Nietzsche.[126] Hence, upon reading Brown's work, it seems curious that Reich does not mention Nietzsche at all, while Marcuse makes only brief, passing references to his philosophical endeavor.[127]

It is important to mention, however, that the link between Freud and Nietzsche has been with psychoanalysis or, more dramatically, has haunted psychoanalysis from the very beginning. After all, Freud admits having read Nietzsche.[128] In the early days of the Vienna Psychoanalytic Society, several sessions had been devoted specifically to the study of the similarities between Nietzsche's philosophy and psychoanalysis.[129] It is also interesting to note that the woman who allegedly inspired Nietzsche to conceive the personality of Zarathustra, Lou Andreas-Salome, eventually became a very close friend of Freud and even practiced psychoanalysis herself.[130]

Moreover, Nietzsche explicitly links his philosophy with the study of the mind, when, in his book *Beyond Good and Evil*, he proclaims that "psychology is once more the path to the fundamental problems."[131] Perhaps Freud has a similar thought in mind when, in the early 1930s, in his *New Introductory Lectures*, he states that there are only two discipline open to gaining genuine knowledge of the world: psychology and natural science.[132] In other words, all scientific disciplines that deal with humanity, all social sciences, could, in the final analysis, be reduced to psychology. The resolution of psychological questions can then be considered as the key for unlocking the mysteries of the human condition and the dilemmas of individual and collective nature.

Yet, Freud is far from being an admirer of Nietzsche and, in the 1920s and 1930s, he strove to steer psychoanalysis away from his influence. This perhaps had something to do with the fact that because of Nietzsche's sister, Elisabeth Förster, who was violently anti-Semitic, Nietzsche's writings came to be associated with the proto-Nazi reaction in Germany.[133] However, I think that Freud's disagreements with Nietzsche are also philosophical in character, especially since Freud doubts that a Nietzschean transfiguration of the psyche is possible or even desirable.

Freud definitely does not share the opinion of Nietzsche's Zarathustra that "man is a bridge toward something higher,"[134] since Freud's intention is to make the individual as comfortable as possible with his or her unconscious desires. In other words, Freud thinks that there are limits (maybe not all that clear, but nonetheless present) to psychological transformations. The concept of the *Übermensch* of the future is alien to him. One can perhaps argue that the Primal Father and Moses represent the figures in Freudian discourse where Freud comes close to think of someone like an overman. But, even in these two cases, he relegates their mythical or real existence to the mists of a distant past. I do not think that there is any indication that Freud thinks that such men could emerge in the future, let alone near future.

Such explicit disagreements between Freud and Nietzsche make it challenging for scholars to show similarities between their theoretical positions. Yet so much that is explicit represses or denies that which it carries within itself. As I see it, Brown is aware of the dangers of a reductive comparison between Freud and Nietzsche. This is why he approaches Nietzsche's work in the manner in which Nietzschean insights can strengthen the critical edge of psychoanalysis.

THE DIONYSIAN EGO AND THE RESURRECTION OF THE BODY

In his work *Life Against Death*, Brown uses a Nietzschean interpretation of the Dionysian mode of being for his psychoanalytic critique of Western civilization, a civilization which he labels "the death-in-life."[135] On his reading, psychoanalysis represents a contemporary development of the heretical tradition of thought whose earlier incarnations could be seen in Oriental and Christian mysticism and the Romantic critique of the Enlightenment. The key idea linking these traditions, according to Brown, is the resurrection of the body which, translated in psychoanalytic terms, means the abolition of repression.[136]

Brown builds up his case around Freud's claim that there is no negation in the unconscious; the answer of the unconscious is always "Yes." He interprets this claim to mean that all negations, denials, disavowals, and repressions perpetrated by the ego and supported by the super-ego in the course of daily life serve only to aggravate the psychic health of the individual. In fact, Brown quotes a passage from Freud's *The Ego and the Id*, in which Freud argues that the ego fulfills, not the mandates of Eros, but the mandates of the death drive. In Freud's words, "by ... setting itself up as the love-object, and desexualizing or sublimating the libido of the id, the ego is working in opposition to the purposes of Eros and placing itself at the service of the opposing instinctual trends."[137]

What this means, in other words, is that the activities taken up by the ego regarding libidinal energy, including sublimation, may in fact fuel the intensity of the death drive or, concretely speaking, increase the quota of aggression and violence in civilization. The ego-oriented activities therefore cannot be seen as successful steps for the alleviation of the plight of humanity and for the lessening of its discontent. Put in yet another way, the liberation of the individual cannot come by the way of the ego, nor can it come through one of the ego's favored psychic mechanisms—sublimatory adaptation to the status quo.

If sublimation is not "the way out,"[138] what else is left? What other strategy or practice is there that may lead to a genuine liberation from the pathological elements of civilization? The answer that Brown gives to this question combines Nietzsche and Freud in a way that is reminiscent of Marcuse's and Reich's critical insights.

Brown contends that if negation and sublimation are "forms of dying," then only the full affirmation of the sexual reality of the body can lead to "complete, immediate" life that breaks through the illusions of the status quo.[139] In other words, he proposes that a Dionysian yes-saying ego needs to be constructed in order to replace the repressive ego stamped by the Oedipus complex and burdened by the super-ego.

Brown defines the Dionysian ego as primarily a body-ego, which means that its mode of self-consciousness transcends the mind-body dualism that, in Brown's view, represents the most damaging split in the history of Western thought. Here Brown seems to be heeding the advice of Nietzsche's Zarathustra who proclaims "soul is only a word for something about the body" and "an unknown sage—whose name is *self*. In your body he dwells; *he is your body.*"[140] In other words, the Dionysian ego accomplishes the unification of the supposed opposites, of the spirit and the body, and therefore heals the fateful split that has plagued Western civilization. The spirit or the soul comes to be re-integrated into the body, into the material out of which it was carved under the external pressure of a repressive social and political order, which forced it to deny its libidinal tendencies.

Once this external pressure ceases, the libidinal reality becomes the only true reality. Concretely speaking, this means that every part of the body becomes a source of enjoyment, since the body is no longer partitioned off into "zones" by various prohibitions linked to the imposition of the Oedipus complex.[141] According to Brown, this is the true meaning of the resurrection of the body—in essence, "man is born again," but this time without having to submit to Oedipal renunciations.[142]

In contrast to Nietzsche, Brown thinks that the Dionysian ego does not have to be solitary, since he contends that standing up for the values of emancipation translates into being "hungry, violent [and] lonely"[143] only under the social and political status quo. Brown argues that, through the Dionysian transfiguration of the psyche, civilization organized along patriarchal lines, which necessitates the figure of a lonely non-conformist, gives way to a fraternal political organization. No more are the sons expelled if they disagree with the Father; in fact, now, when even the memory of repressive paternalism has been eliminated, brothers are enabled to establish a new civilization on the basis of equality and reciprocity.[144]

In this connection, Brown quotes the nineteenth century German historian Ranke's statement on the Concert of Europe[145]—"The union of all must rest upon the independence of each single one. Out of separation and independent development will emerge true harmony."[146] In other words, what comes to be played out is not a harmony imposed from above that by necessity generates repression and discontents, but rather a harmony that grows organically out of the new affirmative ways of living.[147]

BROWN, REICH, MARCUSE

My principal claim in this chapter is that Brown, Marcuse, and Reich belong under the banner of the Liberation Thesis because all three considered psychoanalytic thought and practice capable of supplying critical insights, necessary and sufficient to diagnose *and* change existing social and political inequalities. However, though these thinkers are agreed on the contours of the general thesis, to a certain degree they differ in the particulars. This is especially true in terms of Brown's relation to the other two.

Brown and Reich are not in agreement on the issue of genital sexuality. As I have shown, the complete unfolding of genital sexuality is, for Reich, the only way to a genuine social liberation, to a real possibility of transcending the centuries of repression and bringing in the new era grounded in the pursuit of love, work, and knowledge. Brown, however, refers to this kind of liberation as the tyranny of the genital.[148] According to Brown, the privileging of one organ of the body over the others, and the pleasure of this organ—orgasm—over other pleasures, may well represent "sexual liberation in the ordinary sense," but falls short from what needs to be accomplished in order to reverse the pathological tendencies of existing civilization.[149] In fact, for Brown, the exclusive focus on genital pleasure continues psychological repression in a way that mirrors and even contributes to the repression already inherent in the status quo, since what is being denied, in both cases, is the importance of infantile, pre-genital sexuality for psychic health and happiness.

Brown contends that without the re(dis)covery of infantile sexuality, the construction of a Dionysian ego and hence of the new ways of living and being is an illusive dream. This is so, because if the body is to become "the temple," and this seems the *sine qua non* of a Dionysian civilization, then "the activity of any and all of [its] organs" must be seen and felt as yielding pleasure and delight.[150] This in fact is the meaning that Brown assigns to the concept of polymorphous perversity. In other words, it is the "perversity" of a child's play, free, joyful and curious about all possible ways of relating to the world.[151]

Marcuse is less critical of the concept of polymorphous perversity than Reich who thinks that it comes into being only as a reaction to the frustration of the genital path. However, he finds faults in Brown's argument on another account.[152] Marcuse is concerned that Brown's argument (as manifested in *Love's Body*) may lead to the mystification of social reality, and therefore will be of no more than ephemeral significance for the movements for political change that Brown seeks to inspire and motivate. For instance, Marcuse underscores Brown's frequent use of religious and mystical terminology, and points out that religious discourse can hardly be used as the language of emancipation. Marcuse argues that, over the centuries, religious terminology has come to be so identified with repressive reality ("the association of the spirit with the Spirit, the resurrection of the body with Resurrection") that it seems impossible to believe in its liberatory integrity.[153]

In addition, according to Marcuse, religious "salvation" differs distinctly from emancipation advocated by critical psychoanalytic theory. Marcuse maintains that while the goal of the Second Coming is "to abolish or negate" history, the goal that motivates critical theory and practice is the *Aufhebung*, the process in which social and political relations are dialectically raised to a higher level without the reductionist shutting out of the past.[154]

Moreover, Marcuse claims that Brown's extensive reliance on obscure psychoanalytic and mystical symbolism makes it difficult to connect his argument to political struggles and technological advances and drawbacks. For instance, while it may be true that an airplane is a phallic symbol, it is also true that it conveys passengers from Paris to New York in six hours, and Brown does not seem to relate the first dimension with the second.[155] In other words, he remains so wrapped up in the dimension of symbolic that he loses track of the importance of the material social processes for his theory of universal emancipation. And this is precisely why Brown's argument is liable to the charges of mystification. As all the thinkers of the Liberation Thesis affirm, what needs to be done is not to turn one's gaze away from reality in order to delve into the shadowy world of latent meanings, but instead "to transform the latent into the overt content, sex into politics, the subrational into the rational."[156]

In other words, symbolism by itself can hardly effect any changes in the daily reality of exploitation, or, worse still, it may easily be taken for yet another ideology promising the land of plenty, while hiding the reality of deception. Therefore, I would argue that symbolism and the consciousness of it need to be followed by concrete action, by historical practice, because only in this way can the world be changed. As Marcuse points out in *One-Dimensional Man*, "without [this] material force, even the most acute consciousness remains powerless."[157]

In a published reply to Marcuse's critique, Brown defends himself by claiming that "the [only] alternative to reification is mystification."[158] However, if this is the case, then the pillars of the new society that he seeks to construct will be just as steeped in myth and ideology as those of existing society. In other words, only rhetorical but not any real progress will have been made. But then two related questions arise—was it really worth the effort, and how are we to know that?

FROM FREUD TO THE LIBERATION THESIS: A CONCLUSION

As I have shown in chapter 1, in his post-1920 works, Freud conceptualizes the existence of the ineradicable, conflicting duality both in the human psyche and in the social and political processes shaping and being shaped by the psyche. The conflict between Eros and Thanatos, between the self and the other, between the unconscious and the conscious, remains for him the intrinsic aspect of the human predicament. Freud argues that the only possible resolution for this conflict is the establishment of a temporary balance. World is chaos, and no undertaking in the human realm (and there is no other in Freudian world) can order or harmonize the flux. All attempts at such an endeavor are likely to fail.

By positing a duality at the source of all existence, Freud also seems to imply that the relation between the two sides will always be that of inequality, that it will be decided on the basis of the one side's forceful subordination or repression of the other. The victorious side will take up the reigns to dominate the course of life until "the return of the repressed." But the repressed that has returned will, in turn, be vanquished by that which it had repressed, and so on and on, in a cycle that resembles an infinite regress.

In contrast, the theorists I have placed under the banner of the Liberation Thesis—Reich, Marcuse, and Brown—with a caveat that they do differ in certain aspects—all claim that the vicious cycle of Eros and Thanatos could in essence be broken. The cycle could stop repeating itself and a different, new social configuration could then come into existence. This configuration would have at its source the frictionless interlacing of all the parts and would transform Freud's dualism into a dialectical unity.

Perceived in this way, psychoanalysis contains an insight that combines the separated into the united, the many into One. This insight is the concept of Eros and not surprisingly, all three thinkers ground their emancipatory strategies in it, and especially in what they see as its sexual dimension. Eros binds the aggression of Thanatos, and, in a dialectical fashion, raises the tangled bundle to a higher level, a level where unjust social antagonisms are transcended, where a work-democracy, a non-repressive civilization, or a Dionysian play become guiding principles. Reich, Marcuse, and Brown argue that the construction of this sphere is a real potentiality whose actualization remains the work of the future, since the dynamic of subjectivity (that is, human psychology itself), under the conditions noted by these theorists, does not prohibit its ultimate emergence. In Marcuse's words, for those who subscribe to the Liberation Thesis, "the horizon of history is still open."[159]

As I will show in the following chapter, the discourse that remains fully committed to the openness of history and the importance of erotic desire and hence in my opinion represents the best model of conceptualizing political and social change is Lacan's discourse of the hysteric. This is the discourse that could genuinely liberate Oedipus, and, as I will show, psychoanalytic praxis is indispensable in bringing it about on the individual and collective level.

NOTES

1. This is a passage from Marx's first extensive philosophical work, his dissertation *On the Differences between the Natural Philosophy of Democritus and of Epicurus*, quoted in Leszek Kolakowski, *Main Currents of Marxism: Its Rise, Growth, and Dissolution, Volume I, The Founders*, trans. P. S. Falla (Oxford: Clarendon Press, 1978), 104.
2. Karl Marx and Friedrich Engels, *The German Ideology: Part I* in *The Marx-Engels Reader*, ed. Robert Tucker (New York: Norton, 1978), 193, emphasis mine.
3. Wilhelm Reich, *The Function of the Orgasm*, trans. Vincent R. Carfagno (New York: Farrar, Straus and Giroux, 1973), 35.
4. See the section on childhood sexuality in chapter 1.
5. He approvingly quoted Charcot's proclaimation: "*Mais, dans des cas pareils, c'est toujours la chose genitale, toujours! toujours! toujours!,*" mentioned by Freud in his *History of the Psychoanalytic Movement*, see Reich, *The Function of Orgasm*, 95–96.
6. Reich, *The Function of Orgasm*, 90.
7. See, for instance, Reich, *Function of Orgasm*, 84–86.
8. Reich, *Function of Orgasm*, 100.
9. Reich, *Function of Orgasm*, 102.
10. In Reich's view, symptoms are formed due to the incomplete or blocked discharges of libidinal energy.
11. Reich was very critical of the psychoanalysts of the second generation, whom he saw as essentially flattening out the full significance and depth of Freud's insights. The same type of criticism directed against the "official" psychoanalytic Establishment is found in Jacques Lacan, as I will show in chapter 3. In fact, both Reich and Lacan were expelled from the International Psychoanalytic Association, the official organization of the psychoanalytic movement.
12. Reich, *Function of Orgasm*, 170–71.
13. Reich, *Function of Orgasm*, 300.
14. Reich, *Function of Orgasm*, 305.
15. See, for instance, the in-depth case history Reich relates in chapter VIII, *Function of Orgasm*, 309–29.
16. Lacan will side with Freud in this respect. In fact, one of Lacan's most important contributions to the study of the psyche is precisely the careful elaboration of how language and the symbolic register as a whole fundamentally and irrevocably shapes human subjectivity. See chapter 3.
17. Reich, *Function of Orgasm*, 311–13.
18. Reich, *Function of Orgasm*, 185.
19. Reich, *Function of Orgasm*, 126–27.
20. Reich, *Function of Orgasm*, 128. Reich also criticizes the rigid, mechanistic application of Freud's schema (the id, the ego, the super-ego) by the analysts of the second generation. In his words, "They operated with it as if it were a concretely established fact. The id was 'wicked,' the superego sat on a throne with a long beard and was 'strict,' and the poor ego endeavored to 'mediate' between the two," *Function of Orgasm*, 124.
21. Reich, *Function of Orgasm*, 213–14.
22. Reich, *Function of Orgasm*, 148. In this statement, one can find the echoes of Freud's three essays on sexuality. See chapter 1.

23. As I will show, Marcuse encounters the same problematic. It is therefore not surprising that in the preface to his book *Eros and Civilization*, he asks the fateful question—"how to speak of liberation to free men?" see *Eros and Civilization: A Philosophical Inquiry into Freud* (Boston: Beacon Press, 1966), xiii.

24. Reich, *Function of Orgasm*, 158–59.

25. Reich, *Function of Orgasm*, 179.

26. Paradoxically, it may be that the individual has a stronger sense of freedom when faced with an external prohibition than when he or she is the final arbiter of prohibitions. Contemporary psychoanalytic theorist Slavoj Žižek refers to this idea (see chapter 5). In contrast to Dostoevski's Ivan Karamazov who claimed that "if there is no God, everything is permitted," Žižek contends that "if there is no God [if there is no signifier], nothing is permitted." This is so because the field of prohibition is no longer limited and circumscribed, but is instead endless, able to spring up when and where least expected, and since the signifying chain is broken, a psychosis may ensue.

27. Reich, *Function of Orgasm*, 179–82.

28. Reich, *Function of Orgasm*, 218–19. An echo of Marxian social theory, no doubt. It is interesting to note that, in one of his earliest works published in the surrealist periodical *Minotaure*, Lacan states something along the same lines. He writes that "the murderous reactions of [psychotic] patients very frequently emerge at a neuralgic point of the social tensions with which they are historically contemporary," quoted in Victor Burgin, *In / Different Spaces* (Berkeley: University of California Press, 1996), 101.

29. Reich, *Function of Orgasm*, 215–16.

30. Reich, *Function of Orgasm*, 220.

31. Reich, *Function of Orgasm*, 223.

32. Reich, *Function of Orgasm*, 226.

33. Quoted in Wilhelm Reich, *The Invasion of Compulsory Sex-Morality* (New York: Farrar, Straus and Giroux, 1971), 12.

34. Quoted in Reich, *Sex-Morality*, 21.

35. Reich, *Sex-Morality*, 28–29.

36. Reich, *Sex-Morality*, 18–19.

37. Reich, *Sex-Morality*, 22–23. I think that Reich's list should be extended to include contemporary American phenomena such as Spring Break, Mardi Gras, Woodstock, Burning Man, Naked Mile, and so on.

38. The credit goes to the young Marx for succinctly formulating the law of pleasure pursuits in capitalist societies. In a section of *The 1844 Economic-Philosophical Manuscripts*, Marx imagines a monologue between the capitalist and the likely consumer—"Dear friend—says the capitalist—I give you what you need, but you know the *condition sine qua non*; you know the ink in which you have to sign yourself over to me: in providing for your pleasure, I fleece you." Marx, *Marx-Engels Reader*, 94.

39. Marx and Engels, *The German Ideology*, in *Marx-Engels Reader*, 150.

40. Marx, "Marx on the History of His Opinions," in *Marx-Engels Reader*, 4.

41. Reich, *Sex-Morality*, 46–47, 94.

42. Reich, *Sex-Morality*, 69–77.

43. Reich, *Sex-Morality*, 135–37.

44. Reich, *Sex-Morality*, 114–17. In my opinion, this hypothesis contains hints of the famous Hegelian master-slave dialectic, which I will discuss in chapter 3 in relation to Lacan's discourse theory (i.e., the discourse of the master).

45. Reich, *Sex-Morality*, 138.

46. Wilhelm Reich, *The Sexual Revolution: Toward a Self-Regulating Character Structure*, trans. Therese Pol (New York: Farrar, Straus, and Giroux, 1974), 74–75.

47. Reich, *Sexual Revolution*, 76.

48. Reich, *Sexual Revolution*, 78–79.

49. Reich, *Sexual Revolution*, 80.

50. Reich, *Sexual Revolution*, 9.

51. Reich, *Sex-Morality*, 153.

52. The concept of the layer should be understood as that which represents a set of specific attitudinal expressions and behaviors.

53. Wilhelm Reich, *The Mass Psychology of Fascism*, ed. Mary Higgins and Chester M. Raphael (New York: Farrar, Straus, and Giroux, 1970), xi–xii.

54. Reich generally refers to these exploitative interests as patriarchal. See the sections of this chapter dealing with Reich's anthropological researches.

55. Reich, *Mass Psychology*, xii–xiv.

56. Reich, *Mass Psychology*, xiv. All that is said about the little man applies to the little woman as well.

57. Reich, *Mass Psychology*, xxvii.

58. Reich, *Mass Psychology*, 146.

59. Reich, *Mass Psychology*, 148.

60. Reich, *Mass Psychology*, xvi.

61. Reich, *Mass Psychology*, 203.

62. Reich, *Mass Psychology*, 202.

63. Reich, *Mass Psychology*, xxi.

64. Reich, *Mass Psychology*, xxi–xxii.

65. Reich, *Mass Psychology*, 236–48. See Vladimir I. Lenin, *State and Revolution* (New York: International Publishers, 1943), 7–20, 69–85.

66. Reich, *Mass Psychology*, 244–45.

67. Reich, *Mass Psychology*, 221.

68. I will revisit this issue in chapter 5 with the reference to the works of contemporary Lacanians.

69. Reich, *Mass Psychology*, 286–87.

70. Reich, *Mass Psychology*, 295–96.

71. Reich, *Mass Psychology*, 334–35.

72. Reich, *Mass Psychology*, 314. In this insight, Reich, to a certain extent, anticipates the agenda of contemporary Green movements.

73. Reich, *Mass Psychology*, 311, 354–55.

74. For a detailed examination of the theoretical contributions of the Frankfurt School, see Douglas Kellner, *Critical Theory, Marxism, and Modernity* (Baltimore: Johns Hopkins University Press, 1989). See also Filip Kovacevic, "Horkheimer and Adorno's Transcendence of the Enlightenment: Critique of Habermas" (paper presented at the annual meeting of the Southwestern Social Science Association, Galveston, Tex., March 2000).

75. After the Nazi seizure of political power in Germany in 1933, the Institute was forced out of its Frankfurt premises. It first re-located to Geneva and then to Paris. The 1938 issue was published in Paris.

76. Herbert Marcuse, "On Hedonism," in *Negations: Essays in Critical Theory*, trans. Jeremy J. Shapiro (Boston: Beacon Press, 1969), 162.

77. Marcuse, "On Hedonism," 186.

78. Marcuse, "On Hedonism," 188.

79. Marcuse, "On Hedonism," 169-75.

80. Marcuse, "On Hedonism," 172.

81. Marcuse, "On Hedonism," 164-65. It is only, says Marcuse, because wants are "themselves already unfree, [that] the false happiness of their fulfillment is possible in unfreedom," 191.

82. Marcuse, "On Hedonism," 187-88. As I show in the following section, Marcuse elaborates the idea of work as play in his book *Eros and Civilization*.

83. Freud, *Civilization and Its Discontents*, 77.

84. Marcuse, *Eros and Civilization*, 26.

85. Marcuse, *Eros and Civilization*, 14-17.

86. Marcuse, *Eros and Civilization*, 45-48.

87. Marcuse, *Eros and Civilization*, 47.

88. Marcuse, *Eros and Civilization*, 199.

89. Marcuse, *Eros and Civilization*, 201.

90. Marcuse, *Eros and Civilization*, 225.

91. Note once again Marx's statement on consumerist pleasures—"In providing for your pleasure, I fleece you," says the capitalist. *Marx-Engels Reader*, 94.

92. Marcuse, *Eros and Civilization*, 227.

93. Marcuse, *Eros and Civilization*, 172-96.

94. Marcuse, *Eros and Civilization*, 198.

95. As I will show in chapter 3, this process of creating new culture symbols is equivalent to that which Lacan calls the construction and/or appropriation of new signifiers, the facilitation of which, I argue, should be considered a key contribution of psychoanalysis as critical theory.

96. Marcuse, *Eros and Civilization*, 161-62.

97. Marcuse, *Eros and Civilization*, 169.

98. Freud, *Civilization and Its Discontents*, 10-21.

99. Marcuse contends that capitalist civilization is in love with death, that is to say, its dominant practices feed and amplify a host of death wishes that, as Freud has shown, populate the unconscious.

100. Marcuse, *Eros and Civilization*, 166.

101. This idea is formulated by Marx in the essay "Private Property and Communism," in *The 1844 Economic and Philosophical Manuscripts*, see *Marx-Engels Reader*, 89, 92. At the same time, it also echoes the sentiments found in the works of the early German Romantic writers, such as Novalis.

102. In an English translation by Richard Wilbur, "there is nothing else but grace and measure / richness, quietness, and pleasure." This verse is taken from Baudelaire's poem "Invitation to the Voyage." See *Invitation to the Voyage: A Poem Illustrated* (New York: Little, Brown & Co., 1997).

103. Marcuse, *Eros and Civilization*, 35, 37–38.

104. Herbert Marcuse, "Repressive Tolerance," in *A Critique of Pure Tolerance*, ed. Robert Paul Wolff (Boston: Beacon Press, 1965), 90–91, 105.

105. Marcuse, *Eros and Civilization*, 92.

106. Marcuse, *Eros and Civilization*, 202.

107. Marcuse, *Eros and Civilization*, xiii.

108. Marcuse, *Eros and Civilization*, 104.

109. This is no doubt another example of repressive desublimation. As Marcuse repeatedly emphasizes, the key repressive aspect of commercialization is that "in exchange for the commodities that enrich their life, the individuals sell not only their labor but also their free time." Marcuse, *Eros and Civilization*, 100.

110. Marcuse, *Eros and Civilization*, 95.

111. Here I recall (as one of many examples) the CNN coverage of the Gulf War and the NATO bombing of Yugoslavia in which the other side (sic!) was unambiguously portrayed as the incarnation of evil.

112. Marcuse, *Eros and Civilization*, 95–97.

113. Marcuse, *Eros and Civilization*, 97.

114. Or, as Marcuse puts it in one of his lectures, "The mechanisms that stifle the need [for radical social change] must first be eliminated, which *presupposes* the need for their elimination." See Herbert Marcuse, "The Problem of Violence and the Radical Opposition," in *Five Lectures: Psychoanalysis, Politics, and Utopia*, trans. Jeremy J. Shapiro and Shierry M. Weber (Boston: Beacon Press, 1970), 99, emphasis mine.

115. Marcuse, "The Obsolescence of the Freudian Concept of Man," in *Five Lectures*, 49.

116. As I will show in chapter 3, the discourse of the hysteric as conceptualized by Lacan is in fact the discourse of the Great Refusal, of transformation of master-signifiers, both in individual and collective matters.

117. Herbert Marcuse, *An Essay on Liberation* (Boston: Beacon Press, 1969), 6.

118. Marcuse, "The End of Utopia," in *Five Lectures*, 77.

119. Herbert Marcuse, *One-Dimensional Man* (Boston: Beacon Press, 1964), 256.

120. Marcuse, *Eros and Civilization*, 105.

121. Marcuse, "The End of Utopia," *Five Lectures*, 66, 78.

122. Marcuse, *Eros and Civilization*, 237.

123. Marcuse, *Eros and Civilization*, 193–96.

124. Marcuse, *Eros and Civilization*, 193, 233.

125. Brown had intended to write *Love's Body* as a sequel to *Life Against Death*, but, as he states in a brief, paragraph-long preface, "the gods decree many surprises; expectations were not realized; God found an opening for the unexpected; that was the way this business turned out." Norman O. Brown, *Love's Body* (New York: Random House, 1966), p. i.

126. As I will show in chapter 4, the emphasis of a similar kind but with very different theoretical consequences, the consequences of which I am critical, is at play in the works of Gilles Deleuze and Felix Guattari.

127. In this respect, see Marcuse, *Eros and Civilization*, 119–24.

128. In a letter to Fliess dated February 1, 1900 Freud even goes so far as to say that he hopes to find in a book by Nietzsche that he had just received "words for much that remains mute in me." *The Complete Letters*, 398. From the context, how-

ever, it appears that Freud was referring to certain personal, family difficulties rather than the theoretical framework of psychoanalysis.

129. Rudnytsky, *Freud and Oedipus*, 198–200; Alexander Etkind, *Eros of the Impossible: The History of Psychoanalysis in Russia*, trans. Noah and Maria Rubens (Boulder, Colo.: Westview Press, 1997), 26–27.

130. For a lucid presentation of Andreas-Salome's very eventful life, see Etkind, *Eros of the Impossible*, 8–38.

131. Quoted in Etkind, *Eros of the Impossible*, 40.

132. Sigmund Freud, *New Introductory Lectures*, trans. Alex Strachey (New York: Norton, 1960), 179.

133. Etkind, *Eros of the Impossible*, 15–16.

134. See also the statement that "man is something that shall be overcome." Friedrich Nietzsche, *Thus Spoke Zarathustra*, trans. Walter Kaufmann (New York: Penguin Books, 1978), 12–16.

135. Norman O. Brown, *Life Against Death: The Psychoanalytic Meaning of History* (Middletown, Conn.: Wesleyan University Press, 1959), 14–15, 316.

136. Brown, *Life Against Death*, 307–8. According to Brown, psychoanalysis represents "the rediscovery of the Orphic or Oriental vision of life as sleep disturbed by dreams, of life as a disturbance in death." Norman O. Brown, *Love's Body* (New York: Random House, 1966), 52. The question is, however, whether psychoanalysis, if its diagnosis of existing social and political conditions is correct, has enough critical or theoretical capacity to provide the conceptual means for their overcoming or change. In other words, the question is whether psychoanalysis can lead to the awakening from the dream that all life is or has been. The answer that I provide in this and subsequent chapters is affirmative.

137. Quoted in Brown, *Life Against Death*, 173. As I will show in chapter 3, Freud's critique of the ego is also strongly emphasized in the work of Jacques Lacan. In fact, the refusal to accept the standards of the ego as the best normative arrangement of the human condition is one of the defining elements of the Liberation Thesis.

138. Freud argues that only the talented few could consider sublimation as a dominant component of their psychological balancing act. See chapter 1.

139. Brown, *Life Against Death*, 173, 175.

140. Nietzsche, *Thus Spoke Zarathustra*, 34, emphasis mine.

141. Brown designates this mode of being as "polymorphous perversity," because it is closely related to the pre-genital, anarchic searches of infantile sexuality.

142. Brown, *Love's Body*, 54.

143. Nietzsche, *Thus Spoke Zarathustra*, 103.

144. Brown, *Love's Body*, 17–19. See also Brown's claim that the true contrary of patriarchy is not matriarchy, but rather fraternity. Brown, *Love's Body*, 11.

145. The Concert of Europe stands for an implicit balance of power agreement among continental European powers that prevented the breakout of a global European war for most of the nineteenth century.

146. Brown, *Love's Body*, 19.

147. This argument is not to be confused with the liberal commonplace about "the invisible hand of the market" that supposedly transmutes all existing particular differences into a universally profitable union. In the liberal arrangement, profitability exists only for the minority that owns the means of production. In contrast,

Brown's conceptualization of harmony is neither externally coordinated, nor hides the reality of exploitation, but instead comes into being organically on the basis of equal and reciprocal relations.

148. Brown, *Life Against Death*, 29.

149. Brown, *Life Against Death*, 59.

150. Brown, *Love's Body*, 225; Brown, *Life Against Death*, 30.

151. As I will show in chapter 3, the activities of the hysteric, whom I consider the primary agent of the drive for political and social change, also reflect the ability to identify with a variety of signifiers. I argue that an openness to the exchangeability of functions is a necessary component of liberation.

152. Marcuse, *Eros and Civilization*, 49–51; Herbert Marcuse, "Love Mystified: A Critique of Norman O. Brown," in *Negations*, 238.

153. Marcuse, "Love Mystified," 230–31.

154. Marcuse, "Love Mystified," 232.

155. Marcuse, "Love Mystified," 235.

156. Marcuse, "Love Mystified," 235.

157. Marcuse, *One-Dimensional Man*, 253.

158. Norman O. Brown, "A Reply to Herbert Marcuse," in *Negations*, 244.

159. Herbert Marcuse, *The Aesthetic Dimension: Toward the Critique of Marxist Aesthetics* (Boston: Beacon Press, 1978), 73.

3

Lacan's Theses

> Consider the flight of a bee. A bee goes from flower to flower gathering nectar. What you discover is that, at the tip of its feet, the bee transports pollen from one flower onto the pistil of another flower. That is what you read in the flight of a bee. . . . But does it read? Does the bee read that it serves a function in the reproduction of phanerogamic plants? . . . In your analytic discourse, you assume that the subject of the unconscious knows how to read. . . . Not only do you assume that it knows how to read, but you assume that it can learn how to read.[1]

> That the subject should come to recognize and to name his desire, that is the efficacious action of analysis. But it isn't the question of recognizing something which would be entirely given, ready to be co-opted. In naming it, the subject creates, brings forth, a new presence in the world.[2]

In the aftermath of the events of May 1968, in an interchange with university students, Jacques Lacan expressed his support for the students' leftist demands, but dodged the question as to whether psychoanalytic insights support the possibility of revolutionary social and political changes.[3] These two statements make Lacan's true position enigmatic. On one hand, Lacan makes clear his sympathy for those who demanded changes in the status quo, both in personal and social matters. Yet, on the other hand, he is unwilling to ally the cause of psychoanalysis explicitly with a radical tradition in social thought.[4]

From the time Lacan began to be known in psychoanalytic circles, this apparently ambiguous quality of his writings has posed a challenge to scholars, especially as they tried to compare Lacan's ideas with other theoretical or philosophical orientations.[5] This challenge confronts me as well in this chapter in which I will attempt to draw out a social and political theory from

Lacan's work and establish its relation to what, in chapter 2, I have called the Liberation Thesis. My principal claim is not only that such a relation exists in a way that could be articulated explicitly, but also that it is not as obviously negative as certain commentators in France and United States have claimed.[6] Luc Ferry and Alain Renaut on one hand and Martin Jay, on the other, reproach Lacan for not supporting the idea of the autonomous ego, which they see as the condition of critical theory and philosophical humanism. However, as I will show in the following section, Lacan agrees with the theorists of the Liberation Thesis that the belief in the ego is closely connected with the belief in the primacy of the Reality Principle, which, translated into non-psychoanalytic terminology, amounts to social conformism and political quietism. As I see it, no radical thinker can support humanism, if these are its end results.

In order to substantiate my claim that Lacan is in fact a radical thinker whose work is grounded in the Freudian orientation also supported by the Liberation Thesis, I have chosen to investigate three aspects of his work. The first aspect that I will discuss concerns Lacan's contributions to ethical theory, and the key problematic that will emerge from this discussion has to do with a set of relationships between desire, pleasure, and the moral law. In this respect, I will show that the ethical theory supported by psychoanalysis offers practical guidelines for individual and social transformation.

The second aspect I will examine is Lacan's discourse theory, which is essentially a product of his attempt to formalize, classify, and explain all relations that "establish a social link."[7] In this respect, I will show that, structurally speaking, the discourse of the analyst possesses precisely the potential needed to transform the dominant sociopolitical discourse—the discourse of the university—into the discourse I see as that of a liberated political subject, the discourse of the hysteric. And lastly, the third aspect I will cover focuses on the logic of sexuation, that is to say, the differentiated masculine and feminine positions in relation to the manner and content of that which can be known of oneself and the world. In this respect, I will argue that the only truly emancipatory sociopolitical perspective is grounded in the feminine pole of sexuation. A careful reader of Lacan may notice that this tripartite division fits roughly with the chronological picture of the early, middle, and late Lacan. I intend to show that each of these periods in Lacan's teaching contains a theoretically relevant relation to the question of psychoanalysis as critical political and social theory, and, most importantly, offers an affirmative answer to it.

THE FAILURES OF EGO PSYCHOLOGY

It seems appropriate to begin the examination of Lacan's treatment of ethics by pointing out what, in his opinion, were the defining characteristics of

Freudian thought on the subject. This is so because Lacan initially made the name for himself on the French intellectual scene as an interpreter of Freud's texts. His early seminars (essentially from 1953 to mid-1960s) clearly make evident his effort to present himself as the (most) faithful reader of Freud. By doing so, Lacan sought to expose what he considered to be serious problems in the theory and practice of the second-generation psychoanalysts, who practiced under the banner of Anglo-American ego psychology (Anna Freud, Heinz Hartmann, Ernst Kris, Rudolf Loewenstein).

The key disagreement between Lacan and the ego psychologists, in fact, involved an issue whose ethical implications were obvious. It had to do with the basic question of psychoanalysis—"What to do in therapy?" or (more technically) "How is the analyst to respond to the analysands' demands?" The techniques of ego psychologists revolved around the goal of the strengthening of the ego, since this was seen as the only way to facilitate the individual's adaptation to social demands. From the perspective of ego psychology, neuroses were the products of a failure to adapt, or, in other words, of a failure on the part of a given individual to subsume himself or herself fully under the functioning of the Reality Principle.[8]

Lacan argued that, on the contrary, this approach to therapy represented a distortion of Freud's best insights. He thought that it represented an essential concealing of radical dimensions of Freudian thought which was brought on by the pragmatic interest of expatriate Continental European psychoanalysts to fit in and find themselves useful in their new homeland, the United States of America.[9] In other words, according to Lacan, the ego psychologists, while pretending to be true heirs to Freud, cleverly muted his emphasis on the discontents of capitalist civilization in exchange for a secure social status in the heartland of capitalism. In Lacan's view, their intellectual production, though voluminous, consisted of nothing else than "old novelties and new junk" whose ultimate purpose was the institution of conformity to the American way of life.[10] As I interpret his comments, Lacan supports both Freud and the theorists of the Liberation Thesis in their claims that a capitalist lifestyle and the psychological attitudes that it brings into existence negate or distort the expression of certain essential aspects of human personality. In fact, for Lacan, the ego—the psychic structure whose strengthening is blessed by liberal capitalism—is "the mental illness of man."[11]

Yet why would this be so? How can it be that something so basic to the history of psychology and philosophy as the concept of the ego is so harshly condemned? On my reading, this question leads to the core of what Lacan refers to as the Freudian discovery. According to Lacan, what Freud discovered was that the psyche is not all of one piece, but is instead divided between the conscious ego functions on one side and the so-called subject of the unconscious on the other.[12] In Lacan's reading, Freud privileged the subject of the unconscious over the ego, because he considered the latter the carrier of the individual's true desires. At the same time, Freud claimed that since the unconscious remains irreducibly different from the ego,[13] true desires are constrained to manifest themselves in the psychic formations most removed from conscious control (dreams, slips of the tongues and the pen, bungled actions, reaction to jokes). It is therefore not hard to see why Lacan insisted that he did nothing but simply follow Freud in asserting that the focus on the ego as the nexus of therapeutic activity was a mistaken path.

For Lacan, the key feature of the ego is the "capacity to fail to recognize" or to mis-recognize the existence of the unconscious.[14] In fact, he postulates that the ego is structured as "a set of defenses, denials, and inhibitions,"[15] and hence that its relations to the unconscious material are generally characterized by self-deception, that is, by repression and negation. In the case of negation, for instance, Lacan agrees with Freud's claim that the negative judgment on the part of the ego can actually be read as the confirmation of an unconscious truth. The fact that somebody *announces* that he or she would never do a certain thing (especially if unwarranted by the preceding conversation) means that he or she has desired doing it.[16] Such a denial, enunciated confidently by the ego, is more likely than not a result of the variety of social pressures and as such masks the truth of the individual's unconscious.

In my opinion, Freud's most dramatic formulation on the topic of the ego is found in one of his introductory lectures on psychoanalysis. Freud states that the "Copernican" revolution in the understanding of the psyche brought about by psychoanalysis is contained in the insight that the ego is not "the master in its own house."[17] In other words, that which acts as the primary motivator of individual behavior is not the conscious pursuit of his or her goals, governed by the ego, but instead the push and pull of desires and drives emanating from the unconscious. The question that I ask is whether psychoanalysis can move forward in its understanding and explanation of mental phenomena and the way they interrelate with social and political affairs, if this insight is swept under the rug as it happens in the work of ego psychologists.

In fact, as Lacan points out, if the famous Freudian formulation of the task of psychoanalysis as facilitating the process of *"wo Es war, soll Ich werden,"* is interpreted alongside the insight on the essential inadequacy of the ego "in its own house," this formulation acquires a meaning that contrasts sharply with traditional interpretations. The formulation, which appeared in *New Introductory Lectures*, has been translated by the editors of the Standard Edition of Freud's works, under the supervision of Anna Freud, as "where the id was, there the ego shall be."[18] Such a translation makes it seem as if the task of psychoanalysis were to replace or substitute the unconscious realm of the id by the mechanisms of the ego, and hence explicitly obtains Freud's blessing for the work of ego psychologists on the building up and strengthening of the ego. This in fact has been the gist of traditional interpretations. But, as Lacan makes clear, this blessing is no more than the artificial product or effect of a bad translation or perhaps of a purposeful, ideological mistranslation.

First of all, Lacan directs his attention to the fact that Freud did not use the definitive articles in his formulation.[19] In other words, he did not write *das Es or das Ich*. If he had done so, then the traditional translation "the id" and "the ego" could be taken as correct, as the examination of Freud's other works on this topic amply shows.[20] However, since this was not the case, Lacan inquires as to whether we are not justified in believing that Freud here meant something other than the expanding of the ego. In fact, in Lacan's retranslation, the dialectic between the subject of the unconscious and the agent of consciousness—the issue with a great deal of ethical significance for psychoanalytic practice and its relation to social and political theory—emerges as Freud's key concern.

Lacan translates "*wo Es war, soll Ich werden*," as "there where *it* was, it is my duty that *I* should come into being."[21] This means that the subject of the unconscious—the *I* that manifests itself in speech—will assume the responsibility for becoming a vehicle for the articulation of the desires of its own unconscious, of the *it* that was formerly denied or repressed by the ego.

As I see it, the most important thing to notice here is that, for Lacan, the standard that needs to be taken as the measure of the truth of the subject's activity is "internal," or, to put it less vaguely, it stems from the particularity of the subject itself. That which one has to conform to is nothing else but one's own desires precisely as they structure the work of one's unconscious. On the other hand, for ego psychologists, the standard for emulation and conformity is external, founded on the forces that are in control of the subject's "reality," that is, the forces that structure its social and political existence.[22] But, on my reading, such a standard, since it remains alien to the I of the subject by excluding its active participation, can never truthfully reflect the particular demands and desires of the subject's unconscious.

Yet, acting in conformity with one's unconscious desires, the proposition that Lacan enshrined as the key precept of the ethics of psychoanalysis, is not an easy one to follow.[23] In fact, Lacan devotes an entire seminar (Seminar VII, 1959–1960) to trying to explain why most people, for the most part, would rather remain deaf to it. I think that Lacan's key concern can be put as follows: why is it precisely that coming into grips with the truth of one's being, as represented in one's unconscious, occasions such a great deal of psychological resistance? The answer to this question, in my opinion, shows to what extent one is justified in considering psychoanalysis a critical political and social theory.

THE PLEASURE PRINCIPLE AS AN OBSTACLE TO *JOUISSANCE*

Lacan claims that Freud's most significant insight on the question of ethics has to do with the affirmation of the creative character of erotic desire.[24] In fact, Lacan states unambiguously that Freud's teaching is "nothing else but a perpetual allusion to the fecundity of eroticism in ethics."[25] In other words, desire is a category of human subjectivity whose unconscious orientation, whether it is recognized or not, structures the coordinates of the ethical field. Even a mental agency such as the super-ego whose function is directed toward the alienation of the subject's desire is steeped in the work of desire, the desire of the Other. The investigation of desire therefore offers itself as the primary path for understanding how the ethical norms and standards of human interactions come into being.

In his approach to studying ethical norms, Lacan sharpens a distinction that in Freud, for instance in his *Beyond the Pleasure Principle*, appears in an implicit way. This distinction refers to the concept of pleasure and the concept of what Lacan calls *jouissance*.[26] To state it dramatically, the functioning of the pleasure principle, according to Lacan, has very little to do with *jouissance*, that is, with a movement toward the fulfillment of desire. In fact, I think that it is not farfetched to say that the two work at cross-purposes. The pleasure principle pushes for the release of tensions, for the regaining of the sense and feeling of mental equilibrium.[27] *Jouissance*, on the other hand, exacerbates tensions and overturns the balance that the pleasure principle ceaselessly works to attain. This is why Lacan sees *jouissance* as being on the side of suffering and pain *(mal)*. Moreover, the word itself in French, in addition to being a general term for enjoyment, has also a connotation of intense pleasure that breaks the bonds of the given: *jouir* is a French verb that means to come, to have an orgasm. Drawing upon this linguistic usage, Lacan affirms that, in contrast to pleasure, *jouissance* is inevitably sexual, or that, in other words, it is motivated by the fulfillment of sexual desire. *Jouissance* therefore can hardly be contained within the pleasure principle; it transcends the pleasure principle toward something else, toward something that is glimpsed beyond it, toward that which Lacan refers to as the real.[28]

In Lacan's theory of the mind, the real is one of the three registers, the other two being the symbolic and the imaginary. The real stands for that which "resists symbolization,"[29] that which, in other words, represents the limit of both the symbolic and the imaginary and hence appears as an ontological gap that cannot be filled by their respective functioning. At the same time, as will become apparent in the following sections, the existence of the real enables the possibility of creation *ex nihilo*, that is of the introduction of new symbolic and imaginary forms into ordinary life. As I will show, this is of particular importance for psychoanalytic social and political theory.

According to Lacan, the symbolic register refers to the signifying networks of language as well as the various discourse structures. It is a register on the basis of which social and political institutions are constructed. The imaginary, the third register, is the register of identifications, both narcissistic and idealizing, and underwrites all ideas positing the existence of totality or perfection. In his later seminars, Lacan represented the linking of the real, the symbolic, and the imaginary by the topological structure known as the Borromean knot.[30] The Borromean knot consists of three rings, connected in the way that appears similar to the five Olympic rings, but with a special feature that the break in one of the rings automatically frees the other two. This conceptualization, for instance, becomes indispensable in Lacan's theory of psychosis, which, as I will discuss in more detail in a later section, is premised on the idea that the psychotic break occasions the dissolution of the imaginary and the separation of the symbolic and the real.[31]

In reference to the establishment of ethical norms, Lacan argues that it is not only *jouissance* that is drawn towards the real, but that something else aims at it as well. This something else is the moral law. Lacan contends that the moral law is, just like *jouissance*, founded "in opposition to pleasure."[32] Both find the source of attraction beyond the workings of the pleasure principle (i.e., beyond the release of tension).[33] Both share a similar relationship towards the real, which, as I pointed out above, conditions the functioning of the two other registers, the symbolic and the imaginary. In other words, *jouissance* and the moral law enable the work of transcendence to be accomplished, that is, they make it possible for something to come into being out of "nothing." Ethics is therefore not psychology, but rather it provides the ground for the possibility of psychology.[34] In other words, as Lacan conceptualizes it, ethics—the existence of moral law—constitutes a fundamental and irreducible dimension of human subjectivity.

THE QUESTION OF *DAS DING*

In order to support his claim that ethical matters are involved in the very possibility of something called a subject, Lacan elaborates the process of the constitution of subjectivity. He refers to some of Freud's earliest works, such as the *Outline for a New Scientific Psychology* (1895) and *Three Contributions to the Theory of Sex* (1905), finding in these works an argument for the presence of "a strange feature" at the core of this process, a feature that he calls *das Ding*.

Lacan defines *das Ding* as something around which "the whole movement of the *Vorstellungen* [that is, mental images and word-representations] turns."[35] It is therefore not a mere object, but that which, beyond all representation, structures the processes of representation. In other words, Lacan's point is that, in order for the subject to come into being, there has to be something in relation to which its representations will be formed, but which, in order that it can act as a support of this relation, must remain outside. This outside is *das Ding*.[36] In other words, *das Ding* provides for the possibility of the subject's representations' forming coherent chains of images and signifiers. Without its presence, no psyche or mind could come into existence.

According to Lacan, one of the basic insights of psychoanalysis is that the law of the pleasure principle governs the chains of mental or psychic representations.[37] This means that *das Ding*, as that which is outside of representations, finds itself beyond the pleasure principle. It therefore stands outside of the utilitarian judgment of the good and bad, and Lacan claims that this puts it in the position of the real in which both the moral law and desire (for *jouissance*) find their aim. Hence both morality and *jouissance* refer to *das Ding*, beyond any utilitarian considerations. In fact, Lacan postulates that paradoxically the attractiveness of an object increases for the subject as this object approaches the limit charted by the nearness of *das Ding*. This is so even though the limit of *das Ding* is the limit of pain.[38] *Das Ding* can hence be conceptualized as the primordially repressed core around which the existence of the subject is oriented.[39]

This conceptualization offers an interesting consequence for anthropological research, especially in terms of the incest taboo. The question of the incest prohibition, as Freud has argued in *Totem and Taboo*, should be considered formative of a social bond, since it imposes a (cultural) law on primordial nature by forcing desire away from the person to which it is initially attached, the mother.[40] What Lacan adds to this is the claim that the incest taboo can also be related to the functioning of *das Ding*. In other words, prohibiting incest means placing the mother in the position of *das Ding*, in the position that can never be reached precisely because the structural position of *das Ding* in relation to the subject makes it impossible.[41]

On my reading, this means that both social and psychological laws work in unison. Lacan seems to imply that what makes incest socially unacceptable is precisely the fact that it is also psychologically unbearable. Moreover, in his view, the former derives from the latter. The psychological non-separation from the mother, considered as a fundamental desire by both Freud and Lacan, is therefore dangerous because it prevents the formation of a social bond. In Lacan's words, it means "the abolition of the whole world of demand," the world which acts as a support for the possibility of a social bond, that is, for the possibility of a discourse.[42] This world of demand remains alien only to psychotics, and it is so because their union with the mother is not affected by a primordial prohibition, which Lacan also refers to as the paternal "No." In other words, the possession of the mother is not prohibited, that is, placed in the position of *das Ding*. As a result, the psychotics (especially in the case of paranoia) are structurally located so close to *das Ding* that they cease to believe in its existence; they are unable to embark upon the search for the object of their desire, since in fact it has never been lost. This is why their imaginary—the chains of identifications and ideals—always presents itself with a great deal of fragility. This of course facilitates the possibility of the dissolution of its ties with the other two registers, the real and the symbolic, which, as I pointed out, is, when it occurs, behaviorally manifested as "a break."[43]

In the non-psychotics, however, the mother is structurally positioned in the realm of *das Ding*. And, in fact, it is not only the mother that one can find there. According to Lacan, (at least) two other figures could be put to stand in its place. Lacan argues that one of them, though historically situated, shows an exemplary way of dealing with the predicament in which one finds oneself as the subject of desire, while the other represents *das Ding* in the mundane reality of modern life. The first figure is the Lady of courtly love, and the second, the neighbor in our everyday existence. I would say that one of the tasks of psychoanalytic social and political theory is to show how a set of practices established in regards to the former apply to our relations with the latter.

COURTLY LOVE, OR HOW SHOULD ONE LOVE ONE'S NEIGHBOR?

It seems to me that what motivated Lacan's attention to different historical expressions of eroticism was Freud's remark in a footnote of his *Three Essays* to the effect that what distinguishes the love life of the ancient world from that of modernity is that the ancients "placed emphasis on the instinct [the drive] itself, while [the moderns] put it on its object."[44] Lacan refers to this remark several times, and, in my reading, it represents a key element or stepping-stone in Lacan's own take on the state of social relations in our time.[45] In fact, Lacan argues that our contemporary age is characterized by the crisis of that which Freud took for granted, namely the crisis or deterioration of our relation to the object (essentially, the other).[46] The question that therefore faces us is whether it is desirable once again to orient oneself toward praising the virtues of the drive (as in antiquity) or whether social strategies could be implemented that would rescue the object from its dismal state in social relations. Here the issue of psychoanalysis as a critical social and political theory comes to the forefront, considering that one of the strategies for rescuing the object is that which has generated considerable amount of thought in psychoanalytic circles—sublimation.

After critiquing the accounts of sublimation by several established psychoanalysts, such as Siegfried Bernfeld, Melanie Klein, and Ella Sharpe, Lacan offers his own succinct definition of the process, which he then applies in reference to concrete historical events. Lacan defines sublimation as "raising the object . . . to the dignity of *das Ding*" and contends that one can find its most dramatic historical articulation in the phenomenon of courtly love.[47]

Courtly love represented a set of social practices structuring the relations between groups of aristocratic men and women in certain parts of France and Germany in the twelfth and thirteenth centuries. In his well-acclaimed book on the subject, Denis de Rougement argued that this short-lived social phenomenon has left an indelible impact on the modern phenomenon of romantic love and hence also on the meaning of intimate relations between contemporary men and women.[48] Lacan's claim is different in that what he emphasizes is the identity in the structural position of the Lady and *das Ding*.[49] In other words, the troubadours considered their Lady as a (sacral) being beyond a certain limit that could not be crossed.[50] In fact, though it is impossible to doubt the intensity and sincerity of the troubadours' sensual passion, it is clear, upon reading their poems, that the Lady, for them, transcended the status of any given feminine object and became an embodiment of the Thing itself. She was in effect *das Ding* that one has always already lost, though without "truly" having it, in the process of the constitution of one's psyche.

Therefore, it is not surprising that all the troubadours "seem to be addressing the same person," a person whose treatment of them, as Lacan points out, was far from kindly and loving.[51] In fact, the relations between the Lady and the troubadour were marked by arbitrariness, capriciousness, and occasionally even outright cruelty. As the troubadour Arnaud Daniel's poem testifies, at times the Lady seemed no less than "an inhuman partner."[52] Lacan claims that these are the features of the troubadour-Lady relationship which justify his point as to the identity of the position of the Lady and *das Ding*, the Thing that is extra-human at the center of human psychology.

What is remarkable, however—and this is why Lacan puts a special emphasis on courtly love—is that, notwithstanding the mistreatment, the troubadours loved the Lady no less. In fact, their love as manifested in sublimated form in their poems grew all the stronger as the Lady's position was shown to be more and more inaccessible. In other words, one can say that the troubadours, though seeing *das Ding* in all its horror, were not repulsed by it, but instead doubled up their subliminatory labors in order to show the presence of their unwavering commitment and love. The crucial implication for psychoanalytic social theory is that since Lacan positions both the Lady and our everyday mundane neighbor as the possible stand-ins for *das Ding*, he implies that the ethically correct approach to the neighbor would be precisely one that incorporates the key components of courtly love.[53] In other words, an ethical action would be that in which the love of one's neighbor would come into being and remain strong despite the knowledge of the neighbor's essentially bad will.

As is obvious, Lacan here approaches one of the New Testament commandments—"love thy neighbor as thyself."[54] Essentially, he seeks to show very complex and serious barriers that such love would need to overcome. This is so, because, as my discussion has indicated, this commandment can be also phrased—with no loss in meaning—as "love thy neighbor as *das Ding*" and even "love *das Ding* as thyself." In other words, love something that is inaccessible and alien in its otherness as if it were the most precious thing that there could possibly be.

Lacan comments on Freud's refusal to accept the possibility of such a social relation ever being established.[55] Freud thought that the death drive (Thanatos) as manifested in aggressive and narcissistic activities would compel one to strike out at one's neighbor even if unprovoked.[56] Even if the neighbor had done nothing wrong, one would be driven to behave aggressively, since the hatred of the neighbor would be motivated by his or her remaining other, distinct from oneself. In fact, it seems to me that, following Freud, one can say that one is driven by one's *jouissance* to seek to colonize the place of the neighbor in order to make him or her yield such a satisfaction. But, in order to obtain this satisfaction, *jouissance* requires the abolishment of distinction between oneself and one's neighbor; it wants the neighbor assimilated into oneself. As argued above, this is not only psychologically unbearable, since the place of the neighbor is the place of *das Ding*, but it is also destructive of the neighbor. In effect, approaching such a situation closely might trigger a psychotic break. No wonder then that Lacan sometimes refers to *jouissance* as impossible to satisfy; the laws of psychic functioning, the pleasure principle centered on the release of tension and inertia, keep it beyond the possibility of fulfillment.

As I see it, psychoanalytic social and political theory confronts here the most pressing question: is there any hope of a possible way out of the endless animosity? Is it possible to transcend the hostility and aggression that crop up in the I-thou, the I-neighbor relation? One answer of course is the Christian one—love. Saints and mystics, for instance, manifest this love in striking ways. St. Francis of Assisi is an obvious example; other saintly figures are of note as well. Lacan mentions Angela de Folignio who drank the water in which she had washed the feet of a leper, and Marie Allacoque who ate the sick person's excrement.[57] These two figures loved and incorporated that which was most repulsive about their fellow being, about their neighbor; in other words, they did not blink in the face of *das Ding*, but, on the contrary, they worshipped it. However, on my reading, the problem with the Christian answer is that it may not elicit reciprocity and therefore proves to be an ineffective social strategy. In other words, the saint or the mystic might end up being taken advantage of; he or she ends up a fool. Another problem is that, in the world without God, the modern (Freudian) world in which God/Father is dead, the saint or the mystic will be a fool by definition.

Lacan says of Freud that he was no fool and I think in saying that, he affirms the same for himself; neither endorses the Christian answer which brings with it being a fool as its ultimate consequence. At the same time, Lacan emphasizes that Freud is not a cynic for whom the empirical reality of aggression represents an eternal law. In other words, he is not a traditional conservative or, in Lacan's description, a knave.[58] Freud's answer is ambiguous. He says that loving one's neighbor is "impossible," but he does not leave it at that: he realizes that something needs to be done about it. In other words, though disagreeing with Marxism, Freud is motivated by humanitarian concerns.[59] After all, Freudian psychoanalysis is a practical endeavor directed toward the enunciation of the cure, that is to say, what is aimed at is a certain transformation of the personality or character. In other words, certain psychological attitudes are encouraged and supported, while others are neutralized or discredited.

THE ETHICAL CONCERNS OF THE PSYCHOANALYTIC CURE

Psychoanalytic techniques have generally been oriented toward the transformation of the suffering of an analysand into the other types of psychological expressions. However, for Lacan, analysis should be specifically formulated as "an invitation to the revelation of [one's] desire."[60] What do you want?—*che vuoi?*—is the most significant question of analysis. What Lacan finds, in this respect, is that what analysands want is precisely to approach that which is the most inaccessible, that which is essentially forbidden, the field of *das Ding*. In fact, Lacan speaks of "a radical desire" which seems to resemble the acephalous functioning of the drive.[61] The goal of this desire is the *jouissance* located beyond the pleasure principle, in the anarchy of subjectivity in the process of being constituted.

In Lacan's view of analysis, what needs to be accomplished under the guidance of this radical desire is the dissolution of one set of signifiers, which underwrites a set of definitive meaning effects, and hence opening up the opportunity for the creation of another set.[62] The set of newly created signifiers enables the analysand to re-constitute or re-structure his or her relations with his or her own past and present as well as with the role that other people may have played in these configurations. However, the process of breaking up the established signifiers (also referred to as the master signifiers) is slow, laborious, and painful. In fact, Lacan isolates two specific barriers or defenses to a kind of analysis that could transform the individual and free him or her from the "illusions on the path of desire."[63]

According to Lacan, these two barriers are no less than the traditional concepts of the good and the beautiful. On my reading, Lacan implies that the concepts of the good and the beautiful represent dangerous foils or traps for the subject in search of the object of his or her true desire. To fall for, or remain enchanted by, the good and the beautiful is in essence to give up searching for the true.

This means that Lacan takes a stand against traditional ethics which grounds the justification of its truth in the pursuit of the good. For Lacan, the pursuit of the good is far from being able to dispel illusions one has accumulated over the years of one's life as to one's unconscious desire. This is so because the good itself is the principal foundation for the functioning of the pleasure principle, that is, it governs the release of tension, the inertia or repetition in psychic behavior. However, in order to get to the goal of desire, in order to break the cycle of repetitions, the pleasure principle needs to be transcended. Therefore, the ethical framework of psychoanalysis, if it truly wants to cure, cannot be pursuit of the good as the standard of desirable behavior. That which can truly transform the set of signifiers that shape one's actions must come from outside of what Lacan calls "the service of goods," that is, its source must be beyond the demands of everyday materialistic existence, or the precepts of the existing social and political status quo.[64] In other words, the good or the goods ordinarily available only tranquilize the individual, making him or her a conformist unwilling to work for individual and social change, since of course the price of change is pain. Pain ruffles up the waters of pleasurable inertia, of "letting it be the way it is."

Hence I think that, in terms of his critique of the good, Lacan is in agreement with the theorists of the Liberation Thesis. The latter, as described in chapter 2, have also drawn a clear distinction between the goods that a present capitalist culture extols as satisfying, but which remain unfulfilling, and something beyond that could provide, if not true gratification, then—and it is no mean thing—the gratification of truth. However, Lacan insists that the formation of a better society is not as simple as establishing the proper manner of organizing needs. Needs are not equivalent to desires: whereas it is reasonable to expect that the former are quantifiable, the latter, being motivated by quality, resist any attempt to do so. This in fact is a point that seems left unconsidered by the Liberation theorists.

Approaching this issue from another direction, I would say that each social entity or product possess a category of value in addition to the use and exchange values identified by Marxian critical theory. This additional category is identified by Lacan as a *jouissance* value, a value derived from the enjoyment of possessing something that others also desire but do not have.[65] Here Lacan does not deviate from Freud's previously noted insight from *Civilization and Its Discontents*. In brief, even if property relations are equalized, the reasons for envy and hatred may not stop from piling up: sexual or intellectual attributes may take the place of the struggle for the just distribution of resources. Desires proliferate and may acquire a thousand different shades; no plan or program could situate them all in a fashion where their fulfillment would be guaranteed.

However, on my reading, this does not mean that Lacan is a moral relativist who throws up his hands saying "one's person's work of art is another person's pornography" and that is about as much as we can say. Lacan does distinguish between true and "false" desires (i.e., illusions).[66] False desires, for instance, are desires satisfied by the pursuit of the good or the beautiful as designated by external social standards without the subject's active participation and contribution. Therefore these desires work as defenses against moving towards the true. The true, in this respect, can be described as that in which the subject confronts its boundedness by the field of *das Ding*, the moment of the (retroactive) comprehension of its dependence on a certain set/chain of signifiers, and a simultaneous push for their re-constitution or re-transcribing. Or, put another way, the field of the true involves recognition that in the signifying chain, the subject exists only as an absence, as something that is not there, but which is necessary for the dynamic movement of the chain.[67] In other words, it precisely because the subject is represented as a lack, as "the missing signifier," that the signifying chain which structures the subject's existence could be re-structured, and the subject's life, its existence and destiny transformed.

SCIENCE AND ETHICS

The fact that the subject is lacking in the signifying chain represents for Lacan a concrete demonstration of the existence of the order of psychic reality that goes beyond the symbolic register, beyond that which is entirely encompassed by the signifier. On the other hand, Lacan locates the paradigmatic manifestation of the symbolic in the discourse of science underwritten as it is by mathematics. This is so because science reveals the power of the signifier *qua* signifier in its push to reorder all there is or could be (nature, world, humanity) along a set of conventional logical rules.[68] The discourse of science as opposed to the discourse of the subject, which manifests the presence of lack, that is, of the unconscious, can admit of nothing beyond its methodology. Its fundamental claim is that eventually with more sophisticated technology all there is, will be symbolized or made predictable. In other words, the discourse of science posits the rationalization of the universe as an infinite, but in essence possible task.

Lacan disagrees and, as I see it, his critique of scientific assumptions, of normal science *à la* Kuhn, resembles that of Marcuse. Lacan claims that science is in its structure one-dimensional, since it remains confined only to one register of thought, the symbolic. The workings of the symbolic correspond to the working of the pleasure principle in the psyche, and this is perhaps how one can explain humanity's fascination with science and its discoveries. It is true that science adds a great deal to the improvement of the human condition in terms of the accumulation of goods, but there are things that its structure makes it blind to. In terms of the study of the mind, Lacan insists that science as practiced in the traditional, mainstream communities of psychologists with particular emphasis on cognitive schemata offers only fragmentary insights. Structurally, the discourse of psychology downplays the significance of the study of the mental registers of the imaginary and the real. Hence, Lacan concludes that only psychoanalysis can provide a methodology that grapples with all three mental registers without reducing them to one or two.

In fact, because the discourse of science refuses to recognize the existence of fields that are beyond its reach, that is, the fields of the real and the imaginary which cannot be designated by conventional scientific notation, Lacan links scientific discourse to the structure of paranoiac psychosis.[69] He explains that what makes for the constitution of individual paranoia is the refusal to accept the imposition of a limit to one's affective attachment to the mother (the mother is not recognized as an object beyond reach, and no such objects are believed to exist). In other words, paranoia comes into being if and when the Name/No of the Father[70] is foreclosed (refused), and therefore the separation process between the child and the mother is not initiated. As a result, the child's imaginary remains constituted in an incomplete way and is subject to potential breaks or dissolutions.[71] Applied to the level of scientific practice this means that, due to the scientific noncomprehension of limits, instruments and tools can be developed whose potential uses would inflict irreparable damage on the life course of humanity. In fact, Lacan refers to his formula "what is foreclosed in the symbolic returns in the real" to explain the development and use of the nuclear bomb.[72]

However, the sole focus on the imaginary register as the antidote to the scientific emphasis of the symbolic is also unable to provide a clear guiding path for ethical activity. Even when the imaginary is constituted in the light of the recognition or avowal of the paternal function, its functioning is not free of troublesome aspects. Otherwise, one would expect all non-psychotics to be people of good will, which is (obviously) not what one encounters in one's daily existence. Lacan's explanation for why this is so is that the imaginary is the order of narcissistic self-absorption. It is that which makes the subject see what he or she wants to see, assuming the position of the ideal ego. For this reason, the imaginary is structured around an antagonistic relationship with the other, the other that serves precisely for the delimitation of one's imaginary by providing an ideal.[73]

The relationship to this other—considering that the other is what the subject desires to be, but also what, at the same time, it is deprived of—is one of envy. The thinking typical of the subject captured in the imaginary register is therefore the one that posits that the other is (always) happy and content, enjoying the type of *jouissance* that brings ultimate fulfillment.[74] In other words, the grass is always greener on the other side of the fence, the side that is beyond one's reach. In terms of ethical activity, this means that the imaginary register cannot be used as the basis of its standards just as the case of science testifies that these standards cannot be derived from the symbolic. As I see it, this is precisely why Lacan argues that the standards of ethics as the guidelines for one's behavior have to be derived from the field of the real.[75] This is why he stresses the significance of practices such as courtly love, which enable the subject to transcend its involvement in the imaginary and symbolic appropriations of the other in order to respect the other as a being in the real, as another subject radically different in its freedom. Hence Lacan, just as the theorists of the Liberation thesis, supports the claim that only a subject which has distanced itself from its narcissistic attachments to possessing goods and controlling their distribution can grant the other a kind of freedom that it is all too willing to grant itself.

ANTIGONE AND THE BEAUTIFUL

Since the order of the good (essentially, the symbolic order or register) obscures the source of ethical rules for the subject, only its transcendence can make visible both the ground of the moral law as well as the fundamental striving of one's desire. Lacan's position is that tapping into and following through this fundamental striving (which is drawn by the field of *das Ding*) is the proper expression of an ethical act. By definition, this will mean entering the field of pain and most likely going against the standards of the daily life of one's community. Here Lacan's argument affirms the contentions of the Liberation Thesis theorists. To follow one's desire is a road to truth under the condition that this desire is in fact a desire that rejects entrapment in materialistic pursuits (that is, the directives of capitalist exchange). True desire, according to Lacan, manifests "a retreat from goods," since only in this way can one approach the field of the real.[76] In other words, only by rejecting that which the given (local) symbolic order offers can a possibility be gained for the creation of a new structure of the subject more closely aligned with the real itself. Such a structure of the subject would make the subject's activities in the world of others and with others more ethical than was the case previously.

Lacan claims that a subject bent on exiting the order of goods will encounter a curious phenomenon. In a word, its actions will acquire the aura of beauty. For Lacan, the beautiful is that which is beyond the good and on the way to the true (the real), but not quite there yet.[77] The beautiful is the last veil hiding the field of *das Ding*. In an unusual reference to Heidegger, Lacan says that the beautiful is the place where "the false metaphors of being (*l'étant; Seiende*) can be distinguished from the position of Being (*l'être; Sein*) itself."[78] As I see it, it is a place of authenticity, a place where the subject's desire begins to unfold itself in a temporality unique to it as opposed to being controlled by the opinion of the "they" (*das Man*).[79] In order to show how the process of this kind is concretely manifested, Lacan refers to Sophocles' tragedy neglected by Freud, *Antigone*.

In Lacan's reading, Antigone transcends the order of the good—the common good established by the political context she inhabits and specifically represented by Creon. It is not so much that she defies the laws of the state in order to protect the values of the family (as Hegel thought) as it is to fulfill what her desire imposes on her. In other words, what motivates her act is not the upholding of the family right over the state right. Instead, it is a passion that she feels for her one and only (irreplaceable) brother (she says herself that she would not have done what she had done for a child or a husband).[80] Antigone therefore follows through the direction of her fundamental desire, which is marking the position of her love for her brother. By doing so, she enters the field of the beautiful, and it is indeed as such that she is described by the Chorus.

According to Lacan, the field of the beautiful that Antigone enters is also the place in between two deaths, the symbolic death and the biological death.[81] This place is essentially the only one providing for the possibility of creating a new symbolic order. It requires shattering the existing symbolic order, embodied in the laws of one's everyday reality, but it is still a step away from the biological death. In other words, this is a place where the subject finds itself stripped of the determinants of identity, having no more support in the symbolic structures that have up till then defined it. The subject encounters itself as what it in reality is, a lack that bears upon itself the inscriptions of signifiers, but does not and should not assume those inscriptions to be its "true" nature. As I see it, it seems appropriate to call this place—the place of awakening, perhaps represented by the image of a phoenix rising out of its own ashes.

Antigone lingers in this space long enough to show the spectator (the one who is moved by the play) both its promise and its limits. The promise of course is the possibility of a radical change in the spectator's (the subject's) identity. In order for this promise to be fulfilled, the subject has to return to the symbolic order that will now have been reconstituted anew profiting from the experience of having been shattered. Just as Plato's philosopher is required to go back to the cave after having glimpsed the Supreme Good in its genuine reality, so the subject must return to the symbolic and use its discourse structures in a way previously closed to it. This is what a set of well-conducted psychoanalytic sessions affords the analysand.

However, as Lacan is quick to point out, the currency in which such changes are paid for is one of intense suffering.[82] In fact, if something is not constructed in the place of that which was lost, the ultimate outcome may well be fatal. The breaking up of the symbolic, together with the accompanying dissolution of the imaginary that had supported it, reveal the real as the traumatic field of *das Ding*. The neighborhood of *das Ding* as the twin source of creation and annihilation is pervaded by the aura of death.

The attitude of Antigone shows this quite clearly. She acts as if her life has already been lost; she insists that for her "the race is over."[83] She finds herself dead to the existing symbolic order whose imperatives she subverts, while at the same time she is unable to construct a new one. She is therefore not afforded a possibility of return, and this—more than any other element in the play—makes her situation tragic, that of a martyr.

Lacan argues that each analysand has to repeat the action of Antigone, but with an ending that makes possible the reintegration into the symbolic order. The analysand suffers the pain of a tragic hero or heroine, but succeeds in the end in dissolving the curse of the gods. In other words, traumatic experiences that determine the analysand's fate could be reconfigured to enable him or her to compose another set of signifiers that would more closely reflect his or her unconscious desires. Even though this outcome cannot bring the possibility of a complete fulfillment, since the real can never be fully articulated by any symbolic configuration, it will still enable the analysand to lead his or her life with more awareness of its possibilities and limitations. The ethical thrust of psychoanalysis is therefore contained in its project of making the analysand learn how to die to one symbolic configuration and then be reborn into another. As such, psychoanalysis in Lacan's interpretation shows itself as an exercise that furthers humanitarian concerns, since it provides for the possibility of a life that is lived in a better and more extensive understanding of oneself and one's modes of expressions. The claims that the Liberation thesis theorists had for psychoanalysis in terms of its ability to facilitate the subversion of alienating status quo is therefore reflected in Lacanian experience as well. Through the actions of those subjects who have been able to develop a critical distance from the status quo in this way, a collective reconfiguration that affects political, economic, and cultural realms could be actualized.

DISCOURSE THEORY AS FRAMEWORK OF SUBVERSION

The key idea that motivates the ethics of psychoanalysis, in my reading of Lacan, is the possibility of the re-constitution of the subject leading to the possibility of the subversion of the symbolic order in general. In order to understand more precisely what such an endeavor entails in terms of what it emphasizes and what it rejects, I think it is necessary consider Lacan's theory of discourse structures. This theory covers the mid-period of Lacan's work, and it was fully formulated about a decade after his seminar on ethics. I interpret the underlying motivation in its formulation as Lacan's desire to formalize in a more specific way the relations of the individual unconscious and the social forms of life. As I will show, in my reading of psychoanalysis as critical theory, one of Lacan's discourse structures—the discourse of the hysteric—represents the most appropriate mode of expression for the radical subject in contemporary social and political life.

It was Heidegger who, in his major work *Being and Time*, argued that discourse represents "a mode of being-with-one-another."[84] To a certain extent, Lacan preserves the key insight of this definition, when he contends that the proper way to conceptualize discourse is to see it as that which establishes a social link by the "utilization of language qua link."[85] In other words, discourse is a linguistic structure that provides the possibility for the subjects to relate to each other. It presupposes non-psychotic psychological development, since, for the psychotic, social links or relations cannot be but illusory and fragile. This is so because, as shown in a previous section, the psychotic has never established a necessary distance from the field of the Other (that is, *das Ding*; the mother) in order to constitute the relations with others in a way that does not reduce their subjectivity to being an expression of the psychotic himself or herself.

Another definition of discourse that Lacan gives is that it is speech "without words."[86] What this means is that words are simply the means through which a given discourse structure produces its meaning effects. In order to uncover the meaning of particular words, one has to discern in which discourse structure they have been articulated.

Lacan sometimes refers to the discourse structures that he formulated as "the four-legged apparatuses," because each structure is made up of four terms and four positions (places).[87] The four terms are: S1—the master signifier; S2—a set of other signifiers, loosely composing a body of knowledge; $—the subject, divided or split by the presence of both conscious and unconscious mental processes; and *a*—the object small *a*, representing the object and cause of the subject's desire and the *surplus jouissance* that motivates the subject to follow its desire. The four positions in which these four terms can be situated are:

agent → other
truth ← production[88]

Lacan claims that one can chronicle the structural emergence of the discourse terms (S1, S2, and *a*) by observing what happens in the process of the constitution of the subject ($). According to Lacan, a signifier (S1) strikes or imposes itself on a given body of other signifiers (S2), which simultaneously leads to the formation of the subject ($) and the separation of a remnant *a* that will configure the various incarnations of the subject's desire.[89] In other words, the signifier S1, in striving to represent the subject ($) for other signifiers (S2), will create a gap that the subject—during his entire existence/life—will be compelled to attempt to fill. The object *a* will show itself to the subject as that which could genuinely fill its lack, that is to say, make it complete and whole. However, the incorporation of the object *a* by the subject will remain illusive, structurally speaking, but for the subject it will appear as the ultimate fulfillment, since the object *a* stands for the lost experience of oneness with the mother (the Other; *das Ding*).

In Lacan's view, all non-psychotic human speech could be situated in four distinct discourse structures. He names these four structures as the discourse of the master, the discourse of the obssessional (also known as the discourse of the university), the discourse of the analyst, and the discourse of the hysteric.[90] Each of the structures is generated by the 90 degree turn of the one that precedes it.[91] Considering that discourse is that which establishes a social link or a social relation, it is to be expected that different discourse structures establish different types of social links. Indeed, Lacan claims that some structures (the discourse of the analyst and the discourse of the hysteric) are more open to the truth of the subject's unconscious and therefore, as I see it, can be used to underwrite social and political changes. In contrast, other structures (the discourse of the master and the discourse of the university) deny or repress this truth or truths, and, as a result, need to be dissolved or re-configured. I see Lacan as stressing this task as one of the most important projects of psychoanalytic theory and practice. I think that in this respect Lacan and the Liberation Thesis theorists are in agreement. They all advocate the elimination of the repression of the truth of a given social and political reality and believe that psychoanalysis has a role to play in revealing the contours of that truth.

THE DISCOURSE OF THE MASTER

Lacan's formalization of the discourse of the master is:

S1 → S2
$ ← a

The interpretation is as follows: The master signifier (S1) is in the position of the speaking agent and is attempting to make a link with the knowledge (S2) in the position of the other. As a result, the object of desire (*a*), carrying *surplus-jouissance*, is produced, while the truth position is marked by the emergence of the split subject ($). The problem with the social link established by the master discourse is that the utterance of S1 can never be the (true) knowledge of the other. According to Lacan, the agent's—the master's—utterance is seen by the other as an imposition from outside, as an order or a command to which the other is compelled to submit. The reason that the master requires the other's submission is to produce the object *a* (the container of the master's *jouissance*) which is unconsciously desired by the master. This desire is unconscious because the master speaks by the means of S1, which, as a signifier, does not admit of any lack (that is, desire). In other words, the master's utterance obscures the existence in the master of the split or divided subject ($), which is designated below S1 in the discourse structure, and is to be interpreted as repressed. The motivation for the repression is the fact that the master (S1) does not want to admit that its utterance is motivated by lack and desire (which in truth it is).

Lacan's conceptualization of the master's discourse is influenced by an interpretation of Hegelian philosophical anthropology by the French philosopher of Russian origin, Alexandre Kojève. Kojève argued that the Master/Slave section in Hegel's *Phenomenology of the Mind* contains an insight in human psychology in that it posits, at the origin of subjectivity, two subjects (in Kojève's terms, two consciousnesses) competing for dominance.[92] Each subject sees the other as an obstacle to its full self-unfolding and therefore desires the other's annihilation. However, in the course of their struggle, both subjects become aware that they have brought into existence the third term, namely, death. In the face of death, one of the subjects yields, and as a result becomes a slave condemned to work, but who, while working, accumulates the true knowledge of social reality. The victor, the subject who remained unaffected by the risk of death, becomes the master. After a while, however, the master realizes his dependence on the work and recognition of the slave, but is unwilling to do anything about it, considering his domination historically justified. However, in contrast to the master's viewpoint, Kojève contended that the future belongs to the slave, since he is the only productive element of the dyad. At the end of history, which Kojeve associated with a Marxist revolution, the slave appropriates the position of the master, not to become the master himself, but instead to transcend the master-slave dialectic once and for all.

As can be seen, the structure of the master's discourse postulated by Lacan follows the Kojevean dynamic closely. The slave (S2) works for the master (S1), producing *jouissance* (*a*), but, at the same time, also revealing that the master himself is lacking something, that he founds his command (S1) on his being a divided subject ($). Eventually the accumulation of knowledge on the part of the slave tips the balance in his favor, and, according to Lacan, the master discourse is transformed into another structure, the structure of the obsessional or of the university. This event is marked by a 90 degrees shift in the discourse structure. The new discourse, in essence, represents the rule of the knowledgeable slave, but, in contrast to Kojeve, Lacan finds as problematic as the master's discourse and therefore impotent to signal the end of history.[93]

THE DISCOURSE OF THE UNIVERSITY

Lacan's formalization of the university discourse is:

$\underline{S2} \rightarrow \underline{a}$
$S1 \leftarrow \$$

The discourse of the university at the social level mirrors in its structure the discourse of the obsessional at the level of the individual.[94] In each case, the agent of speech or utterance is the accumulated body of (systematized) knowledge and ritualistic practices (S2) the purpose of which is to attempt to link up with, or to make an impact on, the object a (the *surplus-jouissance*) in the position of the other. In a certain way, the discourse of the university resembles an attempt at seduction, seduction of the other by the display of the apparent coherence and rigor of one's knowledge.

Just as the theorists of the Liberation Thesis, Lacan here reveals himself as a critic of the contemporary institutions of higher education and the types of educational process that they sponsor. He sees universities not as places where teachers and students are jointly engaged in search for the truth of the human condition, but instead as places of ritualized seduction by knowledge. In other words, students assimilate information provided to them by teachers not only because this information is relevant to the truth of social and political worlds, but also because, in this way, they show their transferential—loving—attachment to teachers.[95] What is produced, as a result, is a subject ($) that is lacking and divided, but who is compelled to seek answers in the type of knowledge that manifests the limited and narrow nature of the university horizons. This knowledge is represented by the term S1 (the master signifier) which finds itself in the position of truth for seeking students or others subject to the dynamic of the university discourse. Lacan takes this state of affairs as a sign that what the university provides cannot answer or respond to the key enigmas encountered by students or by those who desire to know something about truth as opposed to opinion; in his words, "truth is elsewhere."[96]

In other words, Lacan takes the knowledgeable slave, incarnated in the university teacher or scientist, the expert or bureaucrat, as another instance of the master. This is not to say, however, that there is no difference between the types of mastery underwritten by two discourse structures. Whereas the old master grounded his commands in nothing else but his own will ("Thou shalt . . . because I say so"), the new master seeks to justify his position of authority by reference to the whole world of facts, data, statistical techniques and so on. The new master claims to know what the good is, and that this good is at the same time the good of the other. The pretension to know the other's good was not implied in the conduct of the old master who did not particularly care if his good was that of another, so long as it was his own. The new master, in contrast, appeals to the other fervently and relates to him or her as to a precious object of desire (the object *a*). Yet—unfortunately for the other—all the overtures and siren songs are not expressing the desire of the other, but only the desire of the new master himself. According to Lacan, the old tyranny of the naked will, prowess, and brute force has been replaced, in the university discourse, by the new tyranny of knowledge.[97] The structure of control and surveillance has remained in place.

Lacan finds the most problematic aspect of the new master's knowledge in his belief in the possibility of absolute or total knowledge. This in fact is one of the most significant issues in Lacanian epistemology. For Lacan, the structure of truth as such prevents it from being integrated into the postulated totality of knowledge. Truth is the half-said (*mi-dire*) in that one of its parts always remains obscure to the speaking subject. This follows out of Lacan's insistence on the key psychoanalytic division between the conscious and the unconscious. The unconscious, as Freud's German term for it (*das Unbewüsste*) shows, means the unknown or the hidden; as such, it falls out of the subject's scope to know it all. Certain parts of it may be revealed, as my discussion of Lacanian ethics emphasizes, by a close attention to the subject's desire, but such revelation necessarily falls short of the complete elucidation of the structure of the subject's unconscious.

In fact, to explain this aspect of the unconscious, I think it is helpful to refer to one of the earliest Lacan's formulations that the unconscious is structured like a language.[98] In other words, the unconscious in its entirety, just like a language, is beyond the subject's grasp, because the very ability to formulate questions about its scope presupposes the acceptance of the rules of its grammar. Now, if the implicit acceptance of these rules represents a condition for the possibility of questioning, that means that in the activity of questioning, there must always remain something that is unquestioned. To put it succinctly, non-thought allows for the possibility of thought; non-knowledge grounds any possible knowledge. Therefore the totality of absolute knowledge must in the final analysis be false, because it is unable to do justice to—to know—its own ground. In my view, these considerations lead Lacan to affirm the status of truth as *mi-dire* (the half-said) or *pas-tout* (the non-whole or the not-all).

The question that I would raise here is what kinds of implications this essential blindness or falsity of the university discourse has for contemporary social and political life. Is it better or worse than the falsity of the master's discourse? Does it bring us closer to truth or does it obscure truth even further? How does it relate to the issue of individual freedom and the possibility of self-knowledge? I ask these questions, because, in fact, it could be argued that the master's discourse was "better" in all these respects. It could be said, for instance, that while serving the master involved physical bondage, this kind of bondage, at least in theory, allowed a space for the autonomy of individual consciousness and therefore opened up the horizon of rebellion. On the other hand, bondage to university discourse seems to require much more, since it demands not only the disciplining of the body, but also the disciplining and the control of the mind. One could perhaps characterize it as metaphysical bondage. The old master cared only "that it worked,"[99] whereas those who extol university discourse in contemporary circumstances want not only the results, but also the love of those who work for them. In other words, they want their subjects to worship the beauty of their servitude.

What I see reappearing here is the old Freudian distinction between Oedipus and Hamlet, discussed in chapter 1, which relates to their reaction to a psychological predicament that was essentially the same. Apollo, as the typical representative of the master's discourse, punishes Oedipus who is, therefore, justified to believe that he was no more than an unfortunate plaything in the hands of gods and can, in good faith, raise his fist to the sky and curse the gods in return.[100] Hamlet, the thinker, the expert, and so the obsessional *par excellence*,[101] does not have this option; he is the victim of his own libidinally invested super-ego and his crime therefore cannot but end in self-destruction. From this perspective, then, it seems that the university discourse exerts a more controlling influence on the individual and is not necessarily an improvement over the master's discourse.

Lacan does not explicitly side with this perspective, but one can easily imagine him arguing that things have to get worse before they can get better (the kind of argument found in Marx regarding the position of the proletariat, for instance). However, as I see it, for his discourse theory to retain structural coherence, he has to argue that the master's discourse is followed by the university discourse. In other words, the university discourse is a permutation of the master's discourse and not vice versa. This is so because only the university discourse has a structural orientation that allows its transformation into what Lacan calls the discourse of the analyst. Stated in another way, only the university discourse contains a possibility of its being affected and changed by the discourse of psychoanalysis. It will be in vain to try to psychoanalyze the master, but one can and does psychoanalyze obssessionals quite effectively. The master has to become an obsessional in order for psychoanalysis to do its work. Therefore the university discourse, though not necessarily more conducive than the master's discourse in terms of the space for individual freedom and collective subversion, is still a step forward on the road to the nearness of individual and social truth.

THE DISCOURSE OF THE ANALYST

Lacan's formalization of the analyst discourse is:

$\underline{a} \rightarrow \underline{\$}$
$S2 \leftarrow S1$

In this discourse structure, the object *a*, the object-cause of the analysand's or the subject's desire, becomes the agent of speech. In other words, the analyst's position vis-à-vis the analysand becomes that of the love object invested by the libido. The analysand as the divided or lacking subject is in the position of the other, which means that his or her primary focus is to capture or retain that which the analyst has come to represent. Lacan argues that this discourse structure offers the only way to effect a genuine change in the analysand's symptom(s), because it allows the analysand to produce new master signifiers (S1), that is, new determinants of identity and identification. In my view, this means that the analysand is free to construct or reconstruct his or her personality in a way that minimizes deleterious effects, such as inhibitions and anxiety.

What also comes to full expression in the discourse of the analyst is that psychoanalysis as an endeavor for individual and social change is based on the work of love. The analysands change for the love of the analyst, which, in technical terms, is called transference. In fact, as Freud has argued, the treatment of neurosis is successful only if and when the analysand's love of the analyst prevails over the love he or she has for that which makes him or her neurotic. In other words, the *jouissance* obtainable from the object *a*, which materializes itself in the course of analysis, has to lure the analysand away from the *jouissance* of his or her own neurotic symptomatology.

It may appear, however, that due to the key role that the process of transference plays in the analyst discourse, this discourse is not essentially different from the university discourse. After all, one may claim that the analyst discourse also depends on the seductive music of knowledge that the analysand or the student is compelled to march to. Yet, a quick look at the formalization of the two discourse structures shows that the position of knowledge (S2) in each is distinctly different. For the university discourse the body of knowledge (S2) is in the position of agent; in other words, it is that which imposes itself on the other with a maximum degree of urgency and inflexibility. The paths that university knowledge charts need to be invested with the libido (that is, loved) or else—in the position of the truth of the university discourse, we find nothing else but the master signifier (S1). On the other hand, knowledge (S2) in the analyst discourse has a fundamentally different structural role, that is, it is located, not in the position of agent, but in the position of truth. This means that the nature of knowledge imparted by the analyst to the analysand will differ from the knowledge produced by the university discourse, which is, as I have shown, alienated from truth. Knowledge based on truth is precisely the kind of knowledge that the analysand finds himself or herself in need of in order to re-construct his or her personality along different lines.

Lacan claims that the discourse of his seminars and other writings offers an example of the analyst discourse.[102] This is how he accounts for its unmistakably poetic quality that in certain parts borders on the hermetic, but which does not put in question its rigor. In fact, he cautions that the translation or re-playing of his ideas into the discourse of the university, which after all an academic thesis cannot avoid, provides a score of possibilities for misunderstanding and simplistic comprehension. This statement needs to be kept in mind in order to see clearly the limitation of the kind of work produced and transmitted by contemporary university education.

And yet, in my view, without university discourse, as the only discourse that is structurally conducive to the transformative influences of analyst discourse, psychoanalysis as social practice would be reduced to insignificance. In other words, for the analyst discourse to produce meaningful results, the dominant discourse structure in a given society needs to be that of the university. This precisely is the state of affairs in advanced industrial societies, and this is why one could expect psychoanalysis to play an important role in making such societies more open to dealing with the issues of fairness and justice to individual and collective demands.

Even though the beneficial effects of analyst discourse are multiple, it does not represent the final—that is, most desirable—permutation in Lacan's discourse theory. If it were so, one would expect the analysand to remain in analysis for the duration of a lifetime. However, analysis is not a scholastic exercise, one does not engage in it merely for the sake of engaging in it, but instead one expects a certain tangible result from it. According to Lacan, this result is achieved by the production of knowledge that will enable the analysand to move closer towards the answers that his or her neurotic symptoms are in search of. The discourse of the analyst, however, does not produce these answers; it essentially loosens up the structure of the university discourse in a way that allows the analysand to ask questions that are genuinely affecting him or her, those questions that shape his or her unconscious desire.[103]

For Lacan, the prototype of the questioning subject that one encounters at the end of analysis is a figure of the hysteric, and this is why the discourse structure to which the discourse of the analyst gives rise to is called the discourse of the hysteric. In fact, Lacan interprets the entire endeavor of psychoanalysis as aiming at "the hysterization" of the analysand's discourse.[104] In other words, psychoanalysis aims at breaking the analysand's congealed and inauthentic understandings of the self and his or her social world and replaces them by the state of uncertainty that makes it possible to search for and find answers more in line with the particular configuration of his or her unconscious. In the history of philosophy, says Lacan, Socrates was a good example of somebody who skillfully, relying on himself as the object a, induced the conditions of the discourse of the hysteric in those who surrounded him.[105]

THE DISCOURSE OF THE HYSTERIC

Lacan's formalization of the discourse of the hysteric is:
$$\frac{\$}{a} \rightarrow \frac{S1}{S2}$$
(with arrow reversed on bottom: $a \leftarrow S2$)

In the discourse of the hysteric, the agent of speech is the divided subject, the subject who is questioning the orientation of his or her desire. The subject's questions are addressed to an other represented by a master-signifier (S1). In this way, it seems to me that the discourse of the hysteric mirrors the structure of human speech, since, in speech, whatever the subject is expressing about him or herself has to be relayed by signifiers. In other words, the speech of the hysteric takes note of the fact that human beings as such—in all the multifaceted aspects of their life—remain the subject of the signifier, that is, that they can understand their conscious and unconscious life only in light of the set of meaning effects that predate and transcend them.[106]

This insights, far from leading to hopelessness, allows a careful consideration of the subject's own contextual history, embodied in his or her family and sociopolitical situation, which shaped the meanings of his or her unconscious desire. Understanding this desire is precisely the kind of knowledge (S2) that the subject has searched for all along. According to Lacan, such knowledge is generated or produced only through the direct address of the divided subject ($) to a master-signifier (S1). This is so, because the signifier (S1) is the only agency that can represent a subject ($) in human affairs.

In other words, the hysteric sees through the veil of illusion or falsity spawned by the discourse of the master and the discourse of the university. Placing either knowledge (S2), or the object a, in the position of the other (as is the case in these two discourses) grounds the social and political relations of control and ideological manipulation. It does not reveal the primary role that the other, according to my reading of Lacan, should play, which is to represent the subject to another subject. In my view, how and to what extent the other represents the subject will depend on the activities of the subject himself or herself, and here I consider of great importance the stand of the hysteric who directly demands of the other to be represented.

The hysteric confronts the other—the other as the carrier of a specific identity within a signifying chain—and makes his or her demands, which concern the fulfillment of the hysteric's particular configuration of desires. According to Lacan, true knowledge is created when the subject places, in the position of the other, the kind of signifier that represents him or her most closely in accordance with his or her desires. Hence the discourse of the hysteric, which makes this possible, manifests itself as the only discourse structure open to the emergence of true knowledge.

As I see it, there is also another path that Lacan takes to ascertain or confirm the truth-value of the discourse of the hysteric. This path emphasizes the concept of *jouissance*. For Lacan, truth and *jouissance* maintain a relationship of affinity, of kinship. As I have pointed out in previous sections, the key precept of Lacanian ethics is not to give way on one's desire for *jouissance*; precisely there lies the truth of one's subjectivity. Therefore it is not surprising that Lacan would conceptualize truth and *jouissance* as sisters,[107] which I interpret as implying that the commitment to one also entails the commitment to the other. The expectation then is that the commitments of the hysteric both to truth and to *jouissance* would be equally unwavering.

In fact, the examination of the structure of the hysteric's discourse confirms that this is the case. For the hysteric, the object *a*, the fountain of *jouissance*, finds itself in the position of truth. In other words, the hysteric is motivated in his or her search for truth by the prodding of *jouissance* that is to be gained or obtained in the course of such a pursuit. In Lacan's words, truth gives the hysteric a particular "shiver," it brings forth the experiences of enjoyment that can be used as the guideposts of the correctness of his or her conduct.[108] One can say, for instance, that being false or wrong would cut off the hysteric's access to *jouissance*, and this, of course, goes a long way in explaining his or her insistence on truth as the standard of social and political life.

The fact that the hysteric always aims at truth (individual as well as collective) makes Lacan consider it the most desirable of discourses. This means that the social link established by the hysteric's discourse allows for the full unfolding of the subject's possibilities. In my opinion, in holding this position, Lacan affirms the side of psychoanalysis subversive of the social and political status quo. This is so particularly because the forces of the status quo favor the discourse of the university as the discourse of truth. This state of affairs is manifested in the wide-ranging intellectual and material support for the numerous projects of quantitative science. Under the auspices of the university discourse, the public has come to believe in statistical knowledge as the sole incarnation of truth. Though such a claim is daily being upheld (in the mass media, for example), Lacan finds it more akin to a species of mythology than to truth. In other words, just as in the case of witch doctors, the validity of quantitative science is measured by the fact that it offers solutions that work, solutions that, in the conceptualization of Levi-Strauss, function efficiently.[109] Its truth, as argued in a previous section, is entirely in the order of the symbolic, of the chains of signifiers referring to each other, but ignoring their meaning effects. In other words, science in its dominant representations wants to know nothing of the real, the real which remains grounded in the experience of the suffering individual, in those particular objects *a* that make his or her whole being tick with desire. Quantitative science then cannot but cover over both truth and *jouissance* (found in the field of the real), which, in contrast, provide *raison d'etre* for the actions of the hysteric. The hysteric's behavior baffles science, and its truth forever escapes it. As I see it, only psychoanalysis can provide a voice to the hysteric's truth; only psychoanalysis can "hystericize" the discourse of the university and thus make it encounter gaps within the imaginary totality that it seeks to construct.

A THEORY OF SEXUAL DIFFERENCE

There is another element of Lacan's conceptualization of the hysteric that, though discussed briefly in several early seminars, attains a greater degree of clarity and precision in Lacan's later work, especially in *Seminar XX*. In my opinion, this element connects the discourse of the hysteric to the issue of sexual difference, and Lacan's claim that I stress here is that the hysteric's persistent questioning of the social Other is motivated by the search for an answer to the puzzle of sexual identity. The hysteric's principal question is "am I a man or am I a woman?" or "What is it to be a woman?" and this is what makes possible the hysteric's flexibility in his or her relation to the Other.[110]

The hysteric alternately identifies with male and female others, as Freud has shown in *Dora*, his key case study of hysteria.[111] Dora, the young girl in question, identified both with her father and his mistress, Frau K., in her effort to grapple with the meaning of sexual difference in relation to her own sexuality. What generated her suffering was her passionate attempt to understand herself in terms of the male and female figures she interacted with, an attempt that always ended in failure. Something always remained obscure and beyond her reach. This essentially is the paradox of the hysterics. Their non-satisfaction makes them push for more, makes them press the social Other to reveal more and more of that which underlies and governs it. Lacan often said that Freud discovered the unconscious solely thanks to the help of the hysterics. Something in their given symbolic order did not function for them and they manifested what they could of their *jouissance* in their symptoms. These symptoms came from elsewhere that is, precisely, from the unconscious. This is what got Freud up and running (that is, writing).

Lacan notes the fact that the hysterics are typically women. What does this mean?—he asks. Is there something that occurs in the constitution of a woman's psyche that provides for the greater likelihood of a problematic relation with the social Other that is emblematic of hysteria? That there are psychological differences between the sexes that cannot be reduced to or explained by physical sexual characteristics was already postulated by Freud. Freud thought that the path of the girl's understanding of herself as a woman is compounded with difficulties because she has to identify both with and away from her mother.[112] In other words, the girl has to separate herself from the oneness with the mother by identifying with the father (the phallic signifier (Φ) in Lacan's terms). At the same time, however, she has to retain a set of identity links with the mother in order to be able to understand her own role as a woman. This ambiguity in identification is what, in Freud's view, makes female sexuality more open to *jouissance* when compared to male sexuality. In other words, the boy has to identify with the father (the Oedipal and castrating agent) and persist in such identification. He therefore has to own up to his castration as an external limit imposed on his *jouissance*, whereas the girl's re-established links with the mother enable her to sidetrack the father's castrative posture and derive *jouissance* from beyond the paternal law (that is, beyond the symbolic order, in the field of the real).

Lacan considers the possibility of this "supplemental" or "non-phallic" *jouissance* as the principal axis in distinguishing the horizons of female and male sexuality. Women can play with the phallic function, while men remain dominated by it.[113] Man, for Lacan, could be seen as entirely "the creation of [paternal] discourse," while the same cannot be said for woman.[114] This is so because the *jouissance* of woman does not depend entirely on the paternal prohibition; woman can gain her *jouissance* from a more primeval source by identifying with the maternal desire, the desire that is structurally prior to the prohibition. However, in the constitution of the psyche, this desire must be counterbalanced by the paternal prohibition in order to avoid the generation of psychosis, which is the ultimate psychological result of the unbroken unity with the mother. So the question here, as I perceive it, is not that of "either . . . or," but of "both . . . and." This conjunction in identifications is what allows women to deal more effectively than men with the apparent and real gaps and discontinuities in the symbolic order, the order of the social and political status quo.

Lacan avoids the label of (sexual) essentialism by claiming that the experience of "supplemental" *jouissance* is not confined solely to women.[115] Men

Masculine　Feminine

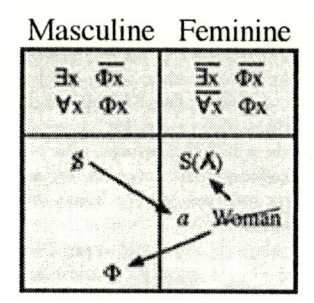

| $\exists x\ \overline{\Phi x}$ | $\overline{\exists x}\ \overline{\Phi x}$ |
| $\forall x\ \Phi x$ | $\overline{\forall x}\ \Phi x$ |

$\$$ → S($\overline{A}$)
a　W̶o̶m̶a̶n̶
Φ

Figure 3.1.
The Sexuation Graph[116]

can also experience it, but it involves a more fundamental psychological or attitudinal transformation than is the case with women. In this respect, Lacan refers to the example of certain mystics and artists, but stresses that this option remains open to other men as well.[117] The *jouissance* of these figures, akin to the *jouissance* of woman, is grounded in the order beyond the symbolic, and entails the transcendence of the laws of the father (the laws of the status quo) in order to be brought into being. In brief, those experiencing supplemental *jouissance* identify with the logic of the feminine position, the logic of the not-all (*pas-tout*), which Lacan formalizes in the so-called sexuation graph. As I will argue in following sections, one of the major tasks of psychoanalysis as critical social and political theory is precisely to make identification with the logic of the not-all, supported by the discourse of the hysteric, accessible to a greater number of people.

The sexuation graph presents, in the symbols of formal logic, the narrative explanation of psychological sexual differences I provided in the previous section. The graph is divided vertically into two sections: the masculine and the feminine.[118] It is also divided into two sections horizontally: the first part concerns four logical equations, while the second presents a topological schema of the relation between the two sexes. Out of four logical equations, two are found on the masculine side, while the other two are on the feminine side.

The two equations on the masculine side establish the conditions of masculinity. The first equation translates as "there exists one who is not a subject to the phallic function" (that is, there is one who is not castrated). This equation finds its consequent in the second equation, which affirms that since there exists one who is not castrated, all the others are subject to castration, that is, to the phallic function. In other words, all men are castrated because the very condition of masculinity is the presence of one who is not. As can be seen, Lacan's formalization here follows closely Freud's myth of the Primal Horde. Freud argued that what makes the Primal Horde united or coherent as a social unit was the presence of the Primal Father who claims access to all women at the expense of his sons. And even when the sons conspire against the Father and murder him, they cannot rid themselves of his influence entirely, because even, in death, the Father continues to be the ground of their morality. In other words, the Father's murder as the source of guilt founds the sons' moral precepts and permeates the norms of the society that they establish. Witness, for instance, the festivals and the ritual slaying of the totem animal, incarnated in various holiday celebrations in our contemporary era.

In Lacan's view, this goes to show that the coherence of the masculine world—the society of sons or brothers as such—is assured by the presence of an element outside of it. In other words, one can claim that the masculine side of sexuation is necessarily bounded or limited. It seems possible therefore to compare the masculine side with the symbolic order itself, which is also grounded by an element that lies outside its reach—*das Ding* (the real). Hence the price of being a man or identifying as a man is equivalent to the price of having a language, of being in the symbolic order, which is to say, it is the price of repression.[119] The entrance into the symbolic order shatters the imaginary union with the mother, the union that the subject will try to re-create during the entire duration of his or her existence by pursuing the union's elusive remnant—the object *a*. One can therefore think of men as doubly castrated once by the phallic function, and the second time by the exigencies of the symbolic order.

The equations on the feminine side of sexuation tell a different story; they are essentially the inverse of the equations on the masculine side. The first equation stands for the claim that, in the feminine world, "there does not exist one who is not castrated." Hence this equation entails the second equation as a consequent—not all are subject to the phallic function. In other words, on the feminine side, there does not exist an element that, by its being excepted, could ground the universal all or the existence of a totality. Hence the misdirection of Freud's puzzled question—"*Was will das Weib?*"— "What does Woman want?" is revealed. This question is misdirected—it is impossible to answer in the way it is asked—precisely because *das Weib* does not exist; there is no universal Woman, only women exist.[120]

Lacan therefore links the feminine side of sexuation to the concept of the non-whole or the not-all (*pas-tout*), while the masculine side is connected to the whole, to the concepts of "false" totality or universality.[121] As I have already shown, for Lacan, the whole is false since the condition of wholeness depends on the exclusion of that which grounds it. On the other hand, truth is the half-said, the non-whole. Truth is covered over by positing totality; it exists only in particular conditions that provide for one's *jouissance*. This is why Lacan claims that the feminine side of sexuation is closer to the notion of truth than the masculine side; the former does not depend on the Father to sanction the conditions of the fulfillment of one's desire. The source of *jouissance* that it establishes may be free of the phallus (Φ). In other words, *jouissance* may be derived not only from the manipulation of the symbolic order, as in the master's or the university discourse, but also from a relation to the real, as in the discourses of the analyst and the hysteric.

The importance of this statement for social theory is seen more clearly when the second part of the graph is examined, the part located underneath the logical equations. Here one finds two topological symbols on the masculine side, and three on the feminine side. The masculine side contains the split or divided subject ($) and the master-signifier (S1) represented by the phallus (Φ). In other words, on the masculine side, one finds both the subject of desire and the key signifier that insures the consistency of the symbolic order. The feminine side contains the object-cause of desire (*a*), the symbol for Woman who does not exist (the barred "Woman" or "*La*" in French), and the symbol for the void or the hole in the Other (S(Ø)). The hole in the Other on the feminine part is the mark of the fact that women or those who identify with the feminine position retain a relation to the real that reveals the symbolic order as incomplete, and its seemingly smooth and coherent functioning as full of gaps, discontinuities, and exclusions.

As I see it, however, the mere explanation of the symbols is not enough to grasp Lacan's take on sexual difference and its implications for social and political life. What must be considered is how the symbols, representing masculine and feminine identity, interact and connect with each other. Only in this way can we come closer to see the obscurities of sexual relations in all their complexity.

To begin with, in the graph, there is only one arrow that leads from the masculine side to the feminine side. This is the arrow linking the divided subject ($) and the object *a*, that is, the desiring subject and the cause of his or her desire. For Lacan, the link of the two, formalized as $◊a, makes up the structure of fantasy.[122] In other words, whoever finds himself or herself on the masculine side approaches the source of his or her sexual attraction as an object fulfilling unconscious fantasy, whose promise is that it will resolve his or her division as subject.

Lacan claims that this is typically how men approach women; in other words, men think they are approaching women as subjects, but actually what they come in contact with is the cause of their desire, a fantasized part-object whose relation to a given woman may be purely coincidental. In other words, this means that what excites man in lovemaking can be best conceptualized as a fetish-object. It is not surprising therefore that Lacan speaks of masculine sexuality as having "a polymorphously perverse" orientation,[123] but without the emancipatory aura that this orientation has acquired in the writings of the theorists of the Liberation Thesis.

The important question to ask at this point, in my opinion, is whether this is also the way that women typically approach men. I interpret Lacan's answer to be negative, considering that the sexuation graph shows that the linkage of the feminine to the masculine is different from the linkage of the masculine to the feminine. In other words, if one sets out to connect to the masculine from the feminine side, one will not stumble upon or be captured by the relation of fantasy ($\$ \Diamond a$). Instead, on this side, one finds two arrows leading out of the position of the feminine subject, the subject which draws its existence from the claim that Woman does not exist, that women speak as a plurality of particular voices. One of the arrows connects directly to the hole in the Other ($S(\emptyset)$) and in this way links female sexuality with supplemental *jouissance* beyond the given symbolic sexual and other practices. This link, as I pointed out above, opens up the possibility of seeing the problematic aspects in the Law of the Father that governs the masculine side.

The other arrow crosses over into the masculine side and connects, not to the divided subject ($\$$), but to the master-signifier, the phallus (Φ), that which, on the masculine side, represents the ruling principle of law and order. This means that women are constantly shifting between two poles, between the signifier that structures the symbolic and the hole that represents the limit, the beyond of that very same signifier. Hence when women relate to men, they do not establish a relation with man as a desiring subject, which is the position out of which men perceive them. Instead, they are attracted by and link up with that in man that transcends any particular man; in other words, women desire the very principle of masculine side, the phallus.

However, the phallus, being a signifier, is something that man as subject finds himself at the mercy of; it is not something that he can freely offer to women. This state of affairs in the relations between men and women motivates Lacan to formulate what, on surface, looks like a paradoxical thesis—"there is no sexual rapport [or relationship]."[124] As I will be explain below, this thesis has profound implications for psychoanalysis as critical social and political theory.

"THERE IS NO SEXUAL RAPPORT."

The thesis that there is no sexual rapport between the sexes primarily means that there is no one-to-one relation or ratio between them. In other words, men's relation to women is not based on the same set of links that grounds women's relation to men. As I pointed out above, the relation of men to women has the structure of fantasy ($\$ \Diamond a$), and therefore one can situate it in the order of the imaginary. On the other hand, the relation of women to men is a relation to the principal signifier (the barred "Woman"), which places it in the order of the symbolic. Hence on the level of structure (that is, on the level of sexuation), men and women want different things from each other, and, based solely on these things, they cannot establish the relation of One, of a certain sort of fusion or unity popularized by, for example, the Romantic movement, but which goes back to Plato. The same also is the case for those who identify with the side of sexuation that differs from their biological sex. Therefore, a woman who identifies with the masculine side may be attracted to her partner because of his physical characteristics (the object *a*), whereas a man who situates himself on the feminine side may be drawn to his partner because of her proficiency in foreign languages or chances for career success (Φ).

In my view, this state of affairs should not be taken as saying anything about the strength and length of such relationships, nor does it affect the frequency of sexual intercourse. Far from saying anything against sex or sexual practices, Lacan only emphasizes that the *jouissance* of two sexes depends on, or is structured by, different components. Or, in other words, if one searches for something that will establish a rapport between the sexes, however provisional it may be, one has to find it in a place other than sexual *jouissance*. To this other place—the place that "stops [the sexual rapport's] not being written"—Lacan gives the designation of love.

THE QUESTION OF LOVE REVISITED

In Lacan's formulation, love is not something that links a man with a woman or a woman with a man, but is instead the relation of a subject of the unconscious to another subject of the unconscious.[125] Considering that the subject is an elusive formation that comes into being through the interplay of particular signifiers, it seems rare and quite miraculous that two subjects would resemble each other to such an extent as to constitute a pair. Hence the presence of love entails an encounter in the strictest sense of the word, which signifies its contingency, since it means the recognition "in the partner [of the] symptoms and affects . . . that mark in each of us the trace of his [her] exile . . . from the sexual relationship."[126] In other words, love is an encounter in the other of that which marks one's own fate as a subject. As such, love has the potential of compensating for the fact that the masculine and the feminine side of sexuation remain radically apart.[127]

As I see it, love, at the level of structure, seems to be able to draw or constitute a non-existent arrow in the sexuation graph between the desiring subject ($), whose typical relation is with the object *a*, and the hole in the Other (S($\emptyset$)), that is *das Ding*. In other words, love means substituting an imaginary relation, not for a relation of the symbolic, underwritten by the feminine side of sexuation, but for a relation of the real.

This is why I think it is important to revisit Lacan's stress on the medieval practice of courtly love as the model for a set of social and political relations that could mitigate the consequences of the absence of sexual rapport. In courtly love, the troubadour liberates his beloved from being an object of his fantasy by elevating her to the position of *das Ding*.[128] In order to do so, he forces himself to follow an artificially designed code that transmutes his desire—and not without pain and suffering—into a symbolic production (a poem, for instance) that breaks the cohesion of the imaginary. The troubadour can therefore see or approach his Lady as a subject in her own right in a way that remains closed to most men who relate to women only on the basis of their sexual fantasies ($◊a).

This, however, is not to say that the troubadour de-sexualizes himself; in fact, his production is as sensual as any physical practice related to sex.[129] Instead, he uses the *jouissance* distilled from fantasies as a means of attaining a knowledge that will articulate for his Lady his own truth as the subject of the unconscious. And, on my reading, it is only this—the revelation of his unconscious—that enables him to prove the truth of that which he yearns most for—the love of his Lady.

In fact, I would say that by willingly submitting himself to the power of the symbolic, to a signifier that will articulate or represent him to an other, the troubadour constitutes in his own practice the discourse of the hysteric. Though he is undoubtedly a subject motivated by desire, the troubadour, just like the hysteric, skillfully avoids the imaginary relation of the subject and the object *a* ($◊a) and, instead, aims for the signifier (S1). Considering that the unconscious itself is structured like a language, that it consists of chains of signifiers structured by one or several master-signifiers, the troubadour's approach enables him to bring to surface (to speak, in other words) those formations and signifiers that shape his conduct and guide his desire.

In my opinion, this approach realizes one of the fundamental aspects of psychoanalytic theory. The troubadour's, or the hysteric's, approach is nothing else but putting into practice in social relations the most important analytic technique, free associations. The crucial value of this technique in accessing directly the sources of one's unconscious desire is something that Freud, Lacan, and the Liberation Thesis theorists all agree on. In other words, "where *it* was, there it is my duty that *I* should come into being," as Lacan translates Freud's dictum *"Wo Es war, soll Ich werden."*[130] The *it* of drives and desires becomes the *I* of speech as a key component in the completion of the individual's foremost ethical task in social and political affairs.

Yet what, in my opinion, appears crucial in the discourse of the hysteric, and is the reason why Lacan reserved highest terms of praise for those who speak it, is a clear recognition that this *I* can never become a signifier. If this were not so, the hysteric would easily turn into yet another master, supported by an S1, since the quarter turn of the hysteric's discourse could transform it into the discourse of the master. This quarter turn would establish the signifier S1 as the speaking agent, which, as I have shown, is the key feature of the master's discourse.

On the other hand, the hysteric, remaining true to the structure of his or her discourse, knows that there is no repair for the split in the subject. This, however, plunges him or her neither into repression nor into a paranoid denial. Instead, the hysteric, as argued above, demands of the signifier S1 the appropriate representation in discourse, and attaches himself or herself to it only if it, in turn, offers the most in terms of affirmation and fulfillment.

SEXUATION AND SOCIETY

The question that I think is necessary to ask at this point is what Lacan's sexuation graph says or does not say about the possibility of social and political changes. What primarily strikes my eye is Lacan's claim that while social and political norms, rules and established ways of life find themselves on the masculine side, the signifier whose presence designates the generation of new social horizons—the signifier representing the hole in the Other, the abyss of destruction and creation—is located on the feminine. Is the feminine then the logic of revolutions? It would appear so, and yet, in that case, this would also mean that a general or systematic plan for a revolution could not be pre-established. This is so, because, on the feminine side, the One is not—in other words, no totality could be formulated—so *the* blueprint for *the* revolution would be out of the question. Does this not entail repudiating the claims of Liberation theorists? I think not. Considering that contingency is involved in revolutionary outcomes, it is possible, from a Lacanian perspective, that the Liberation Thesis is one of those potential mode of revolt that will be ultimately successful. There are no genuine totalities, but there are different ways of organizing social and political life, some of which come to be dominant at a particular historical period. In other words, they cross over onto the masculine side and present themselves as the ground of a new society. However, in my reading of Lacan, I stress his position that there is nothing universal or eternal about the existing status quo, it is only that its master-signifiers (money, exchange value, consumerism, and so on) have captured the determining position in social and political structures. Another set of signifiers (play, exchangeability of functions, Eros, and so on) could replace them and restructure social and political life accordingly.[131]

As I see it, this means that Lacan, just like the theorists of the Liberation thesis, provides criteria for distinguishing between more or less repressive societies, between more or less rigid structuration of the masculine side. As I have shown, in several sections of this Chapter, these criteria are found in

Lacan's discourse theory and especially in the way he chronicles the end of the reign of the master's discourse and the "birth" of the university discourse. By following Lacan's train of thought, I think it is reasonable to conclude that an egalitarian and truly free society would be one in which social and political relations are linked up by the discourse of the hysteric. This discourse allows for the best representation of the subject of the unconscious in the symbolic register, and as such promises to affect social life in a way that reveals and unfolds its hidden or repressed possibilities.

In other words, hysterics are, in my opinion, the proletarians of a Lacanian revolution. Their ways of speaking and acting, their ways of being, subvert the existing status quo, that is, the symbolic register governed by capitalist master-signifiers by bringing to the surface the fact that the Other has no Other, that the structure of the Other is pierced by a hole ($S(\emptyset)$). In other words, hysterics affirm the (Lacanian) fact that there is no smooth transition from the register of the symbolic to the register of the real, since the real cannot be contained by the signifying chain. Hysterics reveal that beyond the given, there lies something more, or, in the language of Heidegger's *Being and Time*, that possibility stands higher (is prior) than actuality.[132]

This ability to make present or bring into being alternative worlds is at the heart of any politics of emancipation, and it is that which I believe links together Lacan's hysterics and the postulated agents of the Liberation Thesis, workers, students, artists. Moreover, at same time, it also grounds ethical parameters for the scope and pace of social and political changes, since hysterics speak and act as governed by unconscious desire—the only carrier of truth in psychoanalytic thought.

THE HYSTERIC AND THE POLITICAL

It is at this point that I think a key question need be addressed—what exactly is a political system that would please the hysteric? For instance, in one of the most recent articulations of Lacanian political theory, Yannis Stavrakakis argues that Lacan gives a nod of approval to contemporary liberal democratic political systems.[133] Stavrakakis bases this claim on what he understands to be a fairly literal analogy between the understanding of the political prevalent in democracies and Lacan's concept of the real. For him, the political can in fact be conceptualized as "a modality of the real."[134] What this means is that the political can never be precisely defined, because any attempt to render it in positive terms (to symbolize it) comes up short. In other words, as soon as one settles on a set of political practices as the true incarnation of governing principles, one has distorted the scope of the political, since all the other possibilities by definition remain unrealized.

Stavrakakis claims that only democracies remain faithful to these unrealized possibilities, since they "legitimize" the existence of the conflict of interests in formulating social and economic policies. In brief, democratic players "agree to disagree"—truth is subject to the marketplace of ideas.

This account seems to me flawed in several respects. In my opinion, Stavrakakis idealizes democratic politics as the place where all voices or possibilities get to be expressed, which is far from being the case since some voices have means at their disposal to be much louder than others. In addition, he simplifies Lacan's ideas by trying to fit them into a framework that reflects the officially sanctioned Western worldview in the post–Cold war world. It is almost as if Stavrakakis were saying "see, Lacan favors contemporary democracies, too." Even though Stavrakakis does not cite Habermas and decries the possibility of Habermasian "ethics of harmony," the implication of his argument is to place Lacan in the same contemporary tradition, to "tranquilize" his ideas the way I think Habermas tranquilized the ideas of the first generation of the Frankfurt School and by implication the theorists of the Liberation Thesis.[135] To paraphrase Slavoj Žižek, whose work will be examined in chapter 5, this move needs to be resisted, no matter how tempting and/or academically profitable not doing so must be.

Perhaps one of the reasons that Stavrakakis does not discern Lacan's affinity with any of the radical thinkers of earlier decades is that his reading of Lacan most extensively relies on the early Lacan, that is, the notions of the split subject and the "lacking" Other.[136] He does not enter into a creative engagement either with Lacan's discourse theory or with the theory of sexual difference. This is perhaps what makes Stavrakakis' account seem simplified: it seems difficult to retain the complexity of Lacanian formulations on the political, if one does not consider the impact of discourses and sexuation both on the articulation of the political and the possibilities of its articulation.

Regarding Stavrakakis' praise of liberal democracies, I think that it is important to stress that democracies "legitimize" the conflict of ideas only to the extent that assures their victory in the struggle against political alternatives. They allow the free marketplace of ideas only to the extent that this marketplace excludes ideas that question their foundation. Liberal democracies cement the freedom of their public sphere by marginalizing or discrediting those who refuse to play the political game by their rules, that is, those who are not democratic according to the pre-established standards, and they do this using all means at their disposal.

As I see it, this means that the consistency of democratic functioning depends on the exclusion or repression of the elements that speak or demonstrate its gaps and failures, such as those in favor of the Liberation Thesis, for instance. Democracies and their intellectual supporters such as Stavrakakis designate these alternatives, which are objectively legitimate (as I have shown in chapter 2) as unrealistic and utopian.[137] Moreover, what reveals the ideological or ungrounded nature of Stavrakakis' argument is the insistence that once these disruptive elements are excluded or barred (socialism, revolutions, and so on), existing liberal democratic political system will provide all that which individuals might need and want. In essence, however, the *a priori* exclusion of the possible truth of political alternatives, negatively designated as utopias, is the condition of the truth of a liberal democracy.

I think this is why Lacan places liberal democracies on the masculine side of sexuation, indicating also that the discourse structure that prevails in them, spoken by political elites, is a modification of the master's discourse, the discourse of the university. This means that Stavrakakis misses an important insight when he construes Lacan's allegiance to contemporary liberal democratic theory. In contrast, what I have shown in my reading is that Lacan favors a political system that is engendered on the feminine side of sexuation, and where the dominant discourse is the discourse of the hysteric. I maintain that this political system, the system that would please the hysteric, is in essence the kind of social and political vision presented by the thinkers of the Liberation Thesis.

LACAN AND THE LIBERATION THESIS

In fact, in my view, what could be a better depiction of the activities of the hysteric than that famous passage from *German Ideology*? In imagining a way of life in a liberated society, Marx and Engels write: "[it is here that] nobody has one exclusive sphere of activity but each can become accomplished in any branch he wishes . . . [it becomes] possible for me to do one thing today and another tomorrow, to hunt in the morning, fish in the afternoon, rear cattle in the evening, criticize after dinner, just as I have a mind, without ever becoming hunter, fisherman, shepherd, or critic."[138] In other words, if we tried to formalize the images and ideas that Marx and Engels weave together in this passage, this formalization would look like a life lived according to the discourse of the hysteric.

In the discourse structure of the hysteric, the subject ($) —motivated by surplus *jouissance* (a)—addresses the signifier S1 (that is, one's identity as a hunter, fisherman, shepherd, or critic) and attaches itself to it in order to gain appropriate representation. As the result of this voluntary attachment, new knowledge of social and political world (S2) is produced. This is the core of that which is praised by Marx and Engels. It involves acquisition of the knowledges of each of the vocations, without mechanistically identifying with them, without being forced into them, as both the master's and university discourse require, considering that they reflect the class division of labor in liberal capitalist economy. In other words, the discourse of the hysteric underwrites individual freedom to change one's choice—one's designations in the symbolic register—at any time that one so desires. It allows the full exercise of one's species-being, of the creative essence of humanity, providing for the possibility of "the casting off of all natural limitations."[139] Therefore, I think that Lacan is in agreement with the Liberation Thesis theorists in that the voluntary exchangeability of functions is indispensable for a fulfilled human existence.[140]

In addition, it seems to me that the establishment of a liberated society coincides with the rejection of the exclusionary nature of the masculine side of sexuation, a move that, as I have shown, Lacan approves of. The evidence to support this claim is not only found in Marcuse's discussions of the non-repressive, erotic civilization and Brown's emphasis on the "resurrection of the body," but is also possible to glimpse in the writings of Marx. For instance, in *The 1844 Economic-Philosophical Manuscripts*, Marx states that communism as such cannot be the final goal of human strivings, since it represents a simple negation of the political and social system based on private property relations (i.e. liberal capitalism).[141] In other words, communism represents no more than a replacement of one type of the political/economic system by its negated underside. In this sense then, communism substitutes one instance of the masculine logic by another; in other words, instead of excluding those without property, the proletariat, the excluded are those who formerly owned property, the bourgeoisie. In fact, this is exactly what happened in the course of the expropriation programs in post-Lenin Soviet Union and other countries of "actually existing socialism," and, in my opinion, helps explain the failure of these countries to come even close to the precepts of the Liberation Thesis. In terms of Lacan's discourse structures, for instance, the systems of these countries, far from representing a step forward, took an unmistakable step backward: their political elites reverted to the open exercise of a discourse more or less concealed in Western democracies, the discourse of the master.

The important point, however, according to both the Liberation Thesis theorists and Lacan, is that anyone interested in human emancipation cannot be content with social and political realities that base themselves on exclusion and repression, either of capitalist or communist kind. As it is one of the fundamental tenets of psychoanalysis that the repressed always returns, one can say that the repression of private property through communism is sure to contain the seeds of reversal into its own opposite, that is, to a society once again governed by private property. In other words, neither communism nor capitalist, neither the master discourse nor the university discourse, can ever break the cycle of repetition that keeps individuals captured by signifiers beyond their conscious and unconscious choosing.

As I have shown, what is to be done, in Lacan's view, is to advance individually and collectively to the discourse of the hysteric by the help of a psychoanalytic working-through of the discourse of the university. It is at this juncture that Lacan, in my opinion, joins Marx and the Liberation Thesis theorists. In other words, Marx says that beyond communism, there is a further development, the coming into being of a social and political space that he defines as "real life," or the onset of true *human* history governed by the desires and wants of those whose historical labor it reflects.[142] This social and political space, according to Marx, is no longer marked by a mediation of any sort; it has nothing that can deny itself to itself, but represents a realm of *freely* evolving possibilities and tasks. In other words, it is an order whose structural location one would expect to find on the feminine side of sexuation, considering that the feminine does not contain a pre-existing limit and remains profoundly aware of the essential contingency of that which is chosen. I contend that this society of liberated real life is linked up by the structures of the hysteric's discourse where the inexhaustible wealth of identificatory signifiers (S1, S2, S3, S4, S5, and so on) is embraced as a matter of course.[143]

CONCLUSION

My intention in this chapter has been to show in what way Lacan's formulations concerning the nature of psychoanalytic endeavor, especially in its ethical and social implications, relate to the key precepts of the Liberation Thesis. I sought to dispel the notion of Lacan as a social reactionary or a thinker who looks disapprovingly at the possibility of radical social and political change. In other words, I wanted to affirm a claim that psychoanalysis in its Lacanian incarnation contains a whole range of concepts and postulates with which it is possible to accomplish a critical interrogation of the existing social and political status quo.

In this respect, I have shown how Lacan's emphasis on the truth value of unconscious desire opens toward an ethical reconstitution of the existing order, a reconstitution that could engender a world of less hostile and antagonistic social relations. I have emphasized his claim that it is possible to restructure dominant social discourses through the intervention of the discourse of the analyst, since this discourse provides a stimulus altogether indispensable for clearing obstacles to direct expression of the relationship between the subject of the unconscious ($) and sets of signifying chains (S1, S2, S3, S4, and so on) through which the subject's desires attain representation. I have demonstrated that the discourse of the hysteric fulfills all the criteria necessary to provide the most fulfilling and ethically justified mode of subject-signifier relationship, and hence establishes a basis for a more fair and just social and political life. I have speculated on how a possible society of hysterics would look and found that, in its essence, it resembles the emancipatory social vision of the Liberation Thesis theorists.

However, I have also shown that even though Lacan's claims do not oppose the general drift of the Liberation Thesis, there are certain differences between the two. In this respect, the most important difference seems to be Lacan's insistence on the contingency and undecidability of social and political change in contrast to the much more linear historical orientation of the Liberation Thesis. Yet, even though Lacan discards the idea that there are systematic blueprints for social change, he does not doubt that the extensive and intensive understanding of oneself and one's world, afforded by psychoanalytic theory and practice, provides a set of *sine qua non* conditions for it. This is seen in his formalization of the discourses of the analyst and the hysteric, as well as in the feminine side of sexuation. In other words, in my opinion, in Lacanian psychoanalysis, one finds concrete tools for social and political practices particularly effective in locating and making known gaps and discontinuities in the liberal democratic status quo, that is, those "weak links" through which the repressed possibilities of emancipation could return.

NOTES

1. Jacques Lacan, *The Seminar of Jacques Lacan, Book XX, Encore: On Feminine Sexuality, The Limits of Love and Knowledge, 1972–1973*, ed. Jacques-Alain Miller, trans. Bruce Fink (New York: Norton, 1998), 37.

2. Jacques Lacan, *The Seminar of Jacques Lacan, Book II, The Ego in Freud's Theory and in the Technique of Psychoanalysis, 1954–1955*, ed. Jacques-Alain Miller, trans. Sylvana Tomaselli (New York: Norton, 1988), 228–29.

3. Jacques Lacan, *Le Seminaire, Livre XVII, L'envers de la Psychanalyse*, ed. Jacques-Alain Miller (Paris: Seuil, 1991), 231, 234; Jacques Lacan, "A Letter to D. W. Winnicot," trans. Jeffrey Mehlman, *October*, no. 40 (Spring 1987): 76–78.

4. Stuart Scheiderman, *Jacques Lacan: The Death of an Intellectual Hero* (Cambridge, Mass.: Harvard University Press, 1983), 157–82.

5. In *Seminar XX*, commenting on the perceived difficulty of following his formulations, Lacan says to his listeners: "If you don't understand [my writings], so much the better—that will give you the opportunity to explain them," 34. In other words, an obstacle motivates one's desire to produce things that can eventually overcome it.

6. For a critique of Lacan stemming out of the French philosophical community, see Luc Ferry and Alain Renaut, *French Philosophy of the Sixties: An Essay on Antihumanism*, trans. Mary H. S. Cattani (Amherst: University of Massachusetts Press, 1990), 185–207. For a critique of Lacan by a scholar sympathetic to the Frankfurt School, see Martin Jay, *Downcast Eyes: The Denigration of Vision in Twentieth Century French Thought* (Berkeley: University of California Press, 1993), 329–70.

7. Jacques Lacan, *The Seminar of Jacques Lacan, Book XX, Encore: On Feminine Jouissance, The Limits of Love and Knowledge, 1972–1973*, ed. Jacques-Alain Miller, trans. Bruce Fink (New York: Norton, 1998), 17.

8. Ernst Kris, "Ego Psychology and Interpretation in Psychoanalytic Therapy," *Psychoanalytic Quarterly* 20, (1951): 15–30.

9. Jacques Lacan, "The Freudian Thing, or The Meaning of the Return to Freud in Psychoanalysis," in *Ecrits: A Selection*, trans. Alan Sheridan (New York: Norton, 1977), 115–16. Lacan's rendering of the myth of Diana and Actaeon in this essay also refers to his conflict with ego psychology. In my reading of the essay's last passage, Lacan refers to the ego psychologists as "the hounds" ready to tear apart Actaeon (that is, Lacan and those who accept his interpretation of Freud), because he had had a glimpse of Diana (that is, truth) in the nude. Hence Lacan counsels the frightened Actaeon "let the pack pass by without hastening your step, Diana will recognize the hounds for what they are," 145. In another text and much less poetically, Lacan refers to ego psychology as "conformist in its aims, barbarous in its doctrine, a complete regression to psychologism, pure and simple," "The Founding Act," trans. Jeffrey Mehlman, *October*, no. 40 (Spring 1987): 102.

10. Lacan, "The Freudian Thing," 131–32. In fact, Lacan says explicitly that the concept of the ego is as relevant for the understanding of the psyche just as much as the concept of the desk. In his words, "of so little use is [the concept of the ego] that I undertake to show that the discourses concerning the ego and the desk (and that is what is at stake) coincide point by point," 132.

11. Jacques Lacan, *The Seminar of Jacques Lacan, Book I: Freud's Papers on Technique, 1953–1954*, ed. Jacques-Alain Miller, trans. John Forrester (New York: Norton, 1988), 16–17.

12. Lacan, *Seminar II*, 8–9, 44.

13. Lacan mirrors this claim in his definition of the unconscious as "the discourse of the Other." See Lacan, *Seminar I*, 85.

14. Lacan, *Seminar I*, 151, 167.

15. Lacan, *Seminar I*, 17.

16. Freud, for instance, interprets an analysand's statement such as "now you'll think I mean to say something insulting, but really I've no such intention," as "a repudiation, by means of projection, of an association that has just emerged [or, in terms of my presentation here, as a negation of the discourse of the subject of the unconscious]." See Sigmund Freud, "Negation," trans. Joan Riviere, in *A General Selection from the Works of Sigmund Freud*, ed. John Rickman (New York: Anchor Books, 1957), 54. Of interest in this respect is also a presentation that the philosopher Jean Hyppolite gave in one of Lacan's seminars. See Jean Hyppolite, "A Spoken Commentary on Freud's 'Negation,'" in Lacan, *Seminar I*, 291–97.

17. Sigmund Freud, *Introductory Lectures on Psychoanalysis*, trans. James Strachey (New York: Norton, 1966), 353.

18. Sigmund Freud, *New Introductory Lectures on Psychoanalysis*, trans. James Strachey (New York: Norton, 1965), 80.

19. Lacan, "The Freudian Thing," 128.

20. The possibility that this was a simple oversight on Freud's part can also be discounted, because it is known that he was a careful and patient stylist and was, moreover, ever ready to notice and comment on the slips of his own unconscious.

21. Lacan, "The Freudian Thing," 129.

22. In some cases, ego psychologists hint that this standard may be even the ego of the analyst, the analyst as the ideally successful "mature" subject. See Lacan, *Seminar I*, 18.

23. Jacques Lacan, *The Seminar of Jacques Lacan, Book VII: The Ethics of Psychoanalysis, 1959–1960*, ed. Jacques-Alain Miller, trans. Dennis Porter (New York: Norton, 1992), 311–25, esp. 314, 319.

24. Lacan, *Seminar VII*, 3.

25. Lacan, *Seminar VII*, 152.

26. Some Lacanian scholars who write in English (i.e., Bruce Fink, Russell Grigg, and Slavoj Žižek) translate *jouissance* as enjoyment. For instance, the title of one of Žižek's well-known books is "Enjoy your Symptom," in the precise sense of relating to one's symptom with *jouissance*. See Slavoj Žižek, *Enjoy Your Symptom: Jacques Lacan in and out of Hollywood* (London: Routledge, 1992). However, the English word "enjoyment" does not have an active quality that is implied in *jouissance*. Therefore, I prefer to leave it in French in my work.

27. Lacan, *Seminar VII*, 27, 31–32, 39–40.

28. In *Beyond the Pleasure Principle* (1920), what Freud finds beyond the pleasure principle is the death drive. Lacan likewise emphasizes the intricate connection between *jouissance* and death. At one point, for instance, Lacan states that *jouissance* implies "the acceptance of death," Lacan, *Seminar VII*, 189.

29. Lacan, *Seminar I*, 66.

30. Jacques Lacan, *The Seminar of Jacques Lacan, Book XXII, The Real, the Symbolic, the Imaginary, 1974–1975*, trans. Jack Stone (draft), Sessions of December 10 and December 17, 1974.

31. Jacques Lacan, *The Seminar of Jacques Lacan, Book III, The Psychoses, 1955–1956*, ed. Jacques-Alain Miller, trans. Russell Grigg (New York: Norton, 1993), 89–101.

32. Lacan, *Seminar VII*, 20.

33. One of the conclusions that presents itself here is that being moral means taking seriously one's *jouissance*, that is, the prompting of one's sexual desire.

34. Lacan, *Seminar VII*, 35–36.

35. Lacan, *Seminar VII*, 57.

36. For instance, Lacan says to the audience of his seminar: "You will not be surprised if I tell you that at the level of the *Vorstellungen*, the Thing [*das Ding*] is not nothing, but literally is not. It is characterized by its absence, its strangeness," *Seminar VII*, 63.

37. Lacan, *Seminar VII*, 61.

38. Lacan, *Seminar VII*, 59–60, 108.

39. Lacan, *Seminar VII*, 54–55.

40. Lacan also cites Claude Levi-Strauss in support of this thesis. *Seminar VII*, 67. See Claude Levi-Strauss, *Structural Anthropology*, trans. Claire Jacobson and Brooke Schoepf (New York: Basic Books, 1967).

41. Lacan, *Seminar VII*, 67–68.

42. Lacan, *Seminar VII*, 68. This is the reason why Lacan does not include the relations of psychotics among the four fundamental discourses (the discourses of the master, the university, the analyst, and the hysteric). See the discussion below.

43. Lacan, *Seminar III*, 44–56, 156–57.

44. Freud, *Three Contributions to the Theory of Sex*, 563, fn. 1. See chapter 1.
45. Lacan, *Seminar VII*, 98–99, 109.
46. Lacan, *Seminar VII*, 127.
47. Lacan, *Seminar VII*, 112.
48. Denis de Rougemont, *Love and the Western World*, trans. Montgomery Belgion (New York: Pantheon, 1956), 108–26. See also Rougemont's later book, *Love Declared: Essays on the Myths of Love*, trans. Richard Howard (New York: Random House, 1963), 30–31.
49. Lacan, *Seminar VII*, 145–51.
50. In his Heideggerian moments, Lacan hints that this relation can perhaps be seen in ontological terms as the link between man and *Sein*. Lacan, *Seminar VII*, 151–52.
51. Lacan, *Seminar VII*, 149.
52. Lacan, *Seminar VII*, 150, 163. For Arnaud Daniel's poem, see 162.
53. On the issue of the neighbor as a stand-in for *das Ding*, see also Lacan's reading of Freud's early work *Outline for a Scientific Psychology* in *Seminar VII*, 39, 51–52.
54. Lacan, *Seminar VII*, 179.
55. Lacan, *Seminar VII*, 184–86, 193–94.
56. Freud, *Civilization and Its Discontents*, 69–70. It is interesting to note that the remarks on the aggressive neighbor relation immediately precede Freud's critique of what he saw as the Marxist wishful thinking—a harmonious society. See *Civilization and Its Discontents*, 70–73.
57. Lacan, *Seminar VII*, 188.
58. Lacan, *Seminar VII*, 183–84.
59. Lacan, *Seminar VII*, 184.
60. Lacan, *Seminar VII*, 221.
61. Lacan, *Seminar VII*, 216.
62. In *Seminar XX*, Lacan defines the signifier as that which "produces a meaning effect," 18. Another definition of the signifier is that the signifier is that which "represents the subject for another signifier." Jacques Lacan, "The Subversion of the Subject and the Dialectic of Desire in the Freudian Unconscious," *Ecrits: A Selection*, trans. Alan Sheridan (New York: Norton, 1977), 316.
63. Lacan, *Seminar VII*, 219.
64. Lacan, *Seminar VII*, 313–15, 318–19.
65. Lacan, *Seminar VII*, 229.
66. Apropos this subject, see chapter 2 and Marcuse's discussion of hedonism.
67. Lacan, *Seminar VII*, 224.
68. Lacan, *Seminar VII*, 236.
69. Lacan, *Seminar VII*, 130–31.
70. This is one of Lacan's most famous puns. In spoken French, *nom-du-père* and *non-du-père* sound the same. See Lacan, *Seminar VII*, 65, ft. 3.
71. The set of identifications with ideals, out of which the imaginary is constituted, is possible only when others are seen as others. For something to be an ideal, it must forever remain other, located somewhere in the beyond.
72. A reminder that the real as the field of *das Ding* is the site of annihilation. Lacan, *Seminar VII*, 131, 233.
73. Jacques Lacan, "The Mirror Stage as Formative of the Function of the I as Revealed in Psychoanalytic Experience," in *Ecrits: A Selection*, 1–7.

74. Lacan, *Seminar VII*, 237. This is why Lacan states that the jealous subject, no matter whether or not his or her jealousy has an objective confirmation, manifests the symptoms of a pathology.

75. On this point, see Alenka Zupancic, *Ethics of the Real: From Kant to Lacan* (London: Verso, 1997).

76. Lacan, *Seminar VII*, 235. Historical examples offered by Lacan to illustrate what "a retreat from goods" looks like in practice are the Native American potlatch ceremonies and the feudal festivals in medieval Europe.

77. Lacan, *Seminar VII*, 216-17.

78. Lacan, *Seminar VII*, 248.

79. This leads me to think that Lacan's order of the good is comparable in meaning to Heidegger's conceptualization of inauthentic existence.

80. Lacan, *Seminar VII*, 254-55. Lacan gives Goethe credit for being first to have noticed this.

81. Throughout *Seminar VII*, Lacan also refers to the Marquis de Sade as the thinker who conceptualized the existence of such a space (the space of the second death) which he thought could reverse the functioning of the ever-repeating cycles of nature. See for instance the Sadean notion of the crime, Lacan, *Seminar VII*, 210-11, 260-61. For Lacan, the vicious cycle, which the carrying out of an ethical act is in the position to break, is that which has to do with the articulations of signifiers, not nature.

82. Lacan, *Seminar VII*, 261-62.

83. Lacan, *Seminar VII*, 272, 282.

84. Martin Heidegger, *Being and Time*, trans. Joan Stambaugh (Albany, N.Y.: SUNY Press, 1997), 150-156.

85. Lacan, *Seminar XX*, 30. As Lacan states, "I designate [the social link] with the term 'discourse' because there is no other way to designate it once we realize that the social link is instated only by anchoring itself in the way in which language is situated over and etched into what the place is crawling with, namely, speaking beings," *Seminar XX*, 54.

86. Lacan, *Seminaire, Livre XVII*, 11.

87. Lacan, *Seminaire, Livre XVII*, 19.

88. Lacan, *Seminar XX*, 17.

89. Lacan, *Seminaire, Livre XVII*, 18.

90. Lacan, *Seminaire, Livre XVII*, 31. See also Lacan, *Seminar XX*, 16; *Jacques Lacan and the Ecole Freudienne, Feminine Sexuality*, ed. Juliet Mitchell and Jacqueline Rose, trans. Jacqueline Rose (New York: Norton, 1982), 160-61, fn. 6. Mitchell and Rose mistakenly identify *Seminar XVIII* as the seminar in which Lacan elaborated his discourse theory.

91. Lacan, *Seminaire, Livre XVII*, 13.

92. Alexandre Kojeve, *Introduction to the Reading of Hegel*, ed. Allan Bloom, trans. James H. Nichols, Jr., (New York: Basic Books, 1969), 3-30.

93. It is important to keep in mind that Lacan pursues simultaneously the sociohistorical and the individual applicability of the discourse structures. This means that the master's discourse, for instance, has played a noteworthy historical role and is, in our contemporary period, being replaced by the university discourse. At the same time, however, Lacan also applies the discourse structures to evaluate ordinary

speech between individuals, or conversations between the analyst and the analysand during a psychoanalytic session.

94. See fn. 88 above.

95. In fact, Lacan suggests that the university discourse should be written as "uni-vers-Cythera," making a reference to Cythera, the legendary Greek island of voluptuous pleasures. Lacan, *Seminar XX*, 48.

96. Lacan, *Seminaire, Livre XVII*, 35.

97. Lacan, *Seminaire, Livre XVII*, 34-35.

98. Lacan, "The Agency of the Letter in the Unconscious or Reason since Freud," in *Ecrits: A Selection*, 147.

99. Lacan, *Seminaire, Livre XVII*, 24.

100. See Sophocles' last play *Oedipus at Colonus*.

101. Recall that what Hamlet really wanted to do was not to rule Denmark, but to study and teach philosophy.

102. Lacan, *Seminaire, Livre XVII*, 45-46.

103. The importance of such a practice is seen in that, for Lacan, "the only sense (i.e., meaning) is the sense of desire," that is, it is only through an understanding of one's desire that one can make sense of one's actions. Lacan, *Seminaire, Livre XVII*, 69. Once again one can witness Lacan's difference from ego psychologists who stressed the reliance on external factors to enable the resolution of neurotic tension.

104. Lacan, *Semaire, Livre XVII*, 35-36. See also Mitchell and Rose, *Feminine Sexuality*, 160-61, fn. 6.

105. Lacan, "The Subversion of the Subject," in *Ecrits: A Selection*, 322-23.

106. Lacan, *Seminaire, Livre XVII*, 53.

107. Lacan, *Seminaire, Livre* XVII, 76.

108. Those who would object to the use of a state of mind or a mood as the standard for the correctness of conduct need only recall that Heidegger considers anxiety as the *sine qua non* condition for the awareness of what it means to be authentic.

109. See chapter 10 in Levy-Strauss, *Structural Anthropology*, 181-202.

110. Note that the hysteric's questioning has nothing to do with biological confusion. It concerns modes of feeling and acting seen in terms of activity and passivity. Lacan, *Seminar III*, 170-80.

111. Sigmund Freud, *Dora: An Analysis of a Case of Hysteria*, trans. James Strachey (New York: Collier Books, 1963).

112. See chapter 1. Consult also Freud's articles "Some Psychical Consequences of the Anatomical Distinction between the Sexes" (1925) and "Female Sexuality" (1931) in *Standard Edition XIX, XX*.

113. Lacan, *Seminar XX*, 74.

114. Lacan, *Seminaire, Livre XVII*, 62, 89.

115. An extension of the same claim is that men can also speak the discourse of the hysteric. In fact, in my opinion, the task of psychoanalysis is to enable them to do so.

116. The sexuation graph as provided here is depicted in Lacan, *Seminar XX*, 78.

117. Lacan, *Seminar XX*, 76, 80. Just as the option remains open to all women to identify with the phallic function and block their own access to the "other" *jouissance*.

118. Kiarina Kordela is one of several scholars who recently argued that the upper portion of Lacan's sexuation graph genders or sexuates Kant's antinomies of pure reason. On this reading, the masculine side stands for the dynamic antinomy and the feminine for the mathematical antinomy. Briefly reviewing Kant, the dynamic antinomy stands for the situation in which two statements are logically true, but are not applicable to the same empirical world. In the mathematical antinomy, on the other hand, both sentences are logically false, since they presuppose that which is to be explained. Kiarina A. Kordela, "Political Metaphysics: God in Global Capitalism (the Slave, the Masters, Lacan, the Surplus)," *Political Theory* 27, no. 6 (1999), 794–96, 798–801. Compare my reading of the graph with Kordela's Kantian account.

119. For instance, the chaos of the pre-symbolic world populated with fragmentary part-objects and inundated with maternal sayings or whisperings.

120. This is why Lacan writes Woman only as barred. Lacan, *Seminar XX*, 80. See also Jacqueline Rose, "Introduction II," in *Feminine Sexuality*, 49–55.

121. In terms of the set theory that Lacan makes use of in his later seminars, the masculine is represented by the closed set, and the feminine by the open set.

122. Lacan, *Seminar XX*, 95, 126. See also Jacques Lacan, *The Seminar of Jacques Lacan, Book XI: The Four Fundamental Concepts of Psychoanalysis*, ed. Jacques-Alain Miller, trans. Alan Sheridan (Norton: New York, 1977), 185–86, 272–73.

123. Lacan, *Seminar XX*, 72.

124. In French, *"il n'y a pas rapport sexuel."* Lacan, *Seminar XX*, 34–35.

125. Lacan, *Seminar XX*, 144.

126. Lacan, *Seminar XX*, 145.

127. Lacan, *Seminar XX*, 45–46.

128. Lacan, *Seminar VII*, 112; Lacan, *Seminar XX*, 69. In other words, as Lacan points out, the troubadour says to his Lady, not "I love you"—*je vous aime*, but "I love to you"—*j'aime à vous*. Lacan, *Seminar XX*, 104.

129. See, for instance, Arnaud Daniel's poem. Lacan, *Seminar VII*, 162.

130. Lacan, "The Freudian Thing," *Ecrits: A Selection*, 128–29, emphasis mine.

131. On this point, see for instance Ernesto Laclau and Chantal Mouffe's arguments in their *Hegemony and Socialist Strategy: Towards a Radical Democratic Politics* (London: Verso, 2001), vii–xix. See also my chapter 5.

132. See the discussion of possibility in Michel Gelven, *A Commentary on Heidegger's Being and Time* (Dekalb: Northern Illionois University Press, 1989), 76–97.

133. Yannis Stavrakakis, *Lacan and the Political* (London: Routledge, 1999), 120–21.

134. Stavrakakis, *Lacan and the Political*, 73, 77.

135. I suspect this is done through the mediation of Ernesto Laclau and Chantal Mouffe, whom Stavrakakis quotes extensively.

136. It seems a misreading of Lacan to talk about the "lack" in the Other, because the lack presupposes the existence of a real or imagined totality, whereas what Lacan means is better conveyed by referring to the hole or the void in the Other.

137. Stavrakakis, *Lacan and the Political*, 107, 111.

138. Marx and Engels, "German Ideology," in *Marx-Engels Reader*, 160.

139. Marx and Engels, "German Ideology," 192.

140. Another concrete example of this way of life—coming from the sphere of the literary—is the life path of Zorba, the main character of Nikos Kazantzakis'

novel *Zorba the Greek*, trans. Carl Wildman (New York: Simon & Schuster, 1952). Especially relevant in this respect are Zorba's description of his numerous travels in Asia Minor and the trades/vocations he learned—"quarrier, miner, pedlar, *comitadji, santuri*-player, *passa-tempo* hawker, blacksmith, smuggler," 73. What I think is important to be notice is that Zorba never accepted to be defined by the single symbolic identity (i.e. blacksmith, miner, instrument player) that contemporary capitalist society considers a necessity for being thought of as an accomplished individual. A similar refusal to be contained (to fit in) and renounce the possibilities of alternative futures is found in the autobiographical account of G. I. Gurdjieff, a Greek-Russian psychic researcher and spiritual teacher. See Gurdjieff's *Meetings with Remarkable Men* (New York: Penguin, 1985).

141. See the work of Yugoslav philosopher Gajo Petrovic, who elaborates this line of thinking. Gajo Petrovic, *Marx in the Mid-Twentieth Century* (New York: Doubleday, 1967).

142. Marx, "The 1844 Economic-Philosophical Manuscripts" in *Marx-Engels Reader*, 92–93. Consider, in this respect, also Marx's claim that socialism "proceeds [in entirely unmediated way] from the *practically and theoretically sensuous consciousness* of man and of nature as the *essence*," 93. Isn't this a further confirmation of the emancipatory nature of Lacan's emphasis on desire and *jouissance* as the building blocks of an ethic?

143. See my discussion in chapter 5.

4

Post-Lacanian Theses

> If we made a psychoanalyst enter into the domains of the productive unconscious, he would feel as out of place with his theater as an actress from the *Comedie-Française* in a factory, a *priest* from the Middle Ages on an assembly line.[1]

> Let me tell you, gentlemen psychoanalysts, you are pitiful exploiters. You don't even have the daring, the inspiration, the joy, the energy, or the pride of your own phallocratic assertions and positions.[2]

In previous chapters I have shown in what way psychoanalysis can be considered a critical theory of society. I have demonstrated that the psychoanalytic understanding of ethics brings with it an impulse toward individual and social transformation and hence cannot remain indifferent to the status quo. I have argued that even those psychoanalytic thinkers whom some scholars have interpreted as apolitical or even reactionary, thinkers such as Jacques Lacan, retain a relationship to an emancipatory theory, which I have labeled the Liberation Thesis, that affirms its case and underscores its relevance and validity.

However, my line of argument remained essentially positive; I was interested in making the case on behalf of psychoanalysis in a way that accentuated its kinship with the philosophical tradition of critique and its commitment to truth, individual truth and the truth of the social world. This led me to postpone an extensive engagement with those who, though belonging to the same tradition, sought to point out the shortcomings of psychoanalysis, especially regarding its potential for social emancipation. My discussion of Wilhelm Reich is perhaps the closest I have come so far in disputing certain conclusions of Freud.

This is why this chapter is particularly important. Here I encounter those who claim that all is not well with psychoanalysis, that, in actuality, psychoanalysis is equipped with a conceptual apparatus that is either obsolete or ineffective in making any progressive impact whatsoever on the existing state of things. These thinkers discern a secret pact between psychoanalysis and forces that enable the perpetuation of the received individual and social reality. Indeed, they ask, to recall one of the opening quotes, what the priest of psychoanalysis is to do where the true possibility of revolt resides, where the production and creation of the new necessarily take place within a movement that shatters what is seen as psychoanalytic dogmatism.

If psychoanalysis, as I have conceptualized it so far, that is, as revolving around the axis of the Liberation Thesis, can be defended against those who refuse to link psychoanalysis and liberation, then it will be conclusively demonstrated that psychoanalysis is not yet another idealist belief system, deceptively seeking to offer, to paraphrase the early Marx, an imaginary consolation in the world's vale of tears. Instead, it will be seen that what psychoanalysis offers is a rigorous theory with practical consequences for individual and social change.

My choice of the critics whom I turn to in this chapter has been guided by the consideration that, having been schooled extensively in psychoanalytic thought, they speak to it rather than at it. In other words, they move from inside out, which is a procedure infinitely more akin to the movement of truth than is playing at being a disinterested observer or commentator who takes things "objectively." All three critics, Gilles Deleuze, Felix Guattari, and Luce Irigaray, have attended Lacan's seminars for many years and relate to conceptual issues that have arisen in those seminars.[3] This is significant because in this way the relevant intricacies of the psychoanalytic endeavor as discussed in the preceding chapters are brought into play once again. If the critique that I will examine in the following pages discloses a set of weak spots in psychoanalytic thought, then I hope that my rebuttal of it can seen as an affirmation that the principal thesis of this work is true; namely, that psychoanalysis, in its Freudo-Lacanian articulation, is in fact a critical social and political theory.

ANTI-OEDIPUS

Anti-Oedipus was the first collaborative work project of Gilles Deleuze and Felix Guattari. At the time of its publication, in the early 1970s, Deleuze was a well known academic philosopher whose interests centered on the radical, "heretical" strands in Western thought (Spinoza, Hume, Nietzsche, Bergson), while Guattari was a psychiatrist with an extensive record of social and political activism. These facts of their personal biography seem to me important because they provide an understanding of the context, the soil, out of which their collaborative work arose. Obviously those who define themselves as radicals will write a different book than those who identify with the status quo, even though the subject they write on is similar. Deleuze and Guattari were influenced by the events of May 1968, and, as those who sympathized with radical demands, they were taken more by their promise than by their failure. Their works, *Anti-Oedipus* and its sequel *A Thousand Plateaus*, can serve, in my opinion, as conclusive proofs of that.

Though my overall claim, as I have argued it in this work, does not differ in terms of its ultimate goal from that which acted as the mainspring of Deleuze and Guattari's thought, I find their work, their claims, their way of getting there, problematic. When compared with the interpretation of Lacan's work I offer in chapter 3 and the methodology and evidentiary basis of the theorists of the Liberation Thesis (chapter 2), their work, it seems to me, does not represent a step forward in terms of a more consistent elaboration of critical political and social theory.

In line with my priorities here, the portion of their work which deserves (and indeed requires) immediate attention is of course their attack on psychoanalytic theory and practice. After all, their work is entitled "anti-Oedipus," and they take care to portray Oedipus not only as one of the most recognizable psychoanalytic symbols (which it no doubt is), but also as synonymous with psychoanalysis itself. Their intention, as I see it, is to present the Oedipal journey (with its emphasis on subordination, guilt, and punishment) as the social fate of psychoanalysis. By doing so, they aim at disputing the credentials of psychoanalysis as critical theory and hence minimizing the possibility of its having anything worthwhile to contribute to the causes of emancipation. For Deleuze and Guattari, psychoanalysis is a product or an outgrowth of the forces of the status quo, and, through its conceptual apparatus and practical application, it augments and multiplies the hold of these forces over the individual psyche and its ability to imagine different social and political worlds. In other words, Oedipus restricts and limits that which is thought possible in the sociopolitical realm.

The principal claim in Deleuze and Guattari's critique of psychoanalysis is what they designate as psychoanalytic "familialism."[4] In other words, this is the idea that the institution of the family (the triadic structure of father-mother-child) represents a necessary mediation for the child's libidinal investments in social and political world. Its implications are that, in its adult life, the child never truly grows up, but continues to perceive all social relations as instances of the family dynamic. For example, the leader, the boss, the general, all stand for the father, while the love-objects substitute for the mother, and so on. According to this line of thought, it is then not surprising that the relations of submission and control are perpetuated in the society at large, considering that the patterns for such relations have been laid down by the libidinal economy of the childhood family triangle.

In contrast, Deleuze and Guattari argue that direct, unmediated libidinal investment in the social field takes place from the very beginning of child's life. They reject the idea of the self-sufficient, autonomous family as the primary determinant of the child's libidinal investments. In fact, they assert that the social is not to be seen through the eyes of the parental schema, but that the opposite is the case: the parental schema is to be seen through the framework of the pre-existing relationship between the libido and the social. In other words, the parents are not "the organizers" of the child's relations to society, but merely the agents used or made instrumental by society to bind the child's libido in a direction favorable to the status quo.[5] This means that Oedipus (the parental/paternal schooling of the child in moral values) should be understood as a derivative phenomenon that is bound up with the specificity of the given sociopolitical order.[6] In other words, one could imagine societies where the Oedipal problematic would not arise. Deleuze and Guattari claim that the psychoanalytic emphasis on the universality of Oedipus is motivated by an ideology that, in the final analysis, supports the prevailing status quo. By positing the necessity of Oedipal relations, psychoanalysis denies or represses the fact that these relations are grounded in a particular set of social and political relations and hence are contingent. In essence, what Deleuze and Guattari are saying is that the psychoanalytic "love of Oedipus" functions as yet another tool in disciplining the individual and making him or her an ideal masochistic subject of a repressive order.[7]

However, in order to understand the true object of Deleuze and Guattari's critique, certain distinctions need to be kept in mind. As I have elaborated in chapter 3, a kind of psychoanalysis supportive of emancipation, which, in my opinion, is Lacanian psychoanalysis, does not in any way support the masochistic or fatalistic attitudes on the part of the individual. On the contrary, by a way of the analyst discourse, it strives to free the individual from the imaginary and symbolic identifications that have caused him or her psychological anguish. In the course of a Lacanian psychoanalysis, the individual recognizes the ways in which a set of signifiers that had thus far structured his or her life could be replaced by the production of new and different signifiers.

Yet it must be noted that Deleuze and Guattari's critique is correct when applied to another branch of psychoanalysis, ego psychology, which has over the years become the major theoretical and practical orientation of the International Psychoanalytic Association (IPA).[8] As I have shown in chapter 3, the major premise of ego psychology is that in order to attain psychological well being, it is necessary for the individual to be fully integrated into and adapted to his or her own social context. In other words, ego psychology attempts to lessen the suffering of the individual by advocating conscious appropriation of the prevailing social and political values. Instead of facilitating the return of the repressed and in this way helping the individual remain faithful to his or her unconscious desire(s), the therapeutic aspects of ego psychology involve the presentation of a set of psychological modalities or attitudes, which define ideal personality types and which the individual is persuaded to identify with. More often than not, these ideal personality types reflect that which the dominant social forces consider ideal; they are the symbols of individual success as defined by the ruling elites, which for obvious reasons do very little to advance the cause of social change.

It is seems to me that Deleuze and Guattari's critique of the IPA as a conservative, even reactionary organization firmly supportive of the viewpoints that deplore the decline of Oedipal power in contemporary society is right on the mark. For instance, it is enough to peruse the work of Alexander Mitscherlich, one of the IPA functionaries, to get a sense of a very clear longing for the establishment of a paternal power that would guarantee stability and order in the midst of contemporary social and economic challenges.[9] However, sociopolitical views such as these, even though they are supported and perpetuated by the major institutional structures within the psychoanalytic movement are not representative of all there is in psychoanalysis. They are particularly not representative of the kind of psychoanalytic theory and practice that I am concerned with in this work. It is perhaps not surprising then that two psychoanalytic figures, whose theoretical frameworks figure prominently here, Wilhelm Reich and Jacques Lacan, have both been expelled from the IPA for not adhering to the dogmas of the psychoanalytic traditionalists, such as the belief in the paternal (Oedipal) benevolence.[10]

In fact, as I have argued in chapter 3, Lacan in particular has shown in what way the IPA leadership has failed to remain faithful to the essence of Freudian teaching. In a single swoop, the IPA has eradicated both the complexity of Freudian ethics and its subversive critique of the existing power relations. As Lacan indicates, perhaps the reasons for this withdrawal from the radical nature of Freud's insights are to be found in the existential situation of those who led the IPA since the death of Freud, most of whom were faced with the precariousness of their refugee status, whether in Britain or in the United States. In other words, in order to justify their utility to the countries that offered them shelter, these psychoanalysts shifted their analytic interests from the primacy of the unconscious desire and the Pleasure Principle to the primacy of the ego and its unproblematic relation to the Reality Principle. In this way, their work became supportive of the dominant political and social ideology.

However, as I have shown in the examination of Lacan's stands on ethics, discourse theory, and the logic of sexuation, Lacan has always resisted the pressures to assimilate his work to the prevailing sociopolitical elites. This is why I disagree with Deleuze and Guattari in their attempt to place Lacan in the repressive project supported by the IPA and articulated in ego psychology. As I see it, Lacan de-emphasized the importance that Freud and some of his early disciples placed on the actual family dynamic of a given analysand. For instance, Lacan's conceptualization of the unconscious involves not only the realm of the imaginary or fantasized daddy-mommy interactions, but also an additional realm, a realm inhabited by signifiers, in other words, by the products of a symbolic order that transcend any particular family. This is why Lacan would most likely not disagree with the claim that Deleuze and Guattari make to expose the failures of traditionalist psychoanalysis, namely the claim that the unconscious is "like an orphan."[11] Lacan's formula that "the unconscious is structured like a language" is, as I read it, the recognition of transfamilial influences that constitute the individual unconscious.[12]

Therefore, in my opinion, one of the principal questions that one should direct towards Deleuze and Guattari's *Anti-Oedipus* is anti *whose* Oedipus? There is no one universal definition or understanding of Oedipus in all of psychoanalysis. There is the Oedipus of the IPA ego psychology whose meaning in relation to social and political conformity is rightly pointed out and critiqued. In this respect, Deleuze and Guattari on one hand and Lacan on the other are in complete agreement, as Lacan's lecture on "the Freudian thing" testifies.[13] All three thinkers reject equating psychoanalytic praxis with a mere "familialism," with the moralistic narrative unfolding of individual parental dynamics. In fact, all three stress the relation of the individual to the symbolic order, of which the family is only one of many concrete manifestations.

However, there are two issues where Deleuze and Guattari's claims conflict with those of Lacan. The first issue has to do with the nature of desire, while the second deals with the relationship between neurosis and psychosis in psychoanalytic discourse. Both, as is clear, go to the heart of the psychoanalytic enterprise as a whole. The elaboration of these two issues leads Deleuze and Guattari to doubt the overall effects of psychoanalysis as the praxis of individual and social emancipation. What I will try to show in the following sections is that it is possible to defend the existence of a positive relation between psychoanalytic theory and practice and the requirements of a critical theory of society.

THE NATURE OF DESIRE

As I have demonstrated throughout the pages of this work, desire is one of the most important concepts in psychoanalysis. Though it is implicit in

Freud's work and explicit in Lacan's, both thinkers subscribe to the perennial definition of desire as a representation of lack.[14] In other words, they see desire as marking the presence of a certain sort of absence that motivates the striving of the subject. The shape of this absence is far from arbitrary, however. It is determined by the specific configuration of the imaginary, the symbolic, and the real orders in the subject's psyche. Lacan designates that which guides desire as the object small *a*, which he understands as the basis of transference in the practice of psychoanalysis as well as in the relations of everyday life. For instance, in the discourse of the analyst (see chapter 3), the desire of the analysand makes possible the work of psychological transformation. In other words, such a transformation, which in effect represents the ethical re-making of the subject, is put in motion by the reaching out of the analysand for the object *a* that he or she supposes is possessed by the analyst. It is thus by taking hold of the acquisitive nature of desire that psychoanalysis provides the framework for the possibility of self-knowledge. As Lacan repeatedly pointed out, the psychoanalytic question *par excellence* is "*Che Vuoi?*" which, translated from Italian, means "what do you want?"[15] What is to be noted is that such an understanding of the task of psychoanalysis remains consistent only under the condition that desire is defined as the presence of a lack.

However, in *Anti-Oedipus*, Deleuze and Guattari disagree with this definition of desire. In other words, they conceptualize desire as a productive force that is *sui generis*, that, in other words, does not depend on any external or outside condition to come into being. For them, desire is geared toward production and not acquisition, toward spontaneous creation rather than filling out of a lack.[16] They speak of the unconscious that knows nothing of the lack, of any sort of need that transcends its own powers of creation and experimentation. This unconscious is free to make or unmake social standards and values, political institutions, economic frameworks without being bound by anything in its past. In fact, the productive unconscious has no past (no accumulation of actually lived histories), since the idea of the past would entail the restriction of possibilities. As I will show in a later section, by attempting to disentangle desire from all social injunctions, by making it independent of existing sociopolitical configurations, Deleuze and Guattari hope to find a way out of the psychological phenomenon of masochism, of desire desiring its own repression, elaborated both by Freud and the Liberation Thesis theorists.[17]

However, as I see it, conceptualizing desire as a productive plenitude, a machine in the strict sense of a term, involves Deleuze and Guattari in a metaphysical commitment with far reaching consequences. In other words, it becomes apparent that desire as plenitude and desire as lack require rather different metaphysical supports which may or may not be compatible with a metaphysic required to ground a critical theory of society.

In other words, Deleuze and Guattari align desire not with the concept of becoming, as does psychoanalysis, but instead with the concept of being. For them, desire is not change or movement, but it is what it is, it produces itself by doubling or proliferation of itself. There is nothing "outside" of it; in fact, all existence is "the story of desire."[18] What may adversely affect critical theory in this definition is, in my view, that desire comes out as a static concept and therefore it becomes difficult to locate the emergence of anything radically new, or to find any standard that could distinguish the old from the new. In other words, if all history is the story of desire, how can distinctions and evaluations of different historical periods be made, especially in terms of their conditions being just or fair or equitable to those who lived through them? While I agree with Deleuze and Guattari that the most important task facing all societies (be they monarchical, democratic, or tribal) is how to make the desires of a collectivity support a given set of sociopolitical arrangements, it seems that defining desire as a ceaseless productive machine which never stops multiplying or proliferating precludes the possibility of using desire as a standard for evaluating the progress of social forms. In other words, if all there is in the social realm is always already a production of desire, how can we speak of liberation of desire in a sense that is not contradictory?

In this respect, I see a striking resemblance between Deleuze and Guattari's concept of desire and Nietzsche's will to power.[19] The attempt to imprint the status of being on becoming (to convert desire as becoming into desire as an instance of being) seems to have been one of the guiding ideas of Nietzsche's philosophy. However, as scholars of Nietzsche, including Heidegger, have shown, a theoretical commitment to the existence of will to power necessitates, in order to remain consistent, an equally strong commitment to the notion of the eternal return of the same. In fact, the eternal return of the same acts as the mode or manner in which will to power manifests itself.[20] This is so because will to power, just like desire in Deleuze and Guattari's sense, can neither be created nor destroyed but enters countless permutations in which its single (solipsistic) voice echoes forever.[21] In other words, whatever (I) was, comes again and again and its repetition represents the only possible form of eternity.

Why would Deleuze and Guattari commit to this metaphysical picture, considering the orientation of their stated political and social convictions? Why would they want to privilege repetition over change, being over becoming? Why the eternal return, and not the movement of changeable and discrete historical periods? Judging from the content of the section 3 of *Anti-Oedipus*, entitled "Savages, Barbarians, Civilized Men," Deleuze and Guattari do not want to dispense with the idea of historical changes altogether. But if that is the case, they do not explain what precisely motivates such changes (from barbarians to civilized men, for instance) if desire is defined as plenitude, as a self-sufficient machine. On one hand, what Deleuze and Guattari gain by this definition is, as pointed out above, the ability to extricate desire from being fundamentally linked to social mechanisms (Oedipus, for instance) and establish its spontaneous and self-sufficient productive character. On the other, they lose the ability to use desire as a standard to locate and distinguish the mechanisms of historical change. Their definition of desire cannot transcend a metaphysical framework that grounds it and, in the final analysis, gets trapped in the eternal return of the same. In contrast, since psychoanalysis starts with an assumption that desire is a product of the lack, it is able to explain historical changes by the differences in the object that desire was directed to.

On another level, if the goal is to develop a critical theory of society, a close resemblance between Deleuze and Guattari's concept of desire and Nietzsche's will to power ought to strike us as problematic. This is so because it is in the nature of will to power to consider itself self-sufficient, and, in its self-sufficiency, to want to set its own standards as it interacts with other wills, that is, it wants to dominate. The relation of one will to another must therefore take shape of a struggle, of a struggle for the control of resources of power. The consequence of defeat is the subjugation to the will that prevails. It is precisely an instance of the master's discourse as defined by Lacan. In other words, the weak, in order to survive, have to mirror the strong, to imitate or identify with the strong. Contrary to the spirit of critical theory, then, all that the weak can hope for is one day to replace the strong rather than to abolish the conditions of domination, of the division into the weak and the strong, altogether.

Such an authoritarian picture of human relations completely denies the value of individual subjectivity, of one's goal to be who one is, to remain faithful to one's inner demands, whether or not they are ordinarily considered "weak" or "strong." In other words, one is forced to identify with whatever is the dominant ideology of success in a given society. Those who do not subscribe to it are considered failures, cowards, good-for-nothing, intellectually inferior and so on. Unfortunately, as I have shown, this viewpoint has even gained a foothold within a strand of psychoanalysis, that is, in ego psychology where the analysand is compelled to identify with the ego of the analyst, of the respectful and successful ideal, Herr Professor Doctor. It is also unfortunate that in light of their definition of desire, Deleuze and Guattari come perilously close to this authoritarian picture as well. To say the least, their theoretical path crosses that of the most disastrous psychoanalytic practitioners, precisely the ones whom they had set out to critique in the first place, the infamous upholders of paternalistic Oedipus.

If, on the other hand, desire is seen as a relation of lack, if it is conceptualized in the manner of Freud and Lacan, then the relevance of desire for

self-transformation and social change seems evident. A desiring subject ($),
a subject who knows that he or she is lacking, will reject the (arrogant) self-
sufficiency of will to power. He or she will work to attain the object of desire (the object *a*) in a way that entails genuine changes in attitudes and behavior, if they are required for attaining his or her goal. Hence the
psychoanalyst, by means of transference, that is, speaking out of the position of the object of desire, will be able to motivate the analysand to develop a more clear-sighted view of his or her symptoms and of what can be
done to work them through. On a social level, the recognition of lack, of
the gaps in social structure filled up by fantasy, and the necessity of a desiring relation with the other can put an end to all ideologies that proclaim
the superiority of social and political status quo.

SCHIZOPHRENIA AS A MODEL OF EMANCIPATION?

In line with their understanding of desire as a self-sufficient productive machine, Deleuze and Guattari claim that schizophrenic, and not neurotic, discourse provides a useful tool in the arsenal of critical theory.[22] They see schizophrenic discourse as expressive of precisely this kind of desire and hence
able to provide for an opportunity to break the hold of existing political and
social arrangements in order to appropriate creative libidinal flows.

According to Deleuze and Guattari, the principal function of every political
and social system is to bind the productive capacity of desire (instantiated in
libidinal flows) and make it serve the system's reproduction; they refer to this
process as coding or territorialization.[23] The key question for them is how to
disentangle the flows of desire from such repressive or distorting use and
make them available for imagining and construction of different political futures, for the imaginary and symbolic orders of a new type of society. They
therefore depict their task as facilitating the de-coding or de-territorializing of
the actual applications of the libido. This of course is to a great extent the task
of all critical theory and as such fits well with the tenor of my work. However,
it seems to me that there are certain problems with the way that Deleuze and
Guattari tackle this task, especially in that their primary claim, on my reading,
is that schizophrenia (a form of psychosis) can serve as a valid model of how
to decode or de-territorialize the captured flows of desire.

This obviously does not mean that Deleuze and Guattari advocate that
everyone turn himself or herself into a schizophrenic in order to experience
the ultimate reaches of freedom and creativity. In their discussion of the psy-
chiatric literature on psychosis, they show that due to tremendous pain and
suffering experienced in schizophrenia, arguing something along those lines
would be tragically irresponsible. However, what they do assert is that one
can learn from the schizophrenic about desire in its pure, non-sublimated

state and, starting with this understanding or insight, begin to understand the genesis of each particular sociopolitical system. In other words, Deleuze and Guattari claim that the schizophrenic gives us an insight into the ground of that within which we live, and which, due to our non-psychotic psychological constitution, we are unable to see (considering that it is the condition of our "normalcy").

In order to gather evidence for this claim, Deleuze and Guattari refer extensively to the writings of various schizophrenic writers and artists, especially to those of the French dramatist and poet Antonin Artaud and the Russian dancer Vaslav Nijinsky. What they want to convey is, it seems to me, well articulated by a statement found in Nijinsky's diary. Nijinsky writes: "I am God I was not God I am a clown of God; I am Apis. I am an Egyptian. I am a red Indian. I am a Negro. I am a Chinaman. I am a Japanese. . . . I am husband and wife in one. I love my wife. I love my husband."[24] In other words, Deleuze and Guattari aim at bringing out the essential fluidity of desire and the contingency of its tangible manifestations and investments. They charge that psychoanalysis, by its insistence on the necessity of a certain standard or orienting point in the construction of identity (be it Oedipus in Freud or the Name-of-the-Father in Lacan), renders falsely the truth of that which it is supposed to uphold, namely, the truth of desire. This, according to Deleuze and Guattari, translates more or less explicitly into the psychoanalytic support for the codifying or territorializing hand of the status quo and hence taints its ability to provide a *bona fide* perspective for social critique. In other words, psychoanalysis itself is revealed as a discipline that needs to be superceded or overcome.

Schizoanalysis is how Deleuze and Guattari call their alternative to psychoanalysis. They claim that the critical potential of this approach far surpasses that of psychoanalysis, since it does not impose any pre-existing frameworks on that which the subject articulates about him or herself. In other words, its main premise is that the subject's identity is always in flux, that it "never stops migrating," and that therefore it should neither be associated with nor represented by specific signifiers.[25] Hence Deleuze and Guattari see the sole task of schizoanalysis as helping to de-code or disentangle the flows of desire, but delegate beyond its scope all normative assessments of desire's subsequent investments.

It is this absence of normative criteria that, on my reading, presents the greatest drawback of schizoanalysis. While it is true that Deleuze and Guattari's understanding of the function of schizophrenia resembles to some extent Lacan's conceptualization of hysteria, what schizoanalysis lacks, as opposed to psychoanalysis, (or what distinguishes the neurotic from the psychotic) is the presence and affirmation of an ethical relation to the other. In other words, schizoanalysis cannot offer a rationale for being (morally) good, that is, for behaving ethically towards others. In contrast, the rationale elaborated by psychoanalysis, which is embodied in the concept of desire aiming at *jouissance* is, as I have shown in chapter 3, constituted in close relations with moral law. The grounding of this rationale is only possible, however, under the condition that desire is defined as a relation of lack, which the other as the possessor of the object *a* (hence, of *jouissance*) appears able to fill. But, as I showed in the previous section, this is not how Deleuze and Guattari conceptualize desire.

It seems to me that ultimately the inability of schizoanalysis to establish and support a set of ethical rules is explained by the distinction Freud drew between the object-libido and the ego-libido.[26] For Freud, the predominance of the latter meant the presence of psychosis. In other words, the psychotic invests libidinally only in the relations of his or her ego with itself, and this is why he or she is able to mistake the world of psychotic creation for ordinary reality. At the same time, the psychotic cannot invest in the relations with others, considering that his or her libido has been taken back or re-invested into the ego, which makes his or her object-libido non-existent. This led Freud to doubt that the psychotics could be treated by psychoanalytic methods, since the mainspring of psychoanalysis, the functioning of transference based on the relation between the lacking subject and the presence of the object *a*, could not be established between the psychotic and the analyst.

Now, on my reading, the ego-libido as defined by Freud carries an undeniable resemblance to Deleuze and Guattari's understanding of desire as will-to-power. In other words, it seems as if, in order to carry out its tasks, schizoanalysis is called upon to make an impact on the analysand's ego-libido, that is, in the final analysis, on his or her will to power. Yet will to power, just like the ego libido, is characterized by an almost complete entanglement in its own (private, as it were) world. Therefore, it is impossible to make it shift its investments, unless one uses superior will, which means nothing else but the forceful imposition of a bond of subordination. If this is the case, then it seems doubtful that schizoanalysis can be considered more emancipatory than psychoanalysis, considering that the only way for it to be successful appears to be for the analysand to submit entirely to the will of his or her schizoanalyst. And even if one is to affirm the necessity and beneficial therapeutic results of this process, one will immediately have to face that perennial question—who educates the educators, or in this context, who schizophrenizes the schizoanalyst? Deleuze and Guattari, unfortunately, do not answer this question and, in this way, leave schizoanalysis without a sound ethical foundation.

INTEREST AND DESIRE

However, even though Deleuze and Guattari's work is open to critique in regards to the issues raised above, they sharpen focus on an aspect of social theory that, in my opinion, Freud and Lacan left insufficient clear. This aspect relates to the conjunction or disjunction of interest and desire within the political configurations of a given social field. A few examples may be of great help in seeing what is at stake here. Namely, let's imagine a person living close to the poverty line, whose interest is essentially one with those who struggle for a more just distribution of wealth, but who votes for or supports the party or parties whose principles glorify the promises of the status quo. In other words, this person's interest and desire work at cross-purposes; his or her desire is for things to be the same, while his or her interest demands changes. Perhaps this example more than any other depicts the situation of a skilled or semi-skilled worker in Western capitalism.

Or, on a more collective level, how about those social movements whose interest demands the breaking up of various hierarchies and systems of subordination, but which, once they attain a degree of political power, devise political structures and institutions no less repressive than those which they fought to replace? Was this not precisely the fate of the Russian revolution? Or, how about a converse situation where somebody who has an interest in the perpetuation of a given system opts to work for its dismantling? Here one thinks of the case of Friedrich Engels, for instance, and many other sons and daughters of the well-to-do parents who supported proletarian revolution.

These questions indeed pose a particularly important challenge to all critical theory and it seems to me that the most praiseworthy quality of Deleuze and Guattari's work is precisely in their having tackled them and having come up with certain interesting propositions. However, I think that these propositions can be integrated into a psychoanalytic critical theory and hence dispute Deleuze and Guattari's claim that they transcend the sphere of psychoanalytic concerns.

Deleuze and Guattari's key proposition in this respect is that they conceptualize the notion of interest as generated by the preconscious, while the notion of desire is rooted in the unconscious. In other words, one may change or claim to have changed one's interests, but if one's desire remains invested in the same objects or institutions, no true social or political change will be made.[27] However, this is not all, since it is at this juncture that Deleuze and Guattari make, what seems to me, their most imaginative move. They assert that not all unconscious desire is by definition radical or rebellious, that there exists a pole of desire which is actually supportive of the establishment of regimes or situations in which desire is repressed or sublimated. In other words, they divide unconscious desire into two poles, poles that embody two different configurations of desire, which they designate as the molar and molecular pole. In this way, on my reading, they move a step forward toward an answer as to why desire would tolerate or even be actively involved in affirming its own repression in the sociopolitical and economic sphere.

In fact, the molar pole of desire is the pole that pushes for the construction of stable identities and systems that block further possibilities of change.[28] Deleuze and Guattari describe desire produced by this pole as "paranoiac, reactionary, and fascistic," since it is here that one encounters that unswerving commitment to "the things as they are and have always been," which appears inexplicable in light of so much injustice and devastation. Here one also finds the source of a widespread psychological tendency to invest in one's national or class superiority and in the exclusion of those who do not belong to it, in order to affirm the certainty and stability of one's identity. The paranoiac desire puts itself at the center and relegates all otherness, all possibilities to be different, to migrate, to leave, and come back, to its periphery as something that is to be prevented at all costs. It represents the internal limit and hence the betrayal of all revolutions that resides in the unconscious itself.

However, to the molar pole supportive of the status quo, Deleuze and Guattari oppose the molecular pole of desire. This pole, which co-exists in the unconscious with the molar pole, produces desire described as "schizoid and revolutionary," since it invests in free, decoded flows, in fragments of identities and structures, in becoming a nomad, a proletarian, a member of a persecuted minority group.[29] In other words, here one sees desire that breaks through the established regimes and institutions and, in its push for creativity, generates new perspective and directions for living and being. The schizoid desire rejects the postulation of pre-established grand purposes and aims; it embodies desire whose essence is found in experimentation. It motivates experimental innovation not only in the limited sphere of *avant-garde* arts, but also in sciences, mathematics, technological design, political institutions, community programs, and so on.[30]

It seems to me, however, that this molar/molecular unconscious dynamic of desire does not represent so much a break with psychoanalytic theory as its extension into a realm of social theory left unexplored, to a certain extent, by Freud and Lacan. In other words, its efforts are oriented toward conceptualizing the relation between unconscious desire and the given elements of a sociopolitical sphere within which individuals find themselves (i.e., are born into). The existence of this dynamic affirms that the struggle for social and political change cannot be won on the level of interests (the region of the preconscious and the ego), since even at the level of the unconscious, its gaining of necessary support (that is, libidinal investment) is precarious. The unconscious itself is a site of struggle between the reactionary and revolutionary poles, and as such produces desire that can and does invest in its own repression, disciplining, and control. Therefore, the dissolution of the ego is not enough to assure the victory of a project for revolutionary social and political change; one also needs to find ways to take a stand against the fascistic unconscious desire.

As I have shown, both psychoanalysis and schizoanalysis facilitate the overcoming of the habitual libidinal dependence on the status quo and seek to neutralize fascistic desire that invests in its own repression. The only difference between the two is to be found in the theoretical justifications of the form and content of the techniques used. Psychoanalysis conceptualizes desire as lack and underwrites the model role of neurosis in understanding sociopolitical genesis, while schizoanalysis approaches desire as plenitude or will and considers psychosis as capable of accessing the most concealed deposits of social formations. As I have indicated in chapter 3, these psychoanalytic precepts allow its technique to position itself on an emancipatory ethical basis. However, as my discussion in this Chapter shows, its therapeutic companion, schizoanalysis, seems unable to subvert the determining role of the authority figure, the schizoanalyst, which weakens its claims for supporting the radical (anti-fascistic) transformation of values.

DESIRE AND CAPITALISM

However, there is one more difficulty that confronts critical theory when one stops to consider the involvement of unconscious desire not in some general or abstract social configuration, but in the actual socioeconomic configuration of the last decades of the twentieth century, that is, when one examines the relations of desire and global capitalism. Deleuze and Guattari hint at this difficulty in the subtitle of both *Anti-Oedipus* and *A Thousand Plateaus* which reads—capitalism and schizophrenia. From the discussion in the previous section, one can conclude that a truly emancipatory desire will possess a schizoid character; it will refuse to solidify itself in any system of rules and relations that does not allow for constant innovation, change, and experimentation. Now, what if a system of social, economic and political relations that we want to take a stand against possesses precisely a type of character that matches the character of that which we see as an agent of its possible dissolution? What if, in other words, capitalism is structurally akin to schizoid desire, or if, at least, it satisfies the cravings of this desire in such a way that it offers desire no motivation to advance beyond it? What if, in the final analysis (and to be more dramatic), capitalism is in fact the end of history, the end of the striving of unconscious desire for its concrete manifestation in material world?

The most pessimistic answer to this question would no doubt state that this means that the tools of critical theory (as discussed so far) are inadequate to deal with the complexity involved in that which would truly spell the transcendence of capitalism. This certainly would be the answer of those who are, for one reason or another, critical of or opposed to emancipatory critical theory. But, on my reading, paradoxically, even Deleuze and Guattari, in a certain respect, come close to agreeing with these critics. They detail the affinity of capitalism with schizoid desire, but do not show clearly how this desire is in fact betrayed by capitalism.[31] In other words, they demonstrate at length why one is to reject as repressive the codes or territorialities of Oedipus, but do not analyze the processes by which capitalism, in the midst of all its apparent decoding of codes and proliferation of inventions, also creates a set of repressive territorialities.

More specifically, Deleuze and Guattari convincingly argue for the illusory nature of "the mommy-daddy" model of psychological causation, but unfortunately do not take on with the same theoretical rigor the illusory promises of capitalist liberation of desire. The more or less brutal extraction of surplus-value, the unequal division of labor, the increase of cultural impoverishment, atomization, social isolation and other ills of capitalism remain in the background and are never fully brought to bear on the postulated similarity between capitalism and the libidinal flows of schizoid desire. Only when such by-products of capitalism are taken into consideration and their deleterious impact on libidinal unconscious investments accounted for, as is done by the psychoanalytically inclined theorists of the Liberation Thesis, can one hope to develop a robust theory and practice for anti-capitalist movements and activities.

PSYCHOANALYSIS AND FEMINISM

If psychoanalysis is indeed a critical social and political theory, as has been my principal task in this work to show, then it must speak in the name of all traditionally unrepresented social groups. Its discourse should raise, in a fair and deliberate manner, the issues of concern to all groups whose representation (or existence) is currently distorted or impaired by capitalist liberal democracy. In other words, psychoanalytic concepts and innovations must not to be prejudicial or biased in any way in their treatment of such groups. Along these lines, in this and following sections, I intend to show that such is the case with a psychoanalytic approach to the questions concerning the largest historically dispossessed group, that is to say, women.

As pointed out by many commentators, psychoanalysis and feminism have historically had an ambivalent, at times even antagonistic relationship. The early feminist theorists, such as Simone de Beauvoir and Betty Friedan, rejected psychoanalysis which they saw as yet another product of a patriarchal culture bent on subordinating women by making them uphold the dominant masculine social and political norms. Starting in the 1970s, however, with the works of Juliet Mitchell, Jackie Rose, Jane Gallop, and others, a certain sense of reconciliation between the two perspectives came into being, motivated especially by these works' explicit preference for Lacan over Freud, for Lacan who, as I have argued, integrated into psychoanalysis the philosophical "revolutions" of the mid-twentieth century (i.e., the linguistic turn, structuralism, French Hegelianism, and so on).[32] This meant that psychoanalysis and feminism were in fact found to be compatible and could work together in a theoretically fruitful way in order to enable the formation of new and different arrangements of social and political forms. This essentially is the thesis that I will try to uphold as well in my examination of the work of one of the most powerful feminist critics of psychoanalysis, the philosopher Luce Irigaray. I understand, however, that, considering the rocky history of the relationship between feminism and psychoanalysis, my attempt at reconciliation is likely be received with a degree of suspicion among the practitioners of either perspective. As Jerry Aline Flieger has said, a psychoanalytic feminist critic (which I consider myself to be) often finds himself or herself in a paradoxical situation of "simultaneously apologizing to other feminists for the use of 'patriarchal' theory and to other psychoanalytic theorists for the revision of that orthodox theory."[33] However, as Flieger's work testifies, this is far from a sufficient reason not to engage in this endeavor, considering that psychoanalytic insights make possible the articulation of the ways of thinking and being that carry the promise of universal emancipation from the miseries of sociopolitical and sexual oppression.

Hence, as I approach Irigaray's critique, my argument will be that psychoanalysis is feminist (in addition to being radical, which I established above), and that therefore there is no reason for any *bona fide* feminism to dismiss the potential of psychoanalysis to provide a conceptual toolbox on the quest for social and political equality. In fact, it may be that the demands of contemporary feminism are best expressed precisely through a critical theory rooted in psychoanalysis.

In my discussion, I will focus extensively on Irigaray's principal early works *Speculum of the Other Woman* and *This Sex Which is Not One*, considering that they formulate a precise and direct critique of psychoanalytic theory. The first part of *Speculum*, for instance, is a critical account of Freud's understanding of femininity, and *This Sex* is a collection of essays written in response to what Irigaray perceived to be deficiencies of Lacanian psychoanalysis. I will try to show that Irigaray's critique could benefit from a more nuanced treatment of both Freud and Lacan in that these two thinkers, for all their shortcomings, have not dismissed, or even remained indifferent to, the concerns of women. My larger thesis is of course that psychoanalysis and feminism can go together in their critical interrogation of the status quo.

SPECULUM OF THE OTHER WOMAN

On my reading, the aim that Irigaray pursues in *Speculum* is to expose Western philosophy as the project of a specifically male subject which left women unable to articulate their own identities and recover or understand that which they may be in their own right, that is, apart from how a male oriented discourse depicts them.[34] Irigaray argues that this male derived discourse of philosophy distorts and mutilates that which forms women's difference, so as to confine women to the order of the same, the allegiance to Oedipus, the dead father of the Primal Horde, the society of brothers, and so on. This discourse has conceptualized woman as "nothing but a receptacle that passively receives [man's] product," so as to deny or negate the possibility of any other discourse (for instance, the one constructed around women as active subjects and creators of the new) challenging its imposed superiority.[35] According to Irigaray, all existing societies represent nothing more than closed systems whose sociopolitical forms reflect the mirror image of their male makers, of their speculative and other activities, while the only female activity that receives social sanction is "the ceaseless 'activity' of mortification," the unyielding repression of all that might be uniquely feminine.[36] What do women in their own right have in contemporary liberal society, asks Irigaray? Certainly not the room of their own, for something like that would require (re)thinking woman as such, and ending her conceptualization as non-man. Irigaray stresses that woman as such continues to be perceived as the opaque substance, as the darkness that "replenishes" and elevates and grounds man. She is the holder of *his* place, and consequently can never have a place of *her* own.[37]

This is truly the other, the hidden, the *Unbewüsst* side of Western civilization which, according to Irigaray, received its first systematic elaboration concurrently with the birth of Western philosophy, with Socrates and Plato.[38] She argues that no theoretical endeavor since the time of Greek thought was able to escape the perpetuation of this way of thinking. This means that for Irigaray the assimilatory and destructive search for the same involving the rejection of genuine otherness is underwritten by the psychoanalytic project as well.

It is at this juncture that I disagree with Irigaray. In other words, it seems to me that psychoanalysis represents an effort precisely to free philosophical or speculative endeavor from speaking about woman from the abstract male dominated academic ivory tower since, chronologically for the first time in Western tradition, it incorporated empirical or analytical knowledge of and by women into its theory. One only needs to note the extent of contributions made to the formulation and clarification of key psychoanalytic concepts by Melanie Klein and Anna Freud, by Marie Bonaparte and Helen Deutsch, by Ruth Mack Brunswick and Jeanne Lampl de Groot, by Joan Riviere and Sabina Spielrein, and these are just several of the better known women psychoanalysts within Freud's immediate circle. It appears that at least at this admittedly general level, psychoanalysis could and did appeal to at least some women who did not see it as the brutal perpetuation of the male centered discourse.

More specifically speaking, however, it is true that some of these women analysts disagreed with Freud regarding his notion of female sexuality, presented in the most consistent form in his lecture on femininity in 1933.[39] I have also found Freud's conceptions lacking in certain respects, as I pointed out in chapter 1, and I plan to revisit my criticisms below. However, it is one thing to find some aspects problematic and quite another to reject or dismiss Freud's treatment of the subject altogether. Even though one may sympathize with the latter, if the motivations are sufficiently understood, I think that the former is a proper route to take.

For Irigaray, Freud's theories are undeniably phallocratic and below I plan to show how and why she has come to this conclusion. As far as I see this matter, however, I think that Freud's theories are open to both a phallocratic and a non-phallocratic reading, which is to say that to a certain extent they are ambiguous or heterogeneous. In other words, one can also offer the readings of Freud and Lacan that would be consistent with the conceptualization of psychoanalysis as critical theory. I think that Irigaray acknowledges this point implicitly by having some of her own conceptions grounded in Lacanian teaching. In my examination of her work, I will particularly stress such points of theoretical interrelation, because I think that they show that Irigaray's relationship with psychoanalysis is more heterogeneous that she is willing to admit. My rationale for doing so is the fact that it seems to me that psychoanalysis and feminism are compatible and directed at the same set of goals oriented around the improvement of individual and social well being for all. Rather than seeing these two perspectives as antagonists, I think that making an effort in trying to configure a type of theoretical arrangement in which they do work together is justified, since it can expose more strikingly the inadequacies of their common enemy, which is the exploitative and unjust social and political status quo.

IRIGARAY AND FREUD

The principal thesis of Irigaray's critique of Freud is that he has reduced feminine sexuality to a derivation of male sexual development. In other words, she argues that Freud takes male sexuality as the basic model of sexual development, which he then uses as a standard to understand and evaluate the vicissitudes of female sexual development. In this respect, Freud's statement that "the little girl is a little man" can perhaps serve as the best illustration of Irigaray's thesis.[40]

Irigaray interprets this statement from Freud's 1933 lecture on female sexuality as the most repressive distortion of the little girl's identity as a little girl. She asserts that Freud dismisses the uniqueness of the little girl's sexual path by equating her with the little man.[41] She reads this equalization as reflecting Freud's agreement with the dominant patriarchal view, which subordinates women to men and can conceptualize women's roles only negatively, as that which men are not.

I agree that this is a plausible reading of Freud's statement. However, I think that by making note of the context in which this statement appears in Freud's lecture, we may perhaps be able to come to a clearer understanding of his intentions. Of particular importance here is the sentence that immediately precedes the statement that "the little girl is a little man," which reads: "With their entrance into the phallic phase the differences between the sexes are *completely eclipsed* by their *agreements*. [And then] We are therefore obliged to recognize that the little girl is a little man."[42] In other words, the reason why the little girl is a little man is because, at the same time, the little man is a little girl. The agreements between the sexes are total; at this point, they are the same and therefore equivalent. Should we therefore not be justified in reading this as the repression of the little man's masculinity just as much as the reduction of the little girl's femininity?

It is true that Freud does not reverse his statement, that he only says that "the little girl is a little man," but what was in question in the lecture was female sexuality, not male.[43] So it seems that he could be granted the benefit of the doubt as to whether he really thought of female sexuality as a mere derivation of male sexuality. In addition, this statement applies only to the phallic stage of sexual development, whereas we are not told what takes place during the oral or the anal stage, which may presumably be manifested differently in the two sexes. And even if this were not the case, one would have to stress the provisional nature of Freud's conclusions, which he himself emphasizes in several places in the course of the lecture.[44] Perhaps Freud's statements in this lecture need to be taken as hypothetical and speculative, which more research into empirical facts and clinical cases may revise or even reverse.[45] In this way, perhaps certain nuances in the reading of Freud's understanding of female sexuality may emerge which would qualify his being seen as simply the follower and hence the reinforcer of the patriarchal drift of Western philosophy.

WOMAN'S ENVY

Though I see Freud as breaking with the patriarchal tradition of thought, I agree with Irigaray that Freud's account of female penis envy is not an adequate way to formulate the direction of the little girl's desire. In his work on feminine sexuality, Freud constantly comes back to this point, since he thinks it the best way to explain the reason why women abandon their primary love interest—the mother—in favor of investing their libido into their relations with the father and other men.[46] Indeed, for Freud, penis envy is the essential factor that carries little girls beyond what can be termed the primary same sex attachment to the object choice of the other sex. More specifically, once the little girl realizes that her mother did not provide her with a penis (as an instance of a thing that preserves the consistency of the body image), she feels betrayed by the mother, rejects her love, and directs her love toward the other parental figure—the father. The little boy, on the other hand, has no need to reject the love for the primary object, but, as a result, his relations with the father become problematic and permeated with the fear of paternal anger (which, as imagined, could lead to the loss of the penis, that is, castration). So, in other words, the entire early childhood dynamic, with repercussions for adult life, revolves around the issue of having or not having the organ called penis.[47] For Freud, those bodies that do not have it desire to fill their lack by finding substitutes in one way or another. In his account, then, in the paths of their sexuality, women are always in search of something that cannot be found or had. And it is here that, as I see it, Freud's account proceeds in a questionable direction and needs to be revised and, along these lines, Irigaray's critique sheds a helpful light.

For, here's the question, how can a mere possession of an organ make such a big difference and lead to such a great deal of value judgment? In fact, as I contend, taking a lead from Lacan, body organs, taken by themselves, cannot have social significance. At best they can be the signposts of individual (solipsistic) narcissism, which marks the order of the imaginary. In order to have a certain meaning in inter-human interaction, organs need to be symbolized. In other words, they need to enter the symbolic order of social and political discourse as signifiers. Therefore Freud is mistaken in his belief that it is the organ that counts in social relations; instead, what counts is the signifier—the signifier of sexual difference, the phallus (Φ).[48]

However, it seems to me that, in order to underwrite her argument about the psychoanalytic complicity in the perpetuation of patriarchy, Irigaray also reduces the phallus to the penis or, in other words, treats the phallus (a signifier) as if it were a body organ, a penis.[49] In a certain sense, she repeats the error of Freud, since, in critiquing him, she remains captured by the limits of his discourse. In other words, Freud's error is not primarily a biased, sexually reductive approach to analysis, but instead what I would call a biased level of analysis, that is, the reduction of the symbolic register to the imaginary.

In other words, neither the little girl nor the little boy (nor any human being, for that matter) possesses the phallus. The phallus, as Lacan points out, stands for the effects of language on a living being; it "designates *as a whole* the effects [of the signifier] on the signified."[50] It therefore cannot be seen as a sign of dominance of one sex over another; both sexes, insofar as they live within language (that is, insofar as the articulation of their needs is accomplished through speech), suffer and undergo the effects of the phallus. These effects are nothing else but the effects of the symbolic order, the consequences of humans being speaking beings (which Lacan designated as a pun—*parlêtre*).

While it is true that the masculine and feminine relation to the phallus differ (as Lacan's sexuation graph, discussed in chapter 3, demonstrates), on my reading, it is not true that the phallic signifier privileges the masculine relation over the feminine. This claim, however, is one of the most prominent among those advanced by Irigaray. She sees women as being debased and subjugated by the phallus, exiled outside its sphere of influence, and "condemned to psychosis or at best hysteria."[51] However, the opposite seems to be the case as well. Masculinity is also and perhaps even more strongly at the mercy of a phallic economy, considering that men are those who must live and enunciate their desires under the threat and hence the fear of (real) castration. In other words, though they do not and cannot possess the phallus, their status as subjects is constituted as if they had it.[52] This is essentially a delusion, a psychotic delusion, but paradoxically not without profound consequences for the fate of masculine sex.[53] Hence, in my opinion, Irigaray's description of woman as the one who "borrows signifiers, but cannot make her mark, or re-mark upon them"[54] can also, and quite legitimately, be applied to men who, guided by psychoanalysis, reject the phallic delusion.

The feminine, on the other hand, is to a certain extent free from this dynamic of fear, considering that one cannot be afraid of losing something one knows (i.e., is certain) that one does not have. This knowledge, perhaps precisely the kind of knowledge that propels toward the creation of new possibilities and fruitful exploration of human experiences, is firmly anchored in the feminine. As a result, it seems reasonable to conclude that psychoanalysis as interpreted by Lacan, far from denigrating the feminine, in fact, privileges it over the masculine. In a way, then, the relation of the phallus to the feminine seems less painful and less prone to engender conflicts than its relation to the masculine.

As I see it, this insight enables a proper understanding of Freud's remark about the feminine super-ego. Freud notes that women have "little sense" of the super-ego justice.[55] This sentence could be interpreted as an instance of male chauvinism, if the super-ego justice was in fact a good thing. But, as I have shown in the discussion of the ethics of psychoanalysis in chapter 3, the super-ego is a psychic entity whose intervention increases rather than diminishes the creative potential of the individual. In other words, the more the individual obeys, the more he or she has to repress, and the more inhibited (that is, alienated from desire) his or her behavior will become. Not speaking, or compromising one's desire is one of the attitudes most contrary to the general tenor of psychoanalytic theory and practice.

MOTHERS AND DAUGHTERS

Another element of Irigaray's critique of psychoanalysis concerns psychoanalytic understanding of family rivalries. Irigaray claims that psychoanalysis, in a theoretical move symptomatic of its male orientation, falsely constitutes mothers and daughters as rivals and, in this way, prevents their coming together into a united female front.[56] While the idea of a united front is an appealing one for the advancement of critical theory and practice, in this particular case, one needs to see whether perhaps this rivalry is not constituted by certain factors in the development of femininity. For instance, Freud argues that it would be difficult for little girls to develop a libidinal relation with a non-female object, if they were not harboring a great deal of hostility toward the primary love object, which is female, the mother. Hence perhaps the presence of hostility, animosity, and rivalries is necessary to establish the relation of the feminine to the masculine, however tenuous and prone to fragmentation and to reversal this relation may be.

Yet I wonder why this should be taken to mean that all love between the mother and the daughter is lost forever. Psychoanalysis, after all, does not recognize the sharp or binary differentiation of feelings into "either . . . or," but instead stresses their fundamental ambivalence. Hence in certain respects hostility is an underside of love, and with continued attention and communication between the two parties, there is no reason why repressed love, the love for the primary object, may not reemerge. In other words, once the traumas of childhood are put into words or signified, the newly formed signifiers may well rearrange existing relationships between the mother and the daughter. Hence rather than perpetuating the rivalry between the mother and the daughter, as Irigaray alleges, I think that psychoanalysis provides concrete tools for its eventual transcendence.

The other principal family rivalry—the one between fathers and sons—is not emphasized by Irigaray, perhaps because she assumes that all men, no matter whether they are fathers or sons, have a common stake in the preservation of patriarchy. However, it seems that the matters are not as simple, considering that in many of his works, Freud underscores the particularly painful conflicts over power between the father and the son. In fact, the murder of the old man of the Horde, which Freud marks as the origin of civilization (civil society) is, in the last instance, nothing else than a direct expression of the father-son rivalry. Hence, as I see it, psychoanalysis can hardly be a well thought out theoretical and practical tool for male domination, when it goes to such lengths to stress the fundamental nature of male-male hostility. Psychoanalysis does not present all men as united front, as Irigaray seems to imply.

On the contrary, as I pointed out above, I think that one ought to see the theory and practice of psychoanalysis as reaching beyond a mere stress on family rivalries of either kind by providing concepts and practical tools which enable the successful resolution and overcoming of such family dramas. In fact, insofar as one remains entangled in one's family situation and its determinations, one has, for all effects and purposes, failed to heed the key psychoanalytic precept—that is, the (conscious) realization of the content and direction of one's unconscious desire. Therefore, I think that one can locate psychoanalysis on the side of the child, the male *and* female child it should be emphasized, aiding them in their quest to understand the conditions of their own constitution as subjects of desire. This of course cannot but involve confronting both the conscious, but also and particularly so, unconscious desire of the parents. The desire of the mother plays initially a more important role considering the maternal prominence as the first love object and therefore the first (imaginary) other. This does not mean, however, that the role of the father is to be neglected, because the functional role of the paternal figure makes possible the constitution of the symbolic Other, that is, the realm of social and political interaction. In both cases, however, psychoanalysis elucidates the position of one's own mother and father in the wider set of structural relations between the other and the Other. The subject has to recognize the manner in which these relations relate to him or her in order to appropriate and hence enunciate consciously his or her desire.

Therefore, it seems to me that all family relations remain riddled with tension, and that the claim that psychoanalysis has a devious and unacknowledged stake in postulating the existence of hostility between the mother and the daughter is doubtful. Irigaray, however, accentuates this claim by arguing that the function of (postulated) hostility is to misrepresent the daughter's relation to the mother and, in this way, erase or obliterate the possibility of a harmonious relation to the origin (the mother) without the mediation or intervention of the masculine.[57] In fact, Irigaray claims it possible to constitute or rather re-constitute the relation between the mother and the daughter *as* women that would be free from all constitutive relation to the other sex.[58] This, in my view, is problematic for the fact that the daughter would not be able to think of herself as separate from the mother without the involvement of another figure, which, though not necessarily male or animate, is the bearer of the phallic signifier since it signifies difference to the mother-child dyad. Otherwise, as explained in chapter 3, the inability to separate from the mother results in psychosis.

It is not true that men are somehow freed from this outcome, either. Indeed, all men would be psychotic if all their life they loved only their mother. Psychosis is avoided precisely by the fact that this love is repressed into the unconscious by the intervention of the paternal figure (whatever this figure may be empirically) and the threat of castration. In other words, not only women, but men as well, have a problematic relation to their origin or beginning. Hence the claim that psychoanalysis confers on men a privileged relation to the origin put forth by Irigaray seems to me problematic.

MULTIPLICITY AND FEMALE SEXUALITY

Even though the general tenor of Irigaray's work is critical of psychoanalysis, one can still discern certain points of resemblance, especially regarding the issue of feminine *jouissance*. Here the question is whether there is a possibility of a unique feminine enjoyment that would, in certain way, transcend the demands of the existing phallic economy. This question is important because if there in fact exists such *jouissance*, it could motivate or underwrite the push for systemic changes in the social and political realm, since its very existence—beyond the Law—would expose the inadequacy of the present master-signifiers. Along these lines, in *Speculum* Irigaray refers to "the plural nature of woman's sex"[59] and opposes it to the singularity of masculine enjoyment. I will try to show that this reference is also not alien to psychoanalysis, which goes to show that psychoanalysis is not oriented toward the elimination of feminine *jouissance*.

In fact, Freud was among the first to bring into focus the existence of two sources of feminine sexual pleasure—the clitoris and the vagina. However, he emphasized the similarity of the clitoris and the penis and neglected to offer a sustained discussion of the importance of vaginal pleasures. I agree with Irigaray that this is one of the principal flaws in his work. Freud's work is incomplete, because it is necessary to offer an account that would elaborate the consequences of the plurality of women's enjoyment by theorizing the interlinking between the vagina and the clitoris. As I see it, solely stressing the undeniable similarities between the clitoris and the penis to the exclusion of vaginal enjoyment offers a very fragmentary picture of feminine *jouissance*. However, Irigaray is not alone in the effort to correct this state of affairs, since, as I will show, Lacan's sexuation graph also addresses the same point and provides for the re-thinking of differences and similarities between masculine and feminine *jouissance*.

The issue of being two rather than being one arises here both in its real and metaphorical aspect. In fact, both aspects converge when Irigaray writes of female genitals as "two lips in continuous contact. Thus, within herself, she is already two—but not divisible into one(s)—that caress each other."[60] For Irigaray, the fact of woman's two-ness makes her an alien or an outcast in a liberal capitalist political system, which is based on the counting of ones, of individuals, of their property and votes. If woman is counted as one, a part of that which she is has to be denied or repressed, and yet the status quo does not allow alternative ways of counting. Therefore woman is a born rebel; the fact of the existence of her multiplicity is a perpetual threat to the status quo. Hence, Irigaray reads Freud's stress on the clitoris as a theoretical move to protect the edifices of the status quo by making disappear that which is truly different and non-existent in the *one* of male sexuality, a pleasure akin to vaginal orgasm.[61]

However, I think that it is important to stress that woman is *both* one and two, which on the level of the body, entails emphasizing the complementary nature of the two organs in female sexuality. Both the clitoris and the vagina are of equal importance for that which means to be a woman and, in all likelihood, both types of pleasures complement each other. This is important because it allows one to theorize the woman's relation to *jouissance* not only as formally different from man's, but materially different as well.

One finds in Lacan a level of analysis that allows for the unfolding of the structural implications of this difference, and there seems to be a great deal of resemblance between his and Irigaray's conclusions. The only difference is to be found in the fact that Irigaray attributes more importance to the dimension of the body as a dimension, which she sees, to a certain extent, removed from the dimension of the signifier. For Lacan, the latter—the operation of the signifying chains—represents the only dimension in which the full impact of sexual differentiation can be embodied.

Hence Irigaray's statement that "men's desire and women's are strangers to each other" is a rough equivalent of one of the insights of Lacan's sexuation graph.[62] However, whereas Irigaray draws upon the dimension of the body to substantiate this insight, the Lacanian framework, while not denying the importance of unconscious identifications with certain bodily realities, stresses the primacy of the relation to language. This perhaps allows Lacan's account more flexibility for positing alternative outcomes, since the relation of human beings to signifiers is amenable to all kinds of political and economic changes. Hence, as I have argued in chapter 3, one should not underestimate the radical nature of Lacan's theory of sexual difference, particularly as it relates to the issue of femininity.

Lacan is just as convinced as Irigaray that if there is any possibility for the break with the status quo, it lies with the feminine. As Lacan explains in his sexuation graph, the feminine is constituted in relation to the void or the hole in the Other, and this constitutive feature leads it to the awareness of the artificial and provisional nature of any symbolic order and provides an unconscious impetus to draw attention to it. As I have stressed throughout this work, this is also a key feature in the constitution of the only possible subject of liberation, the hysteric. The hysteric, the prototypical split subject ($), demands to be represented by a given master signifier (S1), and it is only in this relation that a true subversion can take place, considering that imposing language on human beings is inevitable. Hence one can say that the feminine with its structural resemblance to the discourse of the hysteric is highly regarded in psychoanalytic theory. In fact, Irigaray's statement that the position of the feminine provides a glimpse into "a sort of expanding universe to which no limits could be fixed and which would not be incoherence either,"[63] which she considers one of the key points of her feminist reading, is entirely consistent with Lacanian formulations regarding the nature of feminine *jouissance*.[64]

IRIGARAY AND LACAN

While I try to stress compatibility between psychoanalysis and feminism, since I think that only in a combined effort they can provide a necessary critical potential for breaking through the liberal ideology of the status quo, Irigaray insists that the relation between the two is one of divergent aims and more or less explicit hostility. As I have shown, this reading is justified when certain aspects of Freud's understanding of femininity are considered. However, on my reading, Lacan has reconfigured these areas of contention in a way that makes it possible to speak of Lacanian feminism.[65] Hence I think that he has emancipated psychoanalysis from the charge that, as Irigaray claims, it reflects the centuries-old philosophical prejudice against women. In other words, in psychoanalysis the feminine does not occur "only within models and laws devised by male subjects,"[66] but is also conceptualized by male *and* female subjects with a strong commitment to the political and social emancipation of women.

Here I think one should consider the implications of Lacan's reference to the feminine as "the not-all" (*pas-tout*). As I see it, this reference underscores the freedom of the feminine from the dictates of the existing symbolic order. The feminine contains a structural link with a realm beyond the symbolic, with a realm out of which the new and alternative types of the symbolic can and have emerged. Hence it seems problematic to interpret Lacan's designation of the not-all as prejudicial to the status of the feminine. The position of the not-all does not translate into the position of "a lack, a fault or flaw," interpreted as something that is not worth anything, as a nothing that is to be discarded.[67]

This interpretation could only work if Lacan had been a champion of the symbolic order as it is manifested in contemporary social and political affairs. In contrast, however, Lacan spent a great deal of time in his seminars explaining the inconsistency and randomness of the structures and institutions of the symbolic (the Other). In this respect, his principal claim is that "there is no Other of the Other," that nothing could complete the void or the hole in the Other.[68] Hence to be the not-all from the standpoint of the symbolic is closer to the truth of the human condition than to be entirely enclosed by it, as is the case with the masculine. As the bearer of something that does not fit, the feminine is the pioneer of the new. Therefore, I would argue that Lacan's position regarding the feminine confirms the radical nature of psychoanalysis and its critical approach to the position of women in contemporary society.

In fact, psychoanalysis stresses that the feminine can and does transform the existing configurations of power and law. It confirms one of Irigaray's principal theses that "from a feminine locus, nothing can be articulated without a questioning of the symbolic itself."[69] This insight is precisely what Lacan underscores in *Seminar XX*. Hence, as I see it, transcending Irigaray's critique of psychoanalysis, there exists a set of common concerns and compatible articulations in both psychoanalysis and feminism.

There is, however, another issue that contains the potential of seriously undermining any collaborative relationship between psychoanalysis and feminism. This issue relates to the question as to whether psychoanalytic concepts allow for a genuinely transformative historical change. Irigaray notes that with his emphasis on structures and their representations in schemas, graphs, and pictures, Lacan seems to have downplayed the historical contingency of the human condition.[70] One could perhaps discern in Irigaray the echoes of anti-Establishment slogans of the May 1968 Movement. "Structures do not walk the streets" chanted the Parisian students, protesting the formalistic nature of academic philosophy and social theory. This charge of formalism assumes that structuralist explanatory frameworks cannot account for any dynamic political and social events. However, as applied to psychoanalysis, both Freud and Lacan stressed the dynamic nature of their conceptualizations of the life of the psyche and its activities. For instance, Freud justified it by reference to the vicissitudes of the drives, while Lacan stressed the lure of *jouissance* beyond any particular symbolic representation.

In fact, one needs only be reminded of Lacan's discourse theory, discussed in chapter 3, in order to see that Lacan assigned a great deal of importance to certain historical factors (the role of universities, the function of modern science and technology) in precipitating the emergence of the university discourse as the most dominant social link in contemporary societies. The fact that the discourse of the university was able to dislodge the discourse of the master as the prevalent social and political discourse clearly reveals that both are historically grounded. It also provides a justification for one of my key contentions that it is reasonable to believe that the discourse of the university, as worked-through by the discourse of the analyst, could be transformed into the discourse of the hysteric. This is very important because, as I have argued in chapter 3, the hysteric is the most appropriate contemporary heir of the Marxian liberated or free individual.

Hence I think it legitimate to conclude that the formalization of psychoanalytic theory does not stifle or distort the multiple and particular configuration of each subject of desire. Rather it enables the transmission of psychoanalytic teaching in a way that makes it more attentive to understanding the sources of unconscious determination; it establishes the ways of reading desire that can serve as useful pointers on the road to individual and social self-understanding. In fact, contrary to what Irigaray contends, I think that Lacanian theory underwrites her conceptualization of the unconscious as "the reservoir of a yet-to-come," as a source of new and different ways of shaping individual and social existence.[71] For instance, the articulations of the subject which is closest to the expression of unconscious desire, the articulations of the hysteric, show well enough the unexpected and surprising quality of unconscious formations. On my reading, therefore there is no basis for Irigaray's fear that psychoanalysis reduces everything to an endless repetition of the same within a system in which nothing can *truly* happen.

However, I agree with Irigaray that certain Lacan's students—the Lacanians of the second generation, let's say—have sought to hide their inadequate understanding of psychoanalytic theory by the unquestioned and repetitious invocations of Lacan's formulas.[72] This is an unfortunate, though not an entirely unexpected, development in the history of psychoanalytic movement. One needs only recall how the proponents of ego-psychology (many of them Freud's own immediate disciples, such as Heinz Hartmann and Ernst Kris) distorted some of Freud's most significant discoveries regarding the functioning of the psyche.[73] The implications of this phenomenon are clear: just because one has studied with Lacan or is certified as Lacanian analyst does not mean that the problems and contradictions in one's work stem from Lacan's own theorizing. The fault, manifested perhaps as a certain rigidity or one-sidedness in conceptual articulation, may lie with a particular interpretation, that is, with its pragmatic orientation, rather than with Lacan's theory *per se*.

Hence I would caution against Irigaray's approach to critique Lacan by critiquing the work of his students. For instance, regarding the issue of feminine sexuality, Irigaray offers a very incisive critique of the works by two Lacanian analysts, Eugenie Lemoine-Luccioni and Moustafa Safouan. However, she does not trace unambiguously a theoretical link between Lemoine-Luccioni, Safouan, and Lacan. Hence, the argument still remains to be made whether the problems of the former two stem from Lacan's own enunciations. I would argue that they do not and that, though a theoretical gap may separate Irigaray from Lacan's students, this is not the case when her and Lacan's works are put side by side.

In fact, if one recalls one of the main claims of Irigaray's writings on the feminine, such as, for instance, that it represents "a threat to every fetishistic economy," one will realize how close her own statements are to Lacan's understanding of the position of the feminine.[74] As I have argued in chapter 3, the feminine, for Lacan, is something that disrupts the network of the existing symbolic relations and provides for a possibility of the emergence of a new and different configuration. Lacan therefore is not and should not be thought of as an anti-feminist (or even as an afeminist) theorist. His psychoanalytic work stresses the importance of the position of the feminine in our indubitably patriarchal society and provides a coherent critical groundwork for a theory of social and political change based on the identification with the feminine (the not-all) attitude towards the others and the world. It is only from the standpoint of the not-all that we perceive or at least get an inkling of the beyond of our social reality; it is only in this way that the boundedness and arbitrariness of social reality come into view and become the material for thought and action.[75]

PSYCHOANALYSIS AND ITS CRITICS

My intention in this chapter has been to engage with those critics of psychoanalysis who disputed the status of psychoanalysis as critical social and political theory. The key criticisms of psychoanalysis came from what were essentially two theoretical angles—the Nietzschean-poststructuralist angle and the feminist angle. The Nietzscheans—Deleuze and Guattari—argued that psychoanalysis (both in theory and practice) remains bogged down in the liberal capitalist discourses of political, social, and economic power and that therefore its operation, far from breaking down these discourses, contributes to their perpetuation. However, I have shown that the form and content of the concepts of psychoanalysis as interpreted by Lacan reveals that their primary orientation is, on the contrary, to challenge the prevailing status quo by showing the contingent and arbitrary nature of its foundations. In fact, I claim that psychoanalysis is a more appropriate conceptual tool for understanding the tasks facing radical social critique than that which Deleuze and Guattari offer in its stead, schizoanalysis. This is so, because, on my reading, schizoanalytic approach to desire is unable to account for ethical relations between individuals (here one sees its Nietzschean heritage) and hence it seems to me problematic for imagining alternative political futures. Why would one need an alternative to the capitalist status quo, if that alternative cannot affirm a strong commitment to the well being of others? In contrast, psychoanalysis provides a basis for new non-capitalist ethic by its immersion to the sphere of the erotic, and by conceptualizing the relation with the other centered on the unfolding of *jouissance*.[76]

The second type of critique of psychoanalysis comes from a feminist angle, and its basic argument, exemplified in the writings of Irigaray, is that psychoanalysis advances under the banner of a patriarchal society and does nothing, or very little at best, to improve the position of women and rescue the importance of the feminine position in contemporary social and political discourse. As I have shown, this critique seems unable or unwilling to reveal the full potential of the key psychoanalytic notions regarding feminine sexuality. While I agree with Irigaray that Freud's theory of the feminine needs to be revised and supplemented, it seems to me that psychoanalysis—and this becomes particularly clear in the case of Lacan—assigns the feminine a particularly significant role in theorizing the nature of social and political change and the genesis and emergence of new, more emancipated forms of political life. Therefore, in contrast to Irigaray, I do not see the urgency of separating psychoanalysis from feminism and vice versa; in fact, I think that only a combined effort and mutual interdependence of these two perspectives can construct a challenge serious enough to affect the efficiency of patriarchal articulations.

After this theoretical engagement with the critics of psychoanalysis, I think that an affirmative answer as to the robustness of its critical commitments is difficult to avoid; at the same time, I hope that the rigor of these commitments stands demonstrated as well. As further investigations presented in chapter 5 will show, in my opinion, psychoanalytic theory in its Lacanian cast is the best and most appropriate model for contemporary critical social and political theory. It remains most faithful to the radical spirit of the theorists of the Liberation Thesis and, as I see it, its theoretical and practical contributions can rejuvenate, in the early decades of the twenty-first century, the failing project of the Left.

NOTES

1. Gilles Deleuze and Felix Guattari, *Anti-Oedipus: Capitalism and Schizophrenia*, trans. Robert Hurle Mark Seem, and Helen R. Lane (Minneapolis: University of Minnesota Press, 1983), emphasis in the original, 113.

2. Luce Irigaray, "The Poverty of Psychoanalysis," in *The Irigaray Reader*, ed. Margaret Whitford (Oxford: Blackwell, 1991), 103.

3. Gilles Deleuze, *Negotiations, 1972–1990*, trans. Martin Joughin (New York: Columbia University Press, 1995), 13.

4. They even borrow the term "Holy Family" from the early Marx's lampooning of the young Hegelians to expose to ridicule an implicit affinity between psychoanalysis and the (repressive) paternalism of Christianity. Deleuze and Guattari, *Anti-Oedipus*, 51–52.

5. Deleuze and Guattari, *Anti-Oedipus*, 91, 97. See also Gilles Deleuze and Felix Guattari, *A Thousand Plateaus: Capitalism and Schizophrenia*, trans. Brian Massumi (Minneapolis: University of Minnesota Press, 1987), 29-30. Note that Deleuze and Guattari's argument here borrows to some extent from Reich and Marcuse. See chapter 2.

6. In other words, the individual does not grow up (un)consciously supportive of authoritarian norms because he or she had a strict, unyielding father, but because he or she grew up in a society that conditioned the emergence of strict, unyielding fathers (and mothers who loved them).

7. Deleuze and Guattari quote with approval a fictional account of a psychoanalyst calling in the police (of course, the Establishment power *par excellence*) to throw out an analysand who became too inquisitive, who questioned the psychoanalyst's ready made answer: "It's your father no doubt." *Anti-Oedipus*, 56, fn. 1.

8. Deleuze and Guattari, *Anti-Oedipus*, 45, 80.

9. See Alexander Mitscherlich, *Society without the Father*, trans. Eric Mosbacher (New York: Schocken Books, 1970). See also the discussion in Deleuze and Guattari, *Anti-Oedipus*, 80-81.

10. See Lacan's own commentary of the event in Jacques Lacan, *The Seminar of Jacques Lacan: Four Fundamental Concepts of Psychoanalysis, Book XI*, ed. Jacques-Alain Miller, trans. Alan Sheridan (New York: Norton, 1978), 1-13.

11. Deleuze and Guattari, *Anti-Oedipus*, 49.

12. On the implications of this formula and its relation the subject of the unconscious, see chapter 3.

13. Lacan, "The Freudian thing, or the Meaning of the Return to Freud in Psychoanalysis," in *Ecrits: A Selection*, 114-45.

14. This conceptualization of desire goes back to the dialogue between Socrates and Agathon in Plato's *Symposium*. See Plato, *Symposium* in *Great Dialogues of Plato*, trans. W. H. D. Rouse (New York: Mentor Books, 1956), 198c-200c.

15. See, for instance, Lacan, "The Subversion of the Subject and the Dialectic of Desire in the Freudian Unconscious," in *Ecrits: A Selection*, 301-16.

16. Deleuze and Guattari, *Anti-Oedipus*, 25-26, 111.

17. Deleuze and Guattari, *Anti-Oedipus*, 61-62. See my discussion of Freud's *Group Psychology and the Analysis of the Ego* in chapter 1 and Reich's *Mass Psychology of Fascism* in chapter 2.

18. Deleuze and Guattari, *Anti-Oedipus*, 216.

19. Perhaps this is not all that surprising considering that Deleuze wrote one of the most influential books on Nietzsche in contemporary French philosophy. See Gilles Deleuze, *Nietzsche and Philosophy*, trans. Hugh Tomlinson (London: The Athlone Press, 1983). For an account of the influence that this book had on other French thinkers, see Paul Patton, *Deleuze and the Political* (London: Routledge, 2000), 1-11, 49-67.

20. Martin Heidegger, *Nietzsche, Vol. 2: The Eternal Recurrence of the Same*, trans. David Farell Krell (San Francisco: Harper & Row, 1984), 162-65. See also Ralph Harper, *The Seventh Solitude: Man's Isolation in Kierkegaard, Dostoevsky, and Nietzsche* (Baltimore: Johns Hopkins Press, 1965), 82-83, 91-98.

21. To emphasize the infinity of desire's permutations, Deleuze and Guattari quote with approval Nietzsche's pronouncement that "at root every name in history

is I," and Antonin Artaud's diary entry "I, Antonin Artaud, am my son, my mother, my father, and myself." *Anti-Oedipus*, 86, 15.

22. Deleuze, *Negotiations*, 23.
23. Deleuze and Guattari, *Anti-Oedipus*, 33-34.
24. Quoted in Deleuze and Guattari, *Anti-Oedipus*, 77.
25. Deleuze and Guattari, *Anti-Oedipus*, 81-82, 86.
26. Sigmund Freud, *Introductory Lectures on Psychoanalysis*, trans. James Strachey (New York: Norton, 1966), 517-25.
27. Deleuze and Guattari, *Anti-Oedipus*, 344-49; Deleuze and Guattari, *A Thousand Plateaus*, 214-21.
28. Deleuze and Guattari, *Anti-Oedipus*, 366-67.
29. Deleuze and Guattari, 340-43. In *A Thousand Plateaus*, Deleuze and Guattari describe the production of these two poles of unconscious desire as "arborescent and rhizomatic multiplicities," the former (the products of the molar pole) resembling the regularized, adaptive and generally predictable growth of tree branches, and the latter (the products of the molecular pole) resembling the anarchic and spontaneous growth of rhizomes/roots, see 33-36. On the concept of the rhizome, see *A Thousand Plateaus*, 3-25.
30. Deleuze and Guattari, *Anti-Oedipus*, 368-71.
31. Deleuze and Guattari, 372-73.
32. For an examination of the multi-level meanings of this reconciliation, see the articles in *Feminism and Psychoanalysis*, ed. Richard Feldstein and Judith Roof (Ithaca, N.Y.: Cornell University Press, 1989) and *The (M)other Tongue: Essays in Feminist Psychoanalytic Interpretation*, ed. Shirley Nelson Garner, Claire Kahane, and Madelon Sprengnether (Ithaca, N.Y.: Cornell University Press, 1985). See also Juliet Mitchell, *Psychoanalysis and Feminism* (New York: Random House, 1974).
33. Jerry Aline Flieger, "Entertaining the *Ménage à Trois*: Psychoanalysis, Feminism, and Literature," in *Feminism and Psychoanalysis*, ed. Feldstein and Roof, 185.
34. See for instance the essay "Any Theory of the 'Subject' has always been Appropriated by the 'Masculine'" in *Speculum of the Other Woman*, trans. Gillian C. Gill (Ithaca, N.Y.: Cornell University Press, 1985), 133-46. For a general introduction, see Margaret Whitford, *Luce Irigaray: Philosophy in the Feminine* (London: Routledge, 1991).
35. Irigaray, "The Blind Spot of an Old Dream of Symmetry," in *Speculum*, 18, 22, 111.
36. Irigaray, "The Blind Spot," 127.
37. Irigaray, "Volume-Fluidity," in *Speculum*, 227-28.
38. In fact, the last third of Irigaray's *Speculum* entitled "Plato's *Hystera*" offers an imaginative feminist reading of Platonic dialogues, 243-364.
39. Sigmund Freud, "On Femininity," in *New Introductory Lectures*, trans. James Strachey (New York: Norton, 1964), 113-34.
40. Freud, *New Introductory Lectures*, 118.
41. Irigaray, *Speculum*, 25-26, 48-49.
42. Freud, *New Introductory Lectures*, 118, emphasis mine.
43. As I have shown in chapter 1, Freud discusses the genesis of masculinity in *Three Contributions to the Theory of Sex* and the case histories *Little Hans* and *Wolf man*.

44. See, for instance, the last paragraph of Freud's article where he says that his account is "certainly incomplete and fragmentary." Freud, *New Introductory Lectures*, 135.

45. This also means that it is a mistake on the part of certain Freud's orthodox followers to interpret his conclusions as if they had the status of an unchangeable law. I am grateful for this point to Kitty Holland.

46. Freud, *New Introductory Lectures*, 125-26, 129.

47. It should be stressed that what is first perceived by the little girl is the rupture with the imaginary consistency of the body image (the absence of the organ) rather than the cultural valuation of this absence. An excellent study of this dynamic is made by Robert and Rosine Lefort in *The Birth of The Other*, trans. Marc du Roy, Lindsay Watson, and Leonardo Rodriguez (Urbana: University of Illinois Press, 1994). I owe this point to Ellie Ragland.

48. See Lacan's 1958 lecture at the Max Planck Institute on "The Signification of the Phallus," *Ecrits: A Selection*, 281-91.

49. Ellie Ragland, for instance, argues that Irigaray fails to "accept the structural effects and symbolic nature of the Lacanian phallic signifier," *Jacques Lacan and The Philosophy of Psychoanalysis* (Urbana: University of Illinois Press, 1987), 273-75, 279-81.

50. Lacan, "The Signification of the Phallus," 285, emphasis mine, translation slightly modified. In his lecture on science and truth, Lacan notes that the phallus "arises outside of the limits of the subject's biological maturation," see "Science and Truth," trans. Bruce Fink, *The Newsletter of the Freudian Field* 3, nos. 1 and 2 (Spring/Fall 1989): 23.

51. Irigaray, *Speculum*, 55.

52. The height of the delusion, which brings in its train scores of deplorable social and political consequences, is when men themselves believe it.

53. This delusion is, according to Lacan, brought into being by the all-encompassing character of the mother's desire (that is, the mother as the primary other). See my discussion of psychosis in chapter 3.

54. Irigaray, *Speculum*, 71.

55. Freud, *New Introductory Lectures*, 129, 134. In my opinion, Freud's account is always most problematic when he discusses the beneficial aspects of the super-ego. Both the theorists of the Liberation Thesis and Lacan speak, as it were, with one voice on this point.

56. Irigaray, *Speculum*, 79-83. According to Irigaray, this tendency is found not only in psychoanalysis, but also in other theoretical currents of Western thought.

57. Irigaray, *Speculum*, 83, 104, 106.

58. Irigaray, *Speculum*, 102-3.

59. Irigaray, *Speculum*, 103, ft. 107.

60. Luce Irigaray, *This Sex Which is Not One*, trans. Catherine Porter with Carolyn Burke (Ithaca, N.Y.: Cornell University Press, 1985), 24.

61. Irigaray, "Psychoanalytic Theory: Another Look," in *This Sex*, 41.

62. Irigaray, *This Sex*, 27. For a close discussion of Lacan's sexuation graph, see chapter 3.

63. Irigaray, *This Sex*, 31.

64. Irigaray, *This Sex*, 31.

65. See, for instance, the work of Juliet Mitchell, Jackie Rose, Ellie Ragland, and Jerry Alin Flieger.

66. Irigaray, "Così Fan Tutti," in *This Sex Which is Not One*, 86, emphasis in the original.

67. Irigaray, "Così Fan Tutti," 89.

68. For the most striking presentation of this thesis, see Lacan's "Subversion of the Subject and Dialectic of Desire in the Freudian Unconscious," in *Ecrits: A Selection*, 310–12.

69. Irigaray, "Questions," in *This Sex*, 162.

70. Irigaray, "The Power of Discourse and the Subordination of the Feminine," in *This Sex*, 70; also, Irigaray, "The Poverty of Psychoanalysis," in *The Irigaray Reader*, 79–81.

71. Irigaray, "The Poverty of Psychoanalysis," 82–84.

72. In her article "The Poverty of Psychoanalysis," Irigaray refers to the works of Eugenie Lemoine-Luccioni and Moustapha Safouan. See Eugenie Lemoine-Luccioni, *The Dividing of Women or Woman's Lot*, trans. Marie-Anne Davenport and Marie-Christine Reguis, (London: Free Association Books, 1987) and Moustafa Safouan, "Feminine Sexuality in Psychoanalytic Doctrine," in *Feminine Sexuality*.

73. Consider also the reductive (even naïve) "evolutionist" reading of Marxism found in the works of the early-twentieth-century theoreticians of the German Social Democratic Party, such as Kautsky.

74. Irigaray, *Speculum*, 117.

75. As Lacan pointed out in one of his last seminars, "If I had to incarnate the idea of freedom . . . I would obviously choose a woman . . . since they are not-alls" in Jacques Lacan, *The Seminar of Jacques Lacan, Book XXII, RSI, 1974–1975*, trans. Jack Stone (draft), Session of February 11, 1975. On the same point, see also Jacques Lacan, "Television," trans. Denis Hollier, Rosalind Craus, and Annette Michelson, *October*, no. 40 (Spring 1987): 44–45.

76. On the relation between the other and *jouissance*, see chapter 3.

5

Contemporary Lacanian Theses

The Liberation Thesis Revisited

> I would call "political" something that—in the categories, the slogans, the statements it puts forward—is less a demand of a social fraction or community to be integrated into the existing order than something which touches on a transformation of that order as a whole.[1]

> [I believe that] psychoanalysis is . . . able to provide the foundation of a new political practice . . . addressing the burning question of how we are to reformulate a leftist, anti-capitalist project in our era of global capitalism and its ideological supplement, liberal-democratic multiculturalism.[2]

As I see it, this is the task at hand: the articulation of a leftist model of social and political change in the face of the contemporary triumph of its perennial adversary. What I have argued so far is that psychoanalytic theory and practice have a significant role to play in the formulation of such a model. In chapter 3, I have shown that Lacan enunciates a discourse structure that can subvert the status quo—the discourse of the hysteric. In chapter 4, I have defended the radical potential of Lacan's against the critics who claim it is necessary to go beyond Lacan, to become post-Lacanian, in order to develop a program of action that takes seriously the eradication of political inequality and other social ills. All along, my principal aim has been to demonstrate similarities between Lacan's endeavor and the Freudian engagements of the theorists of the Liberation Thesis, whom I have discussed in chapter 2. My conclusion is that a contemporary leftist whose commitments do not differ from those of Reich and Marcuse would do well to incorporate the elements of Lacanian psychoanalysis into his or her overall radical framework. Moreover, I think that Lacanian theory can explain the past failures of the Left, while at the same time pointing toward a future that may bring about a different outcome.

For this reason, in the present chapter, I examine the contemporary applications or "uses" of Lacanian theory, especially as they relate to the question of how to articulate a realistic alternative to transnational capitalism and its political double, liberal democracy. I investigate the works of three well known Lacanian theorists, Slavoj Žižek, Ellie Ragland, and Alain Badiou, in order to provide for a setting that allows me to discuss, side by side, the project of contemporary Left and the insights of contemporary psychoanalysis. My intention is to show that the fates of both are irrevocably intertwined insofar as, in my opinion, psychoanalytic thought represents an indispensable facet of critical theory of society.

LACAN AND IDEOLOGY

Slavoj Žižek is a Slovenian philosopher whose fame in Western academic circles was sparked by the publication of a study of the ideological underpinnings of capitalist society.[3] Žižek begins this study by emphasizing that there is something wrong, something which does not fit, in the manner in which ordinary people relate to the reality of a capitalist system in which they live. Žižek claims that Marx's statement on the subject—"*Sie wissen das nicht, aber sie tun es*"—"They do not know it, but they are doing it"—illuminates quite well the paradoxical nature of capitalist ideology.[4] In other words, on a certain level, people know the arbitrariness of their social codes, norms, and values, but proceed to act as if they did not know. Psychoanalytically speaking, they disavow the existence of problems and inconsistencies in their reality, manifested, for instance, in terms of political alienation, labor exploitation, corruption, production of cultural trash, and so on.

However, this disavowal, which becomes the basis of social and political life in capitalism, is not without psychological consequences.[5] For instance, Freud argues that the structure of disavowal grounds perversity. In *Three Contributions to the Theory of Sex*, he shows that the pervert knows that the mother does not have the penis (or, in structural terms, that the maternal totality registers a lack), but continues to believe the contrary. This leads him or her to seek "to prove" the truth of that belief by libidinal enjoyment of a fetishistic object which is supposed to be able to fill the perceived maternal lack.[6]

In my opinion, this state of affairs may also provide an insight into Marx's insistence on "the fetishism of commodities" as an essential feature of capitalism. The reason that the individual derives enjoyment from a strong libidinal attachment to commodities, exemplified by the ideological allegiance to the pursuit of property as happiness, is that commodities play a role of the fetishistic object. Compensating for the untruth of disavowal, they prove the validity of individual belief in the consistent, harmonious nature of capitalist totality.

Hence it seems that, on surface, a classic Marxist approach to dealing with ideology is correct. Ideology is, in this view, nothing but a creation of "false consciousness," an illusion that dissolves as soon as people are shown the bias of their knowledge, as soon as a genuine relation to the "true" state of things is established. Yet, as Žižek shows, this approach implies that there is something behind ideology, that it is a kind of veil concealing a wholesome, pristine (unaffected) reality, now distorted beyond recognition by ideological functioning. The implication is that individuals just need to be enlightened as to what they are doing, and they will stop doing it. If, however, we examine the way people relate to certain social phenomena, we will see that this claim is problematic.

Žižek, for instance, focuses on how individuals in capitalist societies deal with that infamous commodity that establishes the relations of equivalence among all the other commodities, i.e., money. Individuals know well that money itself is a social construction, that it has value only within a specific social and political context and that it is nothing "real." In other words, if we were to follow the approach of classical Marxism, we would expect, that since they know all of this, individuals would become emancipated and reject a money-based economic system. But, instead, what do they do? They follow the logic of disavowal—"knowing very well, but. . . ." They live their lives and conduct themselves "as if money, in its material reality, is the immediate embodiment of wealth as such."[7]

I think that the same phenomenon is at work in the attitude that individuals have toward their political leaders. They know that the Leader (the king, the president, the general and so on) is a man like any other, yet they act as if he was the incarnation of political power. In other words, they choose to misrecognize the Leader's empirical reality as an individual by finding in him that which is "in him more than himself," that is, they identify his function in the symbolic register with the reality of his physical presence.[8]

It is precisely because one can know that money is simply a piece of paper, and the Leader is just an individual, and yet be unable to put a stop their paramount significance or, in words of Levi-Strauss, to their "efficiency," in ordinary social life, that one cannot approach ideology as a problem of knowledge or an epistemological deception. In other words, ideology is not an illusion, it is not something that hides or distorts something more complete or harmonious. On the contrary, ideology *is* complete and harmonious: it is a structure in which all lack is seemingly filled, and this is what makes possible its efficiency. This definition of ideology fits the structure of a specific psychological phenomenon, the phenomenon of fantasy, which is written by Lacan as $\$ \lozenge a$.

The completeness of fantasy is made possible by an apparent conjunction of its two terms: the lacking or divided subject ($) and the object-cause of desire (*a*), in which the subject finds something that promises to fill its lack or repair its split.[9] In capitalist societies, money is placed in the position of an object *a*, underwriting the fantasy of wealth as something through which an individual can reach ultimate fulfillment. Likewise, in the realm of politics, the Leader acts as an object *a*, and the fantasy that comes into being relates to individuals' feeling protected from potential internal and external enemies.[10]

What this ultimately means is that our social reality has the nature of fiction. This fiction is not simply an emanation of some more truthful reality, but is social reality itself. What is "false" about it is not that it stands in place of something else, but that it is consistent enough to be the only true reality. In other words, as Žižek puts it, "ideological is not the 'false consciousness' of a (social) being but this being itself insofar as it is supported by 'false consciousness.'"[11] If this is true, then critical theory is confronted with a very difficult question: namely, what is to be done, if ideology is in fact the only reality that we can know?

As I show below, there are four ways of dealing with this predicament, only one of which is, in my opinion, compatible with the aim of today's critical political theory, which is the revival of a Leftist project. As I see it, this "progressive" way of dealing with social ideology mirrors the "successful" end of a Lacanian analysis, which underscores the utility of psychoanalysis for radical thought.

TRAVERSING THE IDEOLOGICAL FANTASY: HOW NOT TO BE EITHER THE CONFORMIST, OR THE CYNIC, OR THE PERVERT

In a Lacanian framework, traversing the ideological fantasy implies the dissolution of the symbolic order by the refusal of the fetishistic object that sustains it, thus enabling the revelation of the disavowed real.[12] The real is the source of alternative political and other articulations, excluded in order for ideology, masked as objective social reality, to be consistent and operative. The inclusion of these articulations is both impossible and impossible to bear from the standpoint of the existing symbolic, since it entails the annihilation of its limits. The hole or void that Lacan discusses at length in *Seminar XXIII* is the principal feature of every symbolic, thus making of *being* a derivative of *non-being* or, in other words, revealing possibility beneath every actuality.[13] This is an insight essential for contemporary critical theory.

In order for the symbolic to appear complete and harmonious, the hole, which, in my understanding, marks the intersection between the symbolic and the real, has to be filled with the object-cause of desire, the *a*. The main function of ideology is precisely to provide an appropriate object *a*. The proletariat for simplistic Marxists, the Law for conservatives, the Nation for nationalists, Christ for Christians are all different examples of an object *a* that effects the closure of the symbolic circuit, and makes the respective ideology seem to possess a key to all sociopolitical mysteries. All are false, but not because they are unable to account for, and explain, phenomena within a specific symbolic structure, but because they, by structural necessity, must claim that they are *it*, the philosopher's stone, the Absolute.

Yet, the fact that one understands that social reality is an unfolding of ideology, a fantasy that has emerged through the presence of a contingent object, which is never *it*, does not mean that individual attitude toward such reality must inexorably acquire a leftist orientation. In fact, as I noted in the previous section, this orientation is only one of four possible attitudes.

The first possible attitude to the contingency of the object, which shapes a given symbolic order (i.e. reality), is defined by Žižek as traditional, since its most distinctive feature is respect for existing symbolic institutions.[14] In other words, even though the decisions and rules that these institutions are based on may be unjust or arbitrary in specific situations, this still does not justify the uncovering of their contingent grounding. The traditional attitude could perhaps be expressed as "I know that the Emperor has no clothes, but for the sake of social peace, I keep silent." Žižek brings up the example of Socrates who, though knowing well that his death sentence was unjust, refused to escape it. He argues that Socrates' respect for the institutions of Athens outweighed his interest in survival.[15] Another, perhaps a more appropriate example, is that of medieval Christian astronomers who saw the inadequacy of Ptolomeic system, and yet decided not to publicize their findings so as not to stain the authority of the Church.

The second possible attitude to the contingent status of object *a* is designated by Žižek as cynical. Here the individual has realized that the Emperor has no clothes (i.e., that the Other does not exist), but is using this knowledge, not to call for the re-thinking of the system's political foundations, but instead for his or her own benefit. In other words, the cynic is using his or her knowledge to fool and manipulate those who still believe. The case in point is Casanova who, in order to seduce a girl he had met, pretended to be a great magician who could materialize a rain storm at will.[16] However, when by accident the ritual succeeded and rain began to fall, Casanova was so shocked—his belief in the non-existence of the Other proved faulty—that he ran away in fear. In other words, the cynic can easily be converted back into the fold by a demonstration of "symbolic efficiency." Moreover, in contemporary political affairs, it seems to be a commonplace for the Leader to promise something to his followers in order to acquire their support, even though he himself does not believe in it. Hence the

Leader is revealed as a cynic who understands the fundamental incompleteness of the symbolic order, but refuses to share this insight.

The third attitude noted by Žižek seems to me to be an inverse image of the naïve, ordinary (empiricist) attitude that approaches the symbolic order as an unproblematic totality, where everything has its place "by nature" and from the time immemorial. A key feature of this attitude, designated as perverse, is a belief that since the nakedness of the Emperor is beyond the doubt, the individual can provide him with that which he lacks. In other words, the individual believes that through his or her actions, he or she can make the Other complete, make the Other really exist. Such a person makes him or herself into the object *a* needed to ground the ideological fantasy.[17]

This conduct, in which the individual presents himself or herself as the instrument of the Other is, in psychoanalytic theory, linked with perversion. Hence, in Žižek's view, all political systems whose structuring principle is the linear unfolding of a totality (such as Stalinism) are perverse. For instance, the Stalinist believes that he is facilitating that which the "objective laws" of history already decree. In other words, his activities are fulfilling the command of the Other insofar he is making it possible for the Other to actualize itself. The Emperor has no clothes, except the ones we can provide him with.[18]

It seems to me that one can discern this logic at work also in various Western "modernization" campaigns in other regions of the world. In other words, the logic of these campaigns was not simply cynical; it was perverse. Even though the "modernization" of these regions provided the West with a variety of economic advantages, what gave ideological consistence to Western campaigns was that they were embarked on for the sake of the "progress" of humanity and for the benefit of all concerned. Westerners were propelled by the belief that their values were unproblematic and their symbolic order without gaps and insufficiencies, while possessing material and other means to impose this belief on others. Moreover, as is easily witnessed in the accounts of World War II, the cynic is far less dangerous than the true believer.

I think that critical theory, as informed by psychoanalysis, must reject each of these three attitudes as unacceptable in dealing with the essential incompleteness of the symbolic order. Neither conformism, nor cynicism, nor perversion is a valid strategy for a critical thinker, when confronted with the hole in the symbolic. This is to say that the path of a critical thinker is the most difficult of all. He or she must not only reject the naïve, everyday understanding of the social and political world, but must at the same time reject all the apparent alternatives, too. In other words, the guiding light on his or her path must be the acceptance of being "non-justified by the Other."[19]

This means, first of all, the refusal on the part of a critical thinker to accept the consistency of any ideological scenario, of any existing political and economic reality. In other words, the awareness of the arbitrary nature of norms and values in the immediate environment must become an indispensable component of his or her theorizing. This is to be contrasted with a historicist move, popular in contemporary theory, which stresses a belief in the particularity of each and every universe of discourse (the discourse of Western capitalism, the discourse of Athenian democracy, the discourse of "actually" existing socialism and so on). This is so, because, as Žižek points out in his critique of two important proponents of historicism, Judith Butler and Ernesto Laclau, the acceptance of the truth of historicism limits the scope of one's radical activity.[20] One is confined to advocating changes only within a given political and economic realm (let's say emphasizing the expressive and inclusionary potential of global capitalism), but one does not have theoretical means to chart possible transitions from one realm to another.

It seems therefore that if one is a historicist, one is implicitly forced to accept that which one appeared to reject, namely that the Other has this Other, that this given symbolic order is self-sufficiently closed in on itself. In this way, historicism reveals itself as yet another (more complex, to be sure) ideological mechanism.

Hence, in my opinion, what seems a necessity in contemporary critical theory—if it is to reduce as much as possible the perpetually reborn ideological dimension of the status quo—is not only to direct its attention to the untapped potentials of existing political/economic/cultural configuration (historicism), but also, and more importantly, to think through the conditions of possibility for the emergence of such a configuration. In other words, what is necessary, and I am in agreement with Žižek on this score, is "to historicize historicism itself."[21] I think that this is precisely a theoretical space in which the concepts of Lacanian psychoanalytic theory can be of immense help.

HISTORICIZING HISTORICISM

Historicizing historicism is another way of designating the search for a principle that provides the structural conditions of possibility for a given empirical content to unfold. Perhaps the first example of this approach in social and political theory was Marx's claim from *Grundrisse* that production is not simply one element in the series "production-distribution-exchange-consumption" characteristic of industrial capitalism, but also and at the same time the principle that structures this series. In other words, the truth of capitalism is to be found in the relations and modes of production, even though production appears (from within the ideological field) as merely one of the component elements.[22] Another articulation of the same approach is found in Claude Lefort's emphasis on the distinction between "the political [*le politique*]" and "politics [*la politique*]."[23] In his formulation, the political is the condition of possibility for something like politics (political institutions, rules, and regulations) to be established. In Lacanian terms, then, the political is a way of articulating the revelation of the hole (or the void) in the symbolic that is subsequently filled with a new object *a*. It emerges in the periods of transition from one type of politics to another (from one "regime" to another), and represents the moment of "the impossible," where any symbolic articulation is possible, since, at this particular moment, the shapes of the future remain undetermined.

If the political is conceptualized in this way, then we can establish a structural similarity between its own constitution and Freud and Lacan's understanding of "primordial repression."[24] It is to be noted that here we are raising the level of abstraction: we are not simply asking about the constitution of politics (a given symbolic order), but instead about the constitution of the political, that is, the constitution of the constitution of politics. And here a fundamental question needs to be asked—what precisely is to be excluded in order for the political as such to come into being?[25]

The precise contours of this exclusion are something that cannot be known or articulated, considering that the exclusion concerns the order of the real. However, what the question itself makes apparent is that a symbolic form (the political) is also contingent. In other words, a contingent mode is not only to be ascribed to symbolic content (politics), which is what is done by historicist accounts. To be more precise, this means that our current global liberal capitalist constellation should not be seen as being susceptible only to a reformist spirit that strives to make its content more inclusive or livable. Instead, its very form should be conceptualized as something contingent that can eventually morph or coagulate into another entirely different symbolic form or universe, once that which it had excluded as its condition of possibility surges forward.

Therefore I think that it is premature to reject any social or political structure as utopian; what is truly utopian is to think that (symbolic) structures will remain the same.[26] Hence a model such as offered by Marx and Engels in *German Ideology* may allow us to glimpse (rather vaguely of course) a structure that could come into being with the re-configuration of the existing symbolic form. As a matter of fact, it seems that this particular structure implies the disappearance of the political as we know it: "society regulates general production and thus makes it possible for me to do one thing today and another tomorrow."[27] In other words, the perennial question of political discourse (in Lasswell's formulation, "who gets what, when, and how") seems to be resolved.

In contemporary political theory, Claude Lefort has chronicled a similar structural transformation in his studies of the transition between feudal and democratic conception of political power.[28] The feudal conceptualization of power posited the unity of the place of power (sovereignty) and the person filling this place. Perhaps Louis XIV's *"L'état, c'est moi"* should be taken as a prototypical articulation of feudal political power. In other words, the king as an individual was the only depository of state power; as Ernst Kantorowicz has demonstrated, the body of the king was in effect split into two: the empirical and the symbolic.[29]

However, through the experiences of American and French Revolutions, the place of power came to be separated from the person who would fill it. According to Lefort, this structural reconfiguration led to a democratic polity.[30] In other words, what grounded a democratic form of society was the idea of the exchangeability of those who held political power: they were conceptualized as being merely the representatives of the new sovereign, the people. The place of power was never again to be stitched or sutured to a particular individual; it was to remain "empty," filled only with temporary occupants.

However, the question of who the people (the real sovereign) were, of who it was that this abstraction included or excluded has remained far from resolved. In a typical liberal narrative, one sees a linear logic at work, which postulates that the concept of the people becomes more and more inclusive over time, until—at the end of history—all individuals are incorporated within a global democratic political order. What is particularly revealing—from a standpoint that seeks to show the collapse of a truly imaginative leftist political thinking—is that one can see the same ideological framework also in the work of those who are considered the representatives of post-Marxist Left, Ernesto Laclau and Chantal Mouffe.

In their widely popular book *Hegemony and Socialist Strategy*, Laclau and Mouffe argue, for instance, that the key contemporary radical strategy should be to take over or hegemonize the "empty" place of power.[31] Only in this way, they assert, will the groups, which are marginalized in the discourse of the status quo, see their social, political, cultural, and other demands met.

As I see it, the problem with this approach is that it leaves unquestioned the fundamental rules of a liberal democratic game.[32] In other words, it assumes that the liberal democratic Other has an Other, that it is a coherent political system that could resolve all its deadlocks and contradictions and, at the same time, remain structurally unchanged. It seems to me that what is implied by Laclau and Mouffe is that one could make transparent to consciousness all one's historical (unconscious) repressions, and still hold on to the set of signifiers that effected those repressions in the first place.

This illusion is contradicted by even the most basic insights gained through psychoanalytic practice. By integrating repressed signifying content, the analysand does not merely add a new outlet to his or her life, but instead retroactively re-works all that he or she has lived and who he or she has become. In a move that resembles the essential mode of Hegelian dialectic, the analysand posits his or her "own presuppositions."[33] He or she realizes that it is the act in the present that determines the interpretative significance or weight of the past, and hence, after analysis, the game is fundamentally different.

In terms of sociopolitical forms, one can perhaps discern the same logic in Rosa Luxemburg's arguments against the Social Democratic evolutionism at the turn of the twentieth century.[34] In her polemic with Eduard Bernstein, the chief German Social Democratic theorist, Luxemburg argued that it is a mistake to wait for the economic and political conditions "to ripen" in order to enact a socialist take-over. In other words, waiting for an appropriate moment means forever deferring the radical subversion of the act. To expect that the Other will change of itself is to overlook (or more cynically, to deny) both its fantasmatic or ideological consistency and its fundamental incompleteness.

These two complementary features of the Other can only be revealed by one's open confrontation with existing symbolic structures, by, what in Luxemburg's argument, is an act of socialist take-over which can retroactively re-write the past in the manner that is favorable to its success. In other words, the Other cannot recognize its own lack until the subject, through his or her refusal to play the game, forces it to do so.

I think that there is no better way to show the Other that its norms and rules are invalid than by being courageous enough to leap out of them.[35] What Lacanian psychoanalysis shows is that the risk that one takes by plunging into "nothingness" will not go unrewarded, since it will propel us toward new creations.[36]

Therefore contemporary critical theory must go beyond the question of how to make certain social, political, economic and other demands recognized by the existing Other, which is the Other of liberalism. As I have shown, such an approach cannot avoid becoming ideological and thus, in essence, conformist, no matter how strongly its proponents protest to the contrary. This is so because the Other that one addresses or recognizes is the Other in whose existence one believes. And if one believes in the existence of the Other of liberalism—which no doubt does have some psychological advantages—one will hardly be capable of formulating an alternative to it.

I think that an alternative to liberalism can only be constructed if one thinks through the constitution of this Other itself, that is, if one is willing to look for structural gaps in the fantasmatic coherence of liberal ideology. As I see it, this is not accomplished by the contemporary post-Marxist theory of Laclau, Mouffe, and Lefort, since their theorizing does not advance beyond the emphasis on the seat of political power as "empty," which is a principal characteristic of liberal democracy.

However, I think that one cannot make this claim the limit-horizon of one's approach, if one comes to it from a psychoanalytic perspective. A psychoanalytic thinker asks a further question, a question that reveals the provisional nature of any notion of limit. He or she seeks that which had to be constitutionally banished, primordially repressed, or foreclosed in order for the limit to be constituted. In the case of political power, for instance, the key psychoanalytic question would be something like this: what is foreclosed by having the seat of political power conceptualized as "empty"?

This seems to me to open a path to two alternatives. The first alternative would be the one in which the seat of political power is filled by an entity that assumes that it is equivalent with it. This is nothing but a feudal notion of political power, where sovereignty is deposited in the person of the king. For instance, in Hegel's *Philosophy of Right*, a constitutional monarchy is judged to be more beneficial than a representative democracy for the harmonious development of civil society. This is so, because the person of the king can act as an exception point whose function is to constitute as a coherent political community that out of which he is excluded.[37]

In other words, a feudal community is structurally more coherent than a democratic one. In fact, it reveals quite well the structure of the symbolic order in general, which in democracy is obscured to some extent by since a democratic system has no clearly discernible exception point. However, this is not to say that such a point does not exist in it, which seems to me a conclusion reached by those who argue that a democratic polity is a political panacea. In fact, the influence of this point, because it is hidden and easily overlooked, is all the more repressive.

What is to be noted here is that both democratic and feudal societies follow the logic of masculine sexuation, which, in Lacanian psychoanalysis, is a path that conceals the true nature of subjectivity and its relation with the Other. In other words, what needs to be accomplished is to theorize a social and political form that would establish itself in a logic grounded in the other side of sexuation, in the feminine. This is why I have stressed the conceptual importance of the discourse of the hysteric for contemporary critical theory. This discourse structure is the closest to that which both Freud and Lacan posit as the only path on which a subject can encounter its truth, the truth of his or her desire. As I have shown in chapter 3, the discourse of the hysteric shares with feminine sexuation the emphasis on the logic of contingency and incompleteness, the logic of the not-all (*pas-tout*).

As I see it, this is the second alternative to conceptualizing the place of political power as "empty." This alternative posits the existence of the place of political power nowhere, which means that the place of power would be found everywhere. This implies a more fundamental social transformation than that undergone in the transition from feudalism to democracy. However, the details of such a society must remain sketchy, considering that its logic differs fundamentally from the ones that we have known.[38] Perhaps the *jouissance* of mystics and artists might offer a glimpse into such a radically new social formation.[39] In my opinion, one of its key precepts would have to be that every activity, every mode of being, acquires a basis in supplemental, non-phallic *jouissance*.[40] Only in this way would the dispersal of power, where the given configurations of signifiers provide the determining point of the symbolic order for a limited time only, find concrete expression in daily life.

To hold that no activity (no signifier and no object) ever can provide for the adequate compensation of the void in the edifice of the social Other is the most recognizable characteristic of the figure of the hysteric. The hysteric refuses to be satisfied by structural necessity; he or she refuses to give unconditional support to that which determines any given symbolic order.

I think that the articulation of this discourse structure is what critical theory needs today in order to provide for an alternative to what Thomas Frank has called "market populism." This particular type of populism stands for the idea that a globalized market can provide the best possible framework for the realization of public needs.[41] As Frank points out, such an uncompromising form of market ideology has found its adherents in all major political parties, movements, and economic organizations in the First World (the global North, as is currently called). Its main promise is nothing other than an ever-lasting *jouissance* in the invisible hand(s) of the divine God, Business.

However, considering the escalation in the number and intensity of protests that follow the meetings of global economic and political elites, which temporarily brought to halt some major U.S. and European power centers (Seattle; Washington, D.C.; Genoa; Barcelona), leading liberal ideologues might soon see the real cracks in their media-constructed popular consensus on the virtues of unrestricted commerce.

It seems reasonable to expect that these protests, playing the proverbial role of the gadfly—the Socratic metaphor that fairly well delineates the situation of the hysteric—will at least to a certain extent challenge self-satisfied Western privileged minorities that have withdrawn into the "virtual" reality of their cyber-caves. Yet their success in bringing about the changes they demand will no doubt encounter what I would call "the rock of *jouissance*." What I mean by the rock of *jouissance* is the *jouissance* of a subject that the existing sociopolitical Other has been able to incorporate into its structures. In other words, the re-fashioning or removal of these structures leads to the loss of *jouissance*, and as such does not offer itself as particularly desirable to the majority of subjects. The key question is then whether Lacanian psychoanalysis can be of any help in dissolving this rock of *jouissance*, this *jouissance* captured or colonized by the Other. Or, put another way, can there be a *jouissance* in the activities of social and political change and if so, how to bring it into existence?

JOUISSANCE AND SOCIAL CHANGE

In one of his last seminars, Lacan says that *jouissance* is "of the real."[42] This is what makes it particularly difficult to affect the way in which *jouissance* is invested in the status quo, since there is no direct way to access the real. One can, in what is a typical psychoanalytic move, work through the symbolic to motivate the production of new signifiers which would in turn reshape the positioning of the object in the orientation of one's desire. However, this procedure will yield only limited results, unless the intricate relation between *jouissance* and the super-ego, representing the demands of the Other, is taken into consideration.

This relation is far from simple. Lacan rejects a simplistic schema, prevalent in some psychoanalytic circles, that the super-ego is the enemy of *jouissance*, or that there is an inverse relation between the two. In fact, he has shown that the super-ego of a given symbolic order remains the firmest agency of *jouissance*, the ultimate reference point of individual and collective enjoyment. As Lacan dramatically put it in *Seminar XX*: "The super-ego is the imperative of *jouissance*—Enjoy!"[43] In other words, it is one's duty to enjoy the received ways of living and thinking, one's nationality, ethnicity, language and whatever else forms the framework of one's life-world.

One can perhaps see in the fascist movements of the twentieth century the ultimate expression of this logic: the rejection of all Others that do not share the same signifiers and imaginary constructions, that do not enjoy as the fascists themselves.[44] It is worth pointing out that liberal multiculturalism also falls prey to the same (sadistic) logic in that only a superficial set of the features of the different Other (the symbolic registers of other cultures) is integrated into its structures, while the features that truly reveal the Other in its otherness are shunned. For example, the typical liberal capitalist subject enjoys Mexican foods on his or her night out, but votes to keep hundreds of thousands of Mexican immigrants deprived of basic social rights, such as a right to education and safe working conditions.

Hence what needs to be done is to disturb the harmonious ways in which *jouissance* has accumulated in the structures of the prevailing system. Once again I think that a reference to the interventions of Socrates is in order. As Lacan points out in his seminar on transference, Socrates claimed that he knew nothing except one thing, what it meant to know what love was.[45] In practical terms, this means that Socrates used his knowledge of love to provide his teachings with a basis that would be impossible or, at least, very difficult to overturn. Placing himself in the position of the beloved, of someone who seems to possess that which others are looking for (which we of course recognize as the object *a*), Socrates was able to make thematic (if not, to create) the gaps and inadequacies in the Athenian political and social system.

In this way, he was able to liberate desire from its being captured by the established ways of *jouissance* and set it on the paths of search for new forms. This is what made his presence in Athens particularly irritating to conservative defenders of law and order who conspired to get him arrested, tried, and executed. Psychoanalytically speaking, Socrates stood for desire that transcended the imperatives of the super-ego, therefore making possible the emergence of the subject ($) that refused to settle, not to rock the boat, to obey and enjoy.

As I have shown in chapter 3, the discourse of the analyst mirrors the Socratic attitude, or what, considering its transformative character, can perhaps more properly be called the Socratic act. In analytic procedure, we also encounter somebody who speaks from the standpoint of knowing something about love. However, the intent of the analyst is not so much the production of the lacking subject ($) as the production of new master signifiers (S_1, S_2, S_3, S_4, and so on) that can restructure the analysand's symbolic, and in this way affect his or her relation with the real, that is, with *jouissance*.

This then is precisely what we are looking for: the possibility or feasibility of dislodging *jouissance* accumulated in social and political structures. The analyst, by making desire emerge, stimulates the creation of new frameworks for the life of the analysand. In fact, as Lacan shows, there is a close relationship between the appearance of a lack and being active or creative.[46] Having been led to confront lack as the essence of being a subject, the analysand must symbolize anew, appropriating new signifiers and making it possible for him or her to minimize repression and denial.

In political contexts, leaders may be induced to play the analyst's role.[47] This is so, because they, just like the analyst, stand for the "subjects-supposed-to-know,"[48] those who, in the eyes of the public, have a certain something that makes them uniquely qualified for the role. This certain something, which inspires trust and commitment, is nothing else but the object *a*. As we know, however, thinking that a given person actually possesses the object *a* is an illusion, a lure. Yet this lure does not necessarily represent deceit. A lure can be used to motivate, to set one on the path of social and political change, and this is the use of a lure that I am aiming at here. Just as, in analysis, the lure of the analyst's knowledge makes the analysand create knowledge for him or herself, I think that the lure of the concentration of power can be used to put into effect its very opposite, the dispersion of power. This can be accomplished when—through the emancipatory activities of the leader or leaders—individuals realize that they themselves are the final repositories of power, the only genuine subjects-supposed-to-know.[49]

For this actually to take place, leaders need to develop a sense of responsibility for those who are inspired to love them. According to Lacan, Plato makes it clear in the *Symposium* that taking seriously this responsibility was very much the axis around which revolved Socrates' relation with Alcibiades. Likewise, since leaders find themselves in the position of the beloved, they are in the position to make demands and implement changes without much opposition. Their words and actions may inspire social changes of the kind that are necessary in order to establish a global community based on justice and fairness. According to Phaedrus, one of the interlocutors in *The Symposium*, the beloved who transforms himself or herself into the lover—substituting passivity for activity as in the case of a leader who returns genuine investment for what he or she knows is the product of a lure—earns the highest praise and admiration amongst the gods.[50]

I see no reason why these claims should be interpreted as the affirmation of charismatic leadership. In fact, what I affirm is a responsible, emancipatory, analyst-type leadership, not leadership based on mystification and cynical manipulation. I am aware that historically the vast majority of leaders have used special powers granted them by the public to further their own private interests, to play out their own (sadistic) fantasies of control and domination. However, this is not a reason not to try to devise a model of leadership that can work for its own eventual dissolution. I think that the leadership dynamic, as conceptualized in psychoanalytic theory, represents such a model and contains the promise for mobilizing *jouissance* for progressive political and social change, even if this promise has to a large extent been unfulfilled. I say "to a large extent" because it seems impossible to deny the fundamental nature of social and political changes brought on by, for instance, the figures of Socrates, Christ, Buddha, and other spiritual leaders.

LEADERSHIP AND THE FEMININE

As I see it, the leader is supposed to possess the object *a*, he or she is structurally located on the feminine side of sexuation. This means that in order to chart out the coordinates of the leader's activities, we can have a recourse to what Lacanian scholars have written about those who identify themselves with the logic of the feminine. One scholar in particular has written about the intricacies of this logic and I propose at this time to examine certain of her claims. Here I am referring to Ellie Ragland.

As has been noted in chapter 3, the designations of the masculine and the feminine in Lacanian theory do not refer to the facts of biology (or even of sociology), but to epistemological positions oriented around the void in the Other. Ragland argues that the masculine and the feminine are derived from attitudes toward two referents Lacan considered crucial for the development of sexuated subjectivity: mother's desire and father's name.[51] The symbolic and imaginary identifications that make up the masculine side of sexuation revolve around the signifier for the father's name (the phallic signifier (Φ), or the Name-of-the-Father). What grounds the masculine is the belief in this signifier's unproblematic nature. In other words, to believe that a signifier is unproblematic is equivalent to believing in its "existence," that is, in the possibility of its unmediated relation to some kind of substantive reality. In concrete terms, one can say that the public or the community that thinks that its leaders or its laws and regulations provide for the best possible world situates itself entirely on the masculine side.

However, as I have repeatedly pointed out, this thinking is faulty because a signifier can only refer to another signifier (which in turn refers to another and so on in an endless signifying chain) and therefore cannot provide for an one-to-one correspondence between the symbolic and what is "beyond" it. This, however, must not be taken to imply that the symbolic and the real are entirely unhooked, which would, incidentally, condemn us to subsisting all alone in a solipsistic, psychotic universe. Instead, what I want to stress is that the phallic signifier (no matter how it is embodied or incarnated) is only a pretender, an impostor, which plays the role of a unifying agency, but whose substantive nature can and does change, since it can never be *it*. For example, the transition from polytheism to monotheism or from one political system to another represents the change in the nature of the phallic signifier. Therefore, to think that the phallic signifier's transformation can come to an end is an illusion, and yet this illusion grounds the masculine position in sexuation. In other words, the masculine denies the possibility of the "rewriting" of the relation between signifiers and the real, which, as Ragland asserts, is the only true measure of social and political change.[52]

Now, we have reached a set of fundamental questions: how is this "rewriting" possible and what motivates its elements to shift from one incarnation to another? As I have demonstrated in chapter 3, to understand this, we need to understand the logic of the other side of sexuation, the logic of the feminine. Ragland argues that one can define the feminine position primarily in terms of that which it is not. For instance, the feminine set of identifications is not grounded in the One of the Name-of-the-Father. This means that the feminine position allows one to glimpse the existence of a certain supplemental configuration beyond the phallus (which Lacan refers to as supplemental *jouissance*). Hence one begins to see the presence of contingency constitutive of every political and social order. This *jouissance*, glimpsed in the beyond, is a motive enough for questioning the status quo and unveiling contingency. As I have argued, the discourse of the hysteric revolves around the search for such *jouissance*. The hysteric overturns the given in order to reach that which appears to him or her as *jouissance* not incorporated into the status quo.

Ragland speculates that the feminine position remains open to discontinuity in the status quo (in the symbolic), because of its relation to the mother's desire.[53] The feminine relates to the maternal desire in a way that is less prohibitory and restrictive, having been structured, to a greater degree than the masculine, around the pre-phallic, partial object-causes of desire (the objects *a*, such as voice, gaze, breast, and so on). These objects rupture the smooth surface of the symbolic exemplified, for instance, in the university discourse where nothing ever 'really' happens, since desire is engaged only in an abstract way.

Therefore the feminine logic of sexuation affirms the true structure of Other, marked by the void or the hole. In other words, the feminine reveals that the Other is, in its true nature, fragmentary, and that the function of every ideological fantasy is to make it appear complete and consistent. The feminine is particularly resistant to the fantasy of the Other without lack, which represents the essence of all totalizing world views.

If the figure of the leader is located on the feminine pole of sexuation, then it appears that this position enables him or her to see through the illusionary coherence of any social or political order. It is true that the leader can react to this knowledge in different ways: he or she can cynically continue to perpetuate the illusion or, in a perverse mode, try to make it into the true reality, and so on. However, as I see it, the only leadership attitude that contemporary critical theory can support is that of sharing the knowledge of the void in the Other with those who, for one reason or another, are unable to notice it.[54]

The leader therefore needs to orient himself or herself along the lines of the analyst discourse, since only the analyst's discourse has at its disposal means to transform a typical liberal subject, constructed along the lines of the university discourse, into the hysteric. This is important, because the hysteric can be described as somebody who, to paraphrase Marcuse's definition of the dialectical process, negates what is, so that what might be can come into existence.

THE HYSTERIC REVISITED

This allegiance of the hysteric to subversion of the status quo, to "placing the question where an answer had previously stopped up any knowledge of lack,"[55] makes him or her, as I argued in chapters 3 and 4, the only genuine agent of contemporary critical theory, if this theory still aims at the Liberation Thesis, i.e., drawing up political and social futures distinct from capitalism (chapter 2). The discourse structure of the hysteric motivates new relations between signifiers and signifieds and, in this way, drives the processes of change. Perhaps one can approach here that puzzling question—what, if anything, can finally satisfy the hysteric? The answer is nothing, except the possibility of trying yet another mode of satisfaction. The hysteric is not satisfied by contemporary constellation of consumerist capitalism, since consumerism does not provide for *jouissance* that breaks out of the framework of the status quo.[56]

One can anticipate the reaction of critics who would see a community of hysterics as permeated by anarchy, perhaps even violent anarchy. These critics see a Hobbesian world of inner impulses translated into the law of the stronger, into might that makes right. But a quick look at the structure of the hysteric discourse should be enough to dispel such fears.[57] There is no doubt that the hysteric is a subversive, somebody who questions the foundations of a given master-signifier (S1), but he or she does so in a way that precludes a violent action accompanying the subversive gesture.[58] The truth of the hysteric's action is contained in the object *a*, the object-cause of desire. The hysteric is perceived by its Other as the holder of this precious object, and therefore as a person whose approving recognition is indispensable. As a result, the hysteric addresses the Other in such a way that the Other is compelled not to retaliate, but instead to produce knowledge (S2), to produce something new that can conceivably address the hysteric's desire. Perhaps, then, one can say that the hysteric's desire perplexes the forces of the status quo by making them confront the fact that there is something beyond, something that needs to be addressed that is not included within the existing universe of discourse, while it, at the same time, limits their reaction in a way that leaves them more or less disarmed.

The only response available to the Other is to produce more signifiers (S2) in the hope that this production will quiet down the hysteric's desire. As we know, this expectation is illusory and its outcome, rather than disposing of the hysteric, disposes of the Other itself.[59] Namely, the presence of more signifiers affects the consistency of a given symbolic order, since there are now more ways (more perspectives) to approach the same social or political issues. In other words, chances increase that some other signifier (a newly created signifier) may displace the one that has oriented the sociopolitical order up until then. In individual analysis, which signifier this will be depends primarily on working out the transference relation with the analyst. In political affairs, as I have stressed already, the qualities of leadership hold a key to successful transformations.

What is also important to keep in mind is that the newly created signifiers (S2) do not only refer to the hysteric's situation, but, transcending the particularity of the hysteric who called them into being, make a claim to universality. In other words, in confronting the Other with its own lack, the hysteric acts on behalf of all those who have been affected by the Other in a negative way. The hysteric takes up the banner of those excluded, of those whose existence throws into doubt the seemingly harmonious processes of the status quo, that is, of those who are unaccounted for by the logic of a given master-signifier. The hysteric demands the inclusion of such individuals and groups, which, if it is to happen, involves not only the restructuring of particular political outcomes, but also of the political framework itself.

MULTICULTURALISM AND ITS DISCONTENTS

It seems to me that one of the key problems with contemporary liberal multiculturalism is that it cannot incorporate the universalizing dimension of the hysteric's discourse. In other words, in a contemporary liberal universe, every group and subgroup is encouraged to assert its own particular identity against the others, but at the price of not being able to show how its particular struggle relates to fundamental questioning of the very order that is supposed to grant its demands.[60] The principle underlying group recognition in liberal democracy is accommodation with the given order rather than the re-evaluation of its mode of being. For example, ecological protest to save the whales is typically confined only to its one particularistic demand and once the officials address this demand, once they promise that whales will not be harmed, the protesters go home.

What is lost in this kind of protest is the universal dimension that could connect the threat to whales to a set of other issues generated by the globalization of capitalism (undocumented immigrants, human rights violations by the Third-World corporate contractors, ghettoization of inner cities in the West, casual and seasonal employment without social benefits, and the list goes on and on). By concentrating on piecemeal effects rather than the overall causes of environmental degradation, the impetus for genuine social and political change dissolves into a multiplicity of issue-specific movements, which the officials of the status quo skillfully play off one against another. In this respect, consider, for instance, the familiar neo-populist argument in Western liberal democracies that there is no money for the health services for migrant workers, because it needs to go to the disadvantaged citizens in the countries themselves.

The same failure to universalize is found in multicultural "identity politics." The fundamental motivation of identity politics is the recognition of one's ethnic or sexual identity by the given status quo, but such demands cannot be made except according to the terms and rules of the system. In other words, one cannot expect identity politics to give voice to or articulate a true parting of the ways with capitalism. In fact, as Žižek points out, identity politics is, in this sense, hardly "political" at all, since it neutralizes the possibility of a true shift in the existing system, a shift which would make superfluous the divisions and subdivisions of the system's categories.[61]

The fact that identity politics, grounded in liberal theory, fails to provide a Kantian perpetual peace (contrary to the claims of its proponents) is shown in the recent global emergence of violent fundamentalist movements under the guise of ethnic and religious nationalism. I would claim that these expressions of brutal nationalism and xenophobia are connected to the general spirit of the liberal discourse, even though, on surface, the parallel between the two appears inconceivable. According to one of Lacan's key formulations, what is foreclosed (made impossible) in the symbolic returns in the real, and so one can interpret the outbreaks of ethnic or religious nationalism in the First and the Third World as the hidden underside of liberal multiculturalist position.[62]

In other words, this means that the question, whether multiculturalism genuinely respects the difference of the Other, is answered negatively. What is respected and cherished in this discourse is the Other, idealized and cleansed of its problematic, real elements (for instance, of the way those who belong to this Other take or receive their *jouissance*). Hence a given, ethnic culture is celebrated for its unusual rituals or practices without seeing the actual pain and suffering that such cultural practices impose on those whose daily life they are a part of. The Other is always the Other of the rainbow-colored costumes and vaguely Romantic myths, rather than the Other whose practices and ways of life may directly clash with liberal prescriptions.[63]

Therefore liberal multiculturalism, under the guise of an ideology of tolerance, actually strives to neutralize genuine difference and force cultural expressions to fit its (disavowed, hidden) mode. As a result of such rules of the liberal symbolic order (globalized today to an unprecedented degree), difference cannot but take the form of grotesque and pitiful explosions of violence. Yet, in order to break this "vicious" circle, it is not sufficient to favor one side of the equation over another (nationalist communitarianism over rootless liberalism, for instance). As I see it, what needs to be done instead is to intervene or make a gesture that will dispense with such an equation altogether, an intervention that will, as Lacan liked to point out about the outcome of a psychoanalytic process, "bring a new presence into the world."[64]

The question as to how this is to be accomplished forces us to outline a direction that contemporary critical theory needs to take, if it is to remain faithful to the Liberation Thesis, discussed in chapter 2. As I have shown above, liberal multiculturalism is crisis-ridden and manipulatively cynical, and therefore cannot be considered as one of the legitimate options for a critical theorist. Yet, if the rules of the present liberal game are to be discarded, in the name of what this is to be done? For whose sake is a critical theorist raising his or her voice, in whose interest and for which standards does he or she advise the refusal of the status quo?

The answer here is that, as Žižek puts it, a critical theorist takes up rhetorical arms, not for the sake of particularistic interest or culture, but for the sake of "the universality to come."[65] One of the biggest problems with liberal multiculturalism is that it denies the existence of an alternative universality, implicitly finding it only in contemporary Western middle-class public opinion. In other words, under the guise of universality, what one is offered is a configuration of particular class interests inextricably tied with the preservation of the status quo. But if one rightfully rejects this kind of universality as false (or, in Hegelian terms, as bad), then where is one to find the carrier of true universality?

My answer to this question is the same as that of Žižek and the theorists of the Liberation Thesis, and this is why I think I am justified in approaching what I call "contemporary Lacanian theses" as an essential re-playing of the problematics of social and political emancipation examined in chapter 2. Žižek contends—and here he is in perfect agreement with Reich, Marcuse, and Brown—that genuine universality is embodied in that segment of society that is materially excluded from the blessings and prosperity of the status quo.[66] The disavowed and rejected carry with them a truth of the given sociopolitical situation.

Perhaps today's paradigmatic case of the excluded social segment with no political voice are undocumented immigrants, already condemned even on the level of semantics by being referred to as "illegal." Beyond the law of the status quo by definition, and compelled by the necessities of that same status quo, undocumented immigrants incarnate the proliferation of economic hierarchies, the repressed truth of capitalism. Their presence and toil behind the glitzy surface of upper middle-class prosperity (and not only in the First World) show to what extent liberal capitalism is far from being "the end of history" panacea that its ideologists make it out to be.

However, what needs to be kept in mind is that no group, merely by belonging to an objective sociological category, can be a guarantor of the process of universal emancipation. In other words, being an undocumented immigrant or a member of the working class does not necessarily entail one's belonging to the *avant-garde*. Even a minimal political change requires a certain degree of "subjectivization," the understanding of one's position in relation to others and the society as a whole, in order to be effective. Hence only those undocumented immigrants who understand themselves as the symptom of a society which they inhabit, but which disavows their existence, can truly push for progressive change. In other words, these are the undocumented immigrants who could take up the position of the hysteric in contemporary capitalist discourse.

Yet it seems necessary to postulate a convergence between two separate groups in order to make such a project successful. The first group represents those undocumented immigrants who understand how their plight bears upon the question of the genuine presence of justice and freedom in the sociopolitical realm of advanced capitalism. In other words, these are the immigrants who loudly proclaim: "We are the true nation; *wir sind das Volk.*"[67]

The second group is composed of those who are integrated in the system of capitalism (and here I would include critical theorists), but who nonetheless firmly state their identification with immigrants. We can imagine this second group chanting under the banner of "We are all undocumented immigrants." As I see it, only the combination of the two groups, considering that they represent the two sides of every genuine universality—the universalization of the particular and the particularization of the universal—can bring about the widespread recognition of the void in the structure of the capitalist Other. In this way, it can also reveal more generally the truth of the Liberation Thesis: liberalism is the ideology of a particular class privileged by the status quo. Out of the exposed void of liberalism new political alternative can emerge, alternatives that can transform the relations of production, distribution, and consumption in ways that eliminate existing privileges.

THE SUBJECT OF TRUTH

It seems to me that, without departing from a Lacanian framework, the issue of universality—which, in my opinion, must be in the forefront of any project of social and political emancipation—can be approached in yet another way. I find the elaboration of this approach in the work of Alain Badiou. Badiou articulates the logic of social change in a way that combines the insights of psychoanalysis with a set of perennial concepts in Western philosophy (truth, being, knowledge, event, and so on).

Badiou begins by postulating the existence of two ontologically different levels of reality: the level of knowledge (that is, the level of ordinary discourse, of particular laws and regulations, in a word, of ideology) and the level of truth (that is, of an event that disrupts and cuts through the smooth and untroubled circulation of the level of knowledge). For Badiou, truth is to be conceptualized as that which "creates a hole in knowledge."[68] In other words, it is the effects of the emergence of a truth that possess the power to transform the level of ordinary knowledge.

In my opinion, what Badiou puts forward can easily be translated into the basic Lacanian categories. The level of knowledge is nothing else but the register of the symbolic, and the emergence of truth is equivalent to the rupture of the real. The relation between truth and knowledge is hence similar to the relation between the real and the symbolic. However, what makes Badiou's work interesting is that he uses these Lacanian categories to formulate a theory which articulates necessary steps in the transformation of the symbolic (that is, the sociopolitical structure) by the advent of the real (that is, its excluded truth).

The key point is that Badiou explores what happens to the individual who witnesses the emergence of a truth. This individual, recognizing the void in the structure of the symbolic order, can no longer be the same as before this experience. For Badiou, he or she individual has, by the power of the witnessed truth, become a subject. This means that "subjectivization" is not a matter of a natural process played out according to the laws of necessity: somebody may live out his or her entire life without ever even glimpsing this dimension. Being a subject means taking a step beyond the hustle and bustle of daily pragmatic interests by remaining faithful to the event of truth, that is, to the emergence and articulation of the different and the new.[69]

Badiou claims that there are no less than four areas of human endeavor in which one can ascertain the emergence of truths: science, art, politics, and love.[70] In each of these truth-engendering practices, one can discern the same structure: the event (the encounter, the idea), followed by the continued commitment or perseverance on the part of those affected to extend and proliferate the event's effects as far and wide as possible. In fact, the principal ethical imperative as formulated by Badiou is to keep going, not to waver in one's fidelity to the event.[71]

The key question here is as follows: in what way is the concept of the subjectivization by the event useful in critical political theory? It seems to me that the utility of this concept lies primarily in enabling the constitution of "a universal address," that is of a political message that can include everybody no matter who they are, no matter what their "identity" is.[72] In other words, what counts in terms of this perspective is one's engagement in a certain process rather than one's substantive determinations. Hence there is freedom for one to make and re-make oneself; there are no social groups privileged or condemned in their objective being. This stress on voluntarism, in my opinion, does not conflict with the tenets of Lacanian psychoanalysis, considering that Lacan has also emphasized the importance of subjective choice in ethical and political matters. In this respect, it seems sufficient to mention the formula which Lacan thought should guide the ethics of psychoanalysis: "do not give up on your desire."[73]

Badiou finds the formal model of the universalizing message of a truth-event in the teachings of St. Paul.[74] The truth-event in this case was the resurrection of Christ, and St. Paul articulated the necessary principles for a community of the faithful to come into being. The subsequent two thousand years of history testify to the "symbolic efficiency" of this articulation, though there is no doubt that it was affected by crises, such as the schism between Eastern and Western Church, the Crusades, the Reformation, the Inquisition, the Bolshevik Revolution, and so on.

Badiou is a declared atheist, but he argues that one can still learn from St. Paul, even if one disagrees with the substance of his message. He contends that what is valuable in St. Paul's teaching is the form or manner in which he presented it to those who were potential believers. According to Badiou, the formal structure of St. Paul's epistles follows a discernable imperative, which can be phrased as "the no . . . but."[75] In essence, he says to his potential followers—"*No*, you are not subject to the particular laws of your community, *but* you are subject to a higher law, a universal law of the Christ event, the law of grace." This approach justifies the rupture with the status quo—since it reveals the limitations of the existing state of affairs—and while *at the same time* offering the elaboration of another possible configuration. This new configuration is, by the nature of its founding principles, more universal than the one or ones that are replaced. It allows for the formation of a realm where the promise of political and social emancipation has a potential of being fulfilled. Yet, as is obvious, the ultimate promises of Christianity proved illusory. One can argue that perhaps this outcome was brought about by the essential betrayal of Christ's exhortations (the Christ event) by the establishment of Church hierarchies.

Notwithstanding the fate of Christianity, I think that the logic of "the no . . . but" seems indispensable in any conceptual schemas of contemporary critical theory. This logic provides support for the break with the existing system *and* guarantees the universal validity of the system to be established. It can therefore escape the pitfalls of theories, such as liberal multiculturalism, which proclaim their universality, while concealing that their positions are in fact grounded in the practices and ways of life of a particular social group or community. As the theorists of the Liberation Thesis claim, critical theory must be universalist and cosmopolitan, or it will not be.

THE EVENT AND THE HYSTERIC

Badiou argues that the truth-event is an essentially random occurrence.[76] The timing of the event cannot be predicted, since the conditions that make it emerge out of the void of the existing situation arise through chance. To me, this is suspect; it seems permeated by the spirit of reaction and passivity in clear contrast with the voluntarism of other aspects of Badiou's work. In fact, I think I can put forth a claim that will not only remedy what I perceive as a weakness in Badiou's conception of the event, but will also tie Badiou's work more affirmatively to a psychoanalytic critical theory that I have articulated throughout this chapter.

In a word, I contend that the truth-event is caused not by the unknown configuration of factors, but by the individual or a group of individuals who are, in their words and deeds, incarnating the discourse of the hysteric. We know that the hysteric represents the prototypical subject with a message to deliver. Technically speaking, the hysteric as a divided subject ($) is motivated to act by the presence of the object *a* in the position of truth. In other words, the truth of a hysteric is the desire that demands the presence of a social and political configuration more conducive for satisfaction, whether one refers to a particular family or any other power dynamic.

The hysteric, in his or her acts, confronts the Other with the fact that neither is complete. For the Other, this means that its claim to universal truth is revealed to be faulty. In other words, fissures in the Other come to the surface and become the foci of collective political strategies. This is what constitutes the event in the dimension of the political; what is seen is that the prevailing political system radically excluded certain political alternatives. Through the activities of the hysteric, these alternatives are recovered and become the models for a new sociopolitical configuration.

However, what needs to be remembered is that no sociopolitical configuration (whatever it may be) can close up the void in the Other. In other words, the emergence of creative alternatives cannot be arrested, unless one is to revert to the discourse of negation and denial, so characteristic of the master's and university discourses. In my opinion, this is far from being a setback for critical theory, especially since the path of change is given direction by the figure of the hysteric. The hysteric assures that changes will be motivated by the demands of desire, by the demands for that which a particular configuration or situation is lacking. Hence one can assume that the changed configuration will be less restrictive than the one that it has replaced. The interventions of the hysteric, as I have pointed out earlier, lead to the creation of signifiers representing new bodies of knowledge, and this means the presence of more possibilities for the satisfaction of social and political demands.

However, even if the discourse of the hysteric is to be taken as causative of the event, the radical dimension of this gesture stands to be obliterated, because what typically happens, as I see it, is that the event's further articulation and the distribution of its effects are taken over by the discourse of the master. This is the discourse structure of those who demand the rapid implementation of what, in their understanding, is that which the hysteric (in the position of an inspired rebel) has revealed to them.

The world that these individuals inhabit is forever changed by the irruption of the event, and they endeavor to codify it in various categories, applications and uses. They speak from the position of new signifiers, which, considering structural differences between the master's discourse and the discourse of the hysteric, is quite soon degraded into the basis of a new ideology or dogma. The idea that something of a different dimension (something of the nature of a truth-event) is possible is struck out as unjustified idealism or, worse yet, as obscure mysticism. In essence, what is rejected is the fact that the origin of the discourse of the master is to be located in the interventions of the hysteric.

Hence, in my opinion, the position of the master, and its modified incarnation as the university discourse, as positions that declare the end to the possibility of radical change, are more likely candidates for mystifying idealism. These two discourses see truth only as embodied in the particular frameworks of already ideologized social life.[77] As I see it, this is their fundamental illusion, because truth has the structure of the not-all (as argued in chapter 3), whereas the structures of contemporary social and political life are guided by the logic of the all, the logic of totality that allows for no gaps. Paradoxically, however, only the logic of the not-all, which links itself to the void in that what-is, in being, is genuinely universal, and, as such, should, in my opinion, be embraced by contemporary critical theory.

The void in the Other is implicated in the universal because universality, I would argue, has no particular content; its determination is purely formal, and it essentially means this is not *it*. This is why the void is illuminated by the hysteric's desire, which also enunciates this fundamental non-satisfaction. The void is precisely that which the repressive discourses of the master and the university have to take into account. However, this can only happen if these discourse structures are transformed, which, as I have argued, is the path made possible by a psychoanalytic critical theory. In other words, according to Lacan's motto, what is at stake in sociopolitical change is the "hysterization" of discourse structures, which is represented by their moving or turning toward the discourse of the hysteric.[78] The discourse of the hysteric is the only discourse structure that, by revealing the void in any given symbolic order, is able to engender new ways of conceptualizing and being in the world. This is why the transmission and teaching of this discourse is the most pressing task that I see for contemporary critical theory in its re-visitation of the Liberation Thesis.

ŽIŽEK, RAGLAND, BADIOU: CONCLUSION

My intention in this chapter has been to show the extent to which a Lacanian framework seems indispensable in formulating a new, reinvigorated project for critical thought. In the works of Žižek, Ragland, and Badiou I have found support for the general thesis that far from being alien to an endeavor of sociopolitical critique, psychoanalysis offers conceptual and practical tools that propel this endeavor forward and that enable it to enter a level of analysis closed to other theoretical approaches. Psychoanalysis makes possible a questioning that goes beyond investigating the assumptions of any given symbolic order, and focuses on what needs to take place in order for the symbolic itself to come into being. In doing so, psychoanalysis opens up a new significant area for critical thinking, since the key question changes from "which of the given symbolic orders is better" to "how to re-formulate the relations between the symbolic and the real." The latter question allows for a radical re-conceptualization of the orders of sociopolitical reality insofar as it underwrites the possibility of bringing into existence something entirely new.

For this task, as I see it, it is fundamental to remember Lacan's claim that every symbolic is marked by a hole or a void, by a point which it cannot integrate and which, in essence, represents its downfall. As I have shown, Žižek, Ragland, and Badiou all seek to unfold the implications of this claim, whether in the realm of ideology, sexuation, or truth. The conclusion that emerges is that proclaiming the ultimate triumph of any sociopolitical system—as is currently done by those in support of liberal capitalist democracy—is an illusion. The excluded part that this illusion attempts to repress emerges as the symptom in all areas of social and political life, and, in revealing the prevailing totality as false (that is, as structured by particularistic interests), it represents the claims of true universality. In their emphasis on the importance of the notion of the universal in social critique, Lacanian theorists demonstrate their closeness to the cause of the theorists of the Liberation Thesis.

However, I think that knowing that contemporary social and political reality is grounded in an illusion is not sufficient to motivate the processes of social change, because of the *jouissance* invested and accumulated in the status quo. The only way to disturb and dissolve this "rock of *jouissance*" is by liberating (sexual) desire, which brings into being the lack of satisfaction with the status quo. As I see it, this is best accomplished by the discourse of the hysteric, and that is why I have designated the hysteric as the most appropriate agent of sociopolitical change. The hysteric, motivated by presence of the precious object *a*, demands of the Other to produce new bodies of signifiers to satisfy his or her desire and, in doing so, makes possible the re-articulation of the relations between the symbolic and the real in the history of humanity.

NOTES

An earlier version of this chapter was published in *Angelaki: A Journal of the Theoretical Humanities*, 8.3:109–31.

1. Alain Badiou, "Politics and Philosophy: An Interview," in *Ethics: An Essay on the Understanding of Evil*, trans. Peter Hallward (London: Verso, 2001), 109.
2. Slavoj Žižek, *The Ticklish Subject: The Absent Center of Political Ontology* (London: Verso, 1999), 3–4.
3. Slavoj Žižek, *The Sublime Object of Ideology* (London: Verso, 1989).
4. The quoted statement is from Marx's *Capital*. See Žižek, *Sublime Object*, 28.
5. One should note that this sentence implies one of the principal lessons of psychoanalysis, which is that the knowledge of truth and its articulation improves

psychological well being or, put in negative terms, the denial or rejection of truth deteriorates the quality of one's life. Along the same lines, one should keep in mind Lacan's formulation that "what is repressed in the symbolic, returns in the real," see Lacan, *The Seminar of Jacques Lacan, Book III: Psychoses*, 85–88, 190.

6. See Sigmund Freud, "The Sexual Aberrations," in *Three Contributions to the Theory of Sex*, 553–79, esp. 566–68.

7. Žižek, *Sublime Object*, 31.

8. The phrase "in you more than you" appears in chapter 20 of Lacan's *Seminar XI*, and Lacan invokes it to locate the place of the object *a*, the object-cause of desire. See Lacan, *The Seminar of Jacques Lacan: Book XI, Four Fundamental Concepts of Psychoanalysis*, 263–76. As will become clear shortly, the object *a* is one of the principal component of fantasy, written as $\$\lozenge a$: the *a* appears to the lacking/divided subject (\$) as something that will fill its lack. On the significance of "the king's *two* bodies," see Slavoj Žižek, *For They Know Not What They Do: Enjoyment as a Political Factor* (London: Verso, 1991), 253–56.

9. See, for instance, Alain Grosrichard, *The Sultan's Court: European Fantasies of the East*, trans. Liz Heron (London: Verso, 1998), where the concept of fantasy figures as the most prominent explanatory tool in the analysis of the accounts of European visitors to the Ottoman Empire, 26–55.

10. One can also think of religion not as an illusion (as did Marx and Freud), but as a fantasy with God in the place of an object *a*. A particularly interesting case in this respect is the sentence "in God we trust" imprinted on U.S. currency. It seems that the Founding Fathers wanted to displace the efficiency of the religious fantasy onto the fantasy of wealth as the best solution to the question of the good life.

11. Žižek, *Sublime Object*, 21, emphasis in the original.

12. Here one should be reminded of the Great Refusal proposed by Herbert Marcuse and discussed at length in chapter 2. See Marcuse, *One-Dimensional Man*, 254–57.

13. Jacques Lacan, *The Seminar of Jacques Lacan, Book XXIII: Le Sinthome*, trans. Luke Thurston (draft), the session of December 9, 1975.

14. Žižek, *For They Know Not*, 249–53. In his analyses, Žižek draws on a work by Octave Mannoni, *Clefs pour L'Imaginaire* (Paris: Editions du Seuil, 1968).

15. I disagree with Žižek's choice of example, because I am not convinced that Socrates chose to die out of respect for Athens. As I see it, his intention was to make a martyr out of himself, and use martyrdom as a means to perpetuate his name and teachings. Nothing makes such an impact on one's disciples as sacrificing one's life for a "hopeless" cause. Another case in point is the crucifixion of Christ.

16. Žižek, *For They Know Not*, 247–48.

17. One should note here that in Lacanian theory, just as in Hegel, existence does not refer to mere being, but to a grounded being. Only a being that is grounded in some sort of notion or principle exists. See Žižek, *For They Know Not*, 60, ft. 34. Existence follows closely the logic of all; however, as I have shown in chapter 3, Lacan's conception of truth privileges that which is the not-all (*pas-tout*), that which does not exist in a given constellation, since it is excluded by it. Hence one of the components of Lacan's kinship with radical, critical theory.

18. Žižek, *For They Know Not*, 252.

Contemporary Lacanian Theses 221

19. Žižek, *The Sublime Object*, 113. See also Slavoj Žižek, "Da Capo Senza Fine," in Judith Butler, Ernesto Laclau, and Slavoj Žižek, *Contingency, Hegemony, Universality: Contemporary Dialogues on the Left*, (London: Verso, 2000), 258.

20. Slavoj Žižek, "Class Struggle or Postmodernism? Yes, Please!" in Butler, Laclau, Žižek, *Contingency, Hegemony, Universality*, 95-97, 108.

21. Žižek, "Class Struggle," 106.

22. As Žižek points out, perhaps this is why production has all but disappeared (or been repressed) from the view of the publics in late capitalist Western world. "Class Struggle," 129, ft. 13. Žižek traces the philosophical elaboration of this approach to Hegel's *Logic* and his category of "oppositional determination." See Slavoj Žižek, "Holding the Place," in Butler, Laclau, Žižek, *Contingency, Hegemony, Universality*, 314-15.

23. Claude Lefort, *Democracy and Political Theory*, trans. David Macey (Minneapolis: University of Minnesota Press, 1988).

24. Žižek, "Class Struggle," 100-101, 110.

25. See Žižek's claims regarding this question, "Class Struggle," 110-11; also, Žižek, "Holding the Place," 327, ft.3.

26. Another common argument against "utopian" thinking seems to be nothing else but an implicit way of conveying that "what one cannot imagine at present, cannot possibly exist." One does not need to be a scholar of psychoanalysis to recognize reckless narcissism as the basis of such a statement.

27. Marx and Engels, "German Ideology," in *Marx-Engels Reader*, 160.

28. See Claude Lefort, "The Logic of Totalitarianism," in *The Political Forms of Modern Society: Bureacracy, Democracy, Totalitarianism*, ed. John B. Thompson, (Cambridge: Polity Press, 1986), 278-82.

29. Ernst Kantorowicz, *The King's Two Bodies* (Princeton, N.J.: Princeton University Press, 1959). This doubling of the king's person made it so difficult for the Jacobins to decide how to proceed with Louis XVI, since, in eliminating his empirical being, what they truly wanted to eliminate or transfer was his symbolic mandate. The same logic was in place in the decision of the Bolsheviks to execute Tsar Nicholas II and his immediate family. See Žižek, *For They Know Not*, 275-76, ft. 36.

30. Lefort, "The Logic of Totalitarianism," 279-80.

31. Ernesto Laclau and Chantal Mouffe, *Hegemony and Socialist Strategy: Towards a Radical Democratic Politics*, (London: Verso, 1985), 149-93. Yannis Stavrakakis, whose work on Lacanian political theory I critiqued in chapter 3, is another theorist in the same tradition.

32. It should of course be apparent that post-Marxism resembles more J. S. Mill's reform liberalism than Marxism proper.

33. On Hegel, see Žižek, *For They Know Not*, 129-32, 190-92.

34. Žižek, *Sublime Object*, 59-60.

35. In Federico Fellini's film *Juliette of the Spirits*, what begins Juliette's emancipation from her repressed condition is her confronting the hallucinated image of her mother with the words—"You can't scare me any more." Upon hearing these words, the maternal image—representing the Other—crumbles into a thousand pieces.

36. And even the dread we feel in challenging the gigantic edifice of the Other has its productive uses. I think that Heidegger articulates an important insight when

he states in "What is Metaphysics?" that "the dread felt by the courageous cannot be contrasted with the joy or even the comfortable enjoyment of a peaceable life. It stands—on the hither side of all such contrasts—in secret union with the serenity and gentleness of creative longing," *Existence and Being*, 343.

37. Žižek, *Sublime Object*, 229. This mirrors one of the formulas on the masculine side of Lacan's sexuation graph. See Lacan, *Seminar XX*, 78–81.

38. That I, as a historically situated individual who is theorizing, can know. Perhaps a Marxian conception of the "withering away" of the state provides a glimpse into the tentative contours of this social form.

39. See Lacan, *Seminar XX*, 75–76.

40. On the concept of supplemental *jouissance*, coined by Lacan in *Seminars XIX* and *XX*, more will be said below. In *The Hysteric's Guide to the Future Female Subject* (Minneapolis: University of Minnesota, 2000), Juliet Flower MacCannell argues that Stendhal offers an example of how one could live out this kind of existence, 217–33. This, to some extent, contradicts her principal argument in the book, which she articulates as aiming at "a possible or potentially *free female* subject—her logic, her ethic, her unconscious," xii. On the contrary, I think that, as the example of Stendhal shows, the focus on the ways of political articulation of supplemental *jouissance* can be made more universal, that is, it can include the search for a potentially free *male* and *female* subject.

41. Thomas Frank, *One Market Under God: Extreme Capitalism, Market Populism, and the End of Economic Democracy* (New York: Doubleday, 2000), xiv. See also Michel Hardt and Antonio Negri, *Empire* (Cambridge, Mass.: Harvard University Press, 2000), 325–50.

42. Lacan, *Seminar XXIII*, the session of February 10, 1976.

43. Lacan, *Seminar XX*, 3. Perhaps the most dramatic cinematic presentation of this idea is found in Pier Paolo Passolini's *Salò*, based on the Marquis de Sade's *The 120 Days of Sodom*, in a scene where the four sadistic protagonists, after a mock marriage ceremony, strip naked a girl and a boy and coerce them into having sex, while they stand in the background fully dressed in conventional business suits. This scene, I think, should be interpreted as Passolini's comment on the super-ego's role in constituting all that passes as conventional or natural within a given society.

44. Slavoj Žižek, *Birokratija i Uzivanje [Bureaucracy and Enjoyment]* (Beograd: Radionica SIC, 1984), 19–26.

45. Jacques Lacan, *The Seminar of Jacques Lacan, Book VIII: Transference*, Trans. Cormac Gallagher (draft), the session of November 16, 1960.

46. Lacan, *Seminar VIII*, the session of November 30, 1960.

47. Jacques-Alain Miller, "Duty and the Drives," *Newsletter of the Freudian Field* 6, nos. 1 and 2 (Spring/Fall 1992): 8–9.

48. Lacan, *Seminar XI*, 225, 230–36.

49. On the qualities of emancipatory leadership from a perspective close to what I am proposing here, see Paulo Freire, *Pedagogy of the Oppressed*, 121–33.

50. Lacan, *The Seminar of Jacques Lacan, Book VIII: Transference*, the session of November 30, 1960. As Lacan points out, the gods represent the judgment of the real.

51. Ellie Ragland-Sullivan, "Seeking the Third Term: Desire, the Phallus, and the Materiality of Language," in *Feminism and Psychoanalysis*, 40–41.

52. Ellie Ragland-Sullivan, *Jacques Lacan and the Philosophy of Psychoanalysis*, (Urbana, Ill.: University of Illinois Press, 1986), 289-90.

53. Ellie Ragland, "Lacan and the Subject of Law: Sexuation and Discourse in the Mapping of *Subject* Positions that give the Ur-Form of Law," *Washington & Lee Law Review* 54, no. 1091 (1997): 1104-7.

54. As I see it, this orientation represents the essence of Paulo Freire's "problem-posing education," which presents the world as changeable and unfinished rather than as a fixed, objectified totality. See Freire, *The Pedagogy of the Oppressed*, 57-74.

55. Ragland, "Seeking the Third Term," p. 53.

56. It may be useful to differentiate between different types of *jouissance*, and to say that the *jouissance* of consumerism is a phallic *jouissance* (conforming to the status quo), while the *jouissance* aimed at by the hysteric is supplemental, that which the phallus cannot offer.

57. See the section on the hysteric discourse in chapter 3.

58. Colette Soler, "History and Hysteria: The Witty Butcher's Wife," *The Newsletter of the Freudian Field* 6, nos. 1 and 2 (Spring/Fall 1992), 30.

59. In my opinion, one can discern a resemblance between the logic of this argument and Marx and Engels's "grave-digger thesis" (*Manifesto of the Communist Party*, 473-83): that is, that the bourgeoisie is, through its self-propelled activities, creating its own grave-diggers. In other words, every social system engenders its own fatal contradictions, but I would add that the trigger for such a process to begin unfolding is the presence of a figure embodying the discourse of the hysteric.

60. Žižek, *The Ticklish Subject*, 202-4, 208.

61. Žižek, *The Ticklish Subject*, 204-5.

62. Žižek, *The Ticklish Subject*, 201-2, 218-19.

63. I agree with Alain Badiou who claims that the multiculuralist so-called respect for the other is false in that only "a good other" is given a tolerant consideration. Badiou articulates the standpoint of a liberal multiculturalist as "I respect differences, but only, of course, in so far as that which differs also respects, just as I do, the said differences." This, then, is the way in which the ideology of multiculturalism justifies to itself and its public "waging war for peace" and "giving no freedom to the enemies of freedom." In the final analysis, Badiou reduces the key precepts of multiculturalism to "become like me and I will respect your difference." Badiou, *Ethics*, 24-25.

64. Jacques Lacan, *Seminar II*, 229. See chapter 3.

65. Žižek, *The Ticklish Subject*, 224.

66. See, for instance, Barbara Ehrenreich's account of the lives of those working in the so-called service sector (waitresses, maids, supermarket employees) in the prosperous West, *Nickel and Dimed: On (Not) Getting by in America* (New York: Henry Holt & Co., 2001). What is truly refreshing about this book is that Ehrenreich actually worked at these jobs in order to be able to describe the plight of the so-called working poor in more accurate and empathetic terms. Her engagement mirrors a kind of commitment I call for in the life of every contemporary critical theorist. In Žižek's terms, it would be an instance of "identification with the symptom," *The Ticklish Subject*, 224.

67. Žižek, *The Ticklish Subject*, 231.

68. Alain Badiou, *Manifesto for Philosophy*, trans. Norman Madarasz (Albany, N.Y.: SUNY Press, 1999), 37; Badiou, *Ethics*, 41-42. See also Jean-Jacques Lecercle, "Cantor,

Lacan, Mao, Beckett, *meme combat*: The Philosophy of Alain Badiou," *Radical Philosophy*, no. 93 (January–February 1999): 6–13.

69. Badiou, *Ethics*, 43, 48–49. In this connection, Badiou wonders whether "this desire of the subject to persevere in his consistency [that is, in his fidelity to truth] is congruent with the animal's desire to grab its socialized chance," 56. Badiou's answer here is negative and, in this, he reveals his Platonist roots.

70. Badiou, *Manifesto for Philosophy*, 33–35.

71. Badiou, *Ethics*, 52. In Badiou's words: "Truth is, as such, indifferent to differences," 27.

72. See "Politics and Philosophy: An Interview with Alain Badiou," in *Ethics*, 109–12.

73. In fact, on the level of structure, the manifestation of unconscious desire and the event are homologous. On Lacanian ethics, see chapter 3.

74. Alain Badiou, *St. Paul: La Fondation de l'Universalisme* (Paris: PUF, 1997); see also Ed Pluth, "The Pauline Event?" *Theory and Event* 3, no. 3 (1999).

75. Badiou, *St. Paul*, 67–68.

76. Badiou, "Politics and Philosophy" in *Ethics*, 122–23. Badiou refers to the event as a kind of the "laicized grace."

77. In our present sociopolitical configuration, the "eternalized" framework is that of multicultural liberalism.

78. Lacan, Jacques, *Le Seminaire, Livre XVII*, 35–36.

Conclusion

> One day she's a seamstress or she's working in a stocking factory, then before you know where you are she's turned into a hair-dresser. You saw the woman at the switch, who shook her fist at us? Bless me, I thought, if it isn't Glafira gone to work on the railway.[1]

My principal task in this work has been to establish in what ways the post-Freudian developments in psychoanalytic theory and practice can aid critical social and political theory in affirming the possibility of alternative social and political arrangements, norms, and values. I have designated this task metaphorically as "liberating Oedipus," by which I meant a normative effort to free the individual from what appear to be eternal and overwhelmingly powerful external and internal forces. One can think of these forces as the curse whose inevitable fulfillment nothing can stop. And even if the things do change in certain ways, these changes may still appear to be contained within the universe of the same, the universe of the curse.

However, throughout the preceding chapters, my intention has been to show that even though the current state of affairs does not look promising, sociopolitical changes as imagined by the theorists of the Liberation Thesis are not to be thought of as historical curiosities, as outdated dreams whose feeble outlines were shattered by the dawning of reality. I have maintained that these sociopolitical changes are still, and perhaps now more than ever, possible, but that their coming into being or actualization necessitates taking seriously the insights of psychoanalysis, including the institutionalization of the discourse of the analyst on a wider scale.

As I have shown, only the discourse of the analyst, the discourse of somebody who knows something about love, can provide a strategic access point for the transformation of what at this time (the early twenty-first century) is the prevailing sociopolitical discourse, the discourse of the university. The discourse of the university is grounded in the belief in the fundamental completeness of the social Other (the status quo as the only possible world) and as such remains incapable of cutting through the layers of dominant ideology, the ideology of liberal capitalist democracy. By disclosing the contingency of the object a, of the component that makes the ideological fantasy (\$◊a) complete and which, in our contemporary universe, is inscribed in terms of monetary success or profitability,[2] by, in other words, making the object a's seeming substantiality vanish, the analyst transforms the discourse of the university into the discourse of the hysteric. He or she dissolves the rock of *jouissance* invested and accumulated in the existing sociopolitical configuration and in this way enables the birth of a desire that transcends the given, a desire that makes those motivated by it push for the changes in the given in the clear manifestation of the discourse of the hysteric.

The discourse of the hysteric is a discourse of those who refuse to be satisfied by that which is being offered by the social Other, and hence demand that the Other produces something else, some other signifiers (S1, S2, S3, S4. . . .), that may satisfy their desire. The emergence of new signifiers opens up the possibility for the articulation of the repressed content and the reconfiguration of the Other in terms of making its institutional structures more conducive to individual and social well being. Thus the figure of the hysteric, in my view, reveals itself as the prototypical agent of radical social critique and the pioneer of structural political changes.

That the fundamental structures orienting the nature of political life do change we have witnessed in the transition between a feudal political structure and a democratic political structure. As I have noted in chapter 4 in reference to the work of Claude Lefort, the defining element, which structured the politics of feudalism, was the existence of an individual who was thought of as the only possible occupant of the place of power (the place of sovereignty). This individual (under many different designations, the most prevalent of which was the king) exercised the ultimate political authority within a given territory as well as empirically (biologically) grounded the processes of succession. The key political principle was, in short, *l'état, c'est moi*. In psychoanalytic terms, the relation between the registers of the symbolic and the real was regulated by the presence of One and hence perhaps can be written as $S(\emptyset) \rightarrow \Phi$, that is, the void in the Other was filled by the highest in the hierarchy of master-signifiers, the phallus.

The political changes instituted by the American and French Revolutions of the late eighteenth century were revolutionary precisely to the extent to which they affected and transformed this feudal configuration of power. The king was either declared irrelevant or physically eliminated and this, according to Lefort, led to the disclosure of a fundamental emptiness at the seat of power (which can be written as S(Ø)). Hence what characterized the new democratic structure was that those who held political power in it were prohibited from being One (Φ), and were simply to consist of a set of temporary political officers representing all the rest of society. The principle here was to be *l'état, c'est nous*. However, this principle could come to life only under the condition that the place of power genuinely remained empty, that is, under the condition that S(Ø) was not filled with any particular content. Lefort and contemporary critical theorists influenced by his work, such as Ernesto Laclau, Chantal Mouffe, and Yannis Stavrakakis, believe this to have been the case and therefore argue that the structure of contemporary liberal democracy does not in any way preclude the realization of the principle of universal emancipation, the rule of the We. The key task that they formulate for critical theory is to motivate and guide the efforts to include or integrate as many social strata as possible into the operations of existing democratic structures.

However, as I have shown in the preceding chapters, I disagree with their claims that contemporary liberal democracy provides a political structure conducive to universal emancipation. This is so, because I see its mechanisms marked by a particularistic content, by an ideological underpinning, which is represented by the belief in the substantial or real nature of particular objects *a*. In fact, the structure of liberal democracy can perhaps can be written as S(Ø) → *a*, where the object *a* that fills the void in the Other (plugging up the place of emptiness through which the new can emerge) is the object of capitalist ideology, that is, the pursuit of financial gain. This means that everything in the political realm of liberal democracy, from vote representation and group recognition to the address of grievances and correcting of historical wrongs, is distorted by the presence of the monetary object that appears as a spectacular ideal image at the limit of the horizon of those who are today considered most successful.

It seems to me that psychoanalytic theory and practice is an indispensable component of a theory of social change, capable of bringing to life the goals and commitments cherished by the Liberation Thesis, precisely because it is geared towards demonstrating the contingent and illusory quality of the object *a*. In the course of psychoanalytic praxis, the object *a* vanishes and the fundamental emptiness at the core of the Other is disclosed. In our contemporary situation, this would mean the recognition of the falsity of satisfaction afforded by money and consumerist practices (the object *a*). At the same time, it would also mean the birth of a desire for something different, something that would not saturate or plug up the void in the Other in the manner of the object *a*.

In my view, this "something" can be represented by a chain of signifiers ($S1$, $S2$, $S3$, $S4$, $S5$ and so on) where the relation of signifiers to one another precludes a possibility of coming to a point of finality and conclusiveness (the end of the quest; Satisfaction with a capital S). The structure of a signifying chain best reflects one of the principal claims of psychoanalytic thought that there is no Other of the Other, that no "genuine" totality (apart from totality that defines fantasy) is possible. And, moreover, it is precisely the dynamic quality of the chain, where no signifier can exhaust the requirements of desire, that motivates a movement from one position in the social configuration to another, from one symbolic identity to another, from the position of contentment with what is to the position of commitment to what could be. Hence the structure of a sociopolitical system where, in contrast to liberal democracy, the lure of the object a is transcended can perhaps be written as $S(\emptyset) \rightarrow S1, S2, S3, S4, S5 \ldots Sn$. It is a structure that on social level mirrors the discourse of the hysteric whose principal component is precisely the attachment of a lacking/desiring subject to a signifier that has the capability of producing new knowledge.[3]

In my opinion, what this kind of orientation means in concrete terms is best seen in Marx and Engels's formulation of the life interests of a free individual, his or her desire to fish in the morning (S1), rear cattle in the afternoon (S2), and criticize after dinner (S3), without being confined by the Other or its psychological representative, the super-ego, to any of these or any other symbolic designations. Pasternak's Glafira or Kazantzakis's Zorba also express the same philosophy of life. Glafira is a hairdresser one day and the next she works on the railroad; Zorba is a miner in the morning and a *santuri* player in the afternoon, and so on. This exchangeability of functions is made impossible by a sociopolitical configuration that, as in liberal democracy, is grounded in the belief in the substantial nature of the object a, that is, the belief that the object a (in this case, money, property, profitability) is *it*. In other words, if I have found *it*, why would I want to do anything else? If being a critic is *it*, what motivates me to fish in the morning or work on the railroad? Clearly the metonymy of desire needs to be kept alive (in other words, lack needs to be sustained) and the best way to do so, as I see it, is to support its explicit linkage to the operation of signifying chains, precisely what is accomplished through psychoanalytic work.

Hence here we can approach an answer to the question that has puzzled (if not plagued) the theorists of the Liberation Thesis. Having directed their work toward the audiences in advanced industrialized societies, their question was how to speak about liberation to groups that already consider themselves free, groups that find the universe of capitalist liberalism as the best possible universe. Why would somebody who considers himself or herself free need to be liberated?[4] Another aspect of the same question was faced by those who, like Paulo Freire, worked toward the social transformation of the Third World countries. Freire's concern was how to enlighten or educate those who were exploited and downtrodden so that they do not follow in the footsteps of their exploiters by, for instance, imitating the latter's set of preferences, by longing for the exploiters' type of freedom and their cultural practices.[5]

It seems to me that the answer to these questions is found in psychoanalytic practice which addresses the issues of contentedness and customary routines by providing for a possibility of dissatisfaction in the given. Dissatisfaction, the hysteric's reaction to what is offered, comes about as a result of realization that whatever makes one contented is based on a set of repressions. These repressions represent the motive sources for new possibilities, which can be freely chosen by the individual once he or she becomes aware of their existence. This is why I consider psychoanalysis to be emancipatory—it makes the individual aware that things do not have to be as they have always been, that a choice and a commitment make a difference, that a fear of the new is inspired more by the resistance of the old than by the dangers of the new, and overall that a world of alienation, injustice, exploitation, and other sociopolitical pathologies is not the only possible world.

Yet, who will in fact make these changes, what agency will put them in place? I think that it is a mistake to search for the agency in any objective social category or group considering that this precludes the possibility of a genuine universality of revolt. In contrast, I would suggest that being an agent of change means following a certain formal structure in one's way of being. This structure I have located in the discourse of the hysteric. Being a hysteric is open to all, but it is made possible to most only through the intervention of the discourse of the analyst. This is why it is not possible "to hystericize" on a wider scale without psychoanalysis being accorded a great share of influence in public life. And hence all those who want to engage themselves critically with the forces of the status quo should also support the establishment of psychoanalytic training schools and institutes as well as the incorporation of psychoanalysis into the regular school curriculum. In this way, the discourse of the analyst will be given a greater space in fulfilling its designated function of breaking the self-sufficiency of the dominant (university) discourse, and psychoanalysis prove that it in fact carries the banner of the advance of human freedom in the history of humanity.

NOTES

1. Boris Pasternak, *Dr. Zhivago*, trans. Max Hayward and Manya Harari (New York: Pantheon Books, 1960), 220.

2. As Lacan points out in regards to one of his rich analysands, "There is nothing more disappointed than a gentleman who is supposed to have attained the pinnacle of his wishes. One only need speak with him for three minutes, frankly, as perhaps

only the artifice of the psychoanalytic couch permits, to know that in the end all that stuff is just the sort of thing he could not care less about and, furthermore, that he is particularly troubled by all sorts of things." Lacan, *Seminar III*, 82.

3. The structural presentation of the discourse of the hysteric is:

$\underline{\$} \to \underline{S1}$
$a \leftarrow S2$

See chapter 3.

4. Herbert Marcuse, "Political Preface 1966," in *Eros and Civilization*, xi–xxviii.

5. Paulo Freire, *Pedagogy of the Oppressed*, 27–57.

Bibliography

Abramson, Jeffrey B. *Liberation and Its Limits: The Moral and Political Thought of Freud.* New York: The Free Press, 1984.

Abramson, Paul R., and Steven D. Pinkerton, *With Pleasure: Thoughts on the Nature of Human Sexuality.* New York: Oxford University Press, 1995.

Badiou, Alain. *Manifesto for Philosophy.* Trans. Norman Madarasz. Albany, N.Y.: SUNY Press, 1999.

———. *Ethics: An Essay on the Understanding of Evil.* Trans. Peter Hallward. London: Verso, 2001.

———. *St. Paul: La Fondation de l'Universalisme.* Paris: PUF, 1997.

Baudelaire, Charles. *Invitation to the Voyage: A Poem Illustrated.* Trans. Richard Wilbur. New York: Little, Brown & Co., 1997.

Bocock, Robert. *Freud and Modern Society: An Outline and Analysis of Freud's Sociology.* New York: Holmes & Meier Publishers, 1976.

Borch-Jacobsen, Mikkel. *The Freudian Subject.* Trans. Catherine Porter. Stanford: Stanford University Press, 1988.

Brown, Norman O. *Life Against Death: The Psychoanalytic Meaning of History.* Middletown, Conn.: Wesleyan University Press, 1959.

———. *Love's Body.* New York: Random House, 1966.

———. "A Reply to Herbert Marcuse," *Negations: Essays in Critical Theory.* Trans. J. J Shapiro. Boston: Beacon Press, 1968.

Burgin, Victor. *In / Different Spaces.* Berkeley: University of California Press, 1996.

Butler, Judith, Ernesto Laclau, and Slavoj Žižek. *Contingency, Hegemony, Universality: Contemporary Dialogues on the Left.* London: Verso, 2000.

Deleuze, Gilles. *Nietzsche and Philosophy.* Trans. Hugh Tomlinson. London: The Athlone Press, 1983.

———. *Negotiations, 1972–1990.* Trans. Martin Joughin. New York: Columbia University Press, 1995.

Deleuze, Gilles and Felix Guattari. *Anti-Oedipus: Capitalism and Schizophrenia*. Trans. Robert Hurley, Mark Seem, and Helen Lane. Minneapolis: University of Minnesota Press, 1977.

———. *A Thousand Plateaus: Capitalism and Schizophrenia*. Trans. Brian Massumi. Minneapolis: University of Minnesota Press, 1987.

Ehrenreich, Barbara. *Nickel and Dimed: On (Not) Getting by in America*. New York: Henry Holt, 2001.

Etkind, Alexander. *Eros of the Impossible: The History of Psychoanalysis in Russia*. Trans. Noah and Maria Rubens. Boulder, Colo.: Westview Press, 1997.

Feldstein, Richard and Judith Roof, eds. *Feminism and Psychoanalysis*. Ithaca, N.Y.: Cornell University Press, 1989.

Ferry, Luc and Alain Renaut. *French Philosophy of the Sixties: An Essay on Antihumanism*. Amherst: University of Massachusetts Press, 1990.

Flieger, Jerry Aline. "Entertaining the Ménage à Trois: Psychoanalysis, Feminism, and Literature," in *Feminism and Psychoanalysis*, edited by Feldstein, Richard and Judith Roof. Ithaca, N.Y.: Cornell University Press, 1989.

Flower MacCannell, Juliet. *The Hysteric's Guide to the Future Female Subject*. Minneapolis: University of Minnesota Press, 2000.

Frank, Thomas. *One Market under God: Extreme Capitalism, Market Populism, and the End of Economic Democracy*. New York: Doubleday, 2000.

Freire, Paulo. *Pedagogy of the Oppressed*. Trans. Myra Bergman Ramos. New York: Continuum, 1970.

Freud, Sigmund. *The Standard Edition of the Psychological Works of Sigmund Freud*. Ed. and Trans. James Strachey. London: Hogarth Press, 1966–1974.

———. *The Basic Writings of Sigmund Freud*. Ed. and Trans. A. A. Brill. New York: Random House, 1938.

———. *Collected Papers*. Trans. James and Alix Strachey. London: Hogarth Press, 1953.

———. *A General Selection from the Works of Sigmund Freud*. Ed. John Rickman. New York: Doubleday, 1957.

———. *Civilization, War, and Death*. Ed. John Rickman. London: Hogarth Press, 1953.

———. *Dora: An Analysis of a Case of Hysteria*. Ed. Phillip Rieff. New York: Collier Books, 1963.

———. *Three Case Histories*. Ed. Phillip Rieff. New York: Collier Books, 1963.

———. *Beyond the Pleasure Principle*. Trans. James Strachey. New York: Bantam Books, 1959.

———. *The Question of Lay Analysis*. Trans. Nancy Procter-Gregg. New York: Norton, 1950.

———. *Group Psychology and the Analysis of the Ego*. Trans. James Strachey. London: The International Psychoanalytic Press, 1922.

———. *The Future of an Illusion*. Trans. W. D. Robson-Scott. New York: Doubleday, 1953.

———. *Civilization and Its Discontents*. Trans. James Strachey. New York: Norton, 1961.

———. *New Introductory Lectures on Psychoanalysis*. Trans. James Strachey. New York: Norton, 1965.

———. *New Introductory Lectures*. Trans. Alex Strachey. New York: Norton, 1960.

———. *The Complete Letters of Sigmund Freud to Wilhelm Fliess*. Ed. and Trans. Jeffrey Moussaieff Masson. Cambridge, Mass.: Harvard University Press, 1985.

Fornari, Franco. *The Psychoanalysis of War*. Trans. A. Pfeifer. Bloomington: Indiana University Press, 1975.
Gelven, Michel. *A Commentary on Heidegger's* Being and Time. Dekalb: Northern Illinois University Press, 1989.
Glover, Edward. *War, Sadism, and Pacifism*. London: Allen and Unwin, 1931.
Grosrichard, Alain. *The Sultan's Court: European Fantasies of the East*. Trans. Liz Heron. London: Verso, 1998.
Gurdjieff, G. I. *Meetings with Remarkable Men*. New York: Penguin, 1985.
Hardt, Michel and Antonio Negri. *Empire*. Cambridge, Mass.: Harvard University Press, 2000.
Harper, Ralph. *The Seventh Solitude: Man's Isolation in Kierkegaard, Dostoevsky, and Nietzsche*. Baltimore: Johns Hopkins University Press, 1965.
Heidegger, Martin. *Being and Time*. Trans. Joan Stambaugh. Albany, N.Y.: SUNY Press, 1997.
———. *Nietzsche, Vol. 2: The Eternal Recurrence of the Same*. Trans. David Farell Krell. San Francisco: Harper & Row, 1984.
Hermann, Imre. "The Use of the Term 'Active' in the Definition of Masculinity: A Critical Study." *International Journal of Psychoanalysis* 16 (April 1935): 219–22.
Horney, Karen. "The Denial of the Vagina," *International Journal of Psychoanalysis* 14 (January 1933): 57–70.
Hyppolite, Jean. "A Spoken Commentary on Freud's 'Negation.'" in Jacques Lacan. *The Seminar of Jacques Lacan, Book I, Freud's Papers on Technique, 1953–1954*. Ed. Jacques-Alain Miller. Trans. John Forrester. New York: Norton, 1988.
Irigaray, Luce. *Speculum of the Other Woman*. Trans. Gillian C. Gill. Ithaca, N.Y.: Cornell University Press, 1985.
———. *This Sex which is Not One*. Trans. Catherine Porter with Carolyn Burke. Ithaca, N.Y.: Cornell University Press, 1985.
———. *The Irigaray Reader*. Ed. Margaret Whitford. Oxford: Blackwell, 1991.
Jay, Martin. *Downcast Eyes: The Denigration of Vision in Twentieth Century French Thought*. Berkeley: University of California Press, 1993.
Jones, Ernest. *The Life and Work of Sigmund Freud*. New York: Basic Books, 1953–1957.
Kantorowicz, Ernst. *The King's Two Bodies*. Princeton, N.J.: Princeton University Press, 1959.
Kazantzakis, Nikos. *Zorba the Greek*. Trans. Carl Wildman. New York: Simon & Schuster, 1952.
Kellner, Douglas. *Critical Theory, Marxism, and Modernity*. Baltimore: Johns Hopkins University Press, 1989.
Kojeve, Alexandre. *Introduction to the Reading of Hegel*. Ed. Allan Bloom. Trans. James H. Nichols. New York: Basic Books, 1969.
Kolakowski, Leszek. *Main Currents of Marxism: Its Rise, Growth, and Dissolution*. Trans. P. S. Falla. Oxford: Clarendon Press, 1978.
Kovacevic, Filip. "Horkheimer and Adorno's Transcendence of the Enlightenment: Critique of Habermas." Paper presented at the annual meeting of the Southwestern Social Science Association, Galveston, Tex., March 2000.
Kordela, A. Kiarina, "Political Metaphysics: God in Global Capitalism (the Slave, the Masters, Lacan, the Surplus)." *Political Theory* 27, no. 6 (1999): 789–839.

Kris, Ernst. "Ego Psychology and Interpretation in Psychoanalytic Therapy." *Psychoanalytic Quarterly* 20 (1951): 15–30.

Lacan, Jacques. *The Seminar of Jacques Lacan, Book I, Freud's Papers on Technique, 1953–1954*. Ed. Jacques-Alain Miller. Trans. with notes John Forrester. New York: Norton, 1988.

———. *The Seminar of Jacques Lacan, Book II: The Ego in Freud's Theory and in the Technique of Psychoanalysis, 1954–1955*. Ed. Jacques-Alain Miller. Trans. Sylvana Tomaselli, with notes John Forrester. New York: Norton, 1988.

———. *The Seminar of Jacques Lacan, Book III: The Psychoses, 1955–1956*. Eed. Jacques-Alain Miller. Trans. with notes Russell Grigg. New York: Norton, 1993.

———. *The Seminar of Jacques Lacan, Book VII: The Ethics of Psychoanalysis, 1959–1960*. Ed. Jacques-Alain Miller. Trans. with notes Dennis Porter. New York: Norton, 1992.

———. *The Seminar of Jacques Lacan, Book VIII, Transference, 1960–1961*. Trans. Cormac Gallagher. Draft.

———. *The Seminar of Jacques Lacan, Book XI: The Four Fundamental Principles of Psychoanalysis, 1964–1965*. Ed. Jacques-Alain Miller. Trans. Alan Sheridan. New York: Norton, 1978.

———. *Le Séminaire, Livre XVII, L'Envers de la Psychanalyse*. Ed. Jacques-Alain Miller. Paris: Seuil, 1991.

———. *The Seminar of Jacques Lacan, Book XX: Encore, On Feminine Sexuality, The Limits of Love and Knowledge, 1972–1973*. Ed. Jacques-Alain Miller. Trans. with notes Bruce Fink. New York: Norton, 1998.

———. *The Seminar of Jacques Lacan, Book XXII: RSI, 1974–1975*. Trans. Jack W. Stone. Draft.

———. *The Seminar of Jacques Lacan, Book XXIII: Le Sinthome, 1975–1976*. Trans. Luke Thurston. Draft.

———. *Ecrits: A Selection*. Trans. Alan Sheridan. New York: Norton, 1977.

———. "Television." Trans. Dennis Hollier, Rosalind Kraus, and Annette Michelson. *October*, no. 40 (Spring 1987): 7–50.

———. "The Founding Act." Trans. Jeffrey Mehlman. *October*, no. 40 (Spring 1987) 96–105.

———. "A Letter to D. W. Winnicot." Trans. Jeffrey Mehlman. *October*, no. 40 (Spring 1987): 76–78.

———. "Science and Truth." *Newsletter of the Freudian Field* 3, nos. 1 and 2 (Spring/Fall 1989): 4–29.

Laclau, Ernesto, and Chantal Mouffe, *Hegemony and Socialist Strategy: Towards a Radical Democratic Politics*. London: Verso, 1985.

Laplanche, Jean. *New Foundation for Psychoanalysis*. Trans. David Macey. London: Blackwell, 1989.

Lecercle, Jean-Jacques. "Cantor, Lacan, Mao, Beckett, *même combat*: The Philosophy of Alain Badiou." *Radical Philosophy*, no. 93 (January–February 1999): 6–13.

Lefort, Rosine, and Robert Lefort. *Birth of the Other*. Trans. Marc Du Ry, Lindsay Watson, and Leonardo Rodriguez. Urbana: University of Illinois Press, 1994.

Lefort, Claude. *Democracy and Political Theory*. Trans. David Macey. Minneapolis: University of Minnesota, 1988.

———. *The Political Forms of Modern Society: Bureaucracy, Democracy, and Totalitarianism*. Ed. John B. Thompson. Cambridge: Polity Press, 1986.

Lemoine-Luccioni, Eugenie. *The Dividing of Women or Woman's Lot*. Trans. Marie Anne Davenport and Marie-Christine Reguis. London: Free Association Books, 1987.

Lenin, Vladimir I. *State and Revolution*. New York: International Publishers, 1943.

Levi-Strauss, Claude. *Structural Anthropology*. Trans. Claire Jacobson and Brooke Schoepf. New York: Basic Books, 1967.

Loewenberg, Peter. "Psychoanalytic Origins of the Nazi Youth Cohort." *American Historical Review*, no. 76 (1971): 1457–1502.

Mann, Thomas. *The Magic Mountain*. Trans. H. T. Lowe-Porter. New York: Alfred Knopf, 1961.

Mannoni, Octave. *Clefs pour L'Imaginaire*. Paris: Seuil, 1968.

Marcuse, Herbert. *Eros and Civilization: A Philosophical Inquiry into Freud*. Boston: Beacon Press, 1955.

———. *One-Dimensional Man: Studies in the Ideology of Advanced Industrial Society*. Boston: Beacon Press, 1964.

———. *Negations: Essays in Critical Theory*. Trans. J. J. Shapiro. Boston: Beacon Press, 1969.

———. *Five Lectures: Psychoanalysis, Politics, Utopia*. Boston: Beacon Press, 1970.

———. "Repressive Tolerance." *A Critique of Pure Tolerance*. Ed. Robert Paul Wolff. Boston: Beacon Press, 1965.

———. *An Essay on Liberation*. Boston: Beacon Press, 1969.

———. *The Aesthetic Dimension: Toward the Critique of Marxist Aesthetics*. Boston: Beacon Press, 1978.

Marx, Karl, and Friedrich Engels. *The Marx and Engels Reader*. Ed. Robert Tucker. New York: Norton, 1977.

Miller, Jacques-Alain. "Duty and the Drives." *Newsletter of the Freudian Field* 6, nos. 1 and 2 (Spring/Fall 1992): 5–15.

Mitchell, Juliet. *Psychoanalysis and Feminism*. New York: Random House, 1974.

Mitchell, Juliet, and Jacqueline Rose, ed. *Feminine Sexuality: Jacques Lacan and the Ecole Freudienne*. New York: Norton, 1982.

Mitscherlich, Alexander. "Group Psychology and the Analysis of the Ego—One Generation Later." *Psychoanalytic Quarterly*, no. 48 (1978): 1–23.

———. *The Society without the Father*. Trans. Eric Mosbacher. New York: Schocken Books, 1975.

Nelson Garner Shirley, Claire Kahane, and Madelon Sprengnether, ed. *The (M)other Tongue: Essays in Feminist Psychoanalytic Interpretation*. Ithaca, N.Y.: Cornell University Press, 1985.

Nietzsche, Friedrich. *Thus Spoke Zarathustra*. Trans. Walter Kaufmann. London: Penguin Books, 1978.

Pasternak, Boris. *Dr. Zhivago*. Trans. Max Hayward and Manya Harari. New York: Pantheon Books, 1960.

Patton, Paul. *Deleuze and the Political*. London: Routledge, 2000.

Petrovic, Gajo. *Marx in the Mid-Twentieth Century*. New York: Doubleday, 1967.

Plato. "Symposium." In *Great Dialogues of Plato*. Trans. W. H. D. Rouse. New York: Mentor Books, 1956.

Pluth, Ed. "The Pauline Event?" *Theory and Event* 3, No. 3 (1999).
Ragland-Sullivan, Ellie. *Jacques Lacan and the Philosophy of Psychoanalysis*. Urbana: University of Illinois Press, 1986.
———. "Seeking the Third Term: Desire, the Phallus, and the Materiality of Language" in *Feminism and Psychoanalysis*, edited by Richard Feldstein and Judith Roof. Ithaca, N.Y.: Cornell University Press, 1989.
———. "Lacan and the Subject of Law: Sexuation and Discourse in the Mapping of Subject Positions That Give the Ur-Form of Law." *Washington & Lee Law Review* 54, no. 1091 (1997).
Reich, Wilhelm. *The Function of the Orgasm*. Trans. V. R. Carfagno. New York: Simon & Schuster, 1973.
———. *The Sexual Revolution: Toward a Self-Regulating Character Structure*. Trans. Therese Pol. New York: Farrar, Straus, and Giroux, 1974.
———. *The Invasion of Compulsive Sex-Morality*. Trans. Werner and Doreen Grossmann. New York: Farrar, Straus, and Giroux, 1971.
———. *The Mass Psychology of Fascism*. Ed. Mary Higgins and Chester M. Raphael. New York: Farrar, Straus, and Giroux, 1970.
Ricoeur, Paul. *Freud and Philosophy: An Essay on Interpretation*. Trans. Dennis Savage. New Haven: Yale University Press, 1970.
Rieff, Philip. *Freud: The Mind of the Moralist*. Chicago: University of Chicago Press, 1959.
Robinson, Paul A. *The Freudian Left: Wilhelm Reich, Geza Roheim, and Herbert Marcuse*. New York: Harper & Row, 1969.
Rougemont, Denis de. *Love and the Western World*. Trans. Montgomery Belgion. New York: Pantheon, 1956.
———. *Love Declared: Essays on the Myths of Love*. Trans. Richard Howard. New York: Random House, 1963.
Roy, Jean. *Hobbes and Freud*. Trans. T. G. Osler. Toronto: Canadian Philosophical Monographs, 1984.
Rudnytsky, Peter L. *Freud and Oedipus*. New York: Columbia University Press, 1987.
Safouan, Mustafa. "Feminine Sexuality in Psychoanalytic Doctrine. " in *Feminine Sexuality: Jacques Lacan and the Ecole Freudienne*, Ed. Juliet Mitchell and Jacqueline Rose. New York: Norton, 1982.
Schneiderman, Stuart. *Jacques Lacan: The Death of an Intellectual Hero*. Cambridge, Mass.: Harvard University Press, 1983.
Soler, Colette. "History and Hysteria: The Witty Butcher's Wife." *Newsletter of the Freudian Field* 6, nos. 1 and 2 (Spring/Fall 1992): 16–33.
Stavrakakis, Yannis. *Lacan and the Political*, London: Routledge, 1999.
Volkan, Vamik. *The Need to Have Enemies and Allies: From Clinical Practice to International Relations*. Northvale, N.J.: Aronson, 1986.
Weil, Mildred W. *Sex and Sexuality: From Repression to Expression*. Lanham, Md.: University Press of America, 1990.
Whitford, Margaret. *Luce Irigaray: Philosophy in the Feminine*. London: Routledge, 1991.
Žižek, Slavoj. *Birokratija i Uzivanje [Bureaucracy and Enjoyment]*. Beograd: Radionica SIC, 1984.

———. *The Sublime Object of Ideology*. London: Verso, 1989.
———. *For They Know Not What They Do: Enjoyment as a Political Factor*. London: Verso, 1991.
———. *Enjoy Your Symptom: Jacques Lacan in and out of Hollywood*. London: Routledge, 1992.
———. *The Ticklish Subject: The Absent Center of Political Ontology*. London: Verso, 1999.
Zupancic, Alenka. *Ethics of the Real: From Kant to Lacan*. London: Verso, 1997.

Index

Acteon, 150n9
aesthetic consciousness, xii
Agathon, 188n14
aggressive drives, 32, 76
Alcibiades, 207
alienated work, xii
Allacoque, Marie, 117
ambivalence, 27, 31–32, 179
ananke, 36
Andreas-Salome, Lou, 94
Antigone xiii, 122–24
antiquity, 9, 115
Apollo, 130
Aristotle, 81
Artaud, Antonin, 189n21
arts, 10
Aufhebung, 83

Bachofen, Johann Jacob, 70
Badiou, Alain, xviii, 194, 214–19, 223n63
Barcelona, 204
Bartok, Bela, 40
Beaudelaire, Charles, 87
Beauvoir, Simone de, 172
Beethoven, Ludvig van, 46
Bergson, Henri, 158
Bernfeld, Siegfried, 116

Bernstein, Eduard, 202
Bonaparte, Marie, 174
Borromean knot, 113
brother-clan, 28
Brown, Norman O., xii–xiii, 60, 93–99, 147, 213
Buddha, 207
Butler, Judith, 199

Camus, Albert, 53n65, 77
capitalism, xii, xvii, 1, 66, 82, 84, 86, 91, 109, 146–47, 169, 171–72, 182, 194–96, 199–200, 213, 219, 228
Casanova, Giacomo, 197
Cassirer, Ernst, 81
castration, 16, 22, 40, 68, 177, 181
cathexis, 14
Charcot, Jean-Martin, 100n5
child behavior, 6, 8, 10, 12
Christ, 197, 207, 216, 220n15
civilization, 1, 29, 37, 43, 79
clitoris, 16, 181–82
Cohen, Hermann, 81
communism, 147–48
condensation, 5
conscience, 31–32
courtly love, 115–16, 141
Creon, 123

239

critical theory, xix, 89–90, 111, 119, 157, 162–63, 171, 194, 196, 198, 212, 218, 220n17
culture, 8, 24, 42–44, 67
Cyrenaics, 81–82

Daniel, Arnaud, 116–17
Darwin, Charles, 28, 54n92
Das Ding, 113–17, 120, 124, 138, 151n36
death, 6–7, 33–35, 127
death drive, xi, 30–31, 33, 65, 124
Deleuze, Gilles, xv, 158–60, 162–72, 186
desire, xv, 4, 9, 11, 13, 27, 111, 114, 118–19, 127, 134, 139, 148, 154n103, 161–64, 166–67, 169–70, 180, 185, 189n29, 210, 227
Deutsch, Helen, 174
Diana, 150n9
Dilthey, Wilhelm, 25
Dionysian ego, xiii, 95–97
displacement, 5
Doctor Schreber, 17
Dora, 17, 21, 135
Dostoevsky, Fyodor, 47, 54n91, 101n26
dreams, 5–7

ego, 38, 42, 48, 109–11, 150n10; ideal, 39; psychology, 108–9
Ehrenreich, Barbara, 223n66
Eliot, T. S., 80
Engels, Friedrich, xv, 69–71, 78, 146, 169, 200, 223n59, 228
envy, 122, 176
Epicureans, 82–83
Eros, xi–xii, 1, 33–36, 48, 60, 83–84, 92–95, 99, 143
ethics, 112, 118–20, 156n142
event, 215–16

family romance, 22, 26, 159
fantasy, xvii, 139–40, 142, 195–96, 220n8, 220n9, 228
fascination, 40
fascism, xii, 77

father, 2–3, 7, 21, 23, 28, 30, 47, 159, 177, 179–80, 188n6, 207–8; primal, 28–29, 40, 68, 71, 94, 137
Fellini, Federico, 220n35
feminine, xiv, xvi–xviii, 15–16, 52n52, 108, 136–37, 139–41, 143, 149, 174, 178–79, 182–84, 186, 203, 207–9
feminism, xvi, 14–15, 172–73, 175, 183–84, 187
Ferry, Luc, 108
Fink, Bruce, 151n26
Flieger, Jerry Aline, 173
Fliess, Wilhelm, x, 2–3, 5, 50n2, 104n128
Flower MacCannell, Juliet, 222n40
Folignio, Angela de, 117
Frank, Thomas, 204
Frankfurt, 80; School, 81, 145
Fraser, Robert, 28
freedom, 77, 79–80, 89, 95, 130, 166, 229
Freire, Paolo, 222n49, 223n54, 228
Freud, Anna, 109–10, 174
Freud, Sigmund, ix–xi, xiii, 1–20, 24–25, 27–38, 46–50, 60–61, 64, 71–72, 76, 83, 93–98, 109–10, 113, 118, 135–36, 157, 161–62, 168, 173, 175–79, 184, 187, 200
Friedan, Betty, 172

Gallop, Jane, 172
genital character, 66
Genoa, 204
German Ideology, xv, xixn10, 146
God, 46–48, 76, 118, 204, 220n10
Goethe, Johann Wolfgang von, 153n80
great refusal, 90
Grigg, Russell, 151n26
group psychology, 36–39, 41
Guattari, Felix, xv, 158–72, 186

Habermas, Jurgen, 145
Hartmann, Heinz, 109, 185
hedonism, 81
Hegel, Georg Wilhelm Friedrich, 20, 45–46, 123, 127, 203

Index

Hegelian logic, 92
Heidegger, Martin, 80, 123, 125, 144, 154n108, 220n36
Hermes, 86
historicism, xvii, 199
Hobbs, Thomas, 28, 45, 57n160, 210
hole, xiv, 140, 144, 155n136, 196, 214
Horkheimer, Max, 80
Horney, Karen, 16–17
Hume, David, 158
Husserl, Edmund, 80
hypnosis, 40
Hyppolite, Jean, 150n16
hysteric, xiv–xvi, xviii–xix, 132, 135, 142–44, 183, 185, 204, 209–10, 219, 229; discourse of the, xiv, xix, 99, 125–26, 133, 149, 193, 203, 216–18

id, 36–37
identification, 41, 48
ideology, xvii, 73, 76, 80, 89, 194, 196–97, 212
illusion, 42, 45
imaginary register, 113, 115, 121, 152n71
incest, 2–3, 26, 52n36, 71, 73
International Psychoanalytic Association (IPA), 160–61
Irigaray, Luce, xvi, 158, 173–76, 181, 183, 185–87

Jay, Martin, 108
jealousy, 2–3, 72
jouissance, x, xix, xixn3, 112–13, 117, 120, 127, 131, 134, 136–37, 139, 141–42, 151n26, 151n28, 181, 183–84, 187, 203–5, 207–8, 210, 212, 219, 226; surplus *jouissance*, 127–28, 146

Kant, Immanuel, 46, 81, 85, 155n118, 211
Karamzov, Ivan, 47, 101n26
Kautsky, Karl, 191n73
Kazantzakis, Nikos, 155n140, 228
Klein, Melanie, 116, 174

Kojève, Alexandre, 127–28
Kordella, Kiarina, 155n118
Kris, Ernst, 109, 185
Kuhn, Thomas, 121

Lacan, Jacques, ix, xii, xvi–xvii, 99, 100n11, 100n16, 101n28, 103n95, 105n137, 107–10, 112–16, 120–26, 128, 132–34, 139, 141, 143, 146–47, 148–49, 149n5, 150n9, 160–65, 167, 169, 173, 175, 177–78, 182–87, 191n75, 193–95, 200, 205–6, 208, 212, 215, 229n2
lack, xv, 127, 163, 206
Laclau, Ernesto, 155n135, 199, 201–2, 227
Lampl de Groot, Jeanne, 174
Laplanche, Jean, 54n92
Lasswell, Harold, 200
Lefort, Claude, 199, 200, 202, 226–27
Lemoine-Luccioni, Eugenie, 185
Lenin, Vladimir I., 78
Levi-Strauss, Claude, 135, 195
liberal democracy, xvii, 44, 75, 145, 149, 211, 227–28
liberal multiculturalism, xviii, 205, 211–12, 213
liberalism, xviii, 202, 212, 214
liberation thesis, xi, xii, xiii, xvii, 1, 12–13, 29, 44, 49–50, 51n6, 59–60, 65, 67, 70, 72, 74–75, 77, 79, 80, 82, 85, 88, 90–91, 97, 98–99, 108–9, 119, 122, 124, 126, 128, 139, 142–43, 145–46, 147–49, 158, 163, 172, 187, 193, 209, 212–14, 216, 218, 225, 227
libidinal rationality, xii
libido, 12–15, 38–39, 43, 85, 160; ego, 14, 168; object, 14, 168
little Hans, 17
Locke, John, 28
Loewenstein, Rudolf, 109
Louis XIV, 201
Luxemburg, Rosa, 202

Mack Brunswick, Ruth, 174
malaise, 43

Malinowski, Bronislaw, 68–69, 70, 72
Mann, Thomas, 55n125
Marcuse, Herbert, ix, xii, xiii, xviii, 60, 80–92, 97–99, 101n23, 121, 147, 193, 209, 213
Marx, Karl, ix, xv, 45–46, 59, 60, 61, 69–70, 71, 74, 78, 101n38, 146–47, 148, 158, 187n4, 194–95, 199, 200, 223n59, 228
masculine, xiv, xvi, xviii, 15, 108, 136–37, 139–41, 143, 178
masochism, 13, 15, 82
master: discourse of the, xiv, 126, 143; signifier, 125, 127–28, 132–33, 139, 210
maternal breast, 11, 43
Mitchell, Juliet, 172
Mitscherlich, Alexander, 55n127
modernity, 9
morality, 2–3, 7, 20, 79, 113
Morgan, Louis H., 70, 71
Moses, 94
mother, 2, 4, 7, 47, 121, 177, 179–80, 190n53, 207
Mouffe, Chantal, 155n135, 201–2, 227

narcissism, 12, 50, 86
Narcissus, 86, 90, 92
Nazis, 76, 94
Neurosis, ix, 9, 12, 35, 62
New Testament, 117
New York, 98
Newtonian physics, 14
Nietzsche, Friedrich, xiii, xv, 93–94, 95–96, 104n128, 158, 164–65, 186, 188n19, 188n21
Nijinsky, Vaslav, 167
Novalis, 103n101

Oedipal relation, x, 16, 47, 73–74, 89
Oedipus, x, 2, 99, 174; anti, 158–59, 162, 164, 171; complex, 1, 23, 30, 50, 60, 73
oral drive, 11
orgasm, 61, 63, 69, 97, 112
Orpheus, 86–87, 90, 92

other, xi, xiv, xv, xvii–xviii, xix, 11, 25–26, 141, 144–45, 150n13, 184, 197–98, 199, 201–4, 209, 210, 212, 217, 226

Paris, 98; Commune, 78
parricide, 3
Passolini, Pier Paolo, 222n43
Pasternak, Boris, 228
pas-tout, xiv, 137, 183, 203, 220n17
penis, 16, 22, 181; envy, 16, 176–77
performance principle, 84
perversion, 40, 198
Phaedrus, 207
phallus, xvi, 136–37, 140, 177–78, 208, 226
phobia, 18–19
Plato, 12, 81–82, 124, 141, 174, 188n14, 206
pleasure principle, 35, 42, 45, 48, 112, 114, 151n28
positivistic knowledge, xiv
primal scene, 22
Prometheus, 86
psychoanalysis, ix, xiii–xv, xviii, 9, 13–14, 17, 19, 44–45, 81, 86, 99, 110–11, 118, 124–25, 132, 157–58, 163, 165, 171, 175, 180, 184, 186–87, 198, 202–3, 218, 219n5, 225, 229
psychoanalyst, xi; discourse of the, xiv, 126, 131–32, 149, 225
psychosis, 121, 180–81, 208
puberty, 12, 16

Ragland, Ellie, xviii, 194, 207–8, 218–19
Ranke, Otto von, 96
Ratman, 17, 21
reaction-formation, 8, 10, 13
real register, 113, 121, 123, 144, 205, 219
reality principle, 26, 84, 108–9
Reich, Wilhelm, ix, xii, 60–70, 72, 74–75, 77, 80, 83–85, 88, 97, 99, 100n11, 100n20, 101n37, 102n54, 157, 161, 193, 213

religion, 45, 47, 97
Renaut, Alain, 108
repetition compulsion, 34–35, 147, 164
repression, 3, 6, 63, 74–75, 87, 99, 200
repressive desublimation, 87–88, 104n109
revolution, 45, 49, 78, 201; Russian, 79
rivalry, 2, 6, 21
Riviere, Joan, 174
Robinson, Paul, ix
Rose, Jackie, 172
Rougemont, Denis de, 116
Rousseau, Jean-Jacques, 11, 12, 28

Sade, Marquis de, 153n81, 222n43
sadism, 13, 66, 76
Safouan, Moustafa, 185
Schiller, Friedrich, 85
schizoanalysis, xvi, 167–68, 171, 186
schizophrenic, xvi, 166–67
science, 120–21, 135
Seattle, 204
sex-economy, 75
sexual difference, xiv, 7, 14, 17, 61, 135, 137; drives, 10, 26, 33; relations, 15, 140
sexuality, 4, 62, 64, 76; female, 16, 175–76, 182; infantile, 10, 97; male, 15, 176, 182
sexuation, xiii–xiv, xvii, 138, 140, 143, 181; graph, 137
Shakespeare's *Hamlet*, 2–4, 7, 9, 20, 29, 60, 77, 130
Sharpe, Ella, 116
Shoshtakovich, Vladimir, 46
signifiers, 118–20, 126, 148, 152n62, 227
Smith, Adam, 14
Socrates, 133, 174, 188n14, 197, 205–7
Sophocles 123; *Oedipus*, 2–4, 7, 9, 20, 60, 130
Soviet Union, xii, 78–79, 147
Spengler, Oswald, 60
Spielrein, Sabina, 174
Spinoza, 158
St. Francis of Assisi, 117

St. Paul, 215–16
Stalin, Joseph V., 78, 198
Stavrakakis, Yannis, 144–46, 155n135, 220n31, 227
Strauss, Leo, 60
sublimation, 10, 67, 95–96, 115
super-ego, xi, 36–39, 48, 87, 89–90, 96, 112, 178, 190n55, 205
symbolic register, 113, 120, 123, 135, 138, 196, 219

taboo, 3, 25, 27
territorialization, 166
Thanatos, xi, 44, 48, 60, 84, 86, 99, 117
Totem and Taboo, 23–24, 31, 32, 114
Trobriand Islands, 68–69, 71
Trotsky, Lev, 57n156
troubadours, 116, 142
truth, xiii, xvii, 119, 126, 128–30, 134–35, 138, 214–15, 218

Übermenschen, xiii, 94
unconscious, 5, 9, 107, 110, 129, 148, 150n13, 162, 169–70
undocumented immigrants, 213–14
university: discourse of the, xiv–xv, 126, 128, 130, 144, 154n95, 184, 217–18

vagina, 16, 181
vegetotherapy, 64
Vienna, 61
void, xiv, xviii, 218

war, 31, 33
work-democracy, 80, 99
Washington, D.C., 204
wo es war, xiii, 110–11, 142
Wolfman, 17, 21–23, 53n70

Zarathustra, 94, 96
Žižek, Slavoj, xvii, 101n26, 145, 151n26, 194–98, 211–13, 218–19, 220n15
Zorba, 155n140, 228

About the Author

Filip Kovacevic is Professor of Political Psychology and Leadership Studies at the University of Montenegro. He has recently returned from a two-year visiting professorship at Smolny College of Liberal Arts in St. Petersburg, Russia, the first liberal arts college in the ex–Soviet Union. His current projects include a book on Lacanian political theory and a collection of essays on ex-Yugoslav literature.

```
BF          Kovacevic, Filip,
175.5         1975-
.033
K68         Liberating Oedipus?
2007

                              35010000504058
$65.00
                   DATE
```

BAKER & TAYLOR

SOUTH UNIVERSITY LIBRARY